in

England, Wales and Scotland
1st Edition

K.Mark Hughes

Contains public sector information licensed under the Open Government Licence v3.0.
https://www.nationalarchives.gov.uk/doc/open-government-licence/version/3/
Sources : https://www.legislation.gov.uk
Know your Traffic Signs - A DfT Guide.

ISBN: 9798877279278 - Paperback - Monochrome images
ISBN: 9798877290693 - Paperback - Colour images

ISBN: 9798877615441 - Hardback - Monochrome images
ISBN: 9798878555395 - Hardback - Colour images

Disclaimer

The information in this book is intended to provide general guidance on traffic law in Great Britain. It is not a substitute for professional legal advice.

The author has made every effort to ensure the accuracy and completeness of the information, but does not guarantee or warrant that it is up to date, correct, or applicable to any specific situation. Consult a suitably qualified professional before taking any action based on the information in this book.

Any liability for actions taken, or not taken, in reliance on material contained in this publication is excluded.

Contents

Foreword

This book is written by a former roads policing officer and traffic law instructor. He has authored several technical legal guides that have been widely used by enforcement officers across Great Britain for nearly 30 years.

φ

The guide aims to simplify the complicated field of road traffic law by offering a comprehensive overview of a wide range of topics. It is designed to help readers understand the basic principles and rules of traffic law, but it does not replace the need for professional legal advice.

Key - *see Chapter 26 Penalties*	
	Non-endorsable Fixed Penalty Notice
	Endorsable Fixed Penalty Notice *Offences in this guide are summary offences except where specified.*
	Local Authority Penalty Charge Notice
	Financial Penalty Deposit Offence
	Graduated Fixed Penalty Offence
	Legislation specific to England, Wales or Scotland. *Where no flags are displayed the legislation applies to all 3 nations.*

Chapter 1 Roads and Public Places

Road
Section 192(1) Road Traffic Act 1988

In **England and Wales** a road includes :-
- any Highway - 'a way over which members of the public have a right to pass and re-pass', and
- any other Road to which the public has access,

and includes bridges over which a road passes.

In **Scotland** a road includes :-
- any road within the meaning of the *Roads (Scotland) Act 1984* :-
  - ○ 'any way (other than a waterway) over which there is a public right of passage (including toll roads), and
  - ○ includes the verge, and any bridge over which, or tunnel through which, the road passes.'

  and any other way to which the public has access, and includes bridges over which a road passes.

A road extends from hedge to hedge or fence to fence including the verge, the footway alongside the carriageway and the carriageway itself. It includes private roads where the public have access.

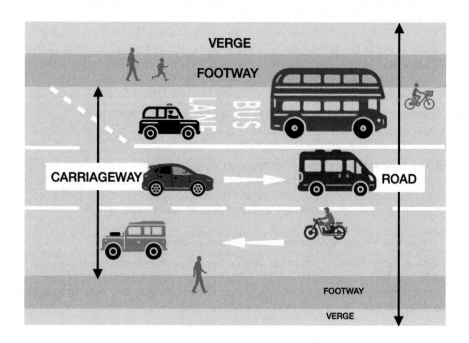

⚠➕ Other Roads
Private Roads and Ways with rights of public access

Public rights of way often cross privately owned land. By definition these are roads for the purpose of the Traffic Acts.

There may also be landowner, local authority or other private rights of access with mechanised vehicles or common law rights to drive animals.

The Traffic Acts include The Road Traffic Act 1988, The Road Traffic Regulation Act 1984 and The Road Traffic Offenders Act 1988.

Private Roads and Ways without rights of public access

Some privately owned roads and paths without any public rights of way are open to the public because the owner has given permission for them to be used or tolerates such access without taking any preventative measures. These routes are sometimes closed for one day a year, with a view to preventing them becoming rights of way. Easements may also exist which provide private rights of access.

Towpaths, paths across land owned by the Forestry Commission and National Trust and sections of the Sustrans National Cycle Network, are available for public use but may not be rights of way.

Similarly in Scotland footpaths created under public path agreements or designated as long distance routes or paths and tracks across local authority land used for recreation, cultural and social activities do not confer any public right of passage and are not roads for the purposes of the *Roads (Scotland) Act 1984* but may still be roads for the purpose of the *Road Traffic Acts*.

Whilst open to the public these ways may be roads for the purpose of the Road Traffic Acts but it may be necessary to prove the following points :-

• it is a definable route or line of communication (a through route) for vehicles or pedestrians,
• the general public have access there (not just the postman etc.),
• the access is enjoyed freely, i.e. it is not gained by overcoming a prohibition or physical obstruction.

Some roads or ways do not afford public rights of access but if the public do have access, on payment or otherwise, then during those times of public access they may fall within the definition of 'Road' being 'other roads or ways to which the public has access'.

Dock, Airfield, Royal Parks and Crown Roads

Various Acts of Parliament may appoint roads within these areas to be roads for the purpose of the *Road Traffic Act* or for certain parts of the Act or at certain times but, in respect of Crown Roads, this may not apply to members of the Crown Forces whilst on duty.

Case Law

Harrison v Hill [1932] SC 13
A private occupation road leading to a farm, if at the time the public have access, is a road.

> *Any road may be regarded as a road to which the public have access upon which members of the public are to be found who have not obtained access either by overcoming a physical obstruction or in defiance of a prohibition express or implied.*

Bowen and Ors v Isle of Wight Council [2021] - High Court (Civ)
Access to a private way by tolerated trespassers, so long as it is not in the face of, or in defiance of, the efforts of the landowner to prevent such access, is sufficient to meet the statutory definition of a road.

The Times, October 23 (1998) HOUSE OF LORDS
Overturning appeals in Clarke v Kato and Others [1996] EWCA Civ 1066 (29/11/1996) and Cutter v Eagle Star Insurance Co Ltd - Save in exceptional circumstances, a car park would not qualify as a road.

Price v DPP [1990] RTR 413
The primary intention of a place does not appear to be of relevance, as in all cases it remains a question of fact whether or not the area is a road to which the public has access, irrespective of whether it is publicly or privately owned.

Cox v White [1976] RTR 248
Whether or not the public have access to a road is a question of fact. If a member of the public has to overcome some form of physical barrier or act in defiance of a prohibition then that will not be considered a road to which the public have access. The question is one of degree, a slight degree of access by the public is not enough to satisfy the definition of road in *section 192 Road Traffic Act 1988*.

Randall v Motor Insurers' Bureau [1968] 1 WLR 190
If any part of a vehicle is on a road, even where it is partly or mostly on some other private land, the vehicle is to be treated as being on a road.

Worth v Brooks [1959] Crim LR 855
Pavements and boundary grass verges by the side of a carriageway were held to form part of the highway which itself constituted a road.

 Definitions

Bridleway

Section 192(1) Road Traffic Act 1988

A highway with public right of way on foot, horseback or leading a horse. A bicycle, not mechanically propelled, may be ridden on a bridleway.

Carriageway

Section 329(1) Highways Act 1980

A highway or part of a highway, not being a cycle track, with a right of way for vehicles.

Section 151(2) Roads (Scotland) Act 1984

A road where the public right of passage includes such a right by vehicle, other than a right by pedal cycle only.

Dual-carriageway road

Schedule 6 Road Traffic RegulationAct 1984

A road part of which consists of a central reservation to separate a carriageway to be used by vehicles proceeding in one direction from a carriageway to be used by vehicles proceeding in the opposite direction.

Footpath

Section 329(1) Highways Act 1980, *Section 192(1) Road Traffic Act 1988*

A highway or way with a public right of way on foot only, but not a footway.

Section 151(2) Roads (Scotland) Act 1984

A road where the public right of passage is by foot only where it is not associated with a carriageway.

Section 192(2) Road Traffic Act 1988

A way over which the public have a right of way on foot only (whether or not associated with a carriageway).

Footway (Pavement)

Section 329(1) Highways Act 1980

Part of a highway, which includes a carriageway, with a public right of way on foot only.

Section 151(2) Roads (Scotland) Act 1984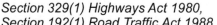

A road where the public right of passage is by foot only where it is associated with a carriageway.

Public Places
Public Place

The term Other Public Place is now used for several offences within the Road Traffic Act 1988.

The following should be considered :-

- are the public in general allowed access or is admission restricted to a particular group?
- can members of the public be expected to be found there?
- were there any members of the public there at the time of the incident? If so, how many?
- can the public drive vehicles there or is it restricted to pedestrians?
- have any prohibitions or restrictions (signs, gates, verbal warnings, etc.) been overcome or ignored?
- are any such prohibitions ever enforced?
- were there any other vehicles at the location?
- is there any separation between vehicles and pedestrians?

Section 1(4) Prevention of Crime Act 1953

Public place includes any highway, or in Scotland any road within the meaning of the *Roads (Scotland) Act 1984* and any other premises or place to which at the material time the public have or are permitted to have access, whether on payment or otherwise.

A location is a public place if people gain access to it in their capacity as members of the public rather than as a person with some form of permission to enter.

Multi storey car parks, hospital car parks and pub car parks during licensing hours have been held to be public places. A pub car park may only be a public place after licensing hours if the public, in fact, do use the car park at that time.

The onus is on the prosecution to prove that the public had access to it, and the best way of doing so is to prove that they actually use it.

Public Road

A Public Road means :-

Section 62(1) Vehicle Excise and Registration Act 1994

- in England and Wales and Northern Ireland, means a road which is repairable at the public expense, and

Section 151 Roads (Scotland) Act 1984

- in Scotland, a road which a roads authority have a duty to maintain.

⚠ Danger To Road Users
Causing Danger To Road Users

Section 22A(1) Road Traffic Act 1988 - 7 years - indictable (triable either way) offence

It is an offence for a person to intentionally and without lawful authority or reasonable cause :-

(a) to cause anything to be on or over a road,

(b) to interfere with a motor vehicle, trailer or cycle, or

(c) to interfere (directly or indirectly) with traffic equipment [1],

in such circumstances that it would be obvious to a reasonable person that to do so would be dangerous.

Dangerous refers to danger either of injury to any person while on or near a road, or of serious damage to property on or near a road. In this section 'Road' does not include a footpath or bridlepath.

Regard shall be had not only to the circumstances of which he could be expected to be aware but also to any circumstances shown to have been within the knowledge of the accused.

[1] Traffic Equipment

• anything lawfully placed on or near a road by a highway authority.

• a traffic sign lawfully placed on or near a road by a person other than a highway authority.

• any fence, barrier or light lawfully placed on or near a road :-

   ○ under *section 174 Highways Act 1980, Public Utilities Street Works Act 1950 or section 65 Street Works Act 1991* (which provide for guarding, lighting and signing in streets at works), or

   ○ by a constable or a person acting under the instructions (whether general or specific) of a chief officer of police.

Anything on or near a road shall, unless the contrary is proved, be deemed to have been lawfully placed there.

Damage to roads etc.

Section 100 Roads (Scotland) Act 1984 - level 3 fine

It is an offence for a person who without lawful authority or reasonable excuse :-

(a) deposits anything whatsoever on a road so as to damage the road,

(b) paints or otherwise inscribes or affixes upon the surface of a road or upon a tree, traffic sign, milestone, structure or works on or in a road, a picture, letter, sign or other mark.

Obstruction

Wilful Obstruction of the Highway

Section 137(1) Highways Act 1980 - 6 months and/or level 3 fine - fixed penalty offence if vehicle

It is an offence for a person, without lawful authority or excuse, if they in any way wilfully obstruct the free passage along a highway.

For the purposes of this section it does not matter if free passage along the highway in question has already been temporarily restricted or temporarily prohibited (whether by a constable, a traffic authority or otherwise).

This offence applies to **vehicles** and obstruction caused by **people** or objects and relates to obstructing the highway itself, not necessarily the obstruction of highway users.

Lawful authority or excuse is wide ranging and can include reasonable exercise of the right to freedom of expression and freedom of assembly.

Consideration should also be given to access for the disabled. See Chapter 36 Page 1 for police powers of arrest.

Interfering with key national infrastructure

Section 7(1) Public Order Act 2023 - 12 months/fine, indictable (triable either way) offence

It is an offence for a person :-

(a) to do an act which interferes with the use or operation of any key national infrastructure in England and Wales, and

(b) they intend that act to interfere with the use or operation of such infrastructure or are reckless as to whether it will do so.

It is a defence for a person to prove that :-

(a) they had a reasonable excuse for the act mentioned in paragraph (a) , or

(b) the act mentioned in paragraph (a) was done wholly or mainly in contemplation or furtherance of a trade dispute.

See Chapter 36 Page 1 for police powers of arrest.

Obstruction by pedestrians (Scotland).

Section 53 Civic Government Scotland Act 1982

It is an offence for a **person** who, being **on foot** in any **public place** :-

(a) obstructs, along with another or others, the lawful passage of any other person and fails to desist on being required to do so by a constable in uniform, or

(b) wilfully obstructs the lawful passage of any other person.

See Chapter 36 Page 2 for police powers of arrest.

Placing a Rope Across a Road

It is an offence for a person for any purpose :-

Section 162 Highways Act 1980 - level 3 fine

• to place any rope, wire or other apparatus across a highway or a road in such a manner as to be likely to cause danger to persons using the highway,

Section 101 Roads (Scotland) Act 1984 - level 3 fine

• to place or cause to be placed in a road rope, wire or other apparatus in such manner as endangers road users.

It is a defence to prove that all necessary means to give adequate warning of danger had been taken.

Depositing Anything on a Highway

Section 148, 161(1) Highways Act 1980 - level 3 fine

It is an offence for a person without lawful authority or excuse to :-

• deposit anything whatsoever on a highway :-

  ○ to the interruption of a user of the highway, *Section 148*, or

  ○ in consequence whereof a user of the highway is injured or endangered, *Section 161(1)*,

Section 129(2) Roads (Scotland) Act 1984 - level 3 fine

• place or deposit anything in a road so as to obstruct the passage of, or to endanger, road users.

Control of stray and other animals

Section 155 Highways Act 1980 - level 3 fine

If any horse, cattle, sheep, goats or swine are found at any time straying or lying on or at the side of a **highway** their **keeper** is guilty of an offence except on any part of a highway passing over any common land, waste or unenclosed ground and where there are rights of pasture at the side of a highway.

Section 98 Roads (Scotland) Act 1984 - level 3 fine

It is an offence for a person to leave an animal on, or allow it so to stray onto, a road other than at a place where that road is running through unenclosed land and it may be seized and detained by the roads authority or by a constable.

It shall be a defence for a person accused of allowing an animal to stray onto a road to prove that he took all reasonable steps to prevent such straying.

Dog without a lead

Section 27 Road Traffic Act 1988 - level 1 fine

It is an offence for a **person** to cause or permit a dog to be on a **designated road** (by an order of the local authority) without the dog being held on a lead except dogs proved to :-

- be kept for driving or tending sheep or cattle in the course of a trade or business,
- have been in use under proper control for sporting purposes.

Fires and Fireworks

Section 161, 161A Highways Act 1980

It is an offence for a **person** without lawful authority or excuse :-

- to light a fire on or over any land forming part of a highway with a carriageway, *S161(2)(a) - level 3 fine*
- to discharge any firearm within 50 feet of the centre of a highway with a carriageway, *S161(2)(b) - level 3 fine*
- to discharge any firework within 50 feet of the centre of a highway with a carriageway, *S161(2)(b) - level 3 fine*
- to light a fire or direct or permit a fire to be lit, without taking reasonable precautions, on any land not forming part of a highway with a carriageway, *Sec 161A(1)(a) - level 5 fine*
- to direct or permit a fire to be lit on any such land, *Sec 161A(1)(b) - level 5 fine*

and in consequence a user of any highway with a carriageway is injured, interrupted or endangered.

It is a defence for the accused to prove :-

- that at the time the fire was lit he was satisfied on reasonable grounds that it was unlikely that users the highway would be injured, interrupted or endangered by, or by smoke from, that fire or any other fire caused by that fire, and
- either :-
  - that both before and after the fire was lit he did all he reasonably could to prevent users of the highway from being injured, interrupted or endangered, or
  - that he had a reasonable excuse for not doing so.

Section 100(c) Roads (Scotland) Act 1984 - level 3 fine

It is an offence for a person who without lawful authority or reasonable excuse to light a fire within, or permit a fire for which he is responsible to spread to within, 30 metres of a road, damages the road or endangers traffic on it.

Road Numbering System

The system of road numbering in Great Britain is based on nine zones numbered from 1 to 9 whose boundaries form nine major arterial roads and the River Thames which radiate from two central points, London and Edinburgh.

Each zone takes its number from the A-road on its anticlockwise boundary. These are :-

- A1 - London to Edinburgh,
- A2 - London to Dover,
- A3 - London to Portsmouth,
- A4 - London to Avonmouth,
- A5 - London to Holyhead,
- A6 - Luton to Carlisle,
- A7 - Carlisle to Glasgow,
- A8 - Edinburgh to Greenock,
- A9 - Grangemouth to Thurso.

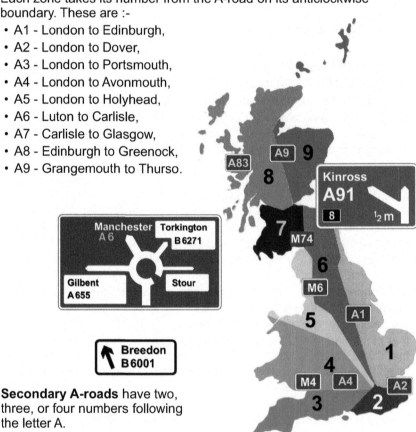

Secondary A-roads have two, three, or four numbers following the letter A.

B-roads conform to the same road numbering zones and have three or four numbers following the letter B.

The numbering system for **motorways** follows the same basic principles but the boundaries differ slightly from those used for A roads.

Some roads cross more than one zone and new roads and changes in route classifications over the years mean that some roads numbers do not conform to the system.

Chapter 2 Vehicles

Vehicle

Oxford English Dictionary

A thing used for transporting people or goods on land.

The term is not defined in the Road Traffic Acts.

Mechanically Propelled Vehicle

Mechanically propelled includes propulsion by internal combustion engine, steam or electricity.

A vehicle will remain mechanically propelled providing motive power can readily be applied or re-applied.

A broken down vehicle does not cease to be a mechanically propelled vehicle. If towed by another vehicle it will also become a trailer.

Motor Vehicle

Section 185 Road Traffic Act 1988

A Motor Vehicle is a mechanically propelled vehicle intended or adapted for use on roads.

A vehicle is intended or adapted for use on a road if a reasonable person would say one of its uses would be a road use.

Adapted can mean fit or suitable as well as altered.

Section 188 Road Traffic Act 1988

A Hovercraft is a motor vehicle.

An e-Scooter (electric scooter) or other powered transporter will fall within the definition of motor vehicle if it can be shown that it is intended or adapted (by its design, construction or by use) for use on the road.

e-Scooters currently on trials across Great Britain are intended for use on the roads and so fulfil the criteria of Motor Vehicle.

Vehicles Not To Be Classed As Motor Vehicles
Section 189(1) Road Traffic Act 1988

The following vehicles are not classed as Motor Vehicles but they remain **Mechanically Propelled Vehicles** and are still subject (except where specifically excluded) to the requirements which apply to mechanically propelled vehicles :-

- a mechanically propelled vehicle being an implement for cutting grass which is controlled by a pedestrian[1] and is not capable of being used or adapted for any other purpose,
- any other mechanically propelled vehicle controlled by a pedestrian[1] specified by regulations,
- an electrically assisted pedal cycle prescribed by regulations,
- Class 1, 2 and 3 Invalid Carriages complying with the prescribed requirements and being used in accordance with the prescribed conditions *(see below and pages 8 and 9)*. *Mechanically propelled invalid carriages are still classed as motor vehicles for the purpose of section 22A RTA 1988 - person causing danger by interfering with a motor vehicle.*

Other Exemptions

Section 20(1)(b) Chronically Sick and Disabled Persons Act 1970
The Use of Invalid Carriages on Highways Regulations 1988

Class 1, 2 and 3 Invalid Carriages complying with the prescribed requirements used in accordance with the prescribed conditions (*see pages 8 and 9*) may be used on footways, footpaths, bridleways and cyclepaths.They are also exempt from the following sections of the *Road Traffic Act 1988* :-

- *sections 1 to 4* - Dangerous and Careless driving offences, Unfit to drive through drink or drugs,
- *section 21* - Prohibition of driving or parking on cycle tracks,
- *section 34* - Prohibition of driving mechanically propelled vehicles elsewhere than on roads,
- *section 83* - Offences relating to selling reflectors and tail lamps,
- *section 163* - Power of police to stop vehicles,
- *section 170* - Duty of driver to stop, report accident and give information or documents, and
- *section 181* - General provisions as to accident inquiries.

[1]**Controlled by a pedestrian** means that the vehicle is either :-

- constructed or adapted for use only under such control, or
- constructed or adapted for use either under such control or under the control of a person carried on it,

but is not for the time being in use under, or proceeding under, the control of a person carried on it.

Other Vehicles

Trailer
Regulation 3 Road Vehicles Lighting Regulations 1989

A vehicle constructed or adapted to be drawn by another vehicle.

Carriage
Section 191 Road Traffic Act 1988

A motor vehicle or trailer is deemed to be a carriage within the meaning of any Act, rule, regulation or byelaw made under any Act of Parliament, and if used as a carriage of any particular class shall for the purpose of any enactment relating to carriages of any particular class be deemed to be a carriage of that class.

Trolley Vehicle and Tramcar
Section 192 Road Traffic Act 1988, Tramcars and Trolley Vehicles (Modification of Enactments) Regulations 1992

Tramcar - any carriage used on any road by virtue of an order under the *Light Railways Act 1896*.

Trolley vehicle - a mechanically propelled vehicle adapted for use on roads without rails under power transmitted to it from some external source (whether or not there is in addition a source of power on board the vehicle).

Duobus - a trolley vehicle adapted to operate under power provided from a source on board when it is not operating from power transmitted to it from some external source, maximum speed 30mph.

Cycle
Section 192(1) Road Traffic Act 1988

A bicycle, a tricycle, or a cycle having four or more wheels, not being in any case a motor vehicle.

Electrically assisted pedal cycles (EAPCs)
Electrically Assisted Pedal Cycle Regulations 1983
The Electrically Assisted Pedal Cycles (Amendment) Regulations 2015

A pedal cycle with two or more wheels (includes tricycle and quad) which is fitted with an electric motor of rated output not exceeding 0.25kW - motor cuts out above 15.5mph (25kph).

Electric Scooter (e-Scooter) used in trials
The Electric Scooter Trials and Traffic Signs (Coronavirus) Regulations and General Directions 2020

In certain areas e-scooters taking part in approved trials may be used on the roads. Only approved rental e-scooters may be used in the trials by agreement with the hosting local public authority.

Privately owned and other e-scooters which do not form part of the trial are not permitted to be used on the road (which includes the footway). See Powered Transporters for further details.

No vehicle licence is required, insurance is arranged by the rental company, helmets are not required to be worn and a full or provisional category AM, A or B driving licence is required - there is no requirement to complete compulsory basic training. The minimum age to drive an e-scooter (which is classed as a category Q vehicle) is 16 years,

The e-scooters are only permitted to be used on carriageways (including cycle lanes) and cycle tracks. They are not permitted on footways (pavements), footpaths, bridlepaths or restricted byways.

Electric scooters used in these trials are classed as **motor vehicles** so the rider is **not exempt** from requirements relating to :-

- drink and drug drive legislation - prescribed limits apply as they do for a car driver, and an e-scooter rider could be breathalysed,
- use of mobile phones whilst riding,
- driving on pavements,
- causing a danger of injury,
- accident obligations including the requirement to stop, report and produce insurance,
- careless/dangerous driving,
- signs and signals.

This list is not exhaustive, other legislation applies as it does to any motor vehicle.

Light Quadricycles (Microcars) L6e
Regulation (EU) No 168/2013

Motor vehicles with 4 wheels and :-

- unladen mass not exceeding 425 kg, (not including batteries on electric vehicles),
- maximum design speed not exceeding 45 km/h (28 mph), and
  - engine cylinder capacity not exceeding 50 cc - spark ignition, or
  - maximum net power output not exceeding 6 kW - diesel, or
  - maximum continuous rated power not exceeding 6 kW - electric motors.

See also Chapter 18 Page 6.

Classification Of Vehicles

Section 185 Road Traffic Act 1988
Regulation 3 Road Vehicles (Construction and Use) Regs 1986

Vehicles constructed or adapted to carry a load or passengers
Invalid Carriage

• Not exceeding 254 kg unladen.
• Designed for the sole use of the disabled.

Motorcycle

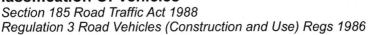

• Not exceeding 410 kg unladen.
• Not more than 3 wheels.

Motor Car

• Goods carrying - Not exceeding 3050 kg unladen.
• Passenger carrying with not more than 7 passenger seats - Not exceeding 3050 kg unladen.
• Passenger carrying with more than 7 passenger seats - Not exceeding 2540 kg unladen.

Heavy Motor Car

• Goods carrying - Exceeding 3050 kg unladen.
• Passenger carrying with not more than 7 passenger seats - Exceeding 3050 kg unladen.
• Passenger carrying with more than 7 passenger seats - Exceeding 2540kg unladen.

Vehicles not constructed or adapted to carry a load or passengers (except water/fuel/batteries/tools)
Motor Tractor

• Not exceeding 7370 kg unladen weight.

Light Locomotive

• Exceeding 7370 kg , not exceeding 11690 kg unladen weight (mobile cranes, fixed plant or agricultural vehicles for example).

Heavy Locomotive

• Exceeding 11690 kg unladen weight.

> **Unladen weight** - The weight of a vehicle or trailer inclusive of the body and all parts (the heavier being taken where alternative bodies or parts are used) which are necessary to or ordinarily used with the vehicle or trailer when working on a road, but exclusive of the weight of water, fuel or accumulators used for the purpose of the supply of power for the propulsion of the vehicle or, as the case may be, of any vehicle by which the trailer is drawn, and of loose tools and loose equipment.

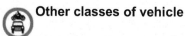 **Other classes of vehicle**

Agricultural Motor Vehicle

- May be of any class of vehicle (except dual purpose vehicle).
- Constructed primarily for off road use and used in connection with agriculture, horticulture, forestry or fisheries.

Agricultural Trailer

- Constructed or adapted and only used for the purpose of agriculture, horticulture or forestry, not being an agricultural trailed appliance.

Articulated Vehicle

- A heavy motor car or motor car not being an articulated bus, with a trailer so attached that part of the trailer is superimposed on the drawing vehicle and, when the trailer is uniformly loaded, not less than 20% of the weight of its load is borne by the drawing vehicle.

Bus

- A motor vehicle which is constructed or adapted to carry more than eight seated passengers in addition to the driver.

Car derived van

- A goods vehicle which is constructed or adapted as a derivative of a passenger vehicle and does not exceed 2000kg laden weight.

Coach

- A large bus with a maximum gross weight of more than 7.5 tonnes and with a maximum speed exceeding 60mph.

Dual Purpose Vehicle

A vehicle constructed or adapted for the carriage both of passengers and of goods, maximum unladen weight not exceeding 2040kg, and either :-

- all wheel drive, or
- permanently fitted with a rigid roof, at least one row of transverse passenger seats to the rear of the driver's seat and fitted with both side and rear windows with a minimum ratio between the size of passenger and stowage areas (eg: some estate cars).

Engineering Plant

- Movable plant or equipment being a motor vehicle or trailer specially designed and constructed for the special purposes of engineering operations, and which cannot, owing to the requirements of those purposes, comply with all the requirements of these Regulations and which is not constructed primarily to carry a load other than a load being either excavated materials raised from the ground by apparatus on the motor vehicle or trailer or materials which the vehicle or trailer is specially designed to treat while carried thereon.

- A mobile crane which does not comply in all respects with the requirements of these Regulations.

Invalid carriage

- A mechanically propelled vehicle the weight of which unladen does not exceed 254 kg and which is specially designed and constructed, and not merely adapted, for the use of a person suffering from some physical defect or disability and is solely used by such a person. *See next page.*

Living Van

- A vehicle used primarily as living accommodation by one or more persons, and which is not also used for the carriage of goods or burden which are not needed by such one or more persons for the purpose of their residence in the vehicle.

Works Trailer

- A trailer designed for use in private premises and used on a road only in delivering goods from or to such premises to or from a vehicle on a road in the immediate neighbourhood, or in passing from one part of any such premises to another or to other private premises in the immediate neighbourhood or in connection with road works while at or in the immediate neighbourhood of the site of such works.

Works Truck

- A motor vehicle (other than a straddle carrier) designed for use in private premises and used on a road only in delivering goods from or to such premises to or from a vehicle on a road in the immediate neighbourhood, or in passing from one part of any such premises to another or to other private premises in the immediate neighbourhood or in connection with road works while at or in the immediate neighbourhood of the site of such works.

Disabled persons vehicles
Motability Motor Cars

A motor car not exceeding 3500kg maximum weight and used by or for the purposes of a disabled person in recipient of Personal Independence Payment, Adult Disability Payment, War Pensioner's Mobility Supplement or Armed Forces Independence Payment may attract a reduced or nil rate of vehicle licence fee and may also benefit from ULEZ exemptions. The car may or may not be adapted.

The user may hold a disabled persons parking permit, a 'Blue Badge' providing exemptions from some parking restrictions (see Chapter 28 Page 8). Vehicles are leased and will be registered to Motability.

Invalid carriages

Invalid Carriages are single seat vehicles specially designed and constructed for the use of a person suffering from some physical defect or disability and solely used by such a person. Vehicles and drivers benefit from exemptions including insurance and testing but may be required to comply with certain conditions.

Invalid carriages not exceeding 254kg unladen

An example was the 'invacar' the 3 wheeled blue microcar which was provided free of charge to disabled drivers. The scheme has since been replaced by the Motability Scheme which provides both cars not classed as invalid carriages (*see above*) and scooters which do fall within this class (*see below*).

Motability Scooters

Use of Invalid Carriages on Highways Regulations 1988
Chronically Sick and Disabled Persons Act 1970

These are Class 1, 2 and 3 Invalid Carriages which must comply with prescribed requirements and be used in accordance with prescribed conditions including use solely by the disabled.

They are not classed as motor vehicles if used as prescribed (except for the purpose of *section 22A Road Traffic Act 1988* - causing danger to road users) and Sections 1 to 4, 21, 34, 83, 163, 170 and 181 of the Road Traffic Act 1988 do not apply (*see Page 2*).

Consider where applicable Section 12 Licensing Act 1872 - drunk on a highway or other public place while in charge of a carriage.

Class 1 Invalid Carriages

• Not exceeding 113.4 kg unladen
• No mechanical propulsion.

Class 2 Invalid Carriages

- Max 113.4 kg unladen.
- Max speed 4mph.
- For use only on footways, footpaths, bridleways and cyclepaths except to cross a carriageway or where there isn't a footway.
- Not permitted on motorway.
- Not classed as a motor vehicle (but is mechanically propelled vehicle).
- Driving licence, Test Certificate and Insurance not required.
- No minimum age.

Class 3 Invalid Carriages

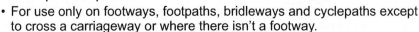

- Max 150 kg unladen, may be increased to 200kg for necessary equipment.
- Max speed 4mph on footway / 8mph on carriageway.
- May be used on footways, footpaths, bridleways, cyclepaths and carriageways but not in active bus or cycle only lanes.
- Not permitted on motorway.
- Not advised to use on dual carriageways but if used (except to cross) where speed limit exceeds 50mph an all round orange flashing beacon is required (*see Chapter 3 Page 17*).
- Not classed as motor vehicle (but is mechanically propelled vehicle).
- Driving licence, Test Certificate and Insurance not required.
- Minimum age 14 years.
- Vehicle excise licence - nil licence.
- Requires a speed indicator, speed limiter (for pavement use), a horn, an efficient braking system, front and rear lights and reflectors, direction indicators able to operate as a hazard warning signal, a rear view mirror.
- Maximum width 0.85 metres.
- Must be registered with DVLA but registration plate not required to be displayed.

Prescribed Conditions

Regulation 4 Use of Invalid Carriages on Highways Regulations 1988

Class 1, Class 2 and Class 3 invalid carriages must only be used by :-

- a person suffering from some physical defect or physical disability,
- some other person for the purposes only of taking the invalid carriage to or bringing it away from any place where work of maintenance or repair is to be or has been carried out to the invalid carriage,
- a manufacturer for the purposes only of testing or demonstrating the invalid carriage,
- a person offering to sell the invalid carriage for the purpose only of demonstrating it, or
- a person giving practical training in the use of the invalid carriage for that purpose only.

Powered Transporters

Unregistered motorised vehicles are becoming a frequent sight on our roads and public places. Such vehicles include :-

- motorised scooters including e-scooters (except rental e-scooters which form part of a government trial),
- motorised boards and cycles (except electrically assisted pedal cycles which are constructed and used in accordance with the regulations),
- quad bikes (although some of these are registered and road legal),
- trials motorcycles and mini race replica motorcycles,
- personal transporters aka Segways.

The legislation does not exempt 'toys'.

Offences

Both the class of vehicle and the place where it is used will determine which offences apply and what powers, including seizure, are available.

Legislation restricting the use of these vehicles may apply to all carriages, all Mechanically Propelled vehicles or only Motor Vehicles.

Additionally it may apply to :-

- use on a Road (including carriageways, footpaths, footways, bridleways, verges, private roads open to the public etc.),
- use on a Public Road (registration and taxation offences),
- use in a Public Place which does not form part of a road including common land and moorland,
- use without permission of the landowner on Private Land which does not form part of a road,
- use on Sites of Special Scientific Interest (SSSI's).

Points of evidence

Points of evidence to note include :-

- characteristics of the vehicle, seats, dimensions, axles, wheels, lights and equipment, propulsion etc.,
- where it is being used (road, public place etc.),
- other traffic or pedestrians using that location, and for what purpose - eg is it used as a shortcut or 'way of passage' or for other reasons,
- frequency of use on a road (including footpaths and footways),
- purpose and length of journey on and off road - from/to etc.

Cases of note which have determined that such vehicles meet the definition of motor vehicle include DPP v Saddington 2000(Go-Ped), Winter v DPP 2002 (electric scooter), Coates v CPS 2011 (Segway).

Automated Vehicles

Section 1 Automated and Electric Vehicles Act 2018
Driving Automation Levels

- Dynamic driving task (DDT) - all the real-time operational and tactile functions required to operate a vehicle in on-road traffic.
- Operational design domain (ODD) - the specific conditions under which an automation system or feature is designed to function.
- Automated driving system (ADS) - encapsulates all the hardware and software collectively capable of performing the entire DDT on a sustained basis.

There are 6 Levels of Driving Automation : -

- **Level 0 – No Driving Automation** The performance by the driver of the entire DDT. *Example - manually controlled vehicles.*
- **Level 1 – Driver Assistance** A driving automation system characterised by the sustained and ODD-specific execution of either the lateral or the longitudinal vehicle motion control subtask of the DDT. *Example - cruise control.*
- **Level 2 – Partial Driving Automation** Similar to Level 1 but characterised by both the lateral and longitudinal vehicle motion control subtasks of the DDT with the expectation that the driver completes the object and event detection and response (OEDR) subtask and supervises the driving automation system. *Example - Adaptive Cruise Control With Stop-and-Go and Lane Centering.*
- **Level 3 – Conditional Driving Automation** The sustained and ODD-specific performance by an ADS of the entire DDT, with the expectation that the human driver will be ready to respond to a request to intervene when issued by the ADS. *Example - vehicles have environmental detection capabilities and can make informed decisions for themselves but still require human override. The driver must remain alert and ready to take control if the system is unable to execute the task.*
- **Level 4 – High Driving Automation** Sustained and ODD-specific ADS performance of the entire DDT is carried out without any expectation that a user will respond to a request to intervene. *Example - vehicles do not require human interaction and can still be manually overridden.*
- **Level 5 – Full Driving Automation** Sustained and unconditional performance by an ADS of the entire DDT. *Example - vehicles do not require human attention and will have no manual steering or speed controls.*

Levels 0, 1, and 2 - the Human monitors the driving environment.
Levels 3, 4, and 5 - the Automated System monitors the driving environment.
Legislation and Codes of Practice will be introduced as the technology evolves.

Stopping Vehicles
Power to Stop - Police and Traffic Officers (HATO)

Section 163 Road Traffic Act 1988

A person :-

- driving a **mechanically propelled vehicle¹** on a **road**, or
- riding a **cycle** on a **road**,

must stop on being required to do so by a constable in uniform or a traffic officer in uniform².

¹ Except Class 2 or 3 Invalid Carriages (mobility scooters) which comply with the prescribed requirements and are being used in accordance with the prescribed conditions. See Page 9.

² Traffic Officer (HATO - Highways Agency Traffic Officer) - designated under s*ection 2 Traffic Management Act 2004* to exercise powers on specified relevant roads whilst on duty in uniform in England and Wales.

No reason to stop is required.

There is **no power to direct vehicles** to another location under this section however a vehicle may be directed to another place for other reasons including :-

- in the case of a traffic survey, to a particular point on or near the road,
- goods vehicles, public service vehicles and motor vehicles adapted to carry more than 8 passengers, up to 5 miles for the purposes of having the vehicle inspected,(s*ection 68 Road Traffic Act 1988*), or
- weighing a motor vehicle and any trailer drawn by it, any distance for the purposes of having the vehicle(s) weighed (s*ection 78 Road Traffic Act 1988*) (compensation if over 5 miles and not overweight), or
- any vehicle to which *EU* or *AETR* rules apply, any distance for the purposes of enabling an inspection of the recording equipment where interference is believed, (s*ection 99ZB Transport Act 1968*), (compensation if over 5 miles and no tachograph offences found).

Fail to stop

Section 163(3) Road Traffic Act 1988 - level 5 fine - (level 3 cycle) - fixed penalty offence

It is an offence for a person :-

- driving a **mechanically propelled vehicle¹** on a **road**, or
- riding a **cycle** on a **road**,

to fail to comply with this section.

Section 17(1)(c)(iiia) Police and Criminal Evidence Act 1984

A constable may enter and search any premises for the purpose of arresting a person for an offence under *Sec 163 Road Traffic Act 1988*.

Other Police Powers

Police powers of arrest - See *Chapter 36 Pages 1 and 2*

Police powers of entry and seizure may be found at :-

Section 165A Road Traffic Act 1988 - See Chapter 2 Page 19

Other Stopping Powers

- A constable (in uniform or otherwise) or a traffic officer in uniform may require any **vehicle** or **cycle** on a **road** to stop when engaged in the regulation of traffic.

- A constable in uniform or a traffic officer in uniform may require a **pedestrian** on a **road** to stop when engaged in the regulation of traffic.

- A constable in uniform may require any **mechanically propelled vehicle** in **any place** to stop when dealing with vehicles used to cause alarm, distress or annoyance.

- *Section 60 Criminal Justice and Public Order 1994* provides powers (subject to authorisation) to a **constable in uniform** to stop a **vehicle** where violence is anticipated or has occurred in a particular location.

- *Sections 43, to 45 Terrorism Act 2000* provide powers to a **constable in uniform** to stop a **vehicle** where when terrorist activity is anticipated in a particular location.

- A constable in uniform may stop any motor vehicle and a stopping officer may stop certain vehicles for the purpose of a roadside test (*see Chapter 12 Page 5*).

Stopping Officers (DVSA)

Section 66B Road Traffic Act 1988

Stopping Officers will typically be DVSA officers with powers in relation to commercial goods and passenger vehicles in respect of :-

- goods and public service vehicle operator's licence checks,
- community authorisations and permit checks,
- cabotage compliance,
- vehicle weight checking,
- roadside vehicle roadworthiness inspections,
- inspection of drivers records and recording equipment,
- driver CPC requirements, and
- HGV road user levy compliance.

They must wear an approved uniform.

Section 66C Road Traffic Act 1988

(1) A person commits an offence if the person, with intent to deceive, impersonates a stopping officer or makes any statement or does any act calculated falsely to suggest that the person is a stopping officer.

(2) A person commits an offence if the person resists or wilfully obstructs a stopping officer who is exercising the powers of a stopping officer.

Regulation of Traffic
Regulation of Vehicles

Section 35 Road Traffic Act 1988 - level 3 fine (NOIP) - 3 points if motor vehicle - fixed penalty offence

Where a constable or a traffic officer[1] is engaged in the regulation of traffic in a **road** it is an offence for a person driving or propelling a **vehicle**[2] to neglect or refuse :-

- *Section 35(1)(a)* to stop the vehicle, or
- *Section 35(1)(b)* to make it proceed in, or keep to a particular line of traffic, or
- *Section 35(2)* in the event of a traffic survey in the vicinity of a road, to stop the vehicle, make it proceed in, or keep to, a particular line of traffic, or to proceed to a particular point on or near the road,

when directed to do so by the constable in the execution of his duty or a traffic officer[1].

There is no requirement for the constable to be in uniform - as when, for example, directing traffic at the scene of an accident when off-duty.

[1] Traffic Officer - designated under Section 2 Traffic Management Act 2004 (usually by the highway authority) to exercise powers on specified relevant roads whilst on duty in uniform.

[2] This Section applies to all vehicles including cycles, horse and trap etc.

Traffic Survey - there is no requirement for the driver to provide any information for the survey - no unreasonable delay shall be caused to a person unwilling to take part.

There is no power to direct vehicles to another location under this section except, in the case of a traffic survey, to a particular point on or near the road.

Regulation of Pedestrians

Section 37 Road Traffic Act 1988 - level 3 fine

It is an offence where a **constable in uniform** or a traffic officer[1] is engaged in the regulation of vehicular traffic in a **road** for a person **on foot** to proceed across or along the carriageway in contravention of a direction to stop.

Interfering with a motor vehicle, trailer or cycle

Section 22A(1)(b) Road Traffic Act 1988 - 7 years - indictable (triable either way) offence

It is an offence for a person to intentionally and without 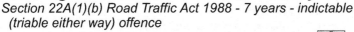 lawful authority or reasonable cause to interfere with a **motor vehicle, trailer or cycle** in such circumstances that it would be obvious to a reasonable person that to do so would be dangerous.

> *Dangerous refers to danger either of injury to any person while on or near a road, or of serious damage to property on or near a road. In this section Road does not include a footpath or bridlepath.*
>
> *Regard shall be had not only to the circumstances of which he could be expected to be aware but also to any circumstances shown to have been within the knowledge of the accused.*

Interfering with vehicles

Section 9(1) Criminal Attempts Act 1981 - 3 months and/or level 4 fine

It is an offence for a person to interfere with :-

- a **motor vehicle**, or
- **trailer**,

or anything carried in or on such a vehicle with the intention of :-

- theft of the motor vehicle or trailer,
- theft of anything carried in or on the motor vehicle or trailer,
- taking the vehicle without consent,

by him or someone else.

> *If it is shown that a person accused of an offence under this section intended that one of those offences should be committed, it is immaterial that it cannot be shown which it was.*

Tampering with motor vehicles

Section 25 Road Traffic Act 1988 - level 3 fine

It is an offence for a person, without lawful authority or reasonable cause, to :-

(a) get on to, or

(b) tamper with the brake or other part of its mechanism of,

a **motor vehicle** which is on a **road or a parking place** provided by a local authority.

Holding or getting on to vehicles in order to be towed or carried

Section 26 Road Traffic Act 1988 - level 1 fine

It is an offence for a person :-

1. for the purpose of being carried, without lawful authority or reasonable cause, to take or retain hold of, or get on to, a **motor vehicle or trailer** while in motion on a **road**, or

2. for the purpose of being drawn, to take or retain hold of a **motor vehicle** or trailer while in motion on a **road**.

Shining Laser at vehicles

Section 1 Laser Misuse (Vehicles) Act 2018 - 5 years and/or max fine - indictable (triable either way) offence

It is an offence for a person to shine or direct a laser beam towards a **vehicle**[1] which is moving or ready to move[2] where the laser beam[3] dazzles or distracts, or is likely to dazzle or distract, the person in control.

It is a defence to show :-

• that the person had a reasonable excuse for shining or directing the laser beam towards the vehicle, or

• that the person :-

  ○ did not intend to shine or direct the laser beam towards the vehicle, and

  ○ exercised all due diligence and took all reasonable precautions to avoid doing so.

A person is taken to have shown a fact mentioned above if sufficient evidence is adduced to raise an issue with respect to it, and the contrary is not proved beyond reasonable doubt.

[1] Vehicle means any vehicle used for travel by land, water or air.
[2] A mechanically propelled vehicle which is not moving or ready to move but whose engine or motor is running is to be treated as ready to move.
[3] Laser beam means a beam of coherent light produced by a device of any kind.

Drivers of horsedrawn carts etc.

Section 65(2) Roads (Scotland) Act 1984

The owner of a drawn vehicle commits an offence if he permits a child of under :-

(a) 14 years of age to drive that vehicle on a road, or

(b) 16 years of age (not being such child as is mentioned in paragraph (a) above) to drive that vehicle on a road other than under the immediate supervision of a person of 18 years of age or more.

Drawn vehicle means a vehicle pulled by one or more draught animals.

Taking vehicles (TDA or TWOC)

Section 12(1) Theft Act 1968 - level 5 fine and/or 6 months

It is an offence for a person, without the consent of the owner or other lawful authority :-

- to take any **conveyance** for his own or another's use, or
- knowing that any conveyance has been taken without such authority, drives it or allows himself to be carried in or on it.

Conveyance includes any conveyance constructed or adapted for the carriage of a person or persons by land, water or air but does not include vehicles controlled by persons not carried in or on them or pedal cycles.

Aggravated Vehicle Taking

Section 12A Theft Act 1968 - 2 years (14 yrs if death results from accident) - disqualification 12 months 3-11 points, indictable (triable either way)

It is an offence for a person to take a **mechanically propelled vehicle** without consent and before it was recovered :-

- the vehicle was driven dangerously on a road or other public place,
- owing to the driving of the vehicle an accident occurred involving injury to any person,
- owing to the driving of the vehicle an accident occurred involving damage to any property other than the vehicle itself, or
- damage was caused to the vehicle.

It is a defence to prove that the accident or damage occurred before a person took it or was carried in the vehicle or he was neither in, on nor in the immediate vicinity when that driving, accident or damage occurred.

Taking vehicles - Scotland

Section 178(1) Road Traffic Act 1988 - 3 months, max fine, 8 points

It is an offence in Scotland for a person to :-

(a) take and drive away a motor vehicle without having either the consent of the owner of the vehicle or other lawful authority, or

(b) knowing that a motor vehicle has been so taken, drives it or allows himself to be carried in or on it without such consent or authority.

Seizure of vehicles
Power to Seize vehicles used to cause alarm, distress or annoyance

Section 59 Police Reform Act 2002
Section 126 Antisocial Behaviour etc. (Scotland) Act 2004

A constable in uniform may seize a motor vehicle[1] where he has reasonable grounds for believing that it is being used or has been used :-

- in contravention of *section 3 Road Traffic Act 1988* (careless and inconsiderate driving), or *section 34 Road Traffic Act 1988* (prohibition of off-road driving), and
- is causing, or is likely to cause, alarm, distress or annoyance to members of the public.

He may, if the motor vehicle is moving, order the person driving it to stop the vehicle.

Before seizing the motor vehicle he must warn the person who appears to be the driver that he will seize it if that use continues or is repeated, and if it appears to him that the use has continued or been repeated after the warning he may then seize and remove the vehicle.

The warning is not required if :-

- the circumstances make it impracticable for him to give the warning, or
- the constable has already on that occasion given a warning in respect of any use of that motor vehicle or of another motor vehicle by that person or any other person, or
- the constable has reasonable grounds for believing that such a warning has been given on that occasion otherwise than by him, or
- the constable has reasonable grounds for believing that the person has already been given such a warning, whether or not by that constable or in respect the same vehicle or the same or a similar use, on a previous occasion in the previous twelve months.

In order to exercise those powers he may enter any premises (except a private dwelling house) on which he has reasonable grounds for believing the motor vehicle to be, and may use reasonable force, if necessary, to seize the vehicle or enter the premises.

*[1] Motor vehicle means **any mechanically propelled vehicle**, whether or not it is intended or adapted for use on roads. Private dwelling house does not include any garage or other structure occupied with the dwelling house, or any land appurtenant to the dwelling house.*

Offence
Section 59(6) Police Reform Act 2002 - level 3 fine
Section 126(6) Antisocial Behaviour etc. (Scotland) Act 2004

It is an offence to fail to stop when ordered to do so by a constable in uniform acting under this section.

If the vehicle is on a road see Section 163 Road Traffic Act 1988 for further powers of entry (see Page 12).

Power to Seize vehicles driven without a licence or insurance etc.

Section 165A Road Traffic Act 1988

A constable in uniform may seize a **motor vehicle** (not an invalid carriage) where :-

- he has required a person under *section 164 Road Traffic Act 1988* to produce his driving licence for examination, the person fails to produce it, and he has reasonable grounds for believing that a motor vehicle is or was being driven by the person in contravention of *section 87(1)* (otherwise than in accordance with a licence, or
- he has required a person under *section 165 Road Traffic Act 1988*, to produce evidence that a motor vehicle is not or was not being driven in contravention of *section 143* (no insurance, the person fails to produce such evidence, and the constable has reasonable grounds for believing that the vehicle is or was being so driven, or
- the person fails to stop the vehicle when required to do so by a constable in uniform under *section 163 Road Traffic Act 1988*, or to stop the vehicle long enough for the constable to make such lawful enquiries as he considers appropriate, and the constable has reasonable grounds for believing that the vehicle is or was being driven in contravention of *section 87(1) or 143* (otherwise than in accordance with a licence or without insurance).

Before seizing the motor vehicle, the constable must warn the driver that he will seize it if the person does not produce his licence immediately, or as the case may be, with evidence that the vehicle is insured or exempt from insurance unless the circumstances make it impracticable for him to do so.

If the vehicle has failed to stop as requested or has driven off, he may seize it at any time within the period of 24 hours beginning with the time at which the condition in question is first satisfied.

The constable may enter any premises (other than a private dwelling house) on which he has reasonable grounds for believing the vehicle to be and may use reasonable force, if necessary, to seize the vehicle or enter the premises.

Private dwelling house does not include any garage or other structure occupied with the dwelling house, or any land appurtenant (related) to the dwelling house.

Seizure Notice

Regulation 4 Road Traffic Act 1988 (Retention and Disposal of Seized Motor Vehicles) Regulations 2005

A constable, on seizing a vehicle shall give a seizure notice to the driver of the vehicle being seized unless the circumstances make it impracticable for him to do so.

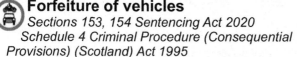

Forfeiture of vehicles
Sections 153, 154 Sentencing Act 2020
Schedule 4 Criminal Procedure (Consequential
Provisions) (Scotland) Act 1995

The courts may deprive an offender of **property** used, or intended for use for the purpose of an offence under the *Road Traffic Act 1988* which is punishable with imprisonment, or an offence of manslaughter or wanton and furious driving (*section 35 Offences Against the Person Act 1861*), by :-

- driving or attempting to drive, or being in charge of a vehicle,
- failure to provide a specimen of breath, blood or urine for analysis under *section 7 Road Traffic Act 1988* during an investigation into whether he had committed an offence whilst driving or attempting to drive or being in charge of a vehicle,
- failing, as the driver, to comply with *sections 170 (2) or (3) Road Traffic Act 1988* (fail to stop, report accident etc),

or by aiding, abetting, counselling or procuring or facilitating the commission of the offences above.

Vehicle Special Orders (VSOs)
Section 44 Road Traffic Act 1988

The Secretary of State may by order authorise, subject to such restrictions and conditions as may be specified by or under the order, the use on roads of Special Vehicles not complying with regulations[1] made under *section 41 of the Road Traffic Act 1988*.

[1]This includes The Road Vehicles (Construction and Use) Regulations 1986, The Road Vehicles (Authorised Weights) Regulations 1998 and The Road Vehicles Lighting Regulations 1989.

Section 44 orders include :-

- *The Road Vehicles (Authorisation of Special Types) (General) Order 2003* the STGO.
- Individual *Vehicle Special Orders*[2] (VSOs).

*Vehicle Special Orders can cover a wide range of vehicles and circumstances. The exemptions these orders provide are dependant on compliance with **ALL** the conditions contained within the order. Failure to comply with any condition negates the exemption and the vehicle/driver/ operator/owner must then comply with all sections of the regulations which would normally apply to the vehicle. Any offence is therefore contrary to the Road Traffic Act 1988, not the Order.*

Individual *Vehicle Special Orders* are not normally publicly circulated. They are usually issued by the Vehicle Certification Agency (VCA). The Order may require a copy to be carried on the vehicle for production.

Chapter 3 Lights

The Road Vehicles Lighting Regulations 1989 specify the fitting, maintenance and use requirements of lighting equipment on all **vehicles** and **trailers** used on the **road.**

Failure to comply with the regulations is an offence contrary to the Road Traffic Act 1988.

Offences

All vehicles

Section 42(a) Road Traffic Act 1988 - fixed penalty offence - level 3 fine

It is an offence for a person to :-

• act in contravention of, or

• fail to comply with

a construction and use requirement as to the lighting equipment and reflectors of **vehicles of any description** used on **roads**, whether or not they are mechanically propelled (no cause or permit offences).

Motor vehicles and their trailers

Section 42(b) Road Traffic Act 1988 - fixed penalty offence
- level 4 fine for goods vehicles and vehicles adapted to carry more than 8 passengers
- level 3 fine in any other case

It is an offence for a person to use on a **road** a **motor vehicle or trailer** :-

• which does not comply with construction and use requirement as to the lighting of vehicles, or

• cause[1] or permit[1] a motor vehicle or trailer to be so used.

[1] Cause and Permit offences are not fixed penalty offences.

Individual Vehicle Special Orders

Exemptions may be applied in special cases by Individual Vehicle Special Orders issued by the Vehicle Certification Agency (VCA) upon application for varying periods up to 5 years are dependant on compliance with **all** conditions contained within the order.

Failure to comply with any condition of the order negates the exemption and the vehicle must then comply with all sections of the Construction Regulations. Any offence is therefore contrary to the Road Traffic Act 1988 and the Lighting Regulations not the Order.

See Page 2-20.

Fitting of Lamps, reflectors, rear markings and devices

Road Vehicles Lighting Regulations 1989

Schedule 1 to these regulations contains the requirements for and exceptions from fitting lamps, reflectors etc. to different classes of vehicle.

Schedules 2 to 21 and Schedule 24 contain the specification for each lamp or reflector including the number required and position. :-

• *Part I* of each schedule relates to obligatory lamps etc.
• *Part II* of each schedule relates to optional lamps.

When is a lamp fitted?

Regulation 4(4) Road Vehicles Lighting Regulations 1989

A lamp shall not be regarded as being a lamp if it is :-

• so painted over or masked that it cannot be readily put to use, or
• an electric lamp which is not provided with any system of wiring by means of which it can be readily be connected with a source of electricity.

Blue warning beacons or special warning lamps remain fitted even if they are covered or not wired up.

Reflective Material

Regulation 3(3) Road Vehicles Lighting Regulations 1989

Material designed to reflect light is to be treated as showing a light and material capable of reflecting an image is not (retro-reflective material is a light but a shiny chrome bumper is not).

Fitting of Obligatory Lamps, reflectors, rear markings and devices

Regulation 18 Road Vehicles Lighting Regulations 1989
Schedule 1 Road Vehicles Lighting Regulations 1989

Every vehicle of a class specified in the tables which follow shall be fitted with the lamp, reflector, rear marking or device which :-

• are of a type specified, and
• comply with the relevant installation, alignment and performance requirements.

The following pages contain the tables referred to.

Fitting of Obligatory Lamps etc.

Motor vehicles with 3 or more wheels
Schedule 1 Table I Road Vehicles Lighting Regulations 1989

Lamp	Exceptions *(See also Exemptions pages 10, 11)*
Front Position	None.
Dim-Dip Device and Running Light	A vehicle having a maximum speed not exceeding 40 m.p.h. A vehicle first used before 01/04/1987. A home forces vehicle. A vehicle which complies with *EC regulation 76/756.*
Dipped Beam Headlamp	A vehicle having a maximum speed not exceeding 15 mph. An agricultural vehicle or works truck first used before 01/04/1986. A vehicle first used before 01/01/1931.
Main Beam Headlamp	A vehicle having a maximum speed not exceeding 25 mph. A vehicle first used before 01/04/1986 being an agricultural vehicle or a works truck. A vehicle first used before 01/01/1931.
Rear Position	None.
Hazard Warning Device	A vehicle not required to be fitted with direction indicators. A vehicle first used before 01/04/1986.
Direction Indicator	An invalid carriage having a max speed not exceeding 4 mph. Any other vehicle having a max speed not exceeding 15 mph. An agricultural vehicle having an unladen weight not exceeding 255kg. A vehicle first used before 01/04/1986 being an agricultural vehicle an industrial tractor or a works truck. A vehicle first used before 01/01/1936.
Side Marker Lamp	A vehicle having a maximum speed not exceeding 25 mph. A passenger vehicle. An incomplete vehicle proceeding for completion or to a place where it is to be stored or displayed for sale. A vehicle first used before 01/04/1991. A vehicle the overall length of which does not exceed 6 m. A vehicle 1st used before 01/04/1996 which complies with *EC Regulation 76/756.*
Rear Retro Reflector	None.
Rear Fog	A vehicle having a maximum speed not exceeding 25mph. An agricultural vehicle or a works truck first used before 01/04/1986. A vehicle first used before 01/04/1980. A vehicle having an overall width not exceeding 1300mm
Stop Lamp	A vehicle having a maximum speed not exceeding 25 mph. An agricultural vehicle or a works truck first used before 01/04/1986. A vehicle first used before 01/01/1936.

Continued over

Fitting of Obligatory Lamps etc. *continued*

Motor vehicles with 3 or more wheels - *continued*
Schedule 1 Table I Road Vehicles Lighting Regulations 1989

Lamp	Exceptions *(See also Exemptions pages 10, 11)*
End-Outline Marker	A vehicle having a max speed not exceeding 25 mph. A motor vehicle having an overall width not exceeding 2100 mm. An incomplete vehicle proceeding to a works for completion or to a place where it is to be stored or displayed for sale. A motor vehicle first used before 01/04/1991.
Rear Registration Plate Lamp	A vehicle not required to be fitted with a rear registration plate. A works truck.
Side Retro Reflector	A vehicle having a maximum speed not exceeding 25 mph. A goods vehicle :- a) 1st used on or after 01/04/1986 the overall length of which does not exceed 6m, or b) 1st used before 01/04/1986 the overall length of which does not exceed 8m. A vehicle primarily constructed for moving excavated material and being used by virtue of an Order under *section 44 of the Act* (abnormal loads - STGO). A passenger vehicle. An incomplete vehicle proceeding to a works for completion or to a place where it is to be stored or displayed for sale. A mobile crane or engineering plant.
Rear Marking	A vehicle having a maximum speed not exceeding 25 mph. A vehicle 1st used before 01/08/1982 the unladen weight of which does not exceed 3050 kg. A vehicle the maximum gross weight of which does not exceed 7500 kg. A passenger vehicle not being an articulated bus. A tractive unit for an articulated vehicle. An incomplete vehicle proceeding to a works for completion or to a place where it is to be stored or displayed for sale. An agricultural vehicle, works truck or engineering plant 1st used before 01/04/1986. A vehicle first used before 01/01/1940. A home forces vehicle. A vehicle constructed or adapted for :- (a) fire fighting or fire salvage, or (b) servicing or controlling aircraft, or (c) heating and dispensing tar or other material for the construction or maintenance of roads, or (d) transporting two or more vehicles or vehicle bodies or two or more boats.

Fitting of Obligatory Lamps etc. *continued*

Solo motor bicycle and motor bicycle combinations
Schedule 1 Table II Road Vehicles Lighting Regulations 1989

Lamp	Exceptions *(See also Exemptions pages 10, 11)*
Front Position	A solo motor bicycle fitted with a headlamp.
Dipped Beam Headlamp	A vehicle first used before 01/01/1931.
Main Beam Headlamp	A vehicle having a maximum speed not exceeding 25 mph. A vehicle first used before 01/01/1972 and having an engine with a capacity of less than 50cc. A vehicle first used before 01/01/1931.
Rear Position Lamp	None.
Rear Registration Plate Lamp	A vehicle not required to be fitted with a rear registration plate.
Rear Retro Reflector	None.
Direction Indicator	A vehicle having a maximum speed not exceeding 25 mph. A vehicle first used before 01/04/1986. A vehicle which is constructed or adapted primarily for use off roads (whether by reason of its tyres, suspension, ground clearance or otherwise) and which can carry only one person or which in the case of a motor bicycle combination can carry only the rider and one passenger in the sidecar.
Stop Lamp	A vehicle having a maximum speed not exceeding 25 mph. A vehicle first used before 01/04/1986 and having an engine with a capacity of less than 50cc. A vehicle first used before 01/01/1936.

Fitting of Obligatory Lamps etc. *continued*

Pedal Cycle
Schedule 1 Table III Road Vehicles Lighting Regulations 1989

Lamp	Exceptions *(See also Exemptions pages 10, 11)*
Front Position	None.
Rear Position	None.
Rear Retro Reflector	None.
Pedal Retro Reflector	A pedal cycle manufactured before 01/10/1985.

Pedestrian Controlled, Horse Drawn, and Track Laying Vehicles
Schedule 1 Table IV Road Vehicles Lighting Regulations 1989

Lamp	Exceptions *(See also Exemptions pages 10, 11)*
Front Position Lamp	None.
Rear Position Lamp	None.
Rear Retro Reflector	None.

Vehicle Drawn Or Propelled By Hand
Schedule 1 Table V Road Vehicles Lighting Regulations 1989

Lamp	Exceptions *(See also Exemptions pages 10, 11)*
Front Position Lamp	A vehicle not exceeding 800mm wide used on a carriageway between sunset and sunrise only :- a) close to the nearside or left hand edge of the carriageway, or b) to cross the carriageway.
Rear Position Lamp	A vehicle fitted with a rear retro reflector A vehicle not exceeding 800mm wide used on a carriageway between sunset and sunrise only :- a) close to the nearside or left hand edge of the carriageway, or b) to cross the carriageway.
Rear Retro Reflector	A vehicle fitted with a rear position lamp. A vehicle not exceeding 800mm wide used on a carriageway between sunset and sunrise only :- a) close to the nearside or left hand edge of the carriageway, or b) to cross the carriageway.

Fitting of Obligatory Lamps etc. *continued*

Trailer Drawn By Motor Vehicle
Schedule 1 Table VI Road Vehicles Lighting Regulations 1989

Lamp	Exceptions *(See also Exemptions pages 10, 11)*
Front Position Lamp	A trailer with an overall width not exceeding 1600mm. A trailer manufactured before 01/10/1985 :- a) whilst being drawn by a passenger vehicle, or b) the overall length of which excluding any drawbar and any fitting for its attachment does not exceed 2300mm. A trailer constructed or adapted for the carriage and launching of a boat.
Front Retro Reflector	A trailer manufactured before 01/10/1990. An agricultural vehicle or a works trailer.
Side Marker Lamp	A trailer the overall length of which, excluding any drawbar and any fitting for its attachment, does not exceed :- a) 6 m, b) 9.15 m in the case of a trailer manufactured before 01/10/1990. An incomplete trailer proceeding to a works for completion or to a place where it is to be stored or displayed for sale. An agricultural vehicle or a works trailer. A caravan. A trailer constructed or adapted for the carriage and launching of a boat. A trailer vehicle manufactured before 01/10/1995 which complies with *EC Regulation 76/756.* (type approval).
End Outline Marker Lamp	A trailer having an overall width not exceeding 2100mm. Incomplete trailer proceeding to works for completion or place where it is to be stored or displayed for sale. Agricultural vehicle or a works trailer. A trailer manufactured before 01/101990.
Rear Marking	A trailer manufactured before 01/08/1982 unladen weight not exceeding 1020 kg. A trailer drawn by a bus. A trailer the maximum gross weight of which does not exceed 3500 kg. An incomplete trailer proceeding to a works for completion or to a place where it is to be stored or displayed for sale. An agricultural vehicle, a works trailer or engineering plant. A trailer drawn by a bus. A Home forces vehicle. A trailer constructed or adapted for :- a) Fire fighting or fire salvage, b) Servicing or controlling aircraft, c) Heating and dispensing tar or other material for construction or maintenance of roads, d) Carrying asphalt or macadam being mixing or drying plant, or e) Transporting two or more vehicles or vehicle bodies or two or more boats.

Continued over

Fitting of Obligatory Lamps etc. *continued*

Trailer Drawn By Motor Vehicle - *continued*
Schedule 1 Table VI Road Vehicles Lighting Regulations 1989

Lamp	Exceptions *(See also Exemptions pages 10, 11)*
Direction Indicator	A trailer manufactured before 01/09/1965. An agricultural vehicle or a works trailer in either case manufactured before 01/10/1990. A trailer drawn by a vehicle which is not required to be fitted with any such lamp.
Side Retro Reflector	Trailer the overall length of which (excluding drawbar) does not exceed 5m. An incomplete trailer proceeding to works for completion or place where it is to be stored or displayed for sale. Engineering plant. Trailer primarily constructed for excavated material and which is being used by virtue of an order under *Section 44* of the Act - (ab loads STGO).
Rear Position Lamp	None.
Rear Registration Plate Light	A trailer not required to be fitted with a rear registration plate.
Stop Lamp	Agricultural vehicle or a works trailer. A trailer drawn by a vehicle which is not required to be fitted with any such lamp.
Rear Fog Lamp	A trailer manufactured before 01/04/1980. A trailer overall width not exceeding 1300mm. Agricultural vehicle or a works trailer. A trailer drawn by a vehicle which is not required to be fitted with any such lamp.
Rear Retro Reflector	None.

Trailer Drawn By a Pedal Cycle
Schedule 1 Table VII Road Vehicles Lighting Regulations 1989

Lamp	Exceptions *(See also Exemptions below)*
Rear Position Lamp	None.
Rear Retro Reflector	None.

Fitting of Optional Lamps etc.

Regulation 20 Road Vehicles Lighting Regulations 1989

Optional Lamps etc. - Motor Vehicles with 3 or more wheels

Part 2 Schedules 2-21 and 24 Road Vehicles Lighting Regs 1989

Lamp	Requirements
Front Position	Any number. White or yellow. Markings not required
Dim-dip devices & running lamps	Any number, No colour requirement. Markings not required.
Dipped-beam headlamps	If 1st used on/after 01/04/1991 -2 in matched pair.otherwise any no. White or yellow.400-1200mm high. Markings not required.
Main-beam headlamps	Any number. White or yellow. Markings if 1st used on/after 01/04/1991.
Front fog lamps	If 1st used on or after 01/04/1991 - max 2 otherwise any number. White or yellow. Markings if 1st used on/after 01/04/1991.
Direction indicators	Maximum 1 pair front - 2 pairs rear, any number side repeaters. Amber (if 1st used before 01/09/1965 may have white - front, red - rear).Markings if 1st used on/after 01/04/1986, (trailer 01/10/1985).
Hazard warning	May be fitted, Tell tale required. Markings not required.
Side marker lamps	Red within 1m of rear or red/white if a trailer. manufactured before 01/10/1990. Any number, Amber. Markings not required.
Rear position	Any number, Red. Markings not required.
Rear fog lamps	if 1st used on/after 01/04/1980 - max 2 otherwise any number. Red - (not connected to brake circuit). Markings required.
Stop lamps	Any number, Red. Markings if 1st used on/after 01/02/1974.
End-outline marker	Any number, Red - rear, White front. Markings not required.
Reversing lamps	Maximum 2. White. Markings if 1st used on/after 01/04/1986 (trailer after 01/10/1985).
Warning beacons	Minimum height 1200mm. Blue, amber, green or yellow. Markings not required.
Side reflectors	Any number (not triangular). Amber (red within 1m of rear). Markings not required.
Reversing lamps	Maximum 2. White. Markings if 1st used on/after 01/04/1986 (trailer after 01/10/1985).
Warning beacons	Minimum height 1200mm. Blue, amber, green or yellow. Markings not required.
Side reflectors	Any number (not triangular). Amber (red within 1m of rear). Markings not required.
Rear reflectors	Any number (triangular only on trailers). Red. Markings not required.
Pedal reflectors	Any number. Amber. Markings not required.
Front reflectors	Any number. White. Markings not required.

Fitting Exemptions

Daytime Exemptions

Regulation 4(3) Road Vehicles Lighting Regulations 1989

Nothing in the regulations shall require any lamp to be fitted between sunrise and sunset to :-

- a vehicle not fitted with any front or rear position lamp (eg: a trials bike or more commonly a trailer),
- an incomplete vehicle proceeding to a works for completion,
- a pedal cycle,
- pedestrian controlled vehicle,
- horse drawn vehicle,
- a vehicle drawn or propelled by hand,
- combat vehicle see also below for night-time exemptions.

Exemptions - Temporarily imported vehicles

Regulation 5 Road Vehicles Lighting Regulations 1989

Nothing in the regulations shall apply to temporarily imported vehicles or vehicles proceeding to a port for export provided they comply with the *Geneva Convention on Road Traffic 1949* (basic front/rear lighting).

Exemptions - Military Vehicles (Home or Visiting Forces)

Regulation 7 Road Vehicles Lighting Regulations 1989

No lights are required to be fitted to such a vehicle whilst being used :-

- on training where 48 hours police notice has been given,
- on manoeuvres specified under the *Manoeuvres Act 1958*.

Convoys - 6 to 12 vehicles not more than 20 metres apart where 48 hours police notice has been given may display only front position lights on the lead vehicle, rear position lights on the tail vehicle and every other vehicle a bright light slung underneath, visible from the rear.

Combat vehicles - the only requirement is two red rear position lamps, two red rear reflectors between sunset and sunrise.

Exemptions - Invalid carriages

Regulation 8 Road Vehicles Lighting Regulations 1989

Class 1 and 2 Invalid carriages (top speed 4 m.p.h.) are exempt from the requirement to fit any lights or reflectors provided that between sunset and sunrise they are confined to the pavements and only used on the carriageway for the sole purpose of crossing the road.

Continued over

Fitting Exemptions *continued*

Towing Exemptions
Vehicles which are towing
Regulation 6(1) and (6) Road Vehicles Lighting Regulations 1989
- Motor vehicles first used before 01/04/1986, and
- Trailers and pedal cycles manufactured before 01/10/1985,

do not require to be fitted any rear position lamp, stop lamp, rear direction indicator, rear fog lamp or rear reflector whilst a trailer fitted with any such lamp is fitted to its rear.

No rear marking is required to be fitted to any vehicle if another vehicle in the combination would obscure such marking.

Vehicles which are being towed
Regulation 6(5) Road Vehicles Lighting Regulations 1989
A trailer manufactured before 01/10/1990 does not require stop lamps or direction indicators to be fitted if the stop lamps and at least one direction indicator on the towing vehicle can be seen from a point 6 metres behind the trailer (NB: the trailer still requires rear position lamps and reflectors).

The daytime exemptions listed on the previous page - a vehicle not fitted with a front or rear position lamp - allows trailers without any lamps fitted to be towed between sunrise and sunset only - (this can also apply if the lighting connections between tow and trailer are not compatible) - many agricultural vehicles take advantage of this exemption.

Broken-down vehicles
Regulation 6(7) Road Vehicles Lighting Regulations 1989
No lights need be fitted nor maintained on a broken-down vehicle being towed between sunrise and sunset.

Between sunset and sunrise only rear position lamps and reflectors need be fitted and maintained.

Regulation 4(4) Road Vehicles Lighting Regulations 1989
A lamp shall not be regarded as being a lamp if it is :-
- so painted over or masked that it cannot be readily put to use, or
- an electric lamp which is not provided with any system of wiring by means of which it can be readily be connected with a source of electricity.

Blue warning beacons and special warning lamps remain fitted even when they are covered or not electrically connected.

Colour Of Lights

Red Lights

Fitting a red lamp or retro reflective material to the front
Regulation 11(1) Road Vehicles Lighting Regulations 1989

No vehicle shall be fitted with a lamp or retro reflective material capable of showing a red light to the front except :-

- red and white from a Fire Service Control Vehicle,
- side marker lamp or side retro reflector,
- reflected light from a retro reflector or material attached to or incorporated in the wheels or tyres of a pedal cycle, pedal cycle trailer or sidecar, solo motor cycle or motorcycle sidecar or an invalid carriage,
- a traffic sign.

Fitting a lamp or retro reflective material other than red to the rear
Regulation 11(2) Road Vehicles Lighting Regulations 1989

No vehicle shall be fitted with a lamp or retro reflective material capable of showing any light to the rear other than a red light except :-

Colour	From
Amber	Direction indicator or side marker lamp
Amber from warning beacon	Road clearance vehicle. Refuse collection vehicle. Breakdown vehicle (a vehicle used to attend an accident or breakdown or to draw a broken down vehicle). Vehicle with max speed not exceeding 25 m.p.h. or from its trailer. Vehicle with width (including load) exceeding 2.9m. Road testing, cleaning, maintenance vehicles. Road apparatus testing, cleansing maintenance and inspection vehicle. Special types section 44 vehicles - abnormal loads (STGO etc.) Vehicle used for escort purposes. Customs and Excise road fuel testing vehicles. Vehicle used for surveying. Vehicle used for statutory removals or immobilisation.
Amber	Reflected from pedal retro reflectors or pedal cycle pedal lamp. From reflectors on a road clearance vehicle.

Orange	• Reflected from HAZCHEM marker boards.
	• Reflected light from orange retro reflective material fitted to the rear of a vehicle used for the following purposes :-
	  - police,
	  - relevant fire or fire and rescue authority,
	  - ambulance purposes, or for the purpose of providing a response to an emergency at the request of an NHS ambulance service,
	  - Driver and Vehicle Standards Agency (DVSA), or
	  - traffic officer (HATO).

White	Reversing lamp. Work lamp.

Continued over

Colour Of Lights *continued*

Fitting a lamp etc. other than red to the rear *continued*

Colour	From
Any	Interior illumination. Illuminated rear registration plate. Route indicator on a bus. Taxi meter light.
	Reflected from wheel/tyre reflectors on a pedal cycle, pedal cycle trailer or sidecar, solo motor cycle or motorcycle sidecar, invalid carriage.
	Reflected light from a registration plate fixed to the rear of a trailer displaying a registration mark assigned to that trailer in accordance with regulations made under *section 15 of the Haulage Permits and Trailer Registration Act 2018.*
Yellow **ZD73 ZLK**	Reflected from rear registration plate. Reflected from prescribed rear marker boards (only on vehicles/ load that require them). Airport vehicles warning beacon. Reflected from a school bus sign or a secondary sign (with the school or authority name or an appropriate safety message) fitted to the rear of a bus. Reflected light from a yellow ECE conspicuity markings (on goods vehicles, buses and large trailers). Reflected light from yellow retro reflective material fitted to the rear of a vehicle used for the following purposes :- - police, - relevant fire or fire and rescue authority, - ambulance purposes, or for the purpose of providing a response to an emergency at the request of an NHS ambulance service, - Driver and Vehicle Standards Agency (DVSA), or - traffic officer (HATO).
Amber / White	From lamp attached to wheel/tyre on pedal cycle, pedal cycle trailer or sidecar.
Blue	Emergency Vehicles (*see next page*), vehicles used for special forces purposes, NHS or Ambulance Trust emergency response vehicles or police purposes.
Blue / White	Police Control vehicle.
Green	Vehicles used by a registered medical practitioner.
Green / White	Ambulance Control vehicle.
White	Fire Control vehicle.
Blue / Yellow / White	Reflected from Euro-plate.

Continued over

Colour Of Lights *continued*

Blue lamps and beacons

Regulation 16 Road Vehicles Lighting Regulations 1989

No vehicle other than an Emergency Vehicle, a vehicle used for special forces purposes or an NHS or Ambulance Trust vehicle primarily used for medical response to emergencies (by virtue of a *Sec 44 Order*), shall be fitted with :-

- a blue warning beacon or special warning lamp (a blue flashing light to the front or rear),
- a device which resembles a blue warning beacon or special warning lamp (whether or not it works).

Blue warning beacons and special warning lamps remain fitted even if they are covered or not wired up.

Emergency Vehicle Definition

Regulation 3 Road Vehicles Lighting Regulations 1989

- Vehicles used for fire and rescue authority or police purposes.
- A vehicle used for ambulance purposes or for the purpose of providing a response to an emergency at the request of an NHS ambulance service.
- Ambulances - vehicles, other than an invalid carriages, which are constructed or adapted for the purpose of conveying sick, injured or disabled persons and which are used for such purposes.
- Blood transfusion and human tissue vehicles.
- Vehicles owned or operated by M.o.D. for bomb disposal, RAF mountain rescue or radiation emergencies.
- Fire salvage vehicle and Forestry Commission or local authority fire fighting vehicle.
- Vehicles used by HM Coastguard or Coastguard Auxiliary Service for the purposes of giving aid to persons in danger or vessels in distress on or near the coast.
- R.N.L.I boat launch vehicles.
- Mine rescue vehicles.
- Mountain rescue vehicles.
- Vehicles under lawful control of HM Revenue and Customs used for investigating serious crime.

Rear Red flashing lights

Regulation 13 Road Vehicles Lighting Regulations 1989

These can only be fitted to vehicles used for police purposes (except rear red flashing lights on pedal cycles).

Rear Marker Boards and Conspicuity Markings

Rear Marker Boards

Regulation 18 Road Vehicles Lighting Regulations 1989
Schedules 1 and 19 Road Vehicles Lighting Regulations 1989

Rear Marker Boards are required to be fitted (subject to exceptions listed in Schedule 1 - *see previous tables*) on goods vehicles which are :-

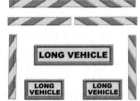

- motor vehicles with gross weight exceeding 7500 kg, and
- trailers with gross weight exceeding 3500 kg.

Different types of marker boards must be displayed according length.

> *It is an offence to display rear marker boards on a vehicle where is not required to do so (see regulation 11 - Fitting a lamp or retro reflective material other than red to the rear).*
>
> *No rear marking is required to be fitted to any vehicle if another vehicle in combination of which it forms part would obscure any such marking.*
>
> *Rear Markings may be replaced by conspicuity markings (see below).*

Conspicuity Markings

Reg 20A Road Vehicles Lighting Regulations 1989, ECE Reg 48

Conspicuity markings are required to be fitted on goods vehicles which are :-

- motor vehicles first used on or after 10/07/ 2011 with gross weight exceeding 7500 kg, and
- trailers manufactured on or after 10/07/2011 with gross weight exceeding 3500 kg,

except an incomplete vehicle proceeding to a works for completion or to a place where it is to be stored or displayed for sale or a motor car or heavy motor car intended to form part of an articulated vehicle.

Full contour marking is mandatory for the rear of vehicles over 2.1m wide and partial contour marking is mandatory for the sides of vehicles which are over 6m in length. However, if the shape, structure, design or operational characteristics of the vehicle make it impossible to meet the applicable contour marking requirements, the vehicle may be fitted with line marking instead. Other vehicles may display conspicuity markings except passengers vehicles (other than a bus) and trailers not exceeding 750 kg g.v.w.

> *It is an offence to display conspicuity marking on a vehicle where is not required or permitted to do so - see regulation 11 (Fitting a lamp or retro reflective material other than red to the rear).*

Signs on Buses Carrying Children
Regulation 17A Road Vehicles Lighting Regulations 1989

No person shall use, cause or permit to be used, on a **road**, a **bus** when it is **carrying a child under 16 years** to or from his school during term time unless prescribed signs are fitted to the front and rear of the bus which are plainly visible to road users ahead and behind the bus (except regular local bus services).

- Secondary signs of the same colour no bigger than the prescribed sign above may also be displayed. These may have the name of the school or education authority or a message relating to the carriage of children or an appropriate road safety message written on them.
- Does not apply to school trips, only to vehicles taking children to and from school at the start and end of the day.
- It is not an offence to leave signs up permanently.
- Hazard warning lights may be used to warn that children under 16 years are entering or leaving the bus or about to do so, (*see Page 25*).

Warning Beacons - Dual Carriageways
Regulation 17 Road Vehicles Lighting Regulations 1989

No person shall use, cause or permit to be used, on an un-restricted dual carriageway (speed limit above 50m.p.h.), any **motor vehicle with four or more wheels having a maximum speed not exceeding 25 m.p.h**. unless it or any trailer drawn by it is fitted with at least one amber warning beacon except :-

- a motor vehicle first used before 01/01/1947,
- a motor vehicle or any trailer being drawn by it when it is crossing such a road in the quickest manner practicable in the circumstances.

Offence
Regulation 26 Road Vehicles Lighting Regulations 1989

No person shall use, cause or permit to be used, on an unrestricted dual carriageway (speed limit above 50m.p.h.), a vehicle which is required to be fitted with at least one warning beacon as above unless every such beacon is kept lit.

Requirements
Schedule 16 Road Vehicles Lighting Regulations 1989

The light from at least 1 beacon (but not necessarily the same beacon) must be visible from any point at a reasonable distance from the vehicle or any trailer drawn by it.

The centre of the lamp must be at least 1200mm from the ground.

Should be constant at between 60 and 240 flashes per minute.

Obscuring Lamps

Construction of Vehicles

Regulation 19 Road Vehicles Lighting Regulations 1989

Every vehicle shall be so constructed that at least part of the apparent surface of any :-

- front and rear position lamp,
- front and rear direction indicator, and
- rear reflector,

required by these Regulations to be fitted is visible when the vehicle is viewed from any point directly in front of or behind the lamp, when every door, tailgate, engine cover, cabs or other moveable point of the vehicle is in a fixed open position.

Obscuring lamps with the load or equipment

Regulation 21 Road Vehicles Lighting Regulations 1989

No person shall use, cause or permit to be used, on a road any vehicle or combination of vehicles which carries a load or equipment which obscures :-

- at all times - any obligatory stop lamp or indicator,
- between sunset and sunrise - any obligatory lamp, reflector or rear marking,
- between sunrise and sunset when visibility is seriously reduced - any obligatory reflector,

unless the obligatory lamp, reflector or rear marking is transferred to a position on vehicle, load or equipment where it is not obscured, or an additional lamp, reflector or rear marking is fitted on the vehicle, load or equipment where it is not obscured.

Lamps to show a steady light

Regulation 13 Road Vehicles Lighting Regulations 1989

No vehicle shall be fitted with a lamp which automatically emits a flashing light except :-

- a direction indicator,
- a headlamp fitted to an Emergency Vehicle or a vehicle used for special forces purposes,
- a warning beacon or special warning lamp,
- a lamp or illuminated sign fitted to a vehicle used for police purposes,
- a green warning lamp used as an anti-lock brake indicator,
- lamps forming part of a traffic sign,
- a front or rear position lamp capable of emitting a flashing light which is fitted to a pedal cycle, or a trailer drawn by, or a sidecar attached to, a pedal cycle.

Projecting Trailers, Loads or Equipment
Regulation 21 Road Vehicles Lighting Regulations 1989

Application
- Between sunset and sunrise, or
- Between sunrise and sunset when visibility is seriously reduced[1] (except in so far as it relates to obligatory reflectors).

Requirements

Projecting Trailers
A trailer not fitted with front position lamps which projects laterally on any side (or its load or equipment projects laterally on any side) more than 400mm from the outermost part of an obligatory front position lamp on any preceding vehicle in the combination - an additional white light showing to the front shall be fitted to the trailer, load or equipment within 400mm of its outer edge.

Load or equipment projecting sideways
If a vehicle's load or equipment projects more than 400mm laterally (sideways) from the outermost part of the obligatory front or rear position lamp on that side then :-
- the obligatory front or rear position lamps shall be transferred to the load or equipment (within 400mm of the edge) to which must also be attached a white front or red rear reflector, or
- an additional front or rear position lamp and a white front or red rear reflector shall be fitted on the vehicle, load or equipment.

Load or equipment projecting to the rear
If a vehicle's load or equipment projects more than 1metre (2m in the case of an agricultural vehicle or a vehicle carrying a fire escape) beyond the rear of the rearmost vehicle in the combination,
- an additional rear position lamp and a red rear reflector visible from a reasonable distance shall be fitted on the vehicle, load or equipment within 1metre (2m in the case of an agricultural vehicle or a vehicle carrying a fire escape) of the rearmost projection.

Load or equipment projecting to the front
If a vehicles' load or equipment projects more than 1m (2m in the case of an Agricultural vehicle or a vehicle carrying a fire escape) beyond the front of the vehicle :-
- an additional front position lamp and a white front reflector visible from a reasonable distance shall be fitted on the vehicle, load or equipment within 1m (2m in the case of an Agricultural vehicle or a vehicle carrying a fire escape) of the foremost projection.

Load or equipment which obscures any obligatory lamp, reflector or rear marking
- Either the obligatory lamp, reflector or rear marking shall be transferred to a position on the vehicle, load or equipment where it is not obscured, or an additional lamp, reflector or rear marking shall be fitted to the vehicle, load or equipment.

Additional side marker lamps - Long Vehicles/ Loads

Regulation 22 Road Vehicles Lighting Regulations 1989

Application

- Between sunset and sunrise, or
- Between sunrise and sunset when visibility is seriously reduced (*see Page 22*).

Requirements

Additional side marker lamps must be fitted and lit on :-

- a vehicle or a combination of vehicles the overall length of which (including any load) exceeds 18.3 m. such that :-
  - ○ one lamp is no more than 9.15 m from the foremost part of the vehicle or vehicles (in either case inclusive of any load),
  - ○ one lamp is no more than 3.05 m from the rearmost part of the vehicle or vehicles (in either case inclusive of any load), and
  - ○ such other lamps as are required to ensure there is not more than 3.05 m between lamps.
- a combination of vehicles the overall length of which (including any load) exceeds 12.2 m but does not exceed 18.3 m and carrying a load supported by any two of the vehicles but not including a load carried by an articulated vehicle such that :-
  - ○ one lamp which is not forward of, or more than 1530 mm rearward of, the rearmost part of the drawing vehicle, and
  - ○ if the supported load extends more than 9.15 m rearward of the rearmost part of the drawing vehicle, one lamp which is not forward of, or more than 1530 mm rearward of, the centre of the length of the load.

Colour

Amber, or :-

- if within 1 m of the rear of the vehicle - red, or
- if the vehicle is a trailer manufactured before 01/10/1990 - white when viewed from the front and red when viewed from the rear.

Exceptions

- A combination of vehicles where any vehicle being drawn in that combination has broken down, or
- A vehicle (not being a combination of vehicles) complying with the requirements and conditions (in relation to the special marking of projections from vehicles) of *Regulation 82 and Schedule 12 of the Construction and Use Regulations.*

Maintenance Of Lamps etc.

It is incorrect To say 'If it is fitted it must work'
It is more accurate to say 'Subject to the exemptions provided, all Obligatory Lamps, Markings and Reflectors as well as specified Optional Lamps and Devices must be in good working order and, in the case of a lamp, clean.'

Maintenance Of Obligatory Lamps, Markings and Reflectors

Regulation 23(1) Road Vehicles Lighting Regulations 1989

No person shall use, cause or permit to be used, on a road, a **vehicle** unless every :-

• Front position lamp,
• Rear position lamp,
• Head lamp,
• Rear registration plate lamp,
• Side marker lamp,
• End outline marker lamp,
• Rear fog lamp,
• Reflector,
• Rear marking,

which is required to be fitted must be in good working order and, in the case of a lamp, clean.

Maintenance Of Obligatory and Optional Lamps and Devices

Regulation 23(2) Road Vehicles Lighting Regulations 1989

No person shall use, cause or permit to be used, on a road, a vehicle unless every :-

• Stop lamp,
• Direction indicator,
• Running lamp,
• Dim dip device,
• Head lamp levelling device,
• Hazard warning device,

which is fitted (required or not) must be in good working order and, in the case of a lamp, clean.

Example

A car is fitted with 3 stop (brake) lamps and 4 rear position lamps. Which need to be maintained?
Answer
All 3 stop lamps and only the 2 rear position lamps that are required to be fitted.

Maintenance Of Lamps - *continued*
Exemptions

Regulation 23(3) Road Vehicles Lighting Regulations 1989

- A rear fog lamp on a vehicle which is part of a combination of vehicles any of which are not required to be fitted with such a lamp.
- A rear fog lamp on a motor vehicle drawing a trailer.
- A defective lamp, reflector, dim-dip device or headlamp levelling device on a vehicle in use on a road between sunrise and sunset if any such lamp became defective during the journey in progress or if arrangements have been made to remedy the defect with all reasonable expedition.
- A lamp, reflector, dim-dip device or headlamp levelling device or rear marking on a combat vehicle in use on a road between sunrise and sunset.

See also :-
- Daytime Exemptions from fitting lamps.

Example

Daytime Exemptions state 'Nothing in the regulations shall require any lamp to be fitted between sunrise and sunset to a vehicle not fitted with any front or rear position lamp'.

This exemption could include trailers and pedal cycles as well as agricultural vehicles where, commonly, no lamps are fitted at all during the day.

- When a lamp is not considered as being fitted.

Example

If a trailer had a lighting board attached but the plug connector to the towing vehicle was not compatible then it would not be considered as fitted as it cannot be readily connected to an electrical supply.

See Regulation 4 Page 2.

*If no lights at all are **fitted** then regulation 23 does not apply.*

If such vehicles were used between sunrise and sunset but in seriously reduced visibility or in other situations where it may be considered dangerous other non-lighting offences could be considered such as dangerous driving.

Between sunset and sunrise these exemptions would not apply.

Movement of lamps and reflectors

Regulation 12 Road Vehicles Lighting Regulations 1989

No person shall use, or cause or permit to be used, on a road any vehicle to which, or to any load or equipment of which, there is fitted a lamp, reflector or marking which is capable of being moved by swivelling, deflecting or otherwise while the vehicle is in motion except :-

- a headlamp which can be dipped only by the movement of the headlamp or its reflector,
- a headlamp which is capable of adjustment so as to compensate for the effect of the load carried by the vehicle,
- a lamp or reflector which can be deflected to the side by the movement of, although not necessarily through the same angle as, the front wheel or wheels of the vehicle when turned for the purpose of steering the vehicle,
- a headlamp or front fog lamp which can be wholly or partially retracted or concealed,
- a direction indicator fitted to a motor vehicle first used before 01/04/1986,
- a work lamp[1],
- a warning beacon,
- an amber pedal retro reflector, or
- retro reflective material or a retro reflector of any colour which is fitted so as to reflect light primarily to one or both sides of the vehicle and is attached to or incorporated in any wheel or tyre of :-
  - a pedal cycle and any sidecar attached to,
  - a solo motor bicycle or motor bicycle combination, or
  - an invalid carriage.

---

[1] Work lamp

A lamp used to illuminate a working area or the scene of an accident, breakdown or roadworks in the vicinity of the vehicle to which it is fitted.

---

[2] Seriously Reduced Visibility

Rule 226 The Highway Code

Generally when you cannot see for more than 100 metres (328 feet).

Use of Lights
Use of Headlamps

Regulation 25 Road Vehicles Lighting Regulations 1989

Obligatory dipped-beam headlamps must be kept lit on a vehicle on a road :-

- during the hours of darkness (1/2 hour after sunset until 1/2 hour before sunrise), except on a restricted road (30 mph or less - 20mph or less in Wales) fitted with street lighting when lit, and
- in seriously reduced visibility[2].

Exemptions

- In seriously reduced visibility[2] if front fog light(s) are kept lit in their place (within 400 mm of edge of the vehicle).
- At all times :-
  - vehicles being drawn by another vehicle,
  - vehicles propelling a snow plough,
  - a parked vehicle.

There is no requirement to switch on fog lights in seriously reduced visibility[2] but it is an offence to have them switched on in conditions other than seriously reduced visibility (see Page 26).

Restrictions on the Use Of Headlamps

Regulation 27 Road Vehicles Lighting Regulations 1989

A headlamp must not be used so as :-

- to be lit when a vehicle is parked, or
- to cause undue dazzle or discomfort to other persons using the road.

Use of Other obligatory lights

Regulation 24 Road Vehicles Lighting Regulations 1989

Every obligatory front and rear position lamp, rear registration plate lamp, side marker lamp and end-outline marker lamp - must be kept lit and unobscured on any vehicle which is on a road :-

- in motion between sunset and sunrise,
- in motion between sunrise and sunset in seriously reduced visibility[1],
- at rest between sunset and sunrise unless certain conditions apply - *see next page.*

Exemptions

- a solo motor bicycle or a pedal cycle being pushed along the left hand edge of a carriageway,
- a pedal cycle waiting to proceed provided it is kept to the left hand or nearside of a carriageway,
- a vehicle parked within signed and lit roadworks.

Lighting of rear registration plates is a requirement of the Road Vehicles (Display of Registration Marks) Regs 2001 not the Lighting Regulations (see Page 21-5).

Parking

Parking Without Lights

Regulation 24 Road Vehicles Lighting Regulations 1989
Schedule 22 Road Vehicles Lighting Regulations 1989

Vehicles of the following classes may park on a road between sunset and sunrise in the circumstances stated without lights :-

• goods vehicles, gross vehicle weight not exceeding 2500 kg,

• passenger vehicles not exceeding 8 passenger seats plus the driver,

• invalid carriages,

• motor cycles or pedal-cycles with or without side car,

providing there is no trailer attached, and the vehicle or load does not require projection lamps.

Circumstances

Parked on a road subject to a speed limit of 30 m.p.h. or less and :-

• in a designated parking area, not in contravention of any enactment, or

• in a lay-by :-

  ◦ whose limits are indicated by dotted lines, or

  ◦ the surface of which is different colour or different texture than road, or

  ◦ whose limits are indicated by a strip or different colour of texture, or

• on a road elsewhere than such a parking area or lay-by if :-

  ◦ it is parked parallel and close to the nearside kerb (either kerb in a one way street), and

  ◦ no part of the vehicle is less than 10 metres from a junction whether on same side of the road or not.

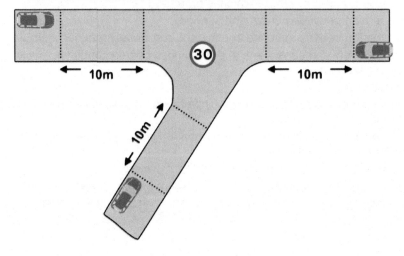

Parking - *continued*

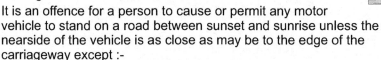

Parking on the nearside between sunset and sunrise

Regulation 101 Road Vehicles (Construction and Use)
Regulations 1986, Section 42 Road Traffic Act 1988

It is an offence for a person to cause or permit any motor vehicle to stand on a road between sunset and sunrise unless the nearside of the vehicle is as close as may be to the edge of the carriageway except :-

- with the permission of a police officer in uniform,
- a vehicle being used for fire brigade or, in England, fire and rescue authority or police purposes or for defence purposes (including civil defence purposes) if compliance with those provisions would hinder or be likely to hinder the use of the vehicle for the purpose for which it is being used on that occasion,
- a vehicle being used for ambulance purposes or for the purpose of providing a response to an emergency at the request of an NHS ambulance service if compliance with those provisions would hinder or be likely to hinder the use of the vehicle for the purpose for which it is being used on that occasion,
- in connection with building or demolition work, repair of another vehicle, removal of obstruction to traffic, repair to roads or utilities,
- in one way streets,
- where waiting or parking is otherwise authorised in recognised parking places, hackney ranks and bus stops.

Use of Headlamps whilst parked

Regulation 27 Road Vehicles Lighting Regulations 1989

A headlamp must not be lit when a vehicle is parked.

Warning Lights on Buses

Regulation 27 Road Vehicles Lighting Regulations 1989

Hazard Warning Lights may be displayed :-

- in the case of a bus, to summon assistance for the driver or any person acting as a conductor or inspector on the vehicle, or
- in the case of a school bus exhibiting the prescribed signs, when stationary and children under 16 years are entering or leaving or about to do so.

Restrictions on the Use Of Lights

Regulation 27 Road Vehicles Lighting Regulations 1989

Light	Prohibition
Headlamp	Used so as to cause undue dazzle or discomfort to other persons using the road. Used so as to be lit when a vehicle is parked.
Front Fog Lamp	Used so as to cause undue dazzle or discomfort to other persons using the road. Used so as to be lit at any time other than in conditions of seriously reduced visibility[1]. Used so as to be lit when a vehicle is parked.
Rear Fog Lamp	Used so as to cause undue dazzle or discomfort to the driver of a following vehicle. Used so as to be lit at any time other than in conditions of seriously reduced visibility[1]. Save in the case of an emergency vehicle, used so as to be lit when a vehicle is parked.
Warning beacon emitting blue light, Special Warning Lamp	Used so as to be lit except :- - at the scene of an emergency, or - when it is necessary or desirable either to indicate to persons using the road the urgency of the purpose for which the vehicle is being used, or - to warn persons of the presence of the vehicle or a hazard on the road.
Amber Warning Beacon	Used so as to be lit :- - except at the scene of an emergency, or - when it is necessary or desirable to warn persons of the presence of the vehicle, or - in the case of a breakdown vehicle, while it is being used in connection with, and in the immediate vicinity of, an accident or breakdown, or while it is being used to draw a broken-down vehicle, or - an abnormal load escort vehicle being used in connection with the escort of abnormal loads which exceed 2.9 metres width or 18.65 metres length (including load) or those authorised under *section 44 of the Act*, or - an escort vehicle being used in connection with the escort of any vehicle (other than an abnormal load) and travelling at a speed not exceeding 25 mph.
Yellow Warning beacon	Used so as to be lit on a road.
Green Warning Beacon	Used so as to be lit except whilst occupied by a medical practitioner registered by the General Medical Council and used for an emergency.

Restrictions on the Use Of Lights *continued*
Regulation 27 Road Vehicles Lighting Regulations 1989

Light	Prohibition
Hazard Warning Lamp	Used other than :- - to warn persons using the road of a temporary obstruction when at rest, or - on a motorway or unrestricted dual-carriageway, to warn following drivers of a need to slow down due to a temporary obstruction ahead, or - in the case of a bus, to summon assistance for the driver or any person acting as a conductor or inspector on the vehicle, or - in the case of a school bus exhibiting the prescribed signs, when stationary and children under 16 are entering or leaving or about to.
Reversing Lamp	Used so as to be lit except for the purpose of reversing the vehicle.
Work Lamp	Used so as to cause undue dazzle or discomfort to the driver of any vehicle. Used so as to be lit except for the purpose of illuminating a working area, accident, breakdown.
Any Other Lamp	Used so as to cause undue dazzle or discomfort to other persons.

> ¹ *Seriously Reduced Visibility*
> *Rule 226 The Highway Code*
> *Generally when you cannot see for more than 100 metres (328 feet).*

🔦 Markings on lights

Certain lamps on vehicles require European Approval Marks :-

•an E with a circle - indicates a device which has been approved to a UN:ECE Regulation,

(E 11)

• an e within a rectangle - indicates a device which has been approved to an EU Directive.

e 11

The number within the circle or rectangle beside the E or e is the distinguishing number of the country that issued the approval, 11 stands for the United Kingdom.

Other numbers and letters also appear adjacent to these markings which identify the type of lamp.

	Lamp		Lamp
A	Front position lamp (or end-outline marker lamp)	11	Front direction indicators (motorcycles only)
C	Dipped-beam headlamp	12	Rear direction indicator (motorcycles only)
R	Main-beam headlamp	13	Side repeater direction indicator (motorcycles only)
S	Sealed-beam headlamp	SM	Side marker lamp
H	Halogen headlamp	R	Rear position lamp
B	Front fog lamp (white or yellow)	B or F	Rear fog lamp (red)
1	Front direction indicator	S1	Stop lamp
1a	Front direction indicator	S2	Stop lamp
1b	Front direction indicator	S3	Centre mounted stop lamps
2a	Rear direction indicator	I	Class I retro reflector
2b	Rear direction indicator	IA	Class IA retro reflector
3	Front-side direction indicator	III	Class III retro reflector (triangular - for trailers only)
4	Front-side direction indicator	IIIA	Class IIIA retro reflector (triangular - for trailers only)
5	Side-repeater direction indicator	R-S1	Rear position lamp which is also a stop lamp
HCR	Halogen headlamp emitting both main and dipped-beam		

Chapter 4 Construction and Use

The Road Vehicles (Construction and Use) Regulations 1986 specify the construction, dimensions, equipment, and maintenance requirements of **motor vehicles and their trailers used on the road.**

Failure to comply with the regulations is an offence contrary to the Road Traffic Act 1988.

Offences
Breach of requirement as to brakes, steering-gear or tyres
Section 41A Road Traffic Act 1988 fixed penalty offence
- level 5 fine + 3 points for goods vehicles or vehicles adapted to carry more than 8 passengers
- level 4 fine + 3 points in any other case

It is an offence for a person to :-

(a) contravene or fail to comply with a construction and use requirement as to **brakes, steering gear or tyres**, or

(b) to use on a **road** a **motor vehicle or trailer** which does not comply with such a requirement, or cause[1] or permit[1] a motor vehicle or trailer to be so used.

[1] Cause and Permit offences are not fixed penalty offences.

See Pages 4 to 14.

Breach of requirement as to weight: goods and passenger vehicles
Section 41B(1) Road Traffic Act 1988 - level 5 fine - fixed penalty offences

It is an offence for a person to :-

(a) contravene or fail to comply with a construction and use requirement as to any description of **weight** applicable to :-

  ○ a goods vehicle[2], or

  ○ a motor vehicle adapted to carry more than eight passengers, or

  ○ a trailer adapted to carry more than eight passengers, or

(b) use on a road a vehicle which does not comply with such a requirement, or cause[1] or permit[1] a vehicle to be so used.

[1] Cause and Permit offences are not fixed penalty offences.

[2] Goods vehicle means a motor vehicle constructed or adapted for use for the carriage of goods, or a trailer so constructed or adapted.

See Page 21 and Chapter 12 Page 1.

Breach of requirement as to speed assessment equipment detection devices. *NOT YET IN FORCE*
Section 41C Road Traffic Act 1988

Breach of requirements as to control of vehicle

Section 41D(a) Road Traffic Act 1988 - level 4 fine + 3 points for goods vehicles or vehicles adapted to carry more than 8 passengers - level 3 fine + 3 points in any other case - fixed penalty offences

It is an offence for a person to :-

* contravene or fail to comply with a construction and use requirement as to not driving a **motor vehicle** in a position which does not give **proper control or a full view** of the road and traffic ahead, or
* cause[1] or permit[1] the driving of a motor vehicle by another person in such a position.

> [1] *Cause and Permit offences are not fixed penalty offences.*
>
> *See Chapter 30 Page 11.*

Breach of requirements as to mobile telephones etc.

Section 41D(b) Road Traffic Act 1988 - level 4 fine + 6 points for goods vehicles or vehicles adapted to carry more than 8 passengers - level 3 fine + 6 points in any other case - fixed penalty offences

It is an offence for a person to :-

* contravene or fail to comply with a construction and use requirement as to not driving or supervising the driving of a **motor vehicle** while using a **hand-held mobile telephone** or other hand-held interactive communication device, or
* cause[1] or permit[1] the driving of a **motor vehicle** by another person using such a telephone or other device.

> [1] *Cause and Permit offences are not fixed penalty offences.*
>
> *See Chapter 30 Page 12.*

Breach of other construction and use requirements

Section 42 Road Traffic Act 1988 - level 4 fine for goods vehicles or vehicles adapted to carry more than 8 passengers - level 3 fine in any other case - fixed penalty offences

It is an offence for a person to :-

(a) contravene or fail to comply with any construction or use requirement other than one within *section 41A(a) or 41B(1)(a), or 41D of this Act*, or

(b) use on a road a **motor vehicle or trailer** which does not comply with such a requirement, or cause[1] or permit[1] a motor vehicle or trailer to be so used.

> [1] *Cause and Permit offences are not fixed penalty offences.*

Exemptions

General

Regulation 4 Road Vehicles (Construction and Use) Regulations 1986

Exemptions from some requirements include :-

- vehicles proceeding to a port for export,
- vehicles which are brought temporarily into the UK by a person resident abroad, or tax free purchases for export,
- visiting forces vehicles,
- vehicles being tested by an examiner,
- pre-1906 designated vintage motorcars and motorcycles,
- towing dollies which are not carrying another vehicle and are being towed during the day at not more than 20 m.p.h.,
- vehicles being removed under a statutory power of removal,
- Tramcars,
- a vehicle being used by a Police Authority which has been authorised by a Chief Constable to perform accident reconstruction duties.

Approval Certificates

Regulation 3A Road Vehicles (Construction and Use) Regulations 1986

Type approved vehicles may be exempt from certain regulations because the approval has equivalent or higher requirements.

Abnormal Loads [1]

The dimensions of vehicles or loads which comply with certain conditions stipulated in the *Construction and Use Regulations, the Authorised Weights Regulations and the Authorisation of Special Types) (General) Order 2003 (STGO)* may be increased. [1]

Individual Vehicle Special Orders [1]

Exemptions may be applied to a wide range of vehicles dependant on compliance with conditions contained within the order. [1]

---

[1] *Failure to comply with **ALL** the conditions of an Order (STGO or Individual Vehicle Special Order) negates the allowance and the vehicle must then comply with the standard requirements of the applicable Regulations.*
See Page 2-20.

Braking systems
Fitting Requirements

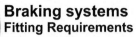

Regulations 15 and16 Road Vehicles (Construction and Use) Regulations 1986, Section 41A Road Traffic Act 1988

Braking systems which fitted in compliance with Regulation 15 or 16 are required on motor vehicles and trailers except :-

(a) a steam propelled locomotive 1st used before 02/01/1933 with an engine which is capable of being reversed (a parking brake is still required),

(b) a trailer which is designed for use and used for street cleansing and does not carry any load other than its necessary gear and equipment,

(ba) a trailer which has a maximum total design axle weight that does not exceed 750 kg,

(bb) an agricultural trailer manufactured before 01/07/1947 with a laden weight not exceeding 4070 kg and drawn as the only trailer by a motor tractor or an agricultural motor vehicle at not more than 10 m.p.h.,

(bc) a trailer drawn by a motor cycle in accordance with *regulation 84*,

(c) an agricultural trailed appliance,

(d) an agricultural trailed appliance conveyor,

(e) a broken down vehicle,

(g) a gritting trailer with a maximum gross weight not exceeding 2000 kg.

Maintenance and Efficiency

Regulation 18(1) Road Vehicles (Construction and Use) Regulations 1986, Section 41A Road Traffic Act 1988

Every part of every braking system and the means of operation fitted to a vehicle shall be maintained in good and efficient working order and be properly adjusted.

Brakes must be maintained if they are fitted even if they are not required.

A brake drum or brake disc are part of the wheel and not the braking system - regulation 3(6).

Exception

Defects on an anti-lock braking system during the journey on which the defect occurred or whilst being driven to a place of repair of the defect.

Application Of Brakes On Trailers

Regulation 19 Road Vehicles (Construction and Use)
Regulations 1986, Section 41A Road Traffic Act 1988

Where a trailer required to be fitted with brakes is drawn by
a motor vehicle the driver shall be in a position to operate the brakes to
the motor vehicle and the trailer unless :-

- the trailer is fitted with overrun brakes, or
- the trailer is a broken down vehicle being drawn in such a manner that
  it cannot be steered by its own steering. (If the vehicle is not broken
  down or otherwise exempt then it cannot, for instance, be towed front
  suspended for delivery without some form of automatic braking system
  fitted).

*In a locomotive a competent person other than the driver may be used to
apply the trailer brakes.*

Unbraked Trailers

Regulation 87(1) Road Vehicles (Construction and Use)
Regulations 1986, Section 41A Road Traffic Act 1988

No person shall use cause or permit to be used on a road an
unbraked wheeled trailer which has a maximum total design axle
weight that does not exceed 750 kg if :-

(a) it is overloaded (its laden weight exceeds its maximum gross
weight), or

(b) the weight of the trailer + load exceeds half the
kerbside weight[K] of the drawing vehicle,

except an agricultural trailer or a trailer mentioned in *paragraph (b), (bb),
(bc), (c), (d), (e), or (g) of regulation 16* above *(see Page 4)*.

*[K] Kerbside Weight of a motor vehicle is the weight of a vehicle when it
carries no person, and a full supply of fuel in its tank, an adequate supply
of other liquids incidental to its propulsion and no load other than the
loose tools and equipment with which it is normally equipped.*

*In other words brakes are required on a small trailer (unless the trailer
falls within another exemption listed above or is an agricultural trailer) if it
is overladen, or if the kerbside weight of the drawing vehicle is less than
twice the total actual weight of the trailer.*

For example :-

- an unbraked trailer which is plated at 500kg max gross weight and
  weighs, with its load, 600kg gross must not be drawn by a motor
  vehicle as the trailer is overweight,
- an unbraked trailer which is plated at 750kg max gross weight and
  weighs, with its load 600kg gross must be drawn by a motor vehicle
  with a kerbside weight of at least 1200kg unless otherwise exempt
  (broken down etc.).

Steering

Regulation 29 Road Vehicles (Construction and Use)
Regulations 1986, Section 41A Road Traffic Act 1988

All steering gear fitted to a motor vehicle shall at all times while the vehicle is used on a road be maintained in good and efficient working order and be properly adjusted.

Springs

Regulation 22 Road Vehicles (Construction and Use) Regulations 1986

Every motor vehicle and every trailer shall be equipped with suitable and sufficient springs between each wheel and the frame of the vehicle.

This regulation does not apply to :-

- a wheeled works truck or a works trailer,
- a wheeled vehicle with an unladen weight not exceeding 4070 kg and which is :-
  - ◦ a motor tractor any unsprung wheel of which is fitted with a pneumatic tyre,
  - ◦ a motor tractor used in connection with railway shunting and which is used on a road only when passing from one railway track to another in connection with such use,
  - ◦ a vehicle specially designed, and mainly used, for work on rough ground or unmade roads and every wheel of which is fitted with a pneumatic tyre and which is not driven at more than 20 mph,
  - ◦ a vehicle constructed or adapted for, and being used for, road sweeping and every wheel of which is fitted with either a pneumatic tyre or a resilient tyre and which is not driven at more than 20 mph,
- an agricultural motor vehicle which is not driven at more than 20 mph,
- an agricultural trailer, or an agricultural trailed appliance,
- a trailer used solely for the haulage of felled trees,
- a motorcycle,
- a mobile crane,
- a pedestrian-controlled vehicle all the wheels of which are equipped with pneumatic tyres,
- a road roller,
- a broken down vehicle, or
- a vehicle first used on or before 01/01/1932.

Tracked vehicles shall have resilient material interposed between the rims of the weight-carrying rollers and the road surface so that the weight of the vehicle, other than that borne by any wheel, is supported by the resilient material and where the vehicle is a heavy motor car, motor car, or trailer (other than a works truck or a works trailer) it shall have suitable springs between the frame of the vehicle and the weight-carrying rollers.

Tyres
Markings on Tyres

Regulation 25 Road Vehicles (Construction and Use) Regulations 1986

A - Section Width - 185mm

B - Aspect Ratio - 65%

C - Construction - Radial

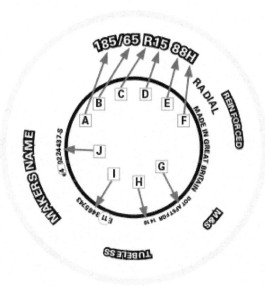

D - Rim Diameter - 15 = 15"

E - Load Index - 88 = 560 kg

F - Speed Rating - H = 130 mph

G - USA Dept. of Transport Codes - n/a

H - Week/Year of Manufacture - 14 10 = 14th week of 2010

I - ECE Tyre Approval Number

J - EC Noise Compliance Approval Number - xxxxxxx-S

XL - Extra Load - the tyre has been reinforced to be able to carry heavier loads than standard tyres of the same dimension - used on heavier vehicles such as SUVs.

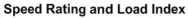

Speed Rating and Load Index

Regulation 25 Road Vehicles (Construction and Use) Regulations 1986

The basic requirement for passenger cars first used on or after 01/04/1991 which are fitted with single wheels is that the load applied to any tyre fitted to the axle of the vehicle shall not exceed that indicated by the load capacity index.

More detailed provisions apply to speed ratings and load index requirements of tyres fitted to :-

• goods vehicles,
• trailers,
• buses,
• engineering plant,
• track-laying vehicles,
• vehicles equipped with tyres of speed category Q,
• works trucks, and
• agricultural motor vehicles, trailers, trailed appliances and trailed appliance conveyors.

The requirements vary by type of vehicle but are basically :-

• the tyre shall be designed and manufactured adequately to support the maximum permitted axle weight for the axle, or
• the tyre shall be designed and manufactured adequately to support the maximum permitted axle weight for the axle when the vehicle is driven at a specified speed.

The requirements do not apply to any tyre fitted to the axle of a broken down vehicle or vehicle proceeding to a place where it is to be broken up, when being drawn by a motor vehicle at a speed not exceeding 20 mph.

Tyre Speed Rating					
Rating	kph	mph	Rating	kph	mph
F	80	49	S	180	112
G	90	56	T	190	118
J	100	62	U	200	124
K	110	68	H	210	130
M	130	81	V	240	149
N	140	87	W	270	168
P	150	93	Y	300	186
Q	160	100	(Y)	>300	>186
R	170	106			

Load Index

The code associated with the maximum load a tyre can carry at the speed indicated by its speed symbol under specified service conditions. At speeds above 130 mph (210 km/h) the rated load must be reduced.

As a rough guide the maximum axle weight of each axle of a vehicle should not exceed the sum of the weight ratings of the tyres on the wheels which are fitted to it.

Load Index

Index	kg	Index	kg	Index	kg
0	45	90	600	180	8000
10	60	100	800	190	10600
20	80	110	1060	200	14000
30	106	120	1400	210	19000
40	140	130	1900	220	25000
50	190	140	2500	230	33500
60	250	150	3350	240	45000
70	335	160	4500	250	60000
80	450	170	6000	260	80000

Tyre Noise

Regulation 25A Road Vehicles (Construction and Use) Regulations 1986, Regulation (EC) No 1222/2009

New replacement tyres (not retreaded or part-worn tyres) with a speed rating of 80km/h (F) or more and a rim diameter 255mm to 634mm (10"to 25"approx) must be marked with an S mark where it is to be fitted to an axle of :-

• a passenger vehicle with 4 wheels or more,

• a goods vehicle,

• a dual-purpose vehicle, or

• a trailer constructed or adapted for use with the above.

Except :-

• T-type temporary-use spare tyres,

• tyres designed only to be fitted to vehicles first registered before 01/10/1990.

Types of Tyres
Pneumatic and Resilient Tyres
Regulation 24 Road Vehicles (Construction and Use) Regulations 1986, Section 41A Road Traffic Act 1988

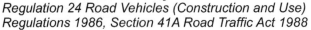

Motor vehicles and trailers, except road rollers, shall be fitted with pneumatic tyres except :-

- motor tractors and locomotives and trailers drawn by them,
- motor cars and heavy motor cars which are vehicles with an unladen weight not exceeding 1020kg (1270kg if electrically propelled), or used mainly for work on rough ground, or fitted with turntable fire escapes, or tower wagons, refuse vehicles, works trucks, or 1st used before 03/01/1933,
- motorcycles which are pedestrian controlled vehicles or works trucks,
- agricultural motor vehicles (not being category T tractors) which are not driven at more than 20 m.p.h.,
- category T tractors (a wheeled agricultural or forestry tractor) which are not driven at more than 40 km/h (25mph),
- trailers which are works trailers, refuse vehicles, or drawn by a heavy motor car which is not required to be fitted with pneumatic tyres, broken down vehicles, or trailers drawn by a vehicle which is not a heavy motor car or a motor car, agricultural trailers manufactured before 01/12/1985, agricultural trailed appliances and trailers used to carry water for a road roller being used in connection with road works.

Re-cut Pneumatic Tyres
Regulation 24 Road Vehicles (Construction and Use) Regulations 1986

Re-cut pneumatic tyres may only be fitted to :-

- locomotives,
- motor tractors with an unladen weight of at least 2540 kg, or a wheel rim diameter of at least 405 mm,
- heavy motor cars,
- motor cars which are goods vehicles and are electrically propelled or have an unladen weight of at least 2540 kg and wheel rim diameter of at least 405 mm,
- agricultural motor vehicles which are not driven at more than 20 m.p.h. with an unladen weight of at least 2540 kg, or a wheel rim diameter of at least 405 mm,
- trailers drawn by a heavy motor car or motor car if the trailer :-
  - has an unladen weight exceeding 2040 kg if it is a living van, or 1020 kg in any other case, or
  - has a gross weight exceeding 2290 kg if it is not constructed or adapted to carry any load, other than plant or other special appliance which is a permanent or essentially permanent fixture,
- trailers drawn by vehicles other than motor cars or heavy motor cars.

Recut tyres must be re-cut in the manufacturers re-cut tread pattern and the cutting process must not cut or expose the fabric.

Mixing of Tyres

Regulation 26 Road Vehicles (Construction and Use)
Regulations 1986, Section 41A Road Traffic Act 1988

Tyres of different construction have different characteristics
which if mixed in certain combinations can be detrimental to the safe
handling of a vehicle. Incorrect combinations can cause oversteer and
uneven braking.

The different types of tyre (marked on the tyre wall) are known as :-

• diagonal-ply or cross-ply,
• bias-belted,
• radial.

Axle Requirements

Pneumatic tyres fitted to :-

• the same axle of a wheeled vehicle, or
• the steerable axles of a wheeled vehicle, or
• the driven axles of a wheeled vehicle which are not steerable,

shall be of the same structure except where a temporary use spare tyre
is fitted to a passenger vehicle with up to 8 passenger seats driven at not
more than 50 m.p.h.

Best to Back Rule

On two axle wheeled motor vehicles fitted with single wheels (saloon
cars, motorcycles, etc.) :-

• if radials are fitted to the front axle, bias-belted or cross-ply tyres shall
  not be fitted to the rear axle, and
• if bias-belted tyres are fitted to the front axle, cross-ply tyres shall not
  be fitted to the rear axle,

except on :-

• vehicles fitted with twin tyres or wide tyres (300 mm in contact with
  road), or
• vehicles with a maximum speed not exceeding 30 m.p.h., or
• vehicles using a temporary use spare (*see below*) in accordance with
  regulations.

Temporary Use Spare Tyres

A temporary use spare tyre may only be fitted to :-

• a passenger vehicle (not being a bus) first used before 01/04/1987,
  and
• a vehicle which complies at the time of its first use with *ECE
  Regulation 64* or *Community Directive 92/23*, or
• a vehicle constructed or assembled by a person not ordinarily
  engaged in the trade or business of manufacturing vehicles of that
  description.

Condition And Maintenance Of Tyres

Regulation 27(1)(a)- (k) Road Vehicles (Con and Use)
Regulations 1986, Section 41A Road Traffic Act 1988

Offence	Exceptions *(See next page)*
A wheeled motor vehicle or trailer fitted with a pneumatic tyre shall not be used on a road, if :-	
(a) the tyre is unsuitable having regard to the use to which the vehicle is being put or to the types of tyres fitted to its other wheels (except where a temporary use spare tyre is fitted to a passenger vehicle with up to 8 passenger seats driven at not more than 50 m.p.h.)	1, 1a, 2, 3, 4
(b) the tyre is not so inflated as to make it fit for the use to which the vehicle is being put	1, 1a, 2, 3, 4
(c) the tyre has a cut in excess of 25 mm or 10% of the section width of the tyre, whichever is the greater, measured in any direction on the outside of the tyre and deep enough to reach the ply or cord	1, 1a, 2, 3, 4, 5
(d) the tyre has any lump, bulge or tear caused by separation or partial failure of its structure	1, 1a, 2, 3, 4, 5
(e) the tyre has any of the ply or cord exposed	1, 1a, 2, 3, 4, 5
(f) the base of any groove which showed in the original tread pattern of the tyre is not clearly visible	1, 1a, 2, 3, 4, 6, 7
(g) Depth of Tread - *see over*	
(h) the tyre is not maintained in such condition as to be fit for the use to which the vehicle or trailer is being put or has a defect which might in any way cause damage to the surface of the road or damage to persons on or in the vehicle or to other persons using the road	None

(i) the tyre is not a retreaded tyre and :-
    (i) the week of manufacture falls more than 10 yrs earlier, or
    (ii) it does not have a week of manufacture marking which complies with **ECE Regulation 30 or 54,**
	8, 10

(j) the tyre is a retreaded tyre and :- • (i) the week of retreading marked on its sidewall falls more than 10 years earlier, or • (ii) it does not have a week of retreading marking.	8, 10
(k) a date marked on the tyre sidewall in accordance with **ECE Regulation 30, 54, 108 or 109** is illegible.	9, 10

Exceptions

None of these exceptions apply to (h)

1 An agricultural motor vehicle (not being a category T tractor) that is not driven at more than 20 m.p.h.

1a A category T tractor (a wheeled agricultural or forestry tractor) that is not driven at more than 40 km/h (25mph).

2 An agricultural trailer.

3 An agricultural trailed appliance.

4 A broken down vehicle or a vehicle proceeding to a place where it is to be broken up, being drawn, in either case, by a motor vehicle at a speed not exceeding 20 m.p.h.

5 In respect of (c), (d) or (e), if the wheel and tyre are designed to run flat and the tyre is marked as such.

6 In respect of (f) only :-
- ○ a three-wheeled motor cycle unladen weight not exceeding 102 kg and maximum speed 12 m.p.h.,
- ○ a pedestrian-controlled works truck.

7 In respect of (f) only - providing the grooves of the tread pattern shall be of a depth of at least 1.6 mm throughout a continuous band comprising the central three-quarters of the breadth of tread and round the entire outer circumference of the tyre (in other words the outer one eighth of the tyre on both sides could be bald with no tread pattern showing) on :-
- ○ passenger vehicles other than motor cycles constructed or adapted to carry no more than 8 seated passengers in addition to the driver,
- ○ goods vehicles with a maximum gross weight which does not exceed 3500 kg, and
- ○ light trailers, not being goods vehicles, first used on or after 03/01/1933.

8 Only applies to tyres fitted :-
- ○ to a front axle of a bus other than a minibus,
- ○ in single configuration on any axle of a minibus,
- ○ to a front axle of a goods vehicle with a maximum gross weight exceeding 3,500 kg.

9 Only applies to :-
- ○ buses (including minibuses),
- ○ goods vehicles with a maximum gross weight exceeding 3,500 kg.

10 Does not apply to vehicles of historical interest used for non-commercial purposes.

Depth of Tread
Regulation 27 Road Vehicles (Construction and Use)
Regulations 1986, Section 41A Road Traffic Act 1988
Wheeled motor vehicle or trailer

A wheeled motor vehicle or trailer fitted with a pneumatic tyre shall not be used on a road, unless :-

Regulation 27(4)(f)

• the grooves of the tread pattern of every tyre are of a depth of at least **1.6 mm** throughout a continuous band comprising the central three-quarters of the breadth of tread and round the entire outer circumference of the tyre fitted to :-

   ○ passenger vehicles other than motor cycles constructed or adapted to carry no more than 8 seated passengers in addition to the driver,

   ○ goods vehicles with a maximum gross weight which does not exceed 3500 kg, and

   ○ light trailers, not being goods vehicles, first used on or after 03/01/1933, or

A Light trailer is a trailer with a maximum gross weight which does not exceed 3500 kg.

Any other motor vehicle or trailer
Regulation 27(1)(g)

• in respect of any other motor vehicle or trailer fitted with a pneumatic tyre :-

   ○ (i) the grooves of the tread pattern of every tyre are of a depth of at least **1mm** throughout a continuous band measuring at least three-quarters of the breadth of the tread and round the entire outer circumference of the tyre, or

   ○ (ii) if the grooves of the original tread pattern of the tyre did not extend beyond three quarters of the breadth of the tread, any groove which showed in the original tread pattern are of a depth of at least 1mm.

Exceptions

• An agricultural motor vehicle that is not driven at more than 20 m.p.h.
• An agricultural trailer.
• An agricultural trailed appliance.
• A broken down vehicle or a vehicle proceeding to a place where it is to be broken up, being drawn, in either case, by a motor vehicle at a speed not exceeding 20 m.p.h.
• A three-wheeled motor cycle unladen weight not exceeding 102 kg and maximum speed 12 m.p.h.
• A pedestrian-controlled works truck.
• A motorcycle with an engine capacity which does not exceed 50 cc.

Dimensions
Overall Length

Regulation 7 Road Vehicles (Construction and Use)
Regulations 1986, Section 42 Road Traffic Act 1988

Motor vehicles
- Wheeled motor vehicles other than buses - 12 metres.
- A bus with two axles - 13.5 m, more than 2 axles - 15 m.
- Tracked motor vehicles - 9.2 metres.

Trailers - *see* [1]
- Drawbar trailer with at least 4 wheels drawn by goods vehicle over 3500kg gross - 12m.
- Agricultural trailer with at least 4 wheels - 12m.
- Semi-trailer (except a car transporter or a semi-trailer which is normally used on international journeys) - 12.2m - *see* [3].
- Composite trailer drawn by a goods vehicle over 3500kg g.v.w. or agricultural motor vehicle - 14.04m.
- Agricultural trailed appliance manufactured on or after 01/12/1985 - 15m including drawbar.
- Any other trailer - 7m.

Combinations
- Motor vehicle + 1 drawbar trailer - *see* [2] - 18.75m.
- Showman's motor vehicle + 1 drawbar trailer where the trailer is living accommodation - 22m.
- Motor vehicle + 2 trailers - 25.9m (motor vehicle 9.2m max, only 1 trailer may exceed 7m).
- Motor vehicle + 3 trailers - 25.9m (motor vehicle 9.2m max, no trailer may exceed 7m).
- Articulated bus and a bus drawing a trailer - 18.75m.
- Articulated vehicle + semi-trailer - *see* [2] - 15.5m - *see* [3].
- Articulated vehicle + semi-trailer which is a low-loader manufactured on or after 01/04/1991 - 18m - *see* [1].
- Articulated vehicle + semi-trailer which is not a low loader and is carrying one or more containers or swap bodies up to a total maximum length of 45 feet as part of an intermodal transport operation - 16.65m.

Exceptions
[1] Except trailers and combinations including trailers constructed and normally used for abnormal length loads or plant trailers for road construction asphalt.
[2] Except combinations involving towing broken down vehicles or trailers constructed and normally used for abnormal length loads.
[3] Up to 14.04m trailer or 16.5m combination (16.69m for car-transporters) if semi-trailer meets turning circle requirements (*Regs 13A or 13B*).

See Regulation 3 Road Vehicles (Construction and Use) Regs 1986 for definition of Overall Length.

Longitudinal Projections
Regulation 82(7) Road Vehicles (Construction and Use)
Regulations 1986, Section 42 Road Traffic Act 1988

No load shall be carried on a vehicle[1] so that the load, or if fitted, special appliance or apparatus, has a :-

• forward projection of a length exceeding 2 metres, or
• rearward projection of a length exceeding 1 metre,

unless the conditions specified[2] are complied with.

[1]Exemptions and differences apply to different vehicles and loads.

Excess Length and Longitudinal Projections

The Construction Regulations - the Road Vehicles (Construction and Use) Regulations 1986 stipulate the dimensions of vehicles and their loads when used on a road.

To exceed these maximums the movement must be authorised either :-

• for standard vehicles, by complying with conditions contained in *Regulation 82* or *Schedule 12 of the Road Vehicles (Construction and Use) Regulations 1986,*
• for special types vehicles, by complying with conditions contained in the *Road Vehicles (Authorisation of Special Types) (General) Order 2003 - (STGO), or*
• by a *Vehicle Special Order* by complying with conditions contained in the order.

> *In any case if the conditions specified are not complied with the movement ceases to be authorised and the vehicle and load must comply to the standard limits required by the regulations.*

Overhang

Regulation 11 Road Vehicles (Construction and Use)
Regulations 1986, Section 42 Road Traffic Act 1988

Overhang applies to the vehicle - not any load carried by it - basically it is the distance from the centre of the rear axle to the rearmost part of the vehicle or, if twin rear axles, from a point 110 mm behind the mid point of the two rearmost axles. This will normally only apply to vehicles which have not been type approved or which have been modified.

Overall Width

Regulation 8 Road Vehicles (Construction and Use)
Regulations 1986, Section 42 Road Traffic Act 1988

The overall width of a vehicle specified below shall not exceed :-

Motor Vehicles

- a locomotive, other than an agricultural motor vehicle - 2.75 metres,

- a refrigerated vehicle or a conditioned container or swap body used to carry goods at controlled temperatures on different modes of transport - 2.60 metres,

- any other motor vehicle - 2.55 metres,

Refrigerated vehicles are specially designed for the carriage of goods at low temperature with sidewalls, including insulation, at least 45 mm thick.

Trailers

- a trailer drawn by a motor vehicle other than a motorcycle - 2.55 metres,

- a trailer drawn by a motor cycle (3 wheeled or 2 wheeled with sidecar) - 1.50 metres,

- a trailer drawn by a two wheeled solo motor cycle - 1.00 metres (*Regulation 84*),

except a broken down vehicle which is being drawn in consequence of the breakdown.

A wheeled agricultural motor vehicle drawing an offset wheeled trailer is treated as one vehicle for width measurement purposes - maximum width 2.55 metres.

This regulation deals only with the actual width of a vehicle not the load (*see later*). Items such as mirrors are not included when measuring the overall width of a vehicle.

See Regulation 3 Road Vehicles (Construction and Use) Regulations 1986 for a more concise definition of Overall Width.

Excess Width and Lateral Projections

The Construction Regulations - the Road Vehicles (Construction and Use) Regulations 1986 stipulate the maximum dimensions of vehicles and their loads when used on a road.

To exceed these maximums the movement must be authorised either :-

- for standard vehicles, by complying with conditions contained in *Regulation 82 or Schedule 12 of the Road Vehicles (Construction and Use) Regulations 1986*, or

- for special types vehicles, by complying with conditions contained in the *Road Vehicles (Authorisation of Special Types) (General) Order 2003 - (STGO)*,

- by a Vehicle Special Order by complying with conditions contained in the order.

In any case if the conditions specified are not complied with the movement ceases to be authorised and the vehicle and load must comply to the standard limits required by the regulations.

Lateral Projections
Regulation 82 Road Vehicles (Construction and Use) Regulations 1986, Section 42 Road Traffic Act 1988

No load shall be carried on a vehicle :-

- so that the overall width of the vehicle together with the width of any lateral projection or projections of its load exceeds 4.3 m, or

- so that the load :-

  ○ has a lateral projection or projections on either side exceeding 305 mm, or

  ○ so that the overall width of the vehicle and of any lateral projection or projections of its load exceeds 2.9 m.

Except this paragraph does not apply to :-

- loose agricultural produce not baled or crated, and

- an indivisible load if the conditions specified in *Schedule 12* are complied with (*see Chapter 14*).

Height

Regulation 9 Road Vehicles (Construction and Use)
Regulations 1986, Section 42 Road Traffic Act 1988

A bus shall not exceed 4.57m (15' 0") overall height.

No other type of vehicle is restricted.

4.57m
15'0"

Height Plates

Regulation 10(1) Road Vehicles (Construction and Use)
Regulations 1986, Section 42 Road Traffic Act 1988

If the overall travelling height of a motor vehicle or its trailer, including load, exceeds 3 metres (9'10") (4m if an EC registered vehicle on an international journey) a notice clearly indicating the height in feet and inches (in characters at least 40mm tall) must be displayed in the cab so that it can be clearly read by the driver, indicating :-

• not less than actual overall travelling height or more than 150mm (6") greater, or
• if high level equipment (hydraulic arms etc.) is fitted, the height at which a warning device would give a visible warning to the driver if exceeded - alarm must set to activate within 1m of overall travelling height.

Reg 10(2) Road Vehicles (Construction and Use) Regulations 1986 [1]

No person shall use or cause or permit to be used on a road a motor vehicle with an overall travelling height exceeding 3m if any letters or numbers are displayed in the cab :-

• where they could be read by the driver, and
• which could be understood as indicating a height associated with the vehicle or any trailer drawn by it,

otherwise than in a notice as required above.

Height Plate Exemptions

Where it is highly unlikely that the driver would encounter any bridge or other overhead structure which is less than 1 metre higher than the overall travelling height or the maximum height of high level equipment when fully extended, allowing for unforeseen diversions or the driver getting lost.

Where document(s) are within easy reach of the driver describing :-

• his route(s) without risk of colliding with any bridge or overhead structure PROVIDING the driver is on that route or is off that route because of an unforeseen diversion, or
• which bridges and structures his vehicle/load could safely pass under and those he could not which are on his route, allowing for unforeseen diversions or the driver getting lost.

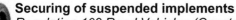
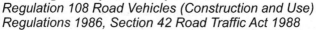

Securing of suspended implements
Regulation 108 Road Vehicles (Construction and Use) Regulations 1986, Section 42 Road Traffic Act 1988

Where a vehicle is fitted with any apparatus or appliance designed for lifting and part of the apparatus or appliance consists of a suspended implement, the implement shall at all times while the vehicle is in motion on a road and when the implement is not attached to any load supported by the appliance or apparatus be so secured either to the appliance or apparatus or to some part of the vehicle that no danger is caused or is likely to be caused to any person on the vehicle or on the road.

Height Warning Devices

Regulations 10A and 10B Road Vehicles (Construction and Use) Regulations 1986, Section 42 Road Traffic Act 1988

A warning device, which gives a visible warning to the driver if a set height is exceeded, is required on the motor vehicle if high level equipment which exceeds 3m when extended (4m if an EC registered vehicle on an international journey) is fitted to a motor vehicle 1st used on or after 01/04/1993 or a trailer manufactured on or after 01/04/1993.

Exceptions
• Agricultural vehicles.
• Industrial tractors.
• Tippers 1st used/manufactured before 01/04/1998 in relation to the tipping part.
• Works trucks and works trailers.
• Vehicles owned by or under orders of armed forces.
• Car transporters.
• Fire brigade vehicles.
• Towed broken down vehicles.
• Vehicles where the equipment height (fully extended) does not exceed the vehicle height or where the high level equipment is fitted with a locking device.
• Where it is highly unlikely that the driver would encounter any bridge or other overhead structure which is less than 1 metre higher than the overall travelling height or the maximum height of high level equipment when fully extended, allowing for unforeseen diversions or the driver getting lost.

CONSTRUCTION AND USE

Weight

Maximum weights are specified in *Regulations 75 to 79* and, in respect of Intermodal Transport Operations, *Schedule 11A of the Road Vehicles (Construction and Use) Regulations 1986*, operating in parallel, the *Road Vehicles (Authorised Weights) Regulations 1998* and, taking into account alternative fuelled vehicles, the *Road Vehicles (Authorised Weight) and (Construction and Use) (Amendment) Regulations 2017.*

The maximum weights permitted by these regulations are subject to the general over-riding condition in regulation 80 Road Vehicles (Construction and Use) Regulations 1986 that plated weights (which may be lower) cannot be exceeded.

Over-riding weight restrictions (Exceeding Plated Weights)

Regulation 80 Road Vehicles (Construction and Use) Regulations 1986, Section 41B(1) Road Traffic Act 1988

No person shall use, or cause or permit to be used, on a road a vehicle :-

- fitted with a plate in accordance with *regulation 66* (Manufacturers Plate), but for which no plating certificate has been issued, if any of the weights shown on the plate is exceeded,
- for which a plating certificate has been issued, if any of the weights shown in the plating certificate is exceeded, or
- required by *regulation 68* (agricultural trailed appliances) to be fitted with a plate, if the maximum gross weight is exceeded.

Excess Weight

The Construction Regulations - the Road Vehicles (Construction and Use) Regulations 1986 and the Road Vehicles (Authorised Weights) Regulations 1998 together stipulate the maximum weights of vehicles and their loads when used on a road.

To exceed these maximums the movement must be authorised either :-

- for standard vehicles, by complying with conditions contained in *regulation 82 or Schedule 12 of the Road Vehicles (Construction and Use) Regulations 1986*, or
- for special types vehicles, by complying with conditions contained in the *Road Vehicles (Authorisation of Special Types) (General) Order 2003 - (STGO), or*
- by a Vehicle Special Order by complying with conditions contained in the order.

In any case if the conditions specified are not complied with the movement ceases to be authorised and the vehicle and load must comply to the standard limits required by the regulations.

4 - 21

Equipment
Mirrors
Fitting

Regulation 33 Road Vehicles (Construction and Use) Regulations 1986, Section 42 Road Traffic Act 1988

Motor vehicles, except road rollers, shall be fitted with a mirror(s) or other device for indirect vision according to their class and date of first use.

Any mirror or other device for indirect vision which is fitted shall, whether or not it is required, comply with the any requirements of these regulations or EC Regulations applicable to that vehicle.

'Mirror' means any device with a reflecting surface, excluding devices such as periscopes, intended to give a clear view to the rear, side or front of the vehicle.

'Devices' for indirect vision mean devices to observe the traffic area adjacent to the vehicle which cannot be observed by direct vision and may include conventional mirrors, camera-monitors or other devices able to present information about the indirect field of vision to the driver.

- Internal mirrors shall have edges protected - wheeled motor vehicles first used on or after 01/04/1969.
- Each mirror shall be fixed so it remains steady under normal driving conditions.
- Exterior mirrors on a vehicle fitted with windows and a windscreen shall be visible to the driver.
- Exterior mirrors less than 2m from ground shall not project more than 20 cm beyond the overall width of the vehicle (or the trailer if wider).
- Interior mirror and exterior driver side mirror shall be capable of being adjusted by the driver when in his driving position.

Exemptions

The following vehicle are exempt from the requirement to fit mirrors :-

- a works truck, a track-laying agricultural motor vehicle, and
- a wheeled agricultural motor vehicle first used before 01/06/1978,

if, in each case, the driver can easily obtain a view to the rear, or :-

- a motor vehicle drawing a trailer, if a person is carried on the trailer so that he has an uninterrupted view to the rear and has an efficient means of communicating to the driver the effect of signals given by the drivers of other vehicles to the rear,
- a pedestrian-controlled vehicle,
- a chassis being driven from the place where it has been manufactured to the place where it is to receive a vehicle body,
- an agricultural motor vehicle unladen weight exceeding 7370 kg which is a track-laying vehicle or a wheeled vehicle first used before 01/06/1978,
- a two-wheeled motor cycle with or without a sidecar attached.

Glass

Maintenance
Regulation 30 Road Vehicles (Construction and Use) Regulations 1986, Section 42 Road Traffic Act 1988

All glass or other transparent material fitted to a motor vehicle shall be maintained in such a condition that it does not obscure the vision of the driver while the vehicle is being driven on a road.

Safety Glass
Regulations 31/ 32 Road Vehicles (Construction and Use) Regulations 1986, Section 42 Road Traffic Act 1988

Safety glass shall be used in all outside windows on passenger and dual purpose vehicles first used on or after 01/01/1959 and specified safety glass of a higher technical specification, marked with either a British Standard mark or an approval mark (or on a vehicle first used before 01/10/1986, a French approval mark), should be fitted on the windscreens and windows alongside the driver on vehicles first used on or after 01/06/1978. (01/09/1978 for caravans).

There are exceptions to the requirement to fit higher specification glass which include security vehicles and vehicles being used for police purposes, motorcycles, temporary windscreens, windows (other than windscreens) of engineering plant, industrial tractors, certain agricultural motor vehicles, windows of the upper deck of a double-decked bus, and windows in the roof of a vehicle.

Tinted Windows
Regulation 32(10) Road Vehicles (Construction and Use) Regulations 1986, Section 42 Road Traffic Act 1988

- All motor vehicles first used before 01/04/1985 - 70%.
- Motor vehicles first used on or after 01/04/1985 - windscreen 75%, Other windows 70%.
- Trailers - 70%.

Measurements should be carried out perpendicular to the surface in accordance with the procedure specified in the appropriate British Standard Specification.

The requirements above have effect in relation to any tint, film or other substance or material applied to a windscreen or window as they have effect in relation to the windscreen or window itself.

Exceptions apply to parts of the windscreen outside the visual reference zone, windows through which the driver could not see the road, and windows, other than rear facing windows and access doors, behind the driver in goods vehicles, buses, locomotives and tractors and all windows behind the driver in an ambulance.

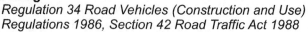

Windscreen wipers and washers
Fitting
Regulation 34 Road Vehicles (Construction and Use)
Regulations 1986, Section 42 Road Traffic Act 1988

Every vehicle fitted with a windscreen shall, unless the driver can obtain an adequate view to the front without looking through the windscreen, be fitted with :-

- one or more efficient automatic windscreen wipers capable of clearing the windscreen so that the driver has an adequate view of the road in front of both sides of the vehicle and to the front of the vehicle, and
- a windscreen washer capable of clearing, in conjunction with the wiper, the area of windscreen swept by the wiper of mud or similar deposits, except (in respect of washers) :-
  - an agricultural motor vehicle 1st used before 01/06/1986,
  - an agricultural motor vehicle 1st used on or after 01/06/1986 driven at not more than 20 m.p.h.,
  - an agricultural motor vehicle (not being a category T tractor) unless it is first used on or after 01/06/1986 and is driven at more than 20 mph,
  - a category T tractor ((a wheeled agricultural or forestry tractor) unless it is first used on or after 01/06/1986 and is driven at more than 40 km/h,
  - a tracked vehicle,
  - a vehicle having a maximum speed not exceeding 20 m.p.h.,
  - a vehicle providing a local service (bus on a regular scheduled service route).

Maintenance
Regulation 34(6) Road Vehicles (Construction and Use)
Regulations 1986, Section 42 Road Traffic Act 1988

Every wiper and washer required to be fitted shall, whilst the vehicle is being used on a road, be maintained in efficient working order and be properly adjusted.

Speedometers
Fitting

Regulation 35 Road Vehicles (Construction and Use)
Regulations 1986, Section 42 Road Traffic Act 1988

Every motor vehicle shall be fitted with a speedometer except :-

• a vehicle having a maximum speed not exceeding 25 mph.,
• a vehicle which, at all times, is unlawful to drive at more than 25 mph.,
• an agricultural motor vehicle (not being a category T tractor) driven at not more than 20 mph.,
• a category T tractor (a wheeled agricultural or forestry tractor) which is not driven at more than 40 km/h (25mph),
• a motor cycle not exceeding 100cc first used before 01/04/1984,
• an invalid carriage first used before 01/04/1984,
• a works truck first used before 01/04/1984,
• any vehicle first used before 01/10/1937,
• a vehicle fitted with an approved tachograph which is required or not.

Vehicles first used on or after 01/04/1984 the speedometer should be capable of indicating the speed in miles/hour and kilometres/hour.

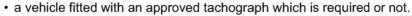

Vehicles may instead comply with EC Regulation (Community Directive) 97/39 or ECE Regulation 39. These directives stipulate the markings, graduations of the speedometer and refer to 75/443/EEC which specifies the tolerances. The indicated speed must never be less than the true speed (it must read exact or high) and between 40km/h and 120km/h the error must not exceed 10% +2.5 m.p.h. high (true speed/10 +4kph).

This means at a true speed of 25mph or 40km/h the speedometer may read 40/10+4 = 8km/h or 5mph high = 30mph indicated.

Maintenance

Regulation 36 Road Vehicles (Construction and Use)
Regulations 1986, Section 42 Road Traffic Act 1988

The speedometer fitted to a vehicle must :-

• be kept free from any obstruction which may prevent it from being easily read, and
• shall at all times it is used on a road be maintained in good working order except if :-
    ◦ the speedometer became defective during the journey being undertaken, or
    ◦ steps have been taken to have the defect remedied by replacement or repair with all reasonable expedition, or
    ◦ the vehicle is fitted with an approved tachograph which is required to be fitted under the *Community Recording Equipment Regulation* (offence is under that regulation).

Audible Warning Instruments
Fitting of Horns and Alarms

Regulation 37(1) Road Vehicles (Construction and Use)
Regulations 1986, Section 42 Road Traffic Act 1988

Every motor vehicle with a maximum speed of more than 20 m.p.h. shall be fitted with an audible warning instrument (horn) except :-

- an agricultural motor vehicle (not being a category T tractor) driven at not more than 20 m.p.h., or
- a category T tractor (a wheeled agricultural or forestry tractor) which is not driven at more than 40 km/h (25mph).

The audible warning instrument fitted to a wheeled vehicle first used on or after 01/08/1973 should be continuous and uniform and not strident.

Nothing in this regulation forbids the use of :-

- a reversing alarm or a boarding aid alarm,
- a theft alarm (but it must incorporate a fully maintained 5 minute cut-out switch when fitted to a vehicle first used on or after 01/10/1982),
- a device used on a bus to summon help for the driver, conductor or inspector,
- a device or apparatus (not two tone horn) designed to emit a sound for the purpose of informing members of the public that goods are on sale. This is permitted between the hours of 1200 hours and 1900 hours (*Regulation 99*).

Use of Horns and Alarms

Regulation 99(1) Road Vehicles (Construction and Use)
Regulations 1986, Section 42 Road Traffic Act 1988

Horns and other warning instruments must not be used :-

- when the vehicle is stationary (other than an emergency involving another vehicle, a reversing alarm or a boarding aid alarm), or
- in motion on a restricted road between 2330 hours and 0700 hours.

Regulation 99(3) Road Vehicles (Construction and Use)
Regulations 1986, Section 42 Road Traffic Act 1988

No person shall sound or cause or permit to be sounded on a road a reversing alarm or a boarding aid alarm unless it is fitted to :-

- a goods vehicle having a maximum gross weight not less than 2000kg,
- a bus,
- engineering plant, a refuse vehicle or a works truck.

They must not emit a sound likely to be confused with that from a pedestrian crossing. A boarding aid alarm means an alarm for a power operated lift or ramp fitted to a bus to enable wheelchair users to board and alight and designed to warn persons that the lift or ramp is in operation.

Two -Tone horns

Fitting
Regulation 37(4) Road Vehicles (Construction and Use) Regulations 1986, Section 42 Road Traffic Act 1988

No vehicle shall be fitted with a bell, gong or two tone horn other than vehicles :-

- used for fire brigade or police purposes,
- used for ambulance purposes or for the purpose of providing a response to an emergency at the request of an NHS ambulance service,
- owned by a body formed primarily for the purposes of fire salvage and used for those or similar purposes,
- owned by the Forestry Commission or local authorities and used from time to time for the purposes of fighting fires,
- owned by Ministry of Defence and used for the purposes of the disposal of bombs or explosives,
- used for the purposes of the Blood Transfusion Service,
- used by HM Coastguard or Coastguard Auxiliary to aid persons in danger or vessels in distress on or near the coast,
- used for the purposes of rescue operations at mines,
- owned by Ministry of Defence and used by RAF Mountain rescue,
- used for mountain rescue purposes,
- owned by R.N.L.I. and used for launching lifeboats,
- under the control of HM Revenue and Customs used from time to time for investigating serious crime,
- owned or operated by Ministry of Defence in connection with radiation accidents or emergencies or for special forces purposes.

Does not include vehicles used for transporting human tissue.

Use
Regulation 99(4) Road Vehicles (Construction and Use) Regulations 1986, Section 42 Road Traffic Act 1988

Nothing in this regulation shall prevent the sounding of 2-tone horns or sirens fitted to a vehicle as permitted above when it is necessary or desirable to do so to indicate to other road users the urgency of the purpose for which the vehicle is being used, or warn other persons of the presence of the vehicle on the road.

Rear under-run Protection for Goods Vehicles
Fitting
Regulation 49 Road Vehicles (Construction and Use)
Regulations 1986, Section 42 Road Traffic Act 1988

Every vehicle to which this regulation applies shall be equipped with a rear under-run protective device or comply with *EU Directive 97/19*

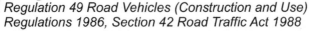

Application
This regulation applies to a wheeled goods vehicle being either :-
- a motor vehicle with a maximum gross weight which exceeds 3500 kg and which was first used on or after 01/04/1984, or
- a trailer manufactured on or after 01/05/1983 with an unladen weight which exceeds 1020 kg.

Exceptions
This regulation does not apply to :-
- a motor vehicle which has a maximum speed not exceeding 15 mph,
- a motor car or a heavy motor car constructed or adapted to form part of an articulated vehicle,
- an agricultural trailer,
- engineering plant,
- a fire engine,
- an agricultural motor vehicle,
- a vehicle fitted at the rear with apparatus specially designed for spreading material on a road,
- a vehicle so constructed that it can be unloaded by part of the vehicle being tipped rearwards,
- a vehicle owned by the Secretary of State for Defence and used for naval, military or air force purposes,
- a vehicle to which no bodywork has been fitted and which is being driven or towed :-
    - for the purpose of a quality or safety check by its manufacturer or a dealer in, or distributor of, such vehicles, or
    - to a place where, by previous arrangement, bodywork is to be fitted or work preparatory to the fitting of bodywork is to be carried out, or
    - by previous arrangement to premises of a dealer in, or distributor of, such vehicles,
- a vehicle which is being driven or towed to a place where by previous arrangement a device is to be fitted so that it complies with this regulation,
- a vehicle specially designed and constructed, and not merely adapted, to carry other vehicles loaded onto it from the rear, *continued over*

Exceptions - *continued*

- a trailer specially designed and constructed, and not merely adapted, to carry round timber, beams or girders, being items of exceptional length,
- a vehicle fitted with a tail lift so constructed that the lift platform forms part of the floor of the vehicle and this part has a length of at least 1 m measured parallel to the longitudinal axis of the vehicle,
- a trailer having a base or centre in a country outside Great Britain from which it normally starts its journeys, provided that a period of not more than 12 months has elapsed since the vehicle was last brought into Great Britain,
- a vehicle specially designed, and not merely adapted, for the carriage and mixing of liquid concrete,
- a vehicle designed and used solely for the delivery of coal by means of a special conveyor which is carried on the vehicle and when in use is fitted to the rear of the vehicle so as to render its being equipped with a rear under-run protective device impracticable, or
- an agricultural trailed appliance.

> *Alternative devices may be fitted to vehicles to which this regulation applies which are fitted with a tail lift, bodywork or other part which renders its being equipped with a rear under-run protective device impracticable.*

Maintenance of rear under-run protective device
Regulation 50 Road Vehicles (Construction and Use) Regulations 1986, Section 42 Road Traffic Act 1988

Every device fitted to a vehicle in compliance with the requirements of *regulation 49* above shall at all times when the vehicle is on a road be maintained free from any obvious defect which would be likely to affect adversely the performance of the device in the function of giving resistance in the event of an impact from the rear.

Sideguards (lateral protection devices) for Goods Vehicles

Lateral protection devices (LPDs) are designed to reduce the likelihood of injury to pedestrians, cyclists and motorcyclists when struck by a vehicle travelling in a forward direction. They are fitted to deflect and to stop people falling underneath the sides of the vehicle and being caught underneath the wheels.

Fitting

Regulation 51(3) Road Vehicles (Construction and Use) Regulations 1986, Section 42 Road Traffic Act 1988

Every vehicle to which this regulation applies shall be securely fitted with a sideguard to give protection on any side of the vehicle where :-

- if it is a semi-trailer, the distance between the transverse planes passing through the centre of its foremost axle and through the centre of its king-pin or, in the case of a vehicle having more than one king-pin, the rearmost one, exceeds 4.5 m, or
- if it is any other vehicle, the distance between the centres of any two consecutive axles exceeds 3m.

Application

This regulation applies to a wheeled goods vehicle being :-

- a motor vehicle first used on or after 01/04/1984 with a maximum gross weight which exceeds 3500 kg, or
- a trailer manufactured on or after 01/05/1983 with an unladen weight which exceeds 1020 kg, or
- a semi-trailer manufactured before 01/05/1983 which has a relevant plate showing a gross weight exceeding 26,000 kg and which forms part of an articulated vehicle with a relevant train weight exceeding 32,520 kg.

This regulation also applies to a wheeled goods vehicle, whether of a description falling within the exceptions below or not, which is a semi-trailer some or all of the wheels of which are driven by the drawing vehicle.

Exceptions

This regulation does not apply to :-

- a motor vehicle which has a maximum speed not exceeding 15 mph,
- an agricultural trailer *,
- engineering plant*,
- a fire engine*,
- an agricultural motor vehicle*,
- a vehicle so constructed that it can be unloaded by part of the vehicle being tipped sideways or rearwards*,

*Vehicles marked * above are also exempt from the requirement to fit spray suppression equipment.* continued over

Exceptions - *continued*

- a vehicle owned by the Secretary of State for Defence and used for naval, military or air force purposes*,
- a vehicle to which no bodywork has been fitted and which is being driven or towed *:-
    - for the purpose of a quality or safety check by its manufacturer or a dealer in, or distributor of, such vehicles,
    - to a place where, by previous arrangement, bodywork is to be fitted or work preparatory to the fitting of bodywork is to be carried out, or
    - by previous arrangement to premises of a dealer in, or distributor of, such vehicles,
- a vehicle which is being driven or towed to a place where by previous arrangement a sideguard is to be fitted so that it complies with this regulation,
- a refuse vehicle*,
- a trailer specially designed and constructed, and not merely adapted, to carry round timber, beams or girders, being items of exceptional length*,
- a motor car or a heavy motor car constructed or adapted to form part of an articulated vehicle,
- a vehicle specially designed and constructed, and not merely adapted, to carry other vehicles loaded onto it from the front or the rear,
- a trailer with a load platform :-
    - no part of any edge of which is more than 60 mm inboard from the tangential plane, and
    - the upper surface of which is not more than 750 mm from the ground throughout that part of its length under which a sideguard would have to be fitted in accordance with paragraph (5)(d) to (g) if this exemption did not apply to it,
- a trailer having a base or centre in a country outside Great Britain from which it normally starts its journeys, provided that a period of not more than 12 months has elapsed since the vehicle was last brought into Great Britain*, or
- an agricultural trailed appliance*.

*Vehicles marked * above are also exempt from the requirement to fit spray suppression equipment.*

Maintenance of Sideguards

Regulation 52 Road Vehicles (Construction and Use) Regulations 1986, Section 42 Road Traffic Act 1988

Every sideguard fitted to a vehicle in compliance with the requirements of *regulation 51* above shall at all times when the vehicle is on a road be maintained free from any obvious defect which would be likely to affect adversely its effectiveness.

Spray Suppression

Fitting
Regulation 64 Road Vehicles (Construction and Use) Regulations 1986, Section 42 Road Traffic Act 1988

Suitable spray suppression equipment (to British Standard or EC 91/226) fitted on each axle is required to be fitted to :-

- motor vehicles exceeding 12000kg gross 1st used on or after 01/04/1986,
- trailers exceeding 3500kg gross manufactured on or after 01/05/1985,
- trailer exceeding 16000kg gross with 2 or more axles whenever manufactured,

except :-

- a motor vehicle with at least 1 front and 1 rear driven axle,
- a motor vehicle whose underside between the wheels is at least 400mm above the ground,
- a works truck and a works trailer,
- a broken down vehicle,
- a motor vehicle which has a maximum speed not exceeding 30 m.p.h.,
- a vehicle exempt from the requirement to fit side guards marked * (*see previous page*),
- a vehicle specially designed for the carriage and mixing of liquid concrete, or
- a vehicle which is being driven or towed to a place where by previous arrangement a device is to be fitted.

Maintenance
Regulation 65 Road Vehicles (Construction and Use) Regulations 1986, Section 42 Road Traffic Act 1988

Every part of every spray suppression device required to be fitted by *regulation 64* shall at all times when the vehicle is on the road be maintained free from any obvious defect which would be likely to affect adversely the effectiveness of the device.

Fuel Tanks
Regulation 39 Road Vehicles (Construction and Use) Regulations 1986, Section 42 Road Traffic Act 1988

Every fuel tank which is fitted to a wheeled vehicle for the purpose of supplying fuel to the propulsion unit or to an ancillary engine or to any other equipment forming part of the vehicle shall be constructed and maintained so that leakage of any liquid or vapour (except pressure relief mechanisms) from the tank is adequately prevented.

This includes the fixing of a fuel cap on petrol or diesel vehicles.

Wings

Regulation 63 Road Vehicles (Construction and Use) Regulations 1986, Section 42 Road Traffic Act 1988

Wings or other similar fittings to catch, so far as practicable, mud or water thrown up by the rotation of its wheels or tracks shall be fitted to :-

- invalid carriages,
- heavy motor cars, motor cars, and motorcycles, not being an agricultural motor vehicle or pedestrian controlled vehicle,
- an agricultural motor vehicle (not being a category T tractor) driven at more than 20 m.p.h.,
- a category T tractor (a wheeled agricultural or forestry tractor) which is driven at more than 40 km/h (25mph),
- trailers - only on the rearmost two wheels,

Exceptions

- Vehicles which comply with *EEC 78/549*,
- A works truck, a living van and a water cart.
- An agricultural trailer drawn by a motor vehicle which is not driven at a speed in excess of 20 m.p.h.
- An agricultural trailed appliance and an agricultural trailed appliance conveyor.
- A broken down vehicle.
- An unfinished vehicle proceeding to a workshop for completion.
- A trailer and the rear wheels of any heavy motor car or motor car drawing a semi-trailer used for or in connection with the carriage of round timber.
- A trailer drawn by a motor vehicle the maximum speed of which is restricted to 20 m.p.h. or less.

Silencers

Fitting

Regulation 54(1) Road Vehicles (Construction and Use) Regulations 1986, Section 42 Road Traffic Act 1988

Every vehicle propelled by an internal combustion engine shall be fitted with an exhaust system including a silencer and the exhaust gases from the engine shall not escape into the atmosphere without first passing through the silencer.

Maintenance

Regulation 54(2) Road Vehicles (Construction and Use) Regulations 1986, Section 42 Road Traffic Act 1988

Every exhaust system and silencer shall be maintained in good and efficient working order and shall not after the date of manufacture be altered so as to increase the noise made by the escape of exhaust gases.

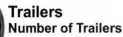

Trailers
Number of Trailers

Regulation 83 Road Vehicles (Construction and Use)
Regulations 1986, Section 42 Road Traffic Act 1988

Trailers may not be drawn by a wheeled vehicle except :-

- a heavy motor car or motor car (including a minibus but no other bus) may draw :-
  - one trailer, or
  - two trailers, if one of them is a towing implement and part of the other is secured to and either rests on or is suspended from that implement,
- a bus, not being an articulated bus or mini-bus, may draw one trailer, if it is a broken down bus only the driver may be carried in the drawn vehicle,
- a motorcycle may draw 1 trailer -
- a motor tractor may draw 1 trailer, or two unladen trailers.
- a locomotive may draw 3 trailers.
- an agricultural motor vehicle may draw :-
  - two unladen agricultural trailers, or
  - two agricultural trailed appliances, or
  - one agricultural trailer (laden or unladen) and one agricultural trailed appliance, or
  - non-agricultural trailers only as permitted by classification of the drawing vehicle above.

A tracked motor vehicle, exceeding 8 m overall length, may only draw a broken down vehicle being recovered.

A broken down, unladen articulated vehicle is treated as one trailer.

A straddle carrier, invalid carriage or an articulated bus may not draw any trailer.

A towed 'agricultural' roller consisting of several separate rollers shall be treated as one appliance.

Discount trailers drawn by a steam powered vehicles used solely for carrying water for the drawing vehicle.

Towing distance

Regulation 86 Road Vehicles (Construction and Use)
Regulations 1986, Section 42 Road Traffic Act 1988

Where a trailer is attached to the vehicle in front of it solely by means of a rope or chain, the distance between the trailer and that vehicle :-

- shall not exceed 1.5m unless the rope or chain is made clearly visible,
- shall not exceed 4.5m in any case.

Tow hitches - Passenger Vehicle coupling devices

*Regulation 86B Road Vehicles (Construction and Use)
Regulations 1986, Section 42 Road Traffic Act 1988*

Any mechanical coupling device which is attached to a light passenger vehicle subject to type approval which is first used on or after 01/08/1998 must comply with *Community Directive 94/20.*

This applies to the tow hitch on the vehicle not to a device which is part of the trailer.

The hitch will bear an E-mark, ECE mark or BS type approval.

Light Passenger Vehicle - Section 85 Road Traffic Act 1988.

Any motor vehicle having at least 4 wheels, an internal combustion engine, not being a goods vehicle but constructed or adapted for use for the carriage of no more than 8 passengers + driver, maximum design speed exceeds 25 km/h. Does not include a quad-bike or vehicle used or intended for use by a fire brigade.

Secondary Couplings on Trailers

*Regulation 86A Road Vehicles (Construction and Use)
Regulations 1986, Section 42 Road Traffic Act 1988*

Trailers must be fitted with :-

• a device designed to stop the trailer automatically in the event of the main coupling detaching whilst in motion and if that device depends on a coupling to the motor vehicle then that coupling should be fitted, or

• if no such device is fitted then a secondary coupling must attach the trailer to the motor vehicle which would, in the event of the main coupling detaching, prevent the drawbar from touching the ground and allow some residual steering of the trailer.

Exemptions

Trailers which are exempt from the requirement to have EEC or ECE braking systems fitted as required by *regulation 15* except that trailers with a maximum total design axle weight not exceeding 750kg which are manufactured on or after 01/01/1997 must comply with this regulation.

Trailers under 750kg manufactured from 01/01/1997 must be stamped with the year of manufacture on the chassis or frame clearly visible from the nearside - regulation 71A.

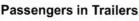
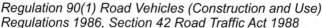

Passengers in Trailers

Regulation 90(1) Road Vehicles (Construction and Use)
Regulations 1986, Section 42 Road Traffic Act 1988

A trailer shall not be used for the carriage of passengers for hire or reward on a road unless the trailer is, or is carrying, a broken down motor vehicle and :-

• the trailer is drawn at a speed not exceeding 30 m.p.h., and
• in the case of a broken down bus, the trailer is drawn by a rigid bar.

Regulation 90(3) Road Vehicles (Construction and Use)
Regulations 1986, Section 42 Road Traffic Act 1988

A wheeled trailer, being a living van with less than 4 wheels or with 4 wheels close coupled, shall not be used for the carriage of any passengers on a road unless the trailer is being tested by :-

• its manufacturer,
• a person who is or has been repairing it,
• a distributor of, or dealer in, trailers.

Close Coupled in relation to wheels on the same side of a trailer, fitted so that at all times while the trailer is in motion they remain parallel to the longitudinal axis of the trailer, and that the distance between the centres of their respective areas of contact with the road surface does not exceed 1 m.

Parking trailers

Regulation 89 Road Vehicles (Construction and Use)
Regulations 1986, Section 42 Road Traffic Act 1988

A trailer shall not be parked on a road when detached from the drawing vehicle unless one at least of the wheels (or tracks) of the trailer is prevented from revolving by the setting of a parking brake or the use of a chain, chock or other efficient device.

Pollution Control
Excessive noise

Regulation 97 Road Vehicles (Construction and Use)
Regulations 1986, Section 42 Road Traffic Act 1988

No motor vehicle shall be used on a road in such a manner as to cause any excessive noise which could have been avoided by the exercise of reasonable care on the part of the driver.

Stopping engine when stationary

*Regulation 98 Road Vehicles (Construction and Use)
Regulations 1986, Section 42 Road Traffic Act 1988*

The driver of a vehicle shall, when the vehicle is stationary, stop the action of any machinery attached to or forming part of it so far as may be necessary for the prevention of noise or exhaust emissions except :-

- when stopped in traffic, or
- in order to examine the working of the machinery following failure, or
- in order to work the machinery for a purpose other than driving the vehicle, or
- machinery connected with gas propulsion units.

Certain Local authorities are now empowered to authorise persons to issue fixed penalty tickets for the offence.

Emissions

*Regulation 61 Road Vehicles (Construction and Use)
Regulations 1986, Section 42 Road Traffic Act 1988*

Every vehicle shall :-

- be constructed and maintained so as not to emit any avoidable smoke or avoidable visible vapour, or
- comply with a relevant EU or ECE directive.

It is an offence for a person to use, cause or permit to be used on a road any motor vehicle from which any smoke, visible vapour, grit, sparks, ashes, cinders or oily substance is emitted if that emission causes or is likely to cause damage to property or injury or danger to any person who is, or who may reasonably expect to be, on the road.

There are numerous technical requirements for vehicle emissions.

Local authorities are empowered to authorise persons to test for emissions providing an Air Quality Management Area (AQMA) has been declared within the boundaries of the authority - Civil Enforcement Officers may issue fixed penalty tickets under a different regulation - Police and DVSA officers may instead issue fixed penalties for offences under section 42 Road Traffic Act 1988.

Closets

*Regulation 62 Road Vehicles (Construction and Use)
Regulations 1986, Section 42 Road Traffic Act 1988*

No wheeled vehicle first used after 15/01/1931 shall be equipped with any closet or urinal which can discharge directly on to a road.

Every tank into which a closet or urinal with which a vehicle is equipped empties, and every closet or urinal which does not empty into a tank, shall contain chemicals which are non-inflammable and non-irritant and provide an efficient germicide.

Safety Measures
Opening Doors

Regulation 105 Road Vehicles (Construction and Use)
Regulations 1986, Section 42 Road Traffic Act 1988

No person shall open or cause or permit to be opened any door of a vehicle on a road so as to injure or endanger any person.

Television Sets

Regulation 109 Road Vehicles (Construction and Use) Regulations 1986

No person shall drive or cause or permit to be driven a motor vehicle on a road if the driver is in such a position as to be able to see, directly or by reflection, a television or similar apparatus used to display anything other than information :-

- about the state of the vehicle or its equipment,
- about the location of the vehicle and the road on which it is located,
- to assist the driver to see the road adjacent to the vehicle,
- to assist the driver to reach his destination, or
- of any sort, provided that the information is displayed on the built-in apparatus of an automated vehicle, which is driving itself and is not requesting the driver to take over control.

Mascots

Regulation 53 Road Vehicles (Construction and Use)
Regulations 1986, Section 42 Road Traffic Act 1988

No mascot, emblem or other ornamental object shall be carried by a motor vehicle in any position where it is likely to strike any person with whom the vehicle may collide unless the mascot is not liable to cause injury to such a person by reason of any projection thereon except :-

- motor vehicles 1st used before 01/10/1937,
- vehicles which comply with *EEC 74/483* or *ECE Reg 26.01.*

Other safety measures

Other measures	Regulation	Chapter / Page
Proper Control	104	30 / 11
Use of Mobile Phones	110	30 / 12
Maintenance and use of vehicles so as not to be a danger		
Condition, Passengers and Loading	100(1)	30 / 14
Security of Loads	100(2)	
Unsuitable Use	100(3)	
Securing of suspended implements	108	30 / 14

Plates and Markings
Manufacturers Plates

Regulation 66 Road Vehicles (Construction and Use)
Regulations 1986, Section 42 Road Traffic Act 1988

The following vehicles shall be equipped with a plate securely attached to the vehicle in a conspicuous and readily accessible position (the plate is usually a black metal plate) :-

- wheeled heavy motor cars or motor cars 1st used on or after 01/01/1968 except :-
  - ○ dual purpose vehicles, agricultural motor vehicles, works trucks, pedestrian controlled vehicles,
  - ○ passenger vehicles (other than buses 1st used on or after 01/04/1982),
- a bus first used on or after 01/04/1982,
- wheeled locomotives or motor tractors first used on or after 01/04/1973 except :-
  - ○ agricultural motor vehicles, industrial tractors, works trucks, engineering plant and pedestrian controlled vehicles,
- wheeled trailers manufactured on or after 01/01/1968 which exceed 1020kg unladen except :-
  - ○ trailers not exceeding 2290kg total weight which are not constructed to carry any load other than permanently fixed plant or special appliances or apparatus,
  - ○ living vans not exceeding 2040kg unladen with pneumatic tyres,
  - ○ works trailers and street cleansing trailers,
  - ○ gritting trailers not exceeding 2000kg gross,
  - ○ agricultural trailers not exceeding 4070kg manufactured before 01/07/1947 drawn by a motor tractor or an agricultural motor vehicle at not more than 10 m.p.h. with no other trailers drawn,
  - ○ trailers not exceeding 750kg total design axle weight,
  - ○ trailers manufactured and used outside GB before use here,
  - ○ agricultural trailed appliances and appliance conveyors,
  - ○ broken down vehicles,
  - ○ trailers being lawfully drawn by motorcycles,
- converter dollies manufactured on or after 01/01/1979.
- vehicles being submitted to or taken away from a type approval exam.

Ministry plates

Regulation 70 Road Vehicles (Construction and Use)
Regulations 1986, Section 42 Road Traffic Act 1988

Every goods vehicle to which the Regulations applyand in respect of which a plating certificate has been issued shall be equipped with a Ministry plate securely affixed, so as to be legible at all times, in a conspicuous and readily accessible position, and in the cab of the vehicle if it has one.

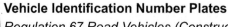

Vehicle Identification Number Plates

Regulation 67 Road Vehicles (Construction and Use) Regulations 1986, Section 42 Road Traffic Act 1988

A wheeled vehicle 1st used on or after 01/04/1980 which is subject to the *Type Approval Regulations* (most production vehicles) shall be equipped with a plate (or tamper proof sticker) in a conspicuous and readily accessible position on a part not normally subject to replacement which shows clearly and indelibly the :-

- Vehicle Identification Number (VIN Number) - usually 17 digits and a mixture of letters and numbers,
- name of the manufacturer,
- Type Approval reference number - this may be on a separate plate.

World Manufacturer Identifier — Vehicle Identifier

YV1FW8250C1067994

Vehicle Descriptor — Year — Chassis Number

The VIN number shall also be stamped on the chassis or frame.

> *If the VIN begins with the letters SABTVRO the VIN has been re-stamped by the Department for Transport. This can mean it has a new body shell or that there's a query over the true identity or age of the vehicle.*

Dimension Plates

Regulation 70B Road Vehicles (Construction and Use) Regulations 1986, Section 42 Road Traffic Act 1988

A plate securely attached to the vehicle in a conspicuous and readily accessible position and containing the particulars as to the dimensions of the vehicle shall be fitted to every :-

- bus or a heavy motor car and which was manufactured after 31/05/1998, or
- trailer manufactured after 31/05/1998 used in combination with the above motor vehicles,

unless it is a goods vehicle fitted with a Ministry plate (*Regulation 70*) or a Manufacturers plate (*Regulation 66*) which show the dimensions.

Speed Limiter Plates

Regulation 70A Road Vehicles (Construction and Use) Regulations 1986, Section 42 Road Traffic Act 1988

Every vehicle which is required to be fitted with a speed limiter shall be equipped with a plate which is in a conspicuous position in the driving compartment and clearly and indelibly marked with the set speed.

Small Motorcycle Plates

Regulation 69 Road Vehicles (Construction and Use) Regulations 1986, Section 42 Road Traffic Act 1988

Motorcycles (not being mowing machines or pedestrian controlled) not exceeding 125cc if 1st used on or after 01/01/1982, (150cc if 1st used between 01/08/1977 and 01/01/1982), shall be equipped with a plate securely fixed and in a readily accessible and conspicuous position.

Marking of weights

Regulation 71 Road Vehicles (Construction and Use)
Regulations 1986, Section 42 Road Traffic Act 1988

Unladen Weight

The unladen weight of a vehicle (other than a tracked agricultural motor vehicle not exceeding 3050 kg unladen weight or a wheeled agricultural motor vehicle) shall be plainly marked in a conspicuous place on the outside of the vehicle on its near side on :-

- a locomotive,
- a motor tractor,
- a bus which is registered under the 1971 Act (or any enactment repealed thereby).

Maximum Gross Weight

The maximum gross weight shall be plainly marked in a conspicuous place on the outside of an unbraked wheeled trailer on its near side except :-

- an unbraked wheeled trailer designed for use and used for street cleansing and does not carry any load other than its necessary gear and equipment,
- an unbraked wheeled trailer which :-
  - is an agricultural trailer manufactured before 01/07/1947,
  - is being drawn by a motor tractor or an agricultural motor vehicle at a speed not exceeding 10 mph,
  - has a laden weight not exceeding 4070 kg, and
  - is the only trailer being drawn,
- a trailer which is being drawn by a motor cycle in accordance with *regulation 84*,
- an agricultural trailed appliance,
- an agricultural trailed appliance conveyor,
- a broken down vehicle,
- a gritting trailer with a maximum gross weight not exceeding 2000 kg.

Marking of date of manufacture of trailers

Regulation 71A Road Vehicles (Construction and Use)
Regulations 1986, Section 42 Road Traffic Act 1988

The year of manufacture shall be marked on the chassis, frame or other similar structure on the nearside of the vehicle, in a clearly visible and accessible position, and by a method such as hammering or stamping, in such a way that it cannot be obliterated or deteriorate on a trailer that :-

- is not a motor vehicle,
- is manufactured on or after 01/01/1997, and
- has a maximum total design axle weight not exceeding 750 kg.

Date of 1st Use
Regulations 3, 4(2) and 4(3) Road Vehicles (Construction and Use) Regulations 1986

The date on which a motor vehicle is first used is :-
- the date of manufacture if :-
  - a vehicle is or has been used under a trade licence other than for delivery between manufacturer and dealer, between dealers or from dealer to customer, demonstration, and testing,
  - a vehicle belonging or which did belong to the crown armed forces or visiting forces,
  - a vehicle used on the road outside Great Britain prior to import,
  - a vehicle used off-road after being sold or supplied by retail before being registered, or
- the date of registration if not one of the vehicles listed above.

Where a motor vehicle was manufactured at least six months before a specified date :-
- a provision applied to vehicles first used on or after that date shall not apply to that vehicle, and
- an exemption from, or relaxation of, a provision applied to vehicles first used before that date shall apply to that vehicle even if it is first used on or after that date.

Type Approval

Vehicle Type Approval is the confirmation that production samples of a type of vehicle, vehicle system, component or separate technical unit will meet specified performance standards.

Individual Vehicle Approval (IVA) is the process of approving individual vehicles against national technical requirements.

The Vehicle Certification Agency (VCA) is the designated UK Type Approval Authority for automotive products under the UN and the GB type approval schemes.

UN Type Approval or UNECE Regulations provide for approval of vehicle systems and separate components, but not whole vehicles.

EU procedures for approving most road vehicles and their parts were set out in the EU framework for passenger and goods vehicles and trailers - *Regulation (EU) 2018/858*. which was retained in domestic law at the end of the transition period and now forms the basis of a new national type-approval framework in Great Britain known as the GB type-approval scheme.

Chapter 5 Seatbelts

Fitting and Maintenance of Anchorage Points and Seatbelts

Regulations 46 to 48 Road Vehicles (Construction and Use) Regulations 1986

Section 42 Road Traffic Act 1988, fixed penalty offence
- level 3 fine,
- level 4 fine for goods vehicles and passenger vehicles with more than 8 passenger seats

It is an offence for a person to :-

(a) contravene or fail to comply with a construction and use requirement as to the fitting and maintenance of anchorage points and seatbelts, or

(b) use on a **road** a **motor vehicle or trailer** which does not comply with such a requirement, or cause[1] or permit[1] a motor vehicle or trailer to be so used.

> [1] *Cause and Permit offences are not fixed penalty offences.*

Fitting Requirements

Regulations 46 and 47 Road Vehicles (Construction and Use) Regulations 1986

Seatbelt anchorage points and seatbelts are required to be fitted to a motor vehicle which is a :-

- bus first used on or after 01/04/1982, (X suffix),
- wheeled motor car first used on or after 01/01/1965, (C suffix),
- three-wheeled motor cycle, unladen weight exceeding 255 kg, first used on or after 01/09/1970 (J suffix), or
- heavy motor car first used on or after 01/10/1988, (F prefix),

other than an excepted vehicle.

> *Not every anchorage point requires a seatbelt.*
> *The type of seatbelt required depends on the vehicle and seat position to which it is fitted.*
> *See the regulation for list of excepted and exempt vehicles.*

Fitting Requirements - Summary
Regulations 46 and 47 Road Vehicles (Construction and Use) Regulations 1986

Vehicle	Requirement
1. Any vehicle first used before 01/04/1982	Anchorage Points and Seatbelts - driver and specified passenger seat.
2. Minibus with not more than 12 seats in addition to driver, motor ambulance, motor caravan, first used on or after 01/04/1982 and before 01/10/1988	Anchorage Points and Seatbelts - driver and specified passenger seat.
3. Minibus (not included in 7 or 8 below) not exceeding 3500kg gross, motor ambulance, motor caravan, first used on or after 01/10/1988	Anchorage Points and Seatbelts - driver and each forward facing front seat.
4. Goods vehicle exceeding 3500kg gross first used on or after 01/10/1988 and before 01/10/2001	Anchorage Points - driver and each forward facing front seat. Seatbelts not required.
5. Goods vehicle exceeding 3500kg gross first used on or after 01/10/2001	Anchorage Points and Seatbelts - driver and all forward facing front seats.
6. Coach first used on or after 01/10/1988 and before 01/10/2001	Anchorage Points and Seatbelts - driver and all exposed forward facing seats.
7. Bus exceeding 3500kg gross, first used on or after 01/10/2001, (not an urban bus)	Anchorage Points and Seatbelts - driver and all forward-facing and rearward-facing seats.
8. Bus not exceeding 3500kg gross, first used on or after 01/10/2001, (not an urban bus)	Anchorage Points and Seatbelts - driver and all forward facing and rearward facing seats.
9. Passenger or dual-purpose vehicle (other than a bus) not in items 2 to 8, first used on or after 01/04/1982	Anchorage Points - every forward facing seat constructed or adapted to accommodate no more than 1 adult Seatbelts - driver and specified passenger seat and, if first used on or after 01/04/1987, any forward-facing front seat alongside the driver's seat and certain forward-facing rear seats
10. Vehicle (other than a bus) not in items 2 to 9, first used on or after 01/04/1982	Anchorage Points - every forward facing front seat and every non-protected seat Seatbelts - driver and specified passenger seat and if first used on or after 01/04/1987 any forward-facing front seat alongside the driver's seat

Maintenance Requirements

Regulation 48 Road Vehicles (Construction and Use)
Regulations 1986

Where a seat belt is required to be fitted (by Regulation 47), the seat belt and every anchorage point, fastening, adjusting device and retracting mechanism (if any) for that belt must comply with the following requirements :-

- all load bearing members of the vehicle and panelling within 30 centimetres of each anchorage point must be free from serious corrosion, distortion or fracture,
- the adjusting device and, if fitted, retracting mechanism of the belt must be maintained to adjust automatically, or manually according to its design,
- the seat belt, anchorages and fastenings shall be maintained free from any obvious defect which would be likely to affect their performance,
- the buckle and fastening mechanisms shall be maintained and kept free from obstructions and, except for disabled person's seat belt, be readily accessible to a person sitting in the seat,
- the webbing of the belt must be maintained free from cuts or other visible faults likely to affect performance,
- the ends of belt must be securely fastened to anchorage points provided,
- a disabled persons belt must be securely fixed to the vehicle or seat so the occupant would be restrained in the event of an accident.

These requirements also apply to :-

- every anchorage point with which a goods vehicle exceeding 3500kg gross first used on or after 01/10/1988 and before 01/10/2001 is required to be provided,
- the mountings of the seat to a vehicle where the seat incorporates integral seat belt anchorages.

Anchorage points provided for seat belts shall be used only as anchorages for the seat belts for which they are intended to be used or capable of being used.

Defences

The above requirements do not apply if :-

- the defect occurred on that journey, or
- steps have been taken to have the defect rectified with all reasonable expedition.

Wearing of Seatbelts - person aged 14 years or more

Offence

Section 14(3) Road Traffic Act 1988 - level 2 fine - fixed penalty offence

It is an offence for a person aged 14 years or more to :-

- drive, or
- ride in the front seat of, or
- ride in the rear seat of,

a **motor vehicle** in contravention of the *Motor Vehicle (Wearing Seat Belts) Regulations 1993.*

No person other than the person actually committing the contravention is guilty of an offence.

Requirement to wear seatbelts (front and rear) - Persons over 14 years

Regulation 5 Motor Vehicles (Wearing Seat Belts) Regulations 1993

Every person aged 14 years or more who is :-

- driving, or
- riding in the front or rear seat of,

any **motor vehicle** (other than a two wheeled motor cycle with or without a side car) shall wear an adult belt where one is available.

Exemptions (persons aged 14 years and over)

Regulation 6 Motor Vehicles (Wearing Seat Belts) Regulations 1993

The following persons are exempt from the requirement to wear an adult seat belt :-

- a person holding a medical certificate,
- the driver of or a passenger in a goods vehicle on a journey not exceeding 50 metres undertaken for delivering or collecting anything,
- a person driving a vehicle while performing a manoeuvre which includes reversing,
- a qualified driver supervising a provisional driver while performing a manoeuvre which includes reversing,
- a person conducting a test of competence to drive and the wearing of a seat belt would endanger himself or any other person,
- a person driving or riding in a vehicle while it is being used for fire brigade (or Fire and Rescue Authority) or police purposes, or for carrying a person in lawful custody including the detained person himself.
- the driver of a licensed taxi while being used for seeking hire, or answering a call for hire, or carrying a passenger for hire, or a private hire vehicle while it is being used to carry a passenger for hire,

- a person riding in a vehicle, being used under a trade licence for the purposes or investigating or remedying a mechanical fault in the vehicle,
- a disabled person wearing a disabled persons belt, or
- a person riding in a vehicle while taking part in a procession organised by or on behalf of the crown or which is commonly or customarily held, or a procession which a notice under *section 11 of the Public Order Act 1986* has been issued,
- the driver of the vehicle if an adult seat belt is not provided,
- a person in the front of a vehicle if no adult belt is available for him in the front,
- a person in the rear of a vehicle if no adult belt is available for him in the rear,
- a person riding in a small or large bus which is being used to provide a local service in a built-up area (where the entire route consists of restricted roads), or
- a person riding in a small or large bus which is constructed or adapted for the carriage of standing passengers and on which the operator permits standing,
- a person riding in a motor ambulance while the person is providing medical attention or treatment to a patient which due to its nature or the medical situation of the patient cannot be delayed.

Explanation

(*Exceptions and exemptions apply in all cases*)

If a seatbelt is fitted in the front or rear of any motor vehicle and the seat is occupied then the belt must be worn - even where there is no legal requirement for a belt to be fitted, if fitted it should be worn.

Each passenger is responsible for wearing a seatbelt except where that passenger is under 14 years old - the responsibility then shifts to the driver (except in large buses or taxis with a fixed partition) - *see later*.

If there are more people than available seatbelts in a vehicle, consideration should be given to the manner in which the unbelted passengers are being carried and whether or not it presents a danger of injury to them or a belted occupant of the vehicle (*section 40A Road Traffic Act 1988*). A belt may not be available if there are too many people in the seat for the belt to be worn (*regulation 2(6)*).

If a seatbelt does not work because of lack of maintenance or it is locked because the vehicle is or had been on a hill, proceedings for fail to wear a seatbelt are unlikely to be successful.

Requirement to notify bus passengers to wear seat belts

Section 15B Road Traffic Act 1988 - level 4 fine

It is an offence for the operator of a bus in which any of the passenger seats are equipped with seat belts to fail to take all reasonable steps to ensure that every passenger is notified that he is required to wear a seat belt at all times when he is in a seat equipped with a seat belt and the bus is in motion.

Notification can be by an official announcement, or audio-visual presentation, made when the passenger joins the bus or within a reasonable time of his doing so or by a sign prominently displayed at each passenger seat equipped with a seat belt.

Exceptions

- A bus used to provide a local service in a built-up area where the entire route consists of restricted roads.
- A bus constructed or adapted for the carriage of standing passengers on which the operator permits standing.

Front Seat Airbags

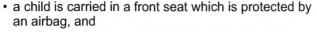

Section 15(2) Road Traffic Act 1988 - level 2 fine - fixed penalty offence

It is an offence for a person, without reasonable excuse, to drive a motor vehicle (other than a bus) on a road where :-

- a child is carried in a front seat which is protected by an airbag, and
- the child is in a rear-facing child restraining device,

unless the air bag has been deactivated or is designed or adapted in such a way that it cannot inflate enough to pose a risk of injury to the child (*section 15(1A)*).

Wearing of Seatbelts - Children in Front seats

Section 15(2) Road Traffic Act 1988 - level 2 fine - fixed penalty offence

It is an offence for a person, without reasonable excuse, to drive a motor vehicle (other than a two wheeled motor cycle with or without a side car) on a road unless any child under the age of fourteen years in the front of the motor vehicle is wearing a seat belt in conformity with the regulations.

Exemptions

Regulation 7 Motor Vehicles (Wearing of Seat Belts by Children in Front Seats) Regulations 1993

- A small child aged 3 years or more who is riding in a bus and is wearing an adult belt if an appropriate seat belt is not available for him in the front or rear of the vehicle.
- A child for whom there is a medical certificate.
- A disabled child who is wearing a disabled person's belt.
- A child riding in a bus :-
  - which is being used to provide a local service (within the meaning of the *Transport Act 1985*) in a built-up area, or
  - which is constructed or adapted for the carriage of standing passengers and on which the operator permits standing.
- A large child if no appropriate seat belt is available for him in the front of the vehicle.

Explanation

(Exceptions and exemptions apply in all cases)

Small children (under 12 years and under 135cm (4'5") tall) MUST wear a child restraint suitable for their height and weight (an appropriate seat belt). If no suitable child restraint is available a small child cannot be carried in the front of a vehicle.

Large children (12 or 13 years old or those under 12 but over 135cm tall) - must wear an adult belt if no suitable child restraint is available. They may however be carried unrestrained in the front of vehicles which are not fitted with belts or where no appropriate seat belt is available in the front.

There is no power to require a child's age or height.

Wearing of Seatbelts - Children in Rear Seats
Section 15(4) Road Traffic Act 1988 - level 2 fine -
fixed penalty offence

It is an offence for a person, without reasonable
excuse, to drive a **motor vehicle** (other than a two
wheeled motor cycle with or without a side car) on a **road** :-

- where seatbelts are fitted in the rear, unless any child under
  the age of 14 years in the rear is wearing a seat belt in conformity with
  the regulations (*section 15(3)(b)*), or
- where no seatbelts are fitted in the rear, whilst carrying a child under
  the age of 3 years in the rear (*section 15(3)(a)*), or
- where the motor vehicle is a passenger car and which has no seat belt
  is fitted in the rear, where :-
  - a child who is under 12 years and less than 150 centimetres in
    height is in the rear, and
  - a front seat is provided with an appropriate seat belt but is not
    occupied by any person. (*section 15(3A)*)

Exemptions
Regulation 9 Motor Vehicles (Wearing of Seat Belts) Regulations 1993
- A large bus,
- A licensed taxi or licensed hire car where rear seats are separated
  from the driver by a fixed partition.

*This is not to say that no seat belt should be worn in such vehicles - if an
adult belt is available it should be worn by children over 3 years however
the driver would not become liable if no belt were worn.*
*Regulation 10 Motor Vehicles (Wearing of Seat Belts) Regulations
1993*
- A child for whom there is a medical certificate,
- A small child aged under 3 years who is riding in a small bus, a
  licensed taxi or a licensed hire car, if no appropriate seat belt is
  available for him in the front or rear of the vehicle (no belt need be
  worn),
- A small child aged 3 years or more who is riding in a licensed taxi, a
  licensed hire car or a small bus and wearing an adult belt if an
  appropriate seat belt is not available for him in the front or rear of the
  vehicle,
- A small child aged 3 years or more who is wearing an adult belt and
  riding in a passenger car or light goods vehicle where the use of child
  restraints by the child occupants of two seats in the rear of the vehicle
  prevents the use of an appropriate seat belt for that child and no
  appropriate seat belt is available for him in the front of the vehicle,
- A small child who is riding in a vehicle being used for the purposes of
  the police, security or emergency services to enable the proper
  performance of their duty,

- A small child aged 3 years or more who is wearing an adult belt and who, because of an unexpected necessity, is travelling a short distance in a passenger car or light goods vehicle in which no appropriate seat belt is available for him.
- A disabled child who is wearing a disabled person's belt or whose disability makes it impracticable to wear a seat belt where a disabled person's belt is unavailable to him.
- A child on a small bus used on a local service in a built up area or which is constructed or adapted for the carriage of standing passengers and on which the operator permits standing.

Explanation

(Exceptions and exemptions apply in all cases)

Small children (under 12 years and under 135cm (4'5") tall) MUST wear a child restraint suitable for their height and weight (an appropriate seat belt). There are a few exceptions which permit the use of an adult belt instead.

If no suitable child restraint is available a child under 3 years cannot be carried in the rear of the vehicle - except in a taxi.

Children 3 years or older may be carried in the rear of vehicles not fitted with any rear seatbelts however in a passenger car which has a vacant front seat with a suitable seat belt or child restraint a child under 12 years and less than 150cm tall must be carried in that front seat rather than left unrestrained in the rear.

Large children (12 or 13 years old or those under 12 but over 135cm tall) - may wear an adult belt if no suitable child restraint is available.

Appropriate Seatbelts for children

Reg 8 Motor Vehicles (Wearing of Seat Belts) Regulations 1993

- For a small child (aged under 12 years and under 135 cm (4'5") in height) is a child restraint suitable for their weight and, if mentioned, height and marked as such with a BS, EU or ECE marking,
- For a large child is a child restraint suitable for their height and weight and marked as such, or an adult seat belt.
- For a person aged 14 years or more - is an adult belt.

Car seats suitable for all sizes of children are available.

High-back booster seats can be used by children weighing 15 to 36kg.

New backless booster seats can be used by children who weigh 22kg or more.

If a child is carried in a rear-facing child seat in the front seat of a car the airbag must be de-activated *(see Page 6).*

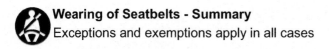 **Wearing of Seatbelts - Summary**
Exceptions and exemptions apply in all cases

Occupant	Vehicle
Children under 3 years	
All vehicles except taxis and buses	**Front and Rear** Must wear a suitable child restraint. If none available then child must not be carried. Air bags must be de-activated where any child is carried in the front in a rear-facing child restraining device.
Small children aged 3 years or more - under 12 years and under 4'5" (135cm)	
All vehicles	**Front** Must wear suitable child restraint. *If none available child cannot be carried in the front of a vehicle.* **Rear** Must wear suitable child restraint if seatbelts fitted in rear. *If no seatbelts fitted in rear child may be carried unrestrained (see *)*
Licensed taxi, a licensed hire car or a bus	An adult belt may be used on a bus if no restraint available. **Rear** An adult belt may be used if a suitable child restraint is not available.
Passenger car or light goods vehicle.	**Front** Must wear suitable child restraint. If none available child cannot be carried in the front of a vehicle. **Rear** An adult belt may be worn when no appropriate seat belt is available :- - because of an unexpected necessity when travelling a short distance, or - where the use of child restraints by the child occupants of 2 seats in the rear prevents the use of an appropriate seat belt.
Children under 12 years and under 4'11" (150cm) *	
Passenger car	**Front** Must wear appropriate seat belt. **Rear** If no seatbelts fitted in rear and there is a front seat available with a suitable restraint then child must use that front seat.
Large Child - 12 or 13 years or 4'5" (135cm) or more	
All vehicles except taxis and buses	**Front** Must wear suitable child restraint or adult belt if available. **Rear** Must wear suitable child restraint or adult belt if available. If no seatbelts fitted in rear child may be carried unrestrained (*see **).
Persons aged 14 years and over	
All vehicles	**Front and Rear** Must wear an adult seat belt if available.

Availability of Seatbelts

Motor Vehicles (Wearing Seat Belts) Regulations 1993
Motor Vehicles (Wearing of Seat Belts by Children in Front Seats)
Regulations 1993 - Schedule 2

If any front seat (other than the driver's seatbelt) is provided with an adult belt (or an appropriate belt in the case of a child) then a front seat belt is available, or any rear seat is provided with an adult belt (or an appropriate belt in the case of a child) then a rear seat belt is available, unless :-

- another person is wearing the belt, or
- a child is occupying the seat and wearing an appropriate restraint for that child and it is impracticable to wear the belt, or
- another person holding a medical certificate is in the seat, or
- a disabled person is in the seat wearing a disabled persons belt and it is impracticable to wear the belt, or
- by reason of a person's disability, it would not be practicable for him to wear the belt, or
- the person is prevented from occupying the seat by the presence of a child restraint which could not be removed without the use of tools unless the person is a child and the restraint is suitable, or
- the seat is specially designed so that :-
  ○ it can be adjusted to increase the space available to carry goods or personal effects, and
  ○ when it is adjusted the seat can not be used as such, and
  ○ it would not be reasonably practicable to carry the goods or personal effects in the vehicle in another way.

Regulation 2(6) and (7) Motor Vehicles (Wearing Seat Belts)
Regulations 1993

A seat shall be regarded as provided with an adult seat belt if it is fixed in such a position that it can be worn by an occupier of that seat.

A seat shall not be regarded as provided with an adult seat belt if the seat belt :-

- has an inertia reel mechanism which is locked as a result of the vehicle being, or having been, on a steep incline, or
- is not maintained in accordance with *regulation 48 Construction and Use Regulations.*

Definitions
Child
•A person under the age of 14 years.
- Large child means a child who is not a small child.
- Small child means a child who is aged under 12 years and under 135 centimetres in height (4'5").

Appropriate Seat Belt
- For a small child is a child restraint suitable for his height and weight and marked as such.
- For a large child - is a child restraint suitable for his height and weight as above or an adult seat belt.
- For a person aged 14 years or more - is an adult belt.

Child restraint
Child restraints, which include baby seats, child seats, booster seats and booster cushions, should bear markings showing the recommended weight of the child, and may show the height.

Seat belt
A belt intended to be worn by a person in a vehicle and designed to prevent or lessen injury to its wearer in the event of an accident to the vehicle and includes, in the case of a restraint, any special chair to which the belt is attached.

Specified passenger's seat
- In the case of a vehicle which has one forward-facing front seat alongside the driver's seat, that seat.
- In the case of a vehicle which has more than one such seat, the one furthest from the driver's seat.
- If the vehicle normally has no seat alongside the driver, the forward-facing front passenger seat which is foremost in the vehicle and furthest from the driver's seat, unless there is a fixed partition separating that seat from the space in front of it alongside the driver's seat.

Non-protected seat
A seat which is not a front seat and the screen zones within the protected area have a combined surface of less than 800 cm2 - *see EC Directive 81/575*

Sideways facing seats
There are no specific legal requirements for sideways facing seats.

Chapter 6 Speed Limiters

Offences

Regulations 36A, 36B, 70A Road Vehicles (Construction and Use) Regulations 1986, Section 42 Road Traffic Act 1988

It is an offence for a person to :-

(a) contravene or fail to comply with a construction and use requirement as to speed limiters and speed limiter plates in accordance with *regulation 36A(4) (graduated penalty), 36B(6)(graduated penalty) or 70A of the Road Vehicles (Construction and Use) Regulations 1986*, or

(b) use on a **road a motor vehicle** or trailer which does not comply with such a requirement, or cause or permit a motor vehicle or trailer to be so used.

> ¹ *Cause and Permit offences are not fixed penalty offences.*

Exemptions

- Goods vehicles which have a relevant speed not exceeding 90 km/h (56 m.p.h.).
- Passenger vehicles which have a relevant speed not exceeding 100 km/h (62mph) (or as the case may be 112.65 km/h (70 m.p.h.)).
- Vehicles being taken to a place where a speed limiter is to be installed, calibrated, repaired or replaced, or to complete the journey during which it has accidentally ceased to function.
- Vehicles owned by the Secretary of State for Defence and used for naval, military or air force purposes.
- Vehicles used for naval, military or air force purposes while being driven by a person for the time being subject to the orders of a member of the armed forces of the Crown.
- Vehicles used for fire and rescue authority, ambulance or police purposes.
- Vehicles which are operated by or on behalf of Her Majesty's Prison Service and used primarily for the purpose of moving Category A prisoners.
- A vehicle which is an emergency tactical response vehicle operated by or on behalf of Her Majesty's Prison Service and used primarily for the purpose of transporting people or equipment (or both) to restore order within Her Majesty's prisons or immigration detention centres.
- Goods vehicles used on a public road for not more than an aggregate of six miles in a calendar week whilst passing between land in the keepers occupation.

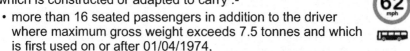 Fitting and Maintenance of Speed Limiters
Passenger Vehicles

Reg 36A(4) Road Vehicles (Construction and Use) Regulations 1986

A speed limiter must be fitted to every passenger motor vehicle which is constructed or adapted to carry :-

- more than 16 seated passengers in addition to the driver where maximum gross weight exceeds 7.5 tonnes and which is first used on or after 01/04/1974,
- more than 8 seated passengers in addition to the driver where maximum gross weight exceeds 7.5 tonnes and which is first used on or after 01/01/1988,
- more than 8 seated passengers in addition to the driver and which is first used on or after 01/01/2005.

Reg 36A(5) Road Vehicles (Construction and Use) Regulations 1986 *

The speed limiter must be sealed and maintained in good and efficient working order and must be set at 100 km/h (62 mph) or 112 km/h (70 mph) for coaches 1st used before 01/01/1988.

Goods Vehicles

Reg 36B(6) Road Vehicles (Construction and Use) Regulations 1986

A speed limiter must be fitted to every goods motor vehicle whose maximum gross weight :-

- exceeds 12 tonnes, first used on or after 01/01/1988,
- exceeds 7.5 tonnes, first used on or after 01/08/1992,
- exceeds 3.5 tonnes, first used on or after 01/01/2005.

Speed limiters are also required to be fitted to vehicles first used between 01/10/2001 and 31/12/2004 which are fitted with Euro III diesel engines with emissions approval on :-

- passenger vehicles with more than 8 passenger seats where the maximum gross weight does not exceed 7.5 tonnes and
- goods vehicles exceeding 3.5 tonnes maximum gross weight but not exceeding 7.5 tonnes.

Excludes many types fitted with engines which are not emissions approved - Ford Transit, LDV etc.

Reg 36B(7) Road Vehicles (Construction and Use) Regulations 1986

The speed limiter must be sealed and maintained in good and efficient working order and must be set at a stabilised speed not exceeding 90 km/h (56 m.p.h.) or 96 km/h (60 mph) for vehicles first used before 01/10/2001 in the 7.5 - 12 tonne weight range.

Speed Limiter Plates

Reg 70A Road Vehicles (Construction and Use) Regulations 1986

Every vehicle which is required to be fitted with a speed limiter shall be equipped with a plate which is in a conspicuous position in the driving compartment and clearly and indelibly marked with the set speed.

Chapter 7 Pedal Cycles

Brakes

Sale of pedal cycle

Section 81 Road Traffic Act 1988 - level 3 fine
Regulation 12 Pedal Cycle (Construction and Use) Regulations 1983

It is an offence for a person to sell supply, offer to sell or supply a **pedal cycle** or an **electrically assisted pedal cycle** unless it is equipped with the required braking system.

Braking Systems

Regulations 4,7 Pedal Cycle (Construction and Use) Regulations 1983

Every **pedal cycle** shall be equipped with at least 1 braking system and if :-

- manufactured before 01/08/1984 if any wheel exceeds 460 mm diameter a total of 2 independent braking systems,
- manufactured on or after 01/08/1984 if saddle height exceeds 635 mm or it has 4 or more wheels a total of 2 independent braking systems.

Only 1 front brake system required if the drive wheel is fixed and does not free-wheel.

Electrically assisted pedal cycles must be fitted with approved braking systems which comply with EU or British Standards.

Maintenance

Section 91 Road Traffic Offenders Act 1988 - level 3 fine
Regulations 5, 10 Pedal Cycle (Construction and Use) Regulations 1983

No person shall ride, or cause or permit to be ridden a **pedal cycle or electrically propelled pedal cycle on a road** unless the braking system required to be fitted is in an efficient working order.

Police Power of Inspection

Regulation 11 Pedal Cycle (Construction and Use) Regulations 1983

Any **constable in uniform** may test and inspect the braking system required to be fitted on a pedal cycle :-

- on a **road**, or
- on any **premises within 48 hours of an accident**, with the consent of the owner of those premises.

Electrically assisted pedal cycles (EAPCs)
Definition

Electrically Assisted Pedal Cycle Regulations 1983

A cycle with two or more wheels which is fitted with :-

- pedals that can be used to propel it, and
- an electric motor of a maximum continuous rated power which does not exceed 0.25kW (250 watts) which cannot propel the vehicle when it is travelling at more than 15.5mph (25kph).

Requirements

An electrically assisted pedal cycle must be :-

- fitted with a plate securely fixed in a conspicuous and readily accessible position showing :-
  - the name of the manufacturer of the vehicle,
  - the nominal voltage of the battery of the vehicle, and the continuous rated output of the motor of the vehicle, or
- visibly and durably marked with :-
  - the name of the manufacturer of the vehicle,
  - the maximum speed at which the motor can propel the vehicle specified in miles per hour or kilometres per hour, and
  - the maximum continuous rated power of the motor of the vehicle specified in watts or kilowatts.

Age Restriction

Section 32 Road Traffic Act 1988 - level 2 fine

It is an offence for a person under the age of 14 years, or knowing or suspecting that a person is under the age of 14 years to cause or permit him, to drive an **electrically assisted pedal cycle on a road**.

Classification

An electrically assisted pedal cycle which is in compliance with the regulations :-

- is not classed as a motor vehicle,
- neither insurance nor a driving licence is required,
- the rider must be at least 14 years old,
- it can be ridden anywhere an unpowered cycle is permitted to go - bus lanes, cycle paths etc.

It does however still fall within the definition of a mechanically propelled vehicle but is exempt from the requirements for registration and vehicle excise duty (road tax). Legislation which does apply includes :-

- Unfit through drink or drugs, and
- Accident Obligation Requirements.

Police Powers

Powers to Stop

Section 163(3) Road Traffic Act 1988 - level 3 fine - fixed penalty

A person riding a **cycle on a road** must stop the cycle on being required to do so by a **constable in uniform** or a traffic officer in uniform designated under s*ection 2 Traffic Management Act 2004.*

If a person fails to comply with this section he is guilty of an offence.

Power of Entry

Section 17(1)(c)(iiia) Police and Criminal Evidence Act 1984

A constable may enter and search any premises for the purpose of arresting a person for an offence under *section 163 of the Road Traffic Act 1988.*

Bells and brake levers

Pedal Bicycles (Safety) Regulations 2010

*These regulations relating to the supply of **new** pedal bicycles, whether assembled or unassembled and include requirements to fit a bell, reflectors and the conventions for hand operated brake levers - **these regulations do not apply to cycles when in use.***

Lights

See Chapter 3 for further details

There is no requirement to fit lights to a pedal cycle between sunrise and sunset, even in seriously reduced visibility however other offences such as dangerous cycling could be considered if the circumstances warrant.

If a front or rear position lamp is fitted fitted however, in conditions of seriously reduced visibility[1], they must be displayed.

> **[1] Seriously Reduced Visibility**
> *Rule 226 The Highway Code*
> *Generally when you cannot see for more than 100 metres (328 feet).*

There is no requirement to display lights at any time on a pedal cycle being pushed along the left-hand edge of a carriageway or whilst waiting to proceed provided it is kept to the left or nearside edge of a carriageway.

Manner of Cycling
Dangerous Cycling

Section 28 Road Traffic Act 1988 (NOIP) - level 4 fine

It is an offence for a person to ride a cycle on a road dangerously.

A person is to be regarded as cycling dangerously if the way he rides falls far below what would be expected of a competent and careful cyclist, and it would be obvious to a competent and careful cyclist that cycling in that way would be dangerous. Dangerous refers to danger of injury to any person, or serious damage to property.

When determining what would be obvious to a competent and careful cyclist regard shall be given not only to the circumstances which he could be expected to be aware but also to any circumstances shown to have been within the knowledge of the accused.

Careless Cycling

Section 29 Road Traffic Act 1988 (NOIP) - level 3 fine

It is an offence for a person to ride a **cycle** on a **road** without due care and attention, or without reasonable consideration for other persons using the road.

Requirement to provide Name and Address

Section 168 Road Traffic Act 1988 - level 3 fine

It is an offence for a person to :-
- refuse to give his name or address, or
- to give a false name or address,

to any person having reasonable grounds for requiring them of the rider of a **cycle** on a **road** who is alleged to have committed an offence of Dangerous or Careless cycling.

Wanton or furious driving or racing

Section 35 Offences Against the Person Act 1861 - 2 years - indictable offence - 3 to 9 points if mechanically propelled vehicle

It is an offence for any person having charge of **any carriage or vehicle**, by wanton or furious driving, or racing, or other wilful misconduct, or by wilful neglect, doing, or causing to be done any bodily harm to any person.

Speed Limits

Generally speed limits apply only to drivers of **motor vehicles** however some temporary limits and limits at special events imposed by orders under *section 14 and 16A Road Traffic Regulation Act 1984* **may** apply to drivers or riders of all vehicles including cycles.

Some local by-laws, particularly in public parks, may also apply to cyclists. Dangerous or Careless cycling may be considered if circumstances warrant.

Traffic Signs

Unless stipulated most Traffic Signs (except speed limit signs - *see above*) apply to riders of pedal cycles, s*ee Chapter 33*.

There are basically 2 types of offences relating to signs :-

- Failure to comply with a sign where (if required) an Act, Regulation, Order, Bylaw, Resolution or Notice or other condition gives legal effect to the sign, and
- Contravention of an Act, Regulation, Order, Bylaw, Resolution or Notice where a sign gives legal effect to the Act, Regulation, Order, Notice etc.

Passengers on bicycles

Section 24(3) Road Traffic Act 1988 - level 1 fine - fixed penalty offence

It is an offence for each of the persons carried on a **bicycle** on a **road** when more than 1 person (including the rider) is carried unless it is constructed or adapted for the carriage of more than 1 person.

Being pulled by a motor vehicle

Section 26(2) Road Traffic Act 1988 - level 1 fine

It is an offence for a person for the purpose of being drawn to take or retain hold of a **motor vehicle or trailer** while in motion on a **road**.

Cycle Racing on Public Ways

Section 31 Road Traffic Act 1988 - level 1 fine

It is an offence for a person to :-

- promote, or
- take part in,

a race or trial of speed on a **public way** between **cycles** unless :-

- the event is authorised,
- it is conducted in accordance with any conditions imposed.

Public way means a highway but does not include a footpath.
Events cannot be authorised on bridlepaths

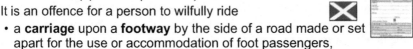 Cycling on footways (pavements) and (in Scotland) footpaths

Section 72 Highways Act 1835 - level 2 fine
  - fixed penalty offence
Section 129(5) Roads (Scotland) Act 1984

It is an offence for a person to wilfully ride

- a **carriage** upon a **footway** by the side of a road made or set apart for the use or accommodation of foot passengers,
- in Scotland, a cycle upon a **footway** by the side of a road **or footpath.**

Exemptions

- Local council vehicles used for maintenance, cleansing etc. of footpaths and verges used in accordance with *Vehicles (Conditions of use on footpaths) Regulations 1963 SI 2126* - (these regulations relate to type of vehicle, times of use, max speed 5 m.p.h. etc.)
- Class 1,2 or 3 Invalid Carriages driven at a maximum of 4 m.p.h.

> *This offence relates to both cycles and motor vehicles and is complete even if committed for a few seconds.*

Cycling on footpaths and bridlepaths

Unless contrary to local bylaws and where there are signs prohibiting such use, a cyclist on a footpath (away from the carriageway) would commit no offence other than a civil trespass or nuisance.

Charges of careless or dangerous cycling could still of course be brought if appropriate or if significant misuse is apparent a charge of public nuisance (common law) could be considered.

A cyclist on a Bridlepath may cycle providing he gives way to horses and pedestrians unless there are Local Orders (accompanied by the appropriate signs) prohibiting such use.

Taking a Pedal Cycle

Section 12(5) Theft Act 1968 - level 3 fine

It is an offence for a person, without the consent of the owner or other lawful authority :-

- to take a **pedal cycle** for his own or another's use, or
- to ride a pedal cycle knowing it to have been taken without such authority.

> *A person does not commit an offence under this section by anything done in the belief that he has lawful authority to do it or that he would have the owner's consent if the owner knew of his doing it and the circumstances of it.*

Chapter 8 Motorcycles

Passengers on motorbicycles

*Section 23(3) Road Traffic Act 1988 - level 3 fine 3 points - fixed
penalty offence*

It is an offence for a person to carry :-

• more than 1 person in addition to the driver on a **motor
bicycle**,

• any person in addition to the driver otherwise than sitting
astride on a proper seat securely fixed to the motorbicycle
and behind the drivers seat (could be facing backwards).

Motorcycle Helmets
No Helmet / Helmet not fastened

*Section 16(4) Road Traffic Act 1988 - level 2 fine -
fixed penalty offence*
*Regulation 4 Motor Cycles (Protective Helmets)
Regulations 1998*

It is an offence for a person to drive or ride a **motorbicycle** on a **road**
without wearing protective headgear.

*Only the person without the helmet can be prosecuted unless he/she is
under 16 in which case an aid/abet charge could be considered.*

Exemptions

• An occupant of a sidecar,
• A follower of the Sikh religion whilst wearing a turban,
• A mowing machine,
• The motorbicycle is (at the time) being propelled by a person on foot.
• Any person driving an electric scooter being used in a trial.

Protective Headgear

A helmet :-

• which bears British Standard approval (it does not have to be the
latest approved helmet standard but must bear a BS mark - these date
from 1956) eg. BS 6658:1985, or

• manufactured for use by motorcyclists which can equal or better
British Standard 6658:1985 or equivalent EEA standard and marked
with that standard, or

• which complies with *UN ECE Regulation 22.05* including the approval,
marking and conformity requirements of that regulation.

which is fitted with a strap which fastens under the jaw and which is
securely fastened.

Motorcycle Visors and Goggles

Requirement

Section 18(3) Road Traffic Act 1988 - level 2
fine - fixed penalty offence
Regulation 4 Motor Cycles (Eye Protectors)
Regulations 1999

It is an offence for a person who drives or rides a **motorbicycle** on a **road** to use eye protectors which :-

• are not of a type prescribed by, or

• are otherwise used in contravention of,

regulations under this section.

Eye Protector means an appliance designed or adapted for use with any headgear or by being attached to or placed upon the head by a person driving or riding on a motorbicycle intended for the protection of the eyes.

Exemptions

• An occupant of a sidecar.

• A mowing machine.

• It is being propelled by a person on foot.

• A visitor on a temporarily imported vehicle.

• Armed forces on duty.

Standards

Motor Cycle (Eye Protectors) Regulations 1999
The Personal Protective Equipment Regulations 2002

Approved eye protectors will usually be marked with British Standard approval marks (4110:1979 or 4110:1999 grades X, XA, YA or ZA),or equivalent EU or ECE standards - *UN ECE Regulation 22.05*

There is of course no requirement that a visor or goggles be used at all. Visors that transmit less than 50% of visible light do not comply with any of the standards above and can not legally be used on the road.

Sale of Visors and Goggles

Section 18(4) Road Traffic Act 1988 - level 3 fine

It is an offence for a person to sell or offer to sell or to hire or offer to hire eye protection for use on a **motorbicycle** which does not meet the requirements above.

Exemption - Sale for export.

Passenger Foot Rests

Regulation 102 Road Vehicles (Construction and Use)
Regulations 1986, Section 42 Road Traffic Act 1988

If any person in addition to the driver is carried astride a **two-wheeled motor cycle** on a **road** (whether a sidecar is attached to it or not) suitable supports or rests for the feet shall be available on the motor cycle for that person.

Motorcycle Exhausts

Markings

Regulation 57A (1 or 4) Road Vehicles (Construction and Use) Regulations 1986, Section 42 Road Traffic Act 1988

The silencer of a **moped or motorbicycle** with or without a sidecar, 1st used on or after 01/01/1985 shall be :-

• the original fitted by the manufacturer (these will normally bear a standard mark except vehicles with a max design speed not exceeding 50km/h), or

• a replacement which is marked with an approved British Standard marking (e.g. BS AU 193/T2 or similar) or an EEC mark or for vehicles with a maximum design speed not exceeding 50 km/h fitted before 01/02/1997 a manufacturers stamp or part number.

A motorcycle shall not be used on a road if it is fitted with an exhaust marked 'Not For Road Use' or similar.

Sale of non-compliant exhausts

Section 1 Motor Cycle Noise Act 1987 - 3 months or level 5 fine

It is an offence for a person in the course of a business to supply, offer or agree to supply, or expose or possess for supplying an exhaust system or a silencer or any component other than a silencer or fixing for such a system for a motorcycle, motor scooter or moped unless marked to comply as above (except for export).

It shall be a defence to show that the accused took all reasonable steps and exercised all due diligence to avoid committing the offence.

Sidestands

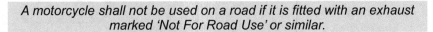

Regulation 38 Road Vehicles (Construction and Use) Regulations 1986, Section 42 Road Traffic Act 1988

No **motor cycle** first used on or after 01/04/1986 shall be fitted with any sidestand which is capable of :-

• disturbing the stability or direction of the motor cycle when it is in motion under its own power, or

• closing automatically if the angle of the inclination of the motor cycle is inadvertently altered when it is stationary.

Sidestand means a device fitted to a motor cycle which, when fully extended or pivoted to its open position, supports the vehicle from one side only and so that both the wheels of the motor cycle are on the ground.

Motorcycle Trailers

Regulation 84 Road Vehicles (Construction and Use)
Regulations 1986, Section 42 Road Traffic Act 1988

All motorcycles

A motorcycle may not :-

• draw more than 1 trailer,

• carry any passengers in the trailer (unless it is towing a broken down motorcycle),

• draw a trailer with an unladen weight exceeding 254kg (unless it is towing a broken down motorcycle).

Solo motorbicycles

2 wheel motorcycle without sidecars may not (unless it is towing a broken down motorcycle) :-

• If not exceeding 125cc, draw any trailer.

• If exceeding 125cc -

  ○ draw a trailer which exceeds 1m overall width,

  ○ allow distance rear axle to rear of trailer to exceed 2.5m,

  ○ draw a trailer, the laden weight of which exceeds two thirds kerbside weight of the motorcycle or a maximum of 150kg.

Must display kerbside weight on m/cycle, and unladen weight on trailer.

Motorcycle Training

Basic Training (CBT)

Section 97(3)(e) Road Traffic Act 1988

A Certificate of Compulsory Basic Training (CBT) is required by **motor bicycle and moped** licence holders before they ride on a road except during the training itself.

Cat B (Car) licence holders who passed their test before 01/02/2001 do not require CBT before riding a moped.

Staged and Direct Access Scheme

A2 Motorcycles

• Direct access - age 19 or over - theory and a practical test.

• Staged access - age 19 or over and two years' experience on an A1 motorcycle - practical test.

A Motorcycles

• Direct access - age 24 years or over - theory and practical tests.

• Staged access - age 21 years or over with two years' experience on an A2 motorcycle - practical test.

Chapter 9 Taxis

Types of Taxi

Taxis may be :-
- Private Hire vehicles which can only pick up pre-booked fares, or
- Hackney carriages which can ply for hire (they can be flagged down).

Taxis are not normally classed as Public Service Vehicles because :-
- they have eight or less passenger seats, and
- they do not operate at separate fares (the whole vehicle is hired).

Licensed taxis may operate as a PSV (running a local service for instance) provided a Special Restricted Operators licence is held - no disc will be displayed but the licence will be held at the company offices.

Licensed PSVs

Section 79A Public Passenger Vehicles Act 1981

Licensed PSVs (a small bus with eight or less passenger seats and normally hired at separate fares) may be used as taxis providing a Private Hire Vehicle licence is held (unless the operators main business is the operation of large buses) and for the purpose of the regulations applying to private hire vehicles are treated as not being PSVs.

Hackney Carriage

Section 38 Town Police Clauses Act 1847
Section 10 Civic Government (Scotland) Act 1982

Any type of wheeled vehicle used in standing or plying for hire in any street and every carriage standing upon any street having thereon any numbered plate required to be fixed upon a hackney carriage, or having thereon any plate resembling or intended to resemble any such plate. (Except PSV's)

A person licensed as a hackney carriage driver may only ply for hire in the district where the licence was issued.

Control

The control of hackney carriages, private hire vehicles and drivers outside London is the responsibility of the local council.

Conditions can be imposed by the regulating authority relating to such things as the type of vehicle used, the condition of the vehicle, use of meters, display of signs and notices, fares, fitness of driver etc.

Powers to inspect Taxis (outside London)

Section 68 Local Government (Miscellaneous Provisions) Act 1976

Section 11 Civic Government (Scotland) Act 1982

Providing the local council has adopted this section of the act a constable may at all reasonable times inspect and test for the purpose of ascertaining its fitness any hackney carriage or private hire vehicle licensed by a district council.

If not satisfied as to the fitness he may by notice in writing suspend the licence until such time as an authorised officer or constable is so satisfied.

Exemptions

- Vehicles from another district as long as they are not made available for hire within the district.
- Vehicles used in connection with a funeral or used wholly or mainly by a funeral director for that purpose.
- Vehicles used in connection with a wedding.

Private Hire vehicles on hire for more than 24 hours do not need to display any plate, disk or notice.

Seatbelts

- Hackney Carriages - Drivers are exempt from the requirement to wear a belt whilst on duty.
- Private Hire - Drivers are exempt only when carrying a passenger for hire.

Passengers in taxis have no special exemptions relating to the use of seatbelts except in regards to small children when an appropriate restraint is not available - under 3 years no restraint is required, over 3 years and an adult belt may be worn.

Basically if they are available they should be worn however where a fixed partition separates front and rear, the driver is not liable for unrestrained children sitting in a rear seat of such a vehicle fitted with rear seat belts.

Touting for Passengers

Section 167 Criminal Justice and Public Order Act 1994 -
level 4 fine

It is an offence for a person in a public place to solicit persons to hire vehicles to carry them as passengers.

Exceptions

- Solicit does not include merely displaying a sign on a vehicle or the driver or of a legitimate service reacting to the approach of a member of the public. (Soliciting is a pro active process.)
- Taxi sharing in licensed taxis.
- Touting for passengers to be carried at separate fares by P.S.V.'s.

Chapter 10 Public Service Vehicles

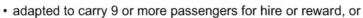

Definition

A Public Service Vehicle is a **motor vehicle** (other than a Tramcar) :-

- adapted to carry 9 or more passengers for hire or reward, or
- adapted to carry 8 or less passengers for hire or reward at separate fares in the course of a passenger carrying business.

Hire or Reward

Section 1(5) Public Passenger Vehicles Act 1981

Includes :-

- payment for any matters which involve the carrying of passengers,
- payment made in consideration of other matters additional to any journey taken,
- payment which confers a right to be carried whether exercised or not.

A shop or hotel providing courtesy buses would come into the definition even if no direct payment was made. The definition is not restricted to profit nor to business use.

Separate fares

Sections 1, 79, 79A and Sched 1 Public Passenger Vehicles Act 1981

Means payment by individuals direct to the operator, an agent or any other person or body.

Even if a group hire a vehicle by a lump sum payment, if the cost is shared amongst the group then separate fares exist although certain arrangements to share the cost, not initiated by the driver or operator are allowed.

Petrol Sharing is permitted without the vehicle being classified as a P.S.V. providing it has 8 or less passenger seats, the total charges made only cover running costs including depreciation and the arrangements are made in advance.

Operators licence

Requirement

Section 12(1) Public Passenger Vehicles Act 1981

Public Service Vehicles shall not be used on a **road** for carrying passengers for hire or reward except under a PSV operators licence or a permit.

Offence

Section 12(5) Public Passenger Vehicles Act 1981 - level 4 fine - fixed penalty offence

It is an offence for an operator to use a Public Service Vehicle on a road for carrying passengers for hire or reward except under a PSV operators licence or permit.

The licence is issued by the traffic commissioner for the area of the operating centre.

Detention and Immobilisation
Regulation 3 Public Service Vehicles (Enforcement Powers) Regulations 2009

Where an authorised person has reason to believe that a vehicle is being, or has been, used on a **road** in contravention of *section 12(1)*, that person may detain the vehicle and its contents.

Authorised person - an examiner appointed by the Secretary of State under section 66A of the Road Traffic Act 1988, or a person acting under the direction of such an examiner.

Operator Licence Disc
Regulation 12 Public Service Vehicles (Operators' Licences) Regulations 1995

An operator licence disc should be displayed on the nearside of the windscreen so that it does not interfere with the driver's view and can be easily read in daylight from the outside the vehicle.

Discs and permits are normally issued by the Traffic Commissioner.

Offence
Section 18(4) Public Passenger Vehicles Act 1981 - level 3 fine

It is an offence for an operator to fail to fix and exhibit an operator's disc on a vehicle used in circumstances such that a PSV operators licence is required.

(Special restricted operators licences issued to taxi firms operating a local service do not have operators discs issued.)

Production of Operator Licence
Regulation 16 Public Service Vehicles (Operators' Licences) Regulations 1995

A police constable, vehicle examiner or any person authorised by the traffic commissioner for any traffic area may require production of a licence or disc from the holder (not driver unless he is also the holder) who may produce it at the operating centre or principal place of business of the holder within 14 days.

Types of PSV Operators Licences and Permits
Licence Vehicles
Section 12(1) Public Passenger Vehicles Act 1981

- **Standard National licence** - Commercial carriage of Passengers operating nationally.
- **Standard International licence** - Commercial carriage of Passengers operating nationally and internationally.
- **Restricted licence** - for small operations with one or two vehicles, constructed to carry not more than eight passengers or vehicles carrying up to 16 passengers not used as part of a passenger transport business, or where passenger carrying vehicles are operated as a sideline and not the main business.
- **Special licence** - to operate a licensed taxi on a local service which is registered with the Traffic Commissioner (for London, a London local service licence or an agreement with London Transport Buses is required).

A Community (EC) Licence is also required for PSVs with 9 or more passenger seats when running an occasional (non-regular) international service.

Permit Vehicles
Section 19 Permits
Section 19 Transport Act 1985
The Section 19 Permit Regulations 2009

Under the Section 19 permit scheme, non-profit making organisations concerned with education, religion, social welfare, recreation and other activities of benefit to the community can make a charge to passengers for providing transport without the need to obtain a PSV Operator's Licence and, in most cases, without the driver having to comply with PCV driver licensing requirements.

Section 19 permits cannot be used to provide services to the general public or on journeys outside the UK.

Community Bus Permits
Section 22 Transport Act 1985
The Community Bus Regulations 2009

Community bus permits, available from the Traffic Commissioner, are issued to groups concerned with social and welfare needs of the community to run a local service on a voluntary non-profit basis. Drivers may be paid. Any size vehicle may be used but the permit will be vehicle specific.

Members of the general public can be carried in the vehicle and the main use would be to give the public a local service. The operator may also use the vehicle for non-local services (eg contract hire) to give financial support to the local operation if allowed by the Traffic Commissioner.

Conduct on Public Service Vehicles
Public Service Vehicles (Conduct of Drivers, Inspectors,
Conductors and Passengers) Regulations 1990

Drivers, Inspectors and Conductors

Section 24(2) Public Passenger Vehicles Act 1981 - level 2 fine

It is an offence for a driver, inspector or conductor to fail to comply with the requirements of the Regulations.

Driver must :-

• stop as closely as possible to the nearside when picking up or setting down passengers at the roadside,

• not speak into a microphone or to anyone by direct communication when moving except for emergencies, safety matters, to the operator or an employee on an operational matter, or to indicate the location (except on an excursion or tour) with occasional short statements.

Driver and Conductor must :-

• take reasonable safety precautions for the passengers,

• give their employers name and address to any police constable or any person having reasonable grounds to require it,

• not smoke unless no passengers carried or on private hire with consent of the operator and hirer.

Conductor must not :-

• distract the driver or obscure his vision without reasonable cause.

Passengers

Section 25(3) Public Passenger Vehicles Act 1981 - level 3 fine

It is an offence for a passenger to fail to comply with the requirements of the Regulations.

Passengers must not :-

• use any door other than indicated,

• endanger safety, impede or cause discomfort to any other person on the vehicle,

• trail or throw anything from the vehicle,

• smoke, carry lighted tobacco etc. contrary to 'no smoking' notices,

• sell or distribute anything without permission,

• speak to the driver whilst the vehicle is in motion except in an emergency or for reasons of safety or to give directions as to the stopping of the vehicle,

• play music to the annoyance of others,

• fail to quit the vehicle on request if full, or having caused a nuisance or if with soiled clothing.

Sporting Events
Alcohol on Public Service Vehicles

Section 1 Sporting Events (Control of Alcohol etc.) Act 1985
It is an offence for a person to :-

- have alcohol in his possession, *Section 1(3) level 3 fine / 3 months*
- to be drunk, *Section 1(4) level 2 fine*
- or for an operator, hirer or their servant or agent to cause or permit carriage of alcohol, *Section 1(2) level 4 fine*

on a public service vehicle used for the principal purpose of carrying passengers for the whole or part of a journey to or from a designated sporting event in England and Wales.

> *Designated sporting event - almost all association football matches taking place at FA grounds.*

Alcohol on other vehicles

Section 1A Sporting Events (Control of Alcohol etc.) Act 1985
It is an offence for a person to :-

- have alcohol in his possession, *Section 1A(3), level 3 fine / 3 months*
- to be drunk, *Section 1A(4) level 2 fine*
- or the driver, keeper, the servant or agent of the keeper, a person to whom it is made available by hire, loan or otherwise to cause or permit carriage of alcohol, *Section 1A(2) level 4 fine*

on a motor vehicle which is not a public service vehicle but is adapted to carry more than 8 passengers, and is being used for the principal purpose of carrying two or more passengers for the whole or part of a journey to or from a designated sporting event.

Power to stop and search vehicle and person

Section 7(2 and 3) Sporting Events (Control of Alcohol etc.) Act 1985
A constable may stop a PSV or other vehicle as above and search such a vehicle and search any person if he has reasonable grounds to suspect an offence is being or has been committed in respect of that vehicle or person.

Designated Sporting Events in Scotland

Sections 18 to 23 Criminal Law (Consolidation) (Scotland) Act 1995
Almost identical provisions apply to designated sporting events in Scotland.

.

Seating and Standing Capacity

Section 26(2) Public Passenger Vehicles Act 1981 - level 2 fine

It is an offence for a person to exceed the standing or seating capacity on a PSV adapted to carry 9 or more passengers which is :-

- stated on a Certificate of initial fitness or conformity issued on or after 01/04/1981,
- in any other case the seating capacity is the number of seats on which the vehicle excise licence fee is calculated.

Children

In double or bench seats 3 children under 14 years (they remain under 14 until the last day of August following their 14th birthday) may share 2 seats providing the seats are not fitted with seatbelts.

A child under 5 who is not occupying a seat does not count as a passenger.

Seating and standing capacity should be clearly marked on the inside of the vehicle.

Standing passengers

Public Service Vehicle (Carrying Capacity) Regulations 1984)

Standing passengers are not allowed :-

- on a PSV with 12 or fewer passenger seats,
- on the steps or upper deck,
- where a notice bans standing.

Warning Lights on Buses

Regulation 27 Road Vehicles Lighting Regulations 1989

Hazard Warning Lights may be displayed :-

- in the case of a bus, to summon assistance for the driver or any person acting as a conductor or inspector on the vehicle, or
- in the case of a school bus exhibiting the prescribed signs, when stationary and children under 16 years are entering or leaving or about to do so.

Chapter 11 Foreign Vehicles

Imported Vehicles
Temporarily Imported Vehicles
Chapter III Convention on Road Traffic - Vienna 08/11/1968

Foreign registered vehicles brought into the UK by a person who is **not resident in the UK** may be used within the UK for 6 months in a 12 month period (in a single visit or several shorter visits) providing :-

- the vehicle's registration certificate is carried by the driver, and, if the vehicle is not registered in the name of an occupant of the vehicle, proof of the driver's right to be in possession of the vehicle,
- the registration number is displayed at the front and rear, however motorcycles need display their registration number only at the rear,
- registration numbers must be displayed in Latin characters and Arabic numerals,
- a distinguishing sign of the country of registration is displayed on the rear of the vehicle,
- the vehicle must be legal for road use in the country of registration.

Concessions

UK residents of any nationality are not entitled to drive foreign registered vehicles in the UK except :-

- students and workers on short term contracts can apply to HMRC before or upon arrival in the UK for a customs relief form C110 (exempting them from the requirement to register the vehicle),
- armed forces personnel and their families,
- diplomatic vehicles,
- persons who work in an (EU) member state and use an EU-registered company vehicle temporarily in the UK and those who lease an EU-registered vehicle and use it temporarily in the UK,
- vehicles being permanently imported (*see below*) **may** be allowed a short period of grace (not for insurance) before registration is completed - this is not a legal concession more of practical one.

Other Vehicles imports

When a person brings a vehicle permanently into the UK from abroad they must :-

- provide HM Revenue and Customs (HMRC) with the vehicle's details within 14 days of its arrival, and pay any VAT or duty due,
- provide proof of vehicle approval where required,
- register, tax, MoT (if required) and insure the vehicle before using it on the road (an 'import pack' is available from www.gov.uk/dvlaforms or by phoning 0300 790 6802).

It is the keeper's responsibility to show they are allowed to use the vehicle in the UK without registering and taxing it.

AA- 957-FR Use of Temporarily Imported Vehicles on the Roads

Exemption from construction regulations

Reg 4(1) Road Vehicles (Construction and Use) Regulations 1986

Exemptions for temporarily imported vehicles :-

- all construction and equipment requirements except length, width and height,
- plates,
- speed limiter requirements,
- marking of weights,
- fitting requirements of lights providing the vehicle complies with the minimum lighting requirements-Convention of Road Traffic at Geneva.

Not exempt from :-

- length, width, height, weight requirements,
- height notices in the cab if over 3m,
- *Part IV* - Conditions relating to Use.

Financial Penalty Deposit Scheme

Section 90A Road Traffic Offenders Act 1988

This scheme enables enforcement authorities to impose on the spot penalties on drivers who commit certain offences relating to use of a motor vehicle or trailer where the person is unable to provide an address in the United Kingdom at which it would be possible to find the person whenever necessary to do so in connection with the proceedings, see *Chapter 26.*

Failure to make immediate payment of financial penalty deposit

Section 90D Road Traffic Offenders Act 1988

Where a person on whom a financial penalty deposit requirement is imposed does not make an immediate payment of the appropriate amount the constable or vehicle examiner may prohibit the driving on a road of any vehicle of which the person was in charge at the time of the offence by giving to the person notice in writing of the prohibition - a direction may be given to move the vehicle to a specified place and subject to conditions.

Powers to prohibit driving of a foreign vehicle

Section 1 Road Traffic (Foreign Vehicles) Act 1972

This section provides power for an examiner or authorised inspector to prohibit the driving of a foreign goods vehicle or foreign public service vehicle for numerous offences detailed in Schedule 2 of the Act including obstruction of the examiner or authorised person and breach of requirements relating to excess weight, drivers hours, condition of vehicle and equipment

Chapter 12 Examination of Vehicles

Weighing vehicles

Powers To Weigh

Section 78(1) Road Traffic Act 1988

An authorised person* may, on production of his authority, require the person in charge of a **motor vehicle** :-

- to allow the vehicle or any trailer drawn by it to be weighed either laden or unladen, and the weight transmitted to the road by any parts of the vehicle or trailer in contact with the road to be tested, and
- for that purpose, to proceed to a weighbridge or other machine for weighing vehicles.

The authorised person may drive the vehicle or do any other thing in relation to the vehicle or its load or the trailer or its load which is reasonably required (except unload it).

> *****Authorised person** means a person authorised by a highway authority (in Scotland, a roads authority) or a constable authorised on behalf of such an authority by a police authority or a chief officer of police.*

Refusal / Obstruction

Section 78(3) Road Traffic Act 1988 - level 5 fine

It is an offence for a person in charge of a **motor vehicle** to :-

- refuse or neglect to comply with a requirement as above, or
- obstruct an authorised person in the exercise of his functions.

Distance

Section 78(6) Road Traffic Act 1988

There is no limit on the distance a vehicle can be directed to a weighbridge however if :-

- at the time the requirement is made the vehicle is more than 5 miles from the weighbridge, and
- the weight is found to be within the limits authorised by law,

a claim may be made.

All visitors must report to the weighbridge

Certificate of weight

Section 79(1) Road Traffic Act 1988

Where a **motor vehicle or trailer** is weighed under *section 78* a certificate of weight must be given to the person in charge of the vehicle exempting him from being weighed again on the continuation of the same journey with the same load.

> *((Actual weight - Permitted weight) ÷ (Permitted weight)) x 100 = Percentage overweight.*

Offence - Excess weight

Section 41B(1) Road Traffic Act 1988 - level 5 fine - fixed penalty

It is an offence for a person to :-

(a) contravene or fail to comply with a construction and use requirement as to any description of weight applicable to a goods vehicle, or a motor vehicle, or trailer adapted to carry more than eight passengers, or

(b) use on a **road** a vehicle which does not comply with such a requirement, or causes[1] or permits[1] a vehicle to be so used.

[1] Cause and Permit offences are not fixed penalty offences.

Defences

Section 41B(2) Road Traffic Act 1988

In any proceedings for an offence under this section in which there is alleged a contravention or failure to comply with a construction and use requirement as to any description of weight applicable to a goods vehicle, it shall be a defence to prove either :-

• that at the time when the vehicle was being used on the road :-

  ○ it was proceeding to a weighbridge which was the nearest available one to the place where the loading of the vehicle was completed for the purpose of being weighed, or

  ○ it was proceeding from a weighbridge after being weighed to the nearest point at which it was reasonably practical to reduce weight to the relevant limit, without causing an obstruction on any road, or

• in a case where the limit of that weight was not exceeded by more than 5% :-

  ○ that the limit was not exceeded at time when loading was originally completed, and

  ○ that since that time no person has made any addition to the load.

Maximum Permitted Weights

Regulations 75 to 78 and Schedule 11 Road Vehicles (Construction and Use) Regulations 1986
Road Vehicles (Authorised Weights) Regulations 1998

Most UK goods vehicles are required to be fitted with plates detailing the maximum permissible weights.

Tables in the Construction and Use Regulations and the Authorised Weight Regulations provide methods of calculating the maximum weight where a plate is not fitted or does not conform, however it should be noted that the methods used are not compatible with each other and it is not permissible to comply with a combination of the Regulations.

Excess Weight Regulations

	Road Vehicles (Construction and Use) Regulations 1986	Road Vehicles (Authorised Weights) Regulations 1998
Exceeding maximum laden weight of vehicle Gross weight	*Reg 75 + Sched 11*	*Reg 4(1)(a) and Schedule 1*
Exceeding maximum laden weight of vehicle and trailer other than articulated vehicles - Train weight	*Reg 76*	*Reg 4(1)(b) and Schedule 2*
Exceeding maximum laden weight of articulated vehicle and trailer - Train weight	*Reg 77 + Sched 11*	*Reg 4(1)(b) and Schedule 2*
Exceeding maximum wheel and axle weights	*Reg 78*	*Reg 4(1)(c) and Schedule 3*
Exceeding maximum weights for closely-spaced axles	*Reg 79 + Sched 11*	*Reg 4(1)(c) and Schedule 3*
C and U Regs 75-79 may be exceeded by *RV (Authorised Weights) Regs* in respect of train and axle weights. A vehicle which complies with *C and U Regs 75-79* is taken to comply with the *RV (Authorised Weights) Regulations*	*Reg 79A*	*Reg 4(2)*
Equalling or Exceeding weights on the Manufacturers Plate (*Reg 66*) where no plating certificate has been issued. (If a vehicle is not required to have a plate fitted under *Reg 66* no excess weight offence under *Reg 80* is committed.)	*Reg 80(1)(a)*	-
Equalling or Exceeding weights on the Plating Certificate (Ministry plate). (Ministry Plated weights should be used in preference to Manufacturers Plate weights)	*Reg 80(1)(b)*	-
Equalling or Exceeding maximum gross weight on agricultural trailed appliance plate (*Regulation 68*).	*Reg 80(1)(c)*	-

The *Authorised Weights Regulations* apply to passenger vehicles with more than 8 passenger seats, goods vehicles and trailers all of which exceed 3500 kg g.v.w. UK weight limits are increased for certain vehicles above C and U limits (up to 44 tonnes on certain 6 axle articulated combinations) but **the regulations do not authorise exceeding plated weights**- even where the weights authorised by these Regulations are not exceeded.

The regulations do not affect the 44 tonne limit for intermodal transport operations (was known as combined transport (rail head) operations).

Further increases are allowed for certain vehicles using low carbon technologies.

The maximum weight for two-axle buses (however powered) is increased by 1.5 tonnes to 19.5 tonnes.

Prohibition Of Overweight Vehicles
Section 70(2) Road Traffic Act 1988

Where a goods vehicle or motor vehicle adapted to carry more than eight passengers has been weighed and it appears that the limit imposed by construction and use requirements has been exceeded or would be exceeded if used on a road or that by reason of excessive overall weight or excessive axle weight on any axle driving the vehicle would involve a danger of injury to any person, an authorised person* may give notice in writing to the person in charge of the vehicle prohibiting the driving of the vehicle on a road until :-

- that weight is reduced to that limit or, as the case may be, so that it is no longer excessive, and
- official notification has been given to whoever is for the time being in charge of the vehicle that it is permitted to proceed.

* Authorised person means a person authorised by a highway authority (in Scotland, a roads authority) or a constable authorised on behalf of such an authority by a police authority or a chief officer of police.

Direction Of Overweight Vehicles

Section 70(3) Road Traffic Act 1988

The authorised person may also by direction in writing require the person in charge of the vehicle to remove it (and, if it is a motor vehicle drawing a trailer, also to remove the trailer) to such place and subject to such conditions as are specified in the direction. The prohibition shall not apply to the removal of the vehicle or trailer in accordance with that direction.

Contravention of prohibitions for being overweight

Section 71(1) Road Traffic Act 1988 - level 5 fine - fixed penalty offence

It is an offence for a person who :-

(a) drives a vehicle in contravention of a prohibition under *section 70*, or

(b) causes or permits a vehicle to be driven in contravention of such a prohibition, or

(c) fails to comply within a reasonable time with a direction under *section 70(3) of this Act.*

A fixed penalty - graduated according to the degree of overloading may be issued. Where no satisfactory address in the UK is provided a financial deposit may also be required. If this is not paid the vehicle may be prohibited. Vehicles prohibited in this manner or under the Road Traffic Act powers above may be immobilised, removed and subsequently disposed of.
Cause or Permit are not fixed penalty offences.

Vehicle testing and inspection
Roadside vehicle testing - all motor vehicles and trailers

Section 67 Road Traffic Act 1988

A police constable in uniform may stop any motor vehicle for the purpose of a test under this section.

A stopping officer (*see Chapter 2 Page 13*) may stop :-

- Passenger vehicles with more than eight passenger seats,
- Goods vehicles and trailers exceeding 3.5 tonnes m.a.m.
- Cat T agricultural or forestry tractors,

for the purpose of a test under this section.

An authorised examiner* may test a **motor vehicle** (including any trailer drawn) on a road for ascertaining compliance with the construction and use requirements (including lighting), and the requirement that the condition of the vehicle is not such that its use on a road would involve a danger of injury to any person, and bringing to the notice of the driver any failure to comply with those requirements.

For the purpose of testing a vehicle under this section he may require the driver to comply with his reasonable instructions and drive the vehicle.

A driver may elect to defer a test to another date and location unless certain circumstances apply (see next page).

* Authorised examiner means :-
- a person appointed under *section 66A Road Traffic Act 1988*,
- a person appointed to examine and inspect public carriages for the purposes of the *Metropolitan Public Carriage Act 1869*,
- a person appointed to act for the purposes of this section by the Secretary of State,
- a constable authorised so to act by or on behalf of a chief officer of police, and
- a person appointed by the police authority for a police area to act, under the directions of the chief officer of police, for the purposes of this section.

An authorised examiner (except an authorised constable) must produce his authority if required to do so.

There are no powers under this section to direct vehicles to another location for the purpose of examination.

See instead Page 1 - weighing motor vehicles and trailers, or

Page 7 - inspection of goods and public service vehicles and motor vehicles adapted to carry more than eight passengers, or

Chapter 16 Page 8 - examination of drivers hours recording equipment which is believed to have been interfered with.

Option for a Deferred Roadside Test
Section 67(6) Road Traffic Act 1988

The **driver** may elect to defer a test to be carried out under this section except where a constable or stopping officer believes :-

• the vehicle has been involved in an accident owing to the presence of the vehicle on a road and it is requisite a test should be carried out forthwith by himself or another and he may detain the vehicle until it has been completed, or

• the vehicle is so defective it ought not be allowed to continue before being tested. The test should be carried out forthwith.

If the Driver is not the Owner the Driver shall supply the owners name and address

---

The **Owner** may :-

• Specify a 7 day period within next 30 days when test can be carried out, (disregard any days spent outside Great Britain) and :-
   ○ if the Owner does specify a period - give 2 days notice in writing, or
   ○ if the Owner does not specify a period - give 7 days notice in writing.

• Specify premises or an area in England, Wales or Scotland where the test may be carried out, and :-
   ○ if the Owner does specify suitable premises or area - give 2 or 7 days notice (as above) and carry out test at those premises or in that area, or
   ○ if the Owner does not specify suitable premises where test can conveniently be carried out - give 2 or 7 days notice (as above) and carry out test at premises specified by the constable or stopping officer.

Obstruction of Authorised Examiner
Section 67(9) Road Traffic Act 1988 - level 3 fine

It is an offence for a person to :-

• obstruct an authorised examiner acting under this section, or
• fail to comply with a requirement of this section.

If the vehicle has been involved in an accident owing to the presence of the vehicle on a road it can be tested at premises with the consent of the owner of the premises within 48 hours of the accident without the consent of the owner of the vehicle.

See Page 11 - Testing vehicles on premises.

Inspection of Goods Vehicles, PSVs, Minibuses etc.

Section 68(6) Road Traffic Act 1988

This section applies to :-

(a) goods vehicles,

(b) public service vehicles, and

(c) motor vehicles which are not public service vehicles but are adapted to carry more than eight passengers.

Power to Inspect

Section 68(1) Part II Road Traffic Act 1988

A vehicle examiner[1] :-

(a) may at any time, on production if so required of his authority, inspect any vehicle to which this section applies and for that purpose detain the vehicle during such time as is required for the inspection, and

(b) may at any time which is reasonable having regard to the circumstances of the case enter any premises on which he has reason to believe that such a vehicle is kept.

The power to enter premises shall not apply in relation to :-

• *motor vehicles which are not public service vehicles but which are adapted to carry more than eight passengers, and*

• *vehicles used to carry passengers for hire or reward only under permits granted under section 19 or 22 of the Transport Act 1985 (use of vehicles by educational and other bodies or in providing community bus services).*

The power to inspect a vehicle includes power to test it and to drive it for the purpose of testing it.

Obstructing an examiner

Section 68(3) Road Traffic Act 1988 - level 3 fine

It is an offence for a person to intentionally obstructs an examiner in the exercise of his powers under *subsection (1)* above.

A driver can also be reported to the Traffic Commissioner for further action.

Directions
Section 68(4) Road Traffic Act 1988
A vehicle examiner[1] or a constable in uniform may at any time require any person in charge of a vehicle to which this section applies and which is stationary on a road to proceed with the vehicle for the purpose of having it inspected under this section to any place where an inspection can be suitably carried out (not being more than **five miles** from the place where the requirement is made).

The power to direct a vehicle for the purposes of such an inspection only applies to goods vehicles, public service vehicles, and motor vehicles which are not public service vehicles but are adapted to carry more than eight passengers.
***It does not apply to other vehicles**.*

Section 68(5) Road Traffic Act 1988 - level 3 fine

A person in charge of a vehicle who refuses or neglects to comply with a requirement made under *subsection (4)* above is guilty of an offence.

A driver can also be reported to the Traffic Commissioner for further action.

[1] Examiner
Section 66A Road Traffic Act 1988
The Secretary of State shall appoint such examiners as he considers necessary for the purpose of carrying out the functions conferred on them by this *Part of this Act, the Goods Vehicles (Licensing of Operators) Act 1995, the Public Passenger Vehicles Act 1981, the Transport Act 1968 and any other enactment.*

Examiners may be DVSA examiners or police officers who have been appointed for the purposes of this section.

Power to prohibit Unfit Vehicles

Section 69(1) and (2) Road Traffic Act 1988

If on inspection of a vehicle under *sections 41, 45, 49, 61, 67, 68 or 77 Road Traffic Act 1988* it appears to :-

- a vehicle examiner* that owing to any defects in the vehicle it is, or is likely to become, unfit for service,
- an authorised constable** that owing to any defects in the vehicle driving it, driving it for any particular purpose or purposes or driving it for any except one or more particular purposes, would involve a danger of injury to any person,

he may prohibit the driving of the vehicle on the road absolutely, or for one or more specified purposes, or except for one or more specified purposes.

* **Vehicle examiner** means an examiner appointed under *section 66A Road Traffic Act 1988*

* ** **Authorised constable** is one who has been authorised to act for the purposes of this section by or on behalf of a chief officer of police (not the same as an authorised examiner under *section 67*).

A prohibition issued under this section by a vehicle examiner shall come into force :-

- as soon as the notice has been given if in his opinion the defects in the vehicle in question are such that driving it, or driving it for any purpose within the prohibition, would involve a danger of injury to any person.
- (unless previously removed under *section 72 of this Act*) at such time not later than 10 days from the date of the inspection as seems appropriate, having regard to all the circumstances.

Contravention of prohibitions for being unfit

Section 71(1) Road Traffic Act 1988 - level 5 fine - fixed penalty offence

It is an offence for a person who :-

(a) drives a vehicle in contravention of a prohibition under *section 69*, or

(b) causes or permits a vehicle to be driven in contravention of such a prohibition.

Where no satisfactory address in the UK is provided a financial deposit may also be required. If this is not paid the vehicle may be prohibited. Vehicles prohibited in this manner or under the Road Traffic Act powers above may be immobilised, removed and subsequently disposed of.

Cause or Permit are not fixed penalty offences.

Immobilisation, Removal and Disposal of Prohibited Vehicles
Schedule 4 Road Safety Act 2006
Road Safety (Immobilisation, Removal and Disposal of Vehicles) Regulations 2009

These Regulations apply with respect to any case where the driving of a vehicle has been prohibited under :-

(a) *section 99A(1) of the Transport Act 1968* (powers to prohibit driving of vehicles in connection with contravention of provisions about drivers' hours),

(b) *section 1 of the Road Traffic (Foreign Vehicles) Act 1972* (powers to prohibit driving of foreign goods vehicles and foreign public service vehicles),

(c) *section 69 or 70 of the Road Traffic Act 1988* (powers to prohibit driving of unfit or overloaded vehicles), or

(d) *section 90D of the Road Traffic Offenders Act 1988* (power to prohibit driving of vehicle on failure to make payment in compliance with financial penalty deposit requirement).

These Regulations do not apply in relation to a vehicle if a current disabled person's badge or current recognised badge is displayed on that vehicle.

Authorised person
Paragraph 10 Schedule 4 Road Safety Act 2006

An authorised person is one who was authorised to prohibit the vehicle under the original enactment. Usually this includes constables, or constables authorised to exercise their powers under the enactment and vehicle examiners appointed under *section 66A of the Road Traffic Act 1988.*

Where the driving of a vehicle has been prohibited an authorised person, or a person acting under his direction may immobilise, remove and subsequently dispose of the vehicle in accordance with the Road Safety (Immobilisation, Removal and Disposal of Vehicles) Regulations 2009.

Testing vehicles on premises
Regulation 74 Road Vehicles (Construction and Use) Regulations 1986

A :-

- police constable in uniform,
- person appointed by the Commissioner of Police of the Metropolis to inspect public carriages for the purpose of the *Metropolitan Public Carriage Act 1869*,
- person appointed by the police authority for a police area to act for the purposes of *section 53 Road Traffic Act 1972*,
- goods vehicle examiner - section 56 *Road Traffic Act 1972*,
- certifying officer or public service vehicle examiner - *section 7 Public Passenger Vehicles Act 1981*, and

may, on production of his authorisation if required,

test and inspect on any vehicle the :-

- brakes,
- steering,
- silencer,
- tyres,

on any premises with the consent of the owner of those premises, and :-

- if the vehicle owner consents - in any circumstances, OR
- if the vehicle owner does not consent :-
  - the vehicle owner is given 48 hours notice in person or 72 hours notice is given by recorded delivery to vehicle owners last known address, or
  - the test is done within 48 hours of a road traffic accident.

Supply of Unroadworthy Vehicles
Section 75(5) Road Traffic Act 1988 - level 5 fine

It is an offence for a person to :-

- sell or supply,
- offer to sell or supply,
- expose for sale,
- alter so as to render,

a motor vehicle or trailer in an unroadworthy condition, that is:-

- it is in such a condition that its use on a road is unlawful in respect of :-
  - brakes, steering gear or tyres, or
  - construction, weight or equipment of the vehicle (including lighting equipment), or
- if it is in such a condition that its use on the road would involve a danger of injury to any person.

Defence
Section 75(6) Road Traffic Act 1988
A person shall not be convicted if he proves :-
- it was supplied or altered for export, or
- he had reasonable cause to believe that the motor vehicle or trailer :-
  - would not be used on a road in Great Britain, or
  - would not be used on a road in Great Britain until it had been put into a condition in which it might be so lawfully used.

Use of the defence by a trade or business
Section 75(6A) Road Traffic Act 1988
The defence above will not apply to a person who, in the course of a trade or business :-
- exposes a vehicle or trailer for sale, unless he also proves that he took all reasonable steps to ensure that any prospective purchaser would be aware that it's use in it's current condition on a road in Great Britain would be unlawful, or
- offers to sell a vehicle or trailer, unless he also proves that he took all reasonable steps to ensure that the person to whom the offer was made was aware of that fact.

Entry to business premises
Section 76 (6) and (7) Road Traffic Act 1988
An authorised examiner* may at any reasonable hour enter premises where in the course of a business, vehicle parts are fitted to vehicles or are supplied, and test and inspect any vehicle or vehicle part found on those premises and may drive any vehicle or draw any trailer.

* Authorised examiner means :-
- a person appointed as an examiner under *section 66A Road Traffic Act 1988*,
- a person appointed to examine and inspect public carriages for the purposes of the *Metropolitan Public Carriage Act 1869,*
- a person appointed to act for the purposes of *section 67 Road Traffic Act 1988* by the Secretary of State,
- a constable authorised so to act (under *section 67 Road Traffic Act 1988*) by or on behalf of a chief officer of police, and
- a person appointed by the police authority for a police area to act, under the directions of the chief officer of police, for the purposes of *section 67 Road Traffic Act 1988.*

An authorised examiner must produce his authority if required to do so (except a constable in uniform).

Obstructing the examiner

Section 76(8) Road Traffic Act 1988 - level 3 fine

It is an offence for a person to obstruct an authorised examiner acting under this section.

Fitting of defective or unsuitable vehicle parts

Section 76(1) Road Traffic Act 1988 - level 5 fine

It is an offence for a person to :-

• fit, or
• cause to be fitted, or
• permit to be fitted,

any vehicle part to a vehicle which, if the vehicle was used on a road, would, by reason of that part :-

• involve a danger of injury to any person,
• be in contravention of any construction and use requirements (including lighting requirement).

Defence

Section 76(2) Road Traffic Act 1988

A person shall not be convicted if he proves :-

• that the vehicle to which the part was fitted was to be exported, or
• that he had reasonable cause to believe that the vehicle :-
  ○ would not be used on a road in Great Britain, or
  ○ would not be used on a road until it had been put into a condition in which it might be so lawfully used.

Sale or Supply of defective or unsuitable vehicle parts

Section 76(3) Road Traffic Act 1988 - level 4 fine

It is an offence for a person to :-

• sell or supply or offer to sell or supply, or
• cause to sell or supply, or
• permit to be sold or supplied,

a vehicle part if he has reasonable cause to believe that the part is to be fitted to :-

• a motor vehicle, or
• a vehicle of a particular class, or
• a particular vehicle,

if that part when fitted to the vehicle would by reason of that part :-

• involve a danger of injury to any person,
• be in contravention of any construction and use requirements (including lighting requirements).

Defence
Section 76(5) Road Traffic Act 1988

A person shall not be convicted if he proves :-

- that the part was supplied for export, or
- that he had reasonable cause to believe that it would not be fitted :-
  - to a vehicle used on a road in Great Britain, or
  - would not be fitted until it had been put into a condition in which it might be so lawfully used.

Entry to Test used vehicles
Section 77(1) Road Traffic Act 1988

An authorised examiner* (under *section 67*) may at any reasonable hour enter premises where used motor vehicles or trailers are supplied in the course of a business and test and inspect any used motor vehicle or trailer found on the premises for the purpose of ascertaining whether it is in an unroadworthy condition for the purpose of *section 75* of the act and he may drive the vehicle or tow the trailer for the purpose of the test.

Obstructing the examiner
Section 77(5) Road Traffic Act 1988 - level 3 fine

It is an offence for a person to obstruct an authorised examiner* acting under this section.

*Authorised examiner means :-

- a person appointed as an examiner under *section 66A Road Traffic Act 1988*,
- a person appointed to examine and inspect public carriages for the purposes of the *Metropolitan Public Carriage Act 1869*,
- a person appointed to act for the purposes of *section 67 Road Traffic Act 1988* by the Secretary of State,
- a constable authorised so to act (under *section 67 Road Traffic Act 1988*) by or on behalf of a chief officer of police, and
- a person appointed by the police authority for a police area to act, under the directions of the chief officer of police, for the purposes of *section 67 Road Traffic Act 1988*.

An authorised examiner must produce his authority if required to do so (except a constable in uniform).

Chapter 13 Dangerous Goods

Carriage of Dangerous Goods

International Transport

European Agreement concerning the International Carriage of Dangerous Goods by Road (ADR)

The ADR agreement allows dangerous goods travelling by road through more than one country to be exempt from the domestic legislation in force in those countries, as long as the requirements of ADR are met in full. Foreign registered vehicles may also travel under ADR while carrying dangerous goods on journeys within the UK(cabotage) without having to conform to domestic legislation.

The ADR is updated regularly (usually every 2 years) and is available on the United Nations website. It contains no provisions for enforcement. Where a vehicle travelling under ADR does not comply in full, the vehicle becomes subject to all domestic requirements.

Regulation 5 Carriage of Dangerous Goods and Use of Transportable Pressure Equipment Regulations 2009

No person is to carry dangerous goods, or cause or permit dangerous goods to be carried, where that carriage is prohibited by ADR, including where that carriage does not comply with any applicable requirement of ADR.

Domestic Transport

Health and Safety at Work etc. Act 1974
Carriage of Dangerous Goods and Use of Transportable Pressure Equipment Regulations 2009

These regulations regulate the carriage of dangerous goods by road and rail in Great Britain and the use of transportable pressure equipment and implement the ADR and the Transportable Pressure Equipment Directive.

Tunnel Restrictions

Vehicles carrying dangerous goods with the restriction code indicated by the sign are prohibited from the tunnel.

Tunnel	Category	Tunnel	Category
Dartford	C	Limehouse	E
Tyne	D	Rotherhithe	E
Clyde	D	East India Dock Road	E
Mersey	D	Heathrow Airport	C or E 0400-2300hrs
Blackwall	E		

Markings

Regulations 6 - 8 Carriage of Dangerous Goods and Use of Transportable Pressure Equipment Regulations 2009

These regulations also stipulate :-

- alternative placarding requirements to the ADR for national carriage operations by UK registered vehicles where dangerous goods are carried in a tank or in bulk,
- additional security requirements to those listed in the ADR.

Classification of Dangerous Goods

Section 2.1.1 ADR

- Class 1 Explosive substances and articles.
- Class 2 Gases.
- Class 3 Flammable liquids.
- Class 4.1 Flammable solids, self-reactive substances and solid desensitized explosives.
- Class 4.2 Substances liable to spontaneous combustion.
- Class 4.3 Substances which, in contact with water, emit flammable gases.
- Class 5.1 Oxidizing substances.
- Class 5.2 Organic peroxides.
- Class 6.1 Toxic substances.
- Class 6.2 Infectious substances.
- Class 7 Radioactive material.
- Class 8 Corrosive substances.
- Class 9 Miscellaneous dangerous substances and articles.

For packing purposes, substances are assigned to packing groups in accordance with the degree of danger they present :-

- Packing group I - substances presenting a high danger.
- Packing group II - substances presenting a medium danger.
- Packing group III - substances presenting a low danger.

The Dangerous Goods List

Chapter 3.2 ADR

The Dangerous Goods List details substances, UN Number, classification code, packing group and Transport Category together with other requirements and the corresponding ADR chapter/section number.

The UN Number is often the easiest way to identify a substance.

Further information is available at http://www.ericards.net/

Chapter 14 Abnormal Loads

Regulations and Orders

The Road Vehicles (Construction and Use) Regulations 1986 and the Road Vehicles (Authorised Weights) Regulations 1998 stipulate the maximum dimensions and weights of vehicles and their loads when used on a **road**.

Together with the *Road Vehicles Lighting Regulations 1989* these regulations are referred to in this chapter as the construction regulations.

Construction and Use Regulations

Regulation 82 Road Vehicles (Construction and Use) Regulations 1986

Authorises movement of standard vehicles with wide or long loads or load projections providing conditions in *Schedule 12* of those regulations are complied with.

Schedule 11A Road Vehicles (Construction and Use) Regulations 1986

Authorises movement of vehicles engaged in Combined Transport Operations (transport by both rail and road) which may exceed the weight limits detailed in *regulations 75 to 79* subject to conditions contained in that Schedule and not exceeding the overall plated weight limits of the vehicle (*regulation 80*).

In both cases if the conditions specified are not complied with, the movement ceases to be authorised and the vehicle and load becomes subject to all the standard requirements of the construction regulations.

Authorised Weights Regulations 1998

Road Vehicles (Authorised Weights) Regulations 1998

The Regulations apply to weights of wheeled motor vehicles and trailers fitted with 'Road friendly suspension' - a suspension system whereby at least 75% of the spring effect is produced by air or other compressible fluid under pressure or an equivalent system.

The weights may not exceed the overall plated weight limits of the vehicle (*regulation 80 Road Vehicles (Construction and Use) Regulations 1986*)

The Regulations do not apply to vehicle combinations that meet the requirements for combined transport in *Schedule 11A to the Road Vehicles (Construction and Use) Regulations 1986*.

The Authorised Weight Regulations operate in parallel to the Construction and Use Regulations but vehicles may only comply with one of the regulations – individual parts of the 2 regulations cannot be combined.

▼ The STGO
Road Vehicles (Authorisation of Special Types) (General) Order 2003

The Road Vehicles (Authorisation of Special Types) (General) Order 2003 - known as the S.T.G.O.- authorises certain types of vehicles to be used on the roads notwithstanding that they or their loads do not fully comply with the construction regulations.

The order authorises movement of vehicles and loads the dimensions or weight of which exceed those authorised in the construction regulations providing the conditions in the order are complied with. It also provides exemptions from other parts of the construction regulations.

If the conditions specified are not complied with, the movement ceases to be authorised and the vehicle and load becomes subject to all the standard requirements of the construction regulations. Offences are contrary to those regulations and the Road Traffic Act 1988.

Vehicle Special Orders

Vehicles which are unable to comply with the STGO order or Construction Regulations can be used on the road if an individual Vehicle Special Order (VSO) has been issued by :-

• *National Highways (formerly Highways England)* - in the case of individual abnormal load movements not covered by the Construction and Use Regulations or the STGO, and

• *The Vehicle Certification Agency (VCA)* regarding divisible loads such as crane ballast outside the scope of the Construction and Use Regulations and the STGO.

Orders are dependant on compliance with conditions
*Failure to comply with **ALL** the conditions negates the allowance and the vehicle must then comply with the standard requirements of the applicable Regulations.*
Any offence is therefore contrary to the Road Traffic Act 1988 not the Order.

ESDAL 2

The Highways England Electronic Service Delivery for Abnormal Loads (ESDAL) system is used to manage abnormal load movements and notifications in England. It can be used by abnormal loads police officers, owners of bridges or structures on or adjacent to the Highways England network and by hauliers when transporting abnormal loads to plot routes and provide notifications.

The system does not extend to Wales or Scotland.

Standard Vehicle movements
Width and lateral projections

Regulation 82, Schedule 12 Road Vehicles (Construction and Use) Regulations 1986, Part 4, Articles 28 - 31 STGO 2003

	Requirement
Lateral Projections of load exceeding 305mm	
Type of Movement	**Con and Use**
Police Notice	2 days [1]
Marker Boards	Yes **S**[1] - *see also next page*
Attendant	No
Speed restrictions	No
Width - indivisible load 2.9 - 3.5 metres	
Type of Movement	**Con and Use**
Police Notice	2 days [1]
Marker Boards	Yes **S**[1]
Attendant	No
Speed restrictions	No
Width - indivisible load +3.5 - 4.3 metres	
Type of Movement	**Con and Use**
Police Notice	2 days [1]
Marker Boards	Yes **S**[1]
Attendant	Yes
Speed restrictions	No
Width - indivisible load +4.3 - 5.0 metres	
Type of Movement	**S.T.G.O**. Part 4
Police Notice	2 days
Marker Boards	No
Attendant	Yes
Speed restrictions	40mph Motorway 35mph Dual carriageway 30mph Single carriageway
Width - indivisible load +5.0 - 6.1 metres	
Type of Movement	**S.T.G.O**. Part 4
Police Notice	2 days
Marker Boards	No
Attendant	Yes
Speed restrictions	40mph Mway / 35mph Dual / 30mph Single carriageway + Secretary of State Consent - VR1 - 10 days

S - side marker boards

[1] Except :-
- carriage of loose agricultural produce not baled or crated,
- vehicles being used for fire brigade, ambulance, police or defence purposes or in connection with the removal of traffic obstructions if compliance would hinder use,
- a vehicle with load exceeding 4.3 metres width which complies with Part 4 of the STGO.

[2] - *BE16 application 2 months in advance for loads outside STGO (ex 6.1m)*

▼ Standard Vehicle movements
Width and lateral projections *continued*

Exceptions

Regulation 82(10) Road Vehicles (Construction and Use) Regulations 1986

In the case of a vehicle being used :-

- for fire brigade or, in England, fire and rescue authority, ambulance or police purposes, or
- for defence purposes (including civil defence purposes), or
- for ambulance purposes, or
- for the purpose of providing a response to an emergency at the request of an NHS ambulance service,
- in connection with the removal of any obstruction to traffic,

if compliance with any provision of this regulation would hinder or be likely to hinder the use of the vehicle for the purpose for which it is being used, that provision does not apply to that vehicle while it is being so used.

Marker Boards for lateral projections

Any projection exceeding 305 mm laterally must be marked with 2 side markers, one visible to the front and one visible to the rear of the vehicle.

Alternatively, it may be marked by day-glow, fluorescent or retro-reflective tape, coloured red, white or yellow (or any combination), so that the point where the width is at its greatest is clearly visible from the front, rear and side of the vehicle. If tape is used, then no retro-reflective material capable of showing red light can be fitted to the front of the vehicle and only red light can be fitted to the rear.

Attendants

An attendant is required where:

- the vehicle width exceeds 3.5 metres,
- the rigid length (excluding the drawing vehicle) exceeds 18.75 metres,
- the total length exceeds 25.9 metres,
- projections exceed 2 metres (front) 3.05 metres (rear),

Where an attendant is needed they can travel in the vehicle according to the STGO or Special Order movement. Alternatively they can travel in an escort vehicle, providing that they are:

- in radio contact with the vehicle concerned,
- are able to see the vehicle concerned during the journey, as far as is reasonably practical.

Where 3 or more loads are travelling in convoy, only the first and last vehicles need an attendant.

Standard Vehicle movements
Length and Longitudinal Projections

Regulation 82 Road Vehicles (Construction and Use) Regulations 1986
Schedule 12 Road Vehicles (Construction and Use) Regulations 1986

	Requirement
Length of the vehicle(s) which bear the load + any projections of the load 18.65 - 27.4 metres (do not measure artic tractive unit)	
Police Notice	2 days
Marker Boards S-side E-End	No
Attendant	Yes
Overall length of vehicle combination + any projections of the load exceeds 25.9 metres	
Police Notice	2 days
Marker Boards S-side E-End	No
Attendant	Yes
Rearward projection 1 - 2 metres	
Police Notice	No
Marker Boards S-side E-End	Render clearly visible
Attendant	No
Rearward projection 2.0 - 3.0 metres	
Police Notice	No
Marker Boards S-side E-End	Yes E
Attendant	No
Rearward projection 3.0 - 3.05 metres	
Police Notice	No
Marker Boards S-side E-End	Yes E S
Attendant	No
Rearward projection exceeds 3.05 metres	
Police Notice	2 days
Marker Boards S-side E-End	Yes E S
Attendant	Yes
Rearward projection exceeds 5.0 metres	
Police Notice	2 days
Marker Boards S-side E-End	Yes E S + additional S
Attendant	Yes

End Marker

A projection exceeding 2 metres to the front or rear of a vehicle must be marked with an end-marker which faces the front or rear of the vehicle.

Side Marker

A projection exceeding 3 metres to the front or rear of a vehicle must (in addition) be marked with side markers to both its right and left hand side, facing out sideways.

continued over

▼ Standard Vehicle movements
Length and Longitudinal Projections *continued*

	Requirement	
Forward projection 1 - 2 metres		
Police Notice	No	
Marker Boards S-side E-End. [1]	No [1]	
Attendant	No	
Forward projection 2.0 - 3.05 metres		
Police Notice	No	
Marker Boards S-side E-End. [1]	Yes E S [1]	
Attendant	Yes (No if [1])	
Forward projection exceeds 3.05 metres		
Police Notice	2 days	
Marker Boards S-side E-End.[1]	Yes E S [1]	
Attendant	Yes (No if [1])	
Forward projection exceeds 4.5 metres		
Police Notice	2 days	
Marker Boards S-side E-End. [1]	Yes E S [1] +additional S	
Attendant	Yes (No if [1])	

End Marker ▼
A projection exceeding 2 metres to the front or rear of a vehicle must be marked with an end-marker which faces the front or rear of the vehicle.

Side Marker ◢◢◢
A projection exceeding 3 metres to the front or rear of a vehicle must (in addition) be marked with side markers to both its right and left hand side, facing out sideways.

[1]- Where the load consists of a racing boat propelled solely by oars - marker boards not required - render clearly visible.

Different requirements apply to straddle carriers.

Exceptions
Regulation 82(10) Road Vehicles (Construction and Use) Regulations 1986

In the case of a vehicle being used :-
- for fire brigade or, in England, fire and rescue authority, ambulance or police purposes, or
- for defence purposes (including civil defence purposes), or
- for ambulance purposes, or
- for the purpose of providing a response to an emergency at the request of an NHS ambulance service,
- in connection with the removal of any obstruction to traffic,

if compliance with any provision of this regulation would hinder or be likely to hinder the use of the vehicle for the purpose for which it is being used, that provision does not apply to that vehicle while it is being so used.

Special Types movements

Part 2 - Special vehicles for haulage, lifting, engineering and vehicle recovery and Part 2 vehicle combinations

Part 2 Articles 12 - 17 Road Vehicles (Authorisation of Special Types) (General) Order 2003

Width and lateral projections

	Requirement
Lateral projection of load exceeds 305mm	
Police Notice	2 days
Marker Boards S-side E-End	Yes S - *see below*
Attendant	No
Other requirements	If side markers not practicable tape may be used at widest points
Overall width of vehicle + any projections of the load exceeds 3 metres	
Police Notice	2 days
Marker Boards S-side E-End	Yes S - if Lateral projection exceeds 305mm
Attendant	No
Overall width of vehicle + any projections of the load exceeds 3.5 metres	
Police Notice	2 days
Marker Boards S-side E-End	Yes S - if Lateral projection exceeds 305mm
Attendant	Yes
Overall width of vehicle + any projections of the load exceeds 5 metres	
Police Notice	2 days
Marker Boards S-side E-End	Yes S - if Lateral projection exceeds 305mm
Attendant	Yes
Other requirements	Secretary of State Consent - VR1 - 10 days

Marker Boards for lateral projections

Any projection exceeding 305 mm laterally must be marked with 2 side markers, one visible to the front and one visible to the rear of the vehicle.

Alternatively, it may be marked by day-glow, fluorescent or retro-reflective tape, coloured red, white or yellow (or any combination), so that the point where the width is at its greatest is clearly visible from the front, rear and side of the vehicle. If tape is used, then no retro-reflective material capable of showing red light can be fitted to the front of the vehicle and only red light can be fitted to the rear.

Special Types movements
Part 2 - Special vehicles for haulage, lifting, engineering and vehicle recovery and Part 2 vehicle combinations

Length and longitudinal projections

	Requirement
Length of the vehicle(s) which bear the load + any projections of the load (do not measure artic tractive unit) exceeds 18.75 metres	
Police Notice	2 days
Marker Boards S-side E-End	No
Attendant	Yes
Overall length of vehicle combination + any projections of the load exceeds 25.9 metres	
Police Notice	2 days
Marker Boards S-side E-End	No
Attendant	Yes
Rearward projection exceeds 1 metre	
Police Notice	No
Marker Boards S-side E-End	No
Attendant	No
Other Requirements	Render clearly visible from rear and sides
Rearward projection exceeds 2 metres	
Police Notice	No
Marker Boards S-side E-End	Yes E or rear
Attendant	No
Rearward projection exceeds 3 metres	
Police Notice	No
Marker Boards S-side E-End	Yes E S
Attendant	No
Rearward projection exceeds 3.05 metres	
Police Notice	2 days
Marker Boards S-side E-End	Yes E S
Attendant	Yes
Rearward projection exceeds 5 metres	
Police Notice	2 days
Marker Boards S-side E-End	Yes E S + additional S
Attendant	Yes

End Marker

A projection exceeding 2 metres to the front or rear of a vehicle must be marked with an end-marker which faces the front or rear of the vehicle.

Side Marker

A projection exceeding 3 metres to the front or rear of a vehicle must (in addition) be marked with side markers to both its right and left hand side, facing out sideways.

continued over

Special Types movements
Part - 2 Special vehicles for haulage, lifting, engineering and vehicle recovery and Part 2 vehicle combinations

Length and longitudinal projections *continued*

	Requirement
Forward projection exceeds 1 metre	
Police Notice	No
Marker Boards S-side E-End	No
Attendant	No
Other Requirements	Render clearly visible front front and sides
Forward projection exceeds 2 metres	
Police Notice	No
Marker Boards. S-side E-End	Yes E
Attendant	Yes
Forward projection exceeds 3 metres	
Police Notice	No
Marker Boards S-side E-End	Yes E S
Attendant	Yes
Forward projection exceeds 3.05 metres	
Police Notice	2 days
Marker Boards S-side E-End	Yes E S
Attendant	Yes
Forward projection exceeds 4.5 metres	
Police Notice	Yes
Marker Boards S-side E-End	Yes E S + additional S
Attendant	Yes

> **End Marker**
> A projection exceeding 2 metres to the front or rear of a vehicle must be marked with an end-marker which faces the front or rear of the vehicle.
>
> **Side Marker**
> A projection exceeding 3 metres to the front or rear of a vehicle must (in addition) be marked with side markers to both its right and left hand side, facing out sideways.

Marker Boards
End Marker

A projection exceeding 2 metres to the front or rear of a vehicle must be marked with an end-marker which faces the front or rear of the vehicle.

Side Marker

A projection exceeding 3 metres to the front or rear of a vehicle must (in addition) be marked with side markers to both its right and left hand side, facing out sideways.

As an alternative to the end marker or side marker boards a different form of marker, authorised in the EU for use on projecting loads, is permitted.

Special Types movements
Part 2 - Special vehicles for haulage, lifting, engineering and vehicle recovery and Part 2 vehicle combinations
Weight

Part 2 Articles 12 - 17 Road Vehicles (Authorisation of Special Types) (General) Order 2003

Conditions	Requirement
Total Weight of vehicle or combination	
Exceeds the maximum authorised axle weight permitted under the construction regulations	No Police Notice required Bridge and Highways Authority notice 2 days and indemnity
Exceeds 44 tonnes	No Police Notice required BHA notice 2 days and indemnity
Exceeds 80 tonnes	2 days Police Notice BHA notice 5 days and indemnity

Conditions on use of and stopping on bridges

Part 2 Article 18 Road Vehicles (Authorisation of Special Types) (General) Order 2003

The driver of a Part 2 vehicle must not cause or permit any part of his vehicle or combination to enter on a bridge if he knows that the whole or part of another Part 2 vehicle or combination is already on the bridge or if he could reasonably be expected to ascertain that fact.

Except in circumstances beyond his control, the driver must not cause or permit the vehicle, or combination, to remain stationary on any bridge.

If a vehicle, total weight exceeding 44 tonnes, is caused to stop on a bridge for any reason, the driver must ensure :-
• that the vehicle or vehicle-combination is moved clear of the bridge as soon as practicable, and
• that no concentrated load is applied to the surface on that part of the road carried by the bridge.

Where the action described above is not practicable and it becomes necessary to apply any concentrated load to the road surface by means of jacks, rollers or other similar means, the driver or other person in charge of the vehicle or vehicle-combination must :-
• before the load is applied to the road surface, seek advice from the bridge or highways authority about the use of spreader plates to reduce the possibility of damage caused by the application of the load, and
• ensure that no concentrated load is applied without using spreader plates in accordance with any advice received.

Special Types movements

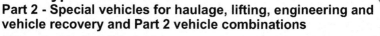

Part 2 - Special vehicles for haulage, lifting, engineering and vehicle recovery and Part 2 vehicle combinations

Abnormal Indivisible Loads

Abnormal indivisible load means a load that cannot without undue expense or risk of damage be divided into two or more loads for the purpose of being carried on a road and that on account of its length, width or height, or weight cannot be carried on a motor vehicle and/or trailer such that the construction regulations are complied with.

Schedule 1 STGO 2003

Additional Requirements for AILVs	Requirement
Overall Dimensions	
Maximum Length 30 metres Maximum Width 6.1 metres	
Category 1 - *Not exceeding weights on the manufacturers plate (Reg 66 C and U) - to a max of 46 tonnes (50 tonnes if 6 axle)*	
Axle limit	Construction regulations limits
Category Marker Boards	Cat 1
Additional Speed restrictions Single carriageway	40 mph
Additional Speed restrictions Dual carriageway	50 mph
Additional Speed restrictions Motorway	60 mph
Category 2 Not exceeding 80 tonnes	
Axle limit	12.5 tonnes max
Category Marker Boards	Cat 2
Additional Speed restrictions Single carriageway	30 mph [1]
Additional Speed restrictions Dual carriageway	35 mph [1]
Additional Speed restrictions Motorway	40 mph [1]
Category 3 Not exceeding 150 tonnes	
Axle limit	16.5 tonnes max
Category Marker Boards	Cat 3
Additional Speed restrictions Single carriageway	30 mph [1]
Additional Speed restrictions Dual carriageway	35 mph [1]
Additional Speed restrictions Motorway	40 mph [1]

Signs and Plates

STGO Category 1, 2 or 3 sign to be exhibited in a clearly visible position at the front of the vehicle.

[1]'SPECIAL TYPES USE' plate which lists the maximum weights at which the vehicle should be driven at speeds from 20mph to 40 mph in 5 mph increments in the opinion of the manufacturer.

Foreign registered abnormal load vehicles usually display 'Convoi Exceptionnel' signs.

CONVOI EXCEPTIONNEL

▼ Special Types movements

Part 2 - Special vehicles for haulage, lifting, engineering and vehicle recovery and Part 2 vehicle combinations

Mobile Cranes

Mobile crane means a motor vehicle which :-

- is specially designed and constructed, or is specially adapted, for the special purposes of lifting operations that cannot safely be carried out by a motor vehicle or trailer that complies in all respects with the construction regulations, and
- has a gross weight of the crane exceeding 12,000 kilograms, and
- has crane apparatus permanently mounted as part of the vehicle chassis design, and
- is operated by a driver or other person riding on it, and
- meets the requirements for registered use as a mobile crane.

Schedule 2 Road Vehicles STGO 2003

A mobile crane which does not comply in all respects with the authorisation requirements for mobile cranes may instead comply with the requirements relating to Engineering Plant in Schedule 3

Additional Requirements for mobile cranes	Requirement
Overall Dimensions	
Maximum Length 30 metres, Maximum Width 6.1 metres	
Maximum Weight of load carrying vehicle - Category A **20 tonnes (2 axle)** **30 tonnes (3 axle) 36 tonnes (4 axle)**	
Axle limit	10 tonnes (11.5 tonnes if driven axle)
Additional Speed restrictions Single/Dual/MWay	40 / 50 / 60 mph
Maximum Weight of load carrying vehicle - Category B **Not exceeding 12.5 x No. axles (tonnes)**	
Axle limit	12.5 tonnes max
Additional Speed restrictions Single/Dual/Motorway	40 / 45 / 50 mph
Maximum Weight of load carrying vehicle - Category C **Not exceeding 150 tonnes**	
Axle limit	16.5 tonnes max
Additional Speed restrictions Single/Dual/|MWay	30 / 35 / 40 mph
Additional Requirements	
A warning beacon should be fitted and must be kept lit :- • when the crane is stationary at the site of the operations at which it is to be used unless there is no reasonable prospect of the presence of the mobile crane causing a hazard to persons using the road (so that it is not necessary or desirable to warn persons of its presence) or it is likely that the use of the beacon could confuse or mislead other road users, • when the crane is unable, on account of the weather conditions or otherwise, to maintain speeds appropriate to the road. No load other than gear and equipment should be carried and no trailer may be towed. A plate should be fitted detailing the maximum weights which should not be exceeded.	

Special Types movements

Part 2 - Special vehicles for haulage, lifting, engineering and vehicle recovery and Part 2 vehicle combinations

Engineering Plant

Engineering plant means any moveable plant or equipment which is a motor vehicle or trailer and which :-

- is specially designed and constructed for the special purposes of engineering operations that cannot safely be carried out by a motor vehicle or trailer that complies in all respects with the construction regulations, and
- is not constructed to carry any load apart from materials that have been excavated and raised from the ground by apparatus on the plant, or materials that the plant is specially designed to treat while carried on the plant, and
- is operated by a driver or other person riding on it, and
- if it is a mobile crane, it does not comply in all respects with the authorisation requirements for mobile cranes.

Schedule 3 Road Vehicles (Authorisation of Special Types) (General) Order 2003

Additional Requirements for engineering plant	Requirement
Overall Dimensions	
Maximum Length 30 metres Maximum Width 6.1 metres Maximum Weight vehicle - 150 tonnes Maximum wheel weight - 11.25 tonnes	
Slow Plant - vehicles which cannot comply with Schedule 1	
Additional Speed restrictions Single/Dual/Motorway	12 / 12 / 30 mph
Cat 1 Vehicles which can comply with Schedule 1 for AILVs in respect of brakes, plates and signs.	
Category Marker Boards	Cat 1
Additional Speed restrictions Single/Dual/Motorway	40 / 50 / 60 mph
Cat 2 or Cat 3 Vehicles which can comply with Schedule 1 for AILVs in respect of brakes, plates and signs.	
Category Marker Boards	Cat 2 or Cat 3
Additional Speed restrictions Single/Dual/Motorway	30 / 35 / 40 mph
Additional Requirements	
No trailer may be towed except a trailer which is engineering plant or a living van or office for site use.	

Special Types movements
Part 2 - Special vehicles for haulage, lifting, engineering and vehicle recovery and Part 2 vehicle combinations
Road Recovery Vehicles

Road recovery vehicle means a vehicle that is specially designed and constructed for the purpose of recovering disabled road vehicles or is permanently adapted for that purpose which is fitted with a crane, winch or other lifting system specially designed to be used for the purpose of recovering another vehicle, and meets the requirements for registered use as a recovery vehicle.

Schedule 4 Road Vehicles (Authorisation of Special Types) (General) Order 2003

Additional Requirements for road recovery vehicles
Maximum Length - 18.75 metres (not including disabled vehicle(s) being towed)
Maximum Width of motor vehicle - the maximum specified in Reg. 8 Construction and Use regulations
Maximum Width of trailer - as above unless a vehicle can only be safely recovered by a wider trailer - to a maximum of 3m
Maximum Weight 3 axle locomotive - 36 tonnes 4 axle locomotive - 50 tonnes Type approved motor vehicle/trailer combination 6 axles - 80 tonnes Other vehicles - the maximum permitted under the construction regulations
Maximum wheel weight - 6.25 tonnes
Maximum axle weight - 12.5 tonnes
Maximum speed whilst towing a disabled vehicle or combination - 30mph on single and dual carriageways, 40mph on motorway
A **warning beacon** should be fitted and lit :- • when the road recovery vehicle is stationary at the scene of the breakdown unless there is no reasonable prospect of the presence of the road recovery vehicle causing a hazard to persons using the road (so that it is not necessary or desirable to warn persons of its presence) or it is likely that the use of the beacon could confuse or mislead other road users, • when the road recovery vehicle is unable, on account of any vehicle or vehicles it is towing, the weather conditions or otherwise, to maintain speeds appropriate to the road.
A **plate** specifying the maximum weight which may be lifted should be fitted.
No load other than gear and equipment should be carried and no trailer may be towed except a disabled vehicle.

Special Types movements
Part 3 - Special vehicles for agriculture

Part 3 Articles 19 - 27 Road Vehicles (Authorisation of
Special Types) (General) Order 2003

Requirement
Total Weight of vehicle or combination
• Wheeled vehicles - the maximum authorised axle weight permitted under the construction regulations • Track- laying motor vehicles - 30 tonnes. If the vehicle exceeds the limits under the construction regulations bridge and highways authority require notification and use on bridges is restricted.
Rearward projection exceeds 4 metres
Police Notice - 24 hrs   Attendant NO
Rearward projection exceeds 6 metres
Police Notice - 24 hrs   Attendant YES
Rearward projection exceeds 12 metres
Police Notice - 24 hrs   Attendant YES + Secretary of State authorisation
Forward projection exceeds 4 metres
Police Notice - 24 hrs   Attendant NO
Forward projection exceeds 6 metres
Police Notice - 24 hrs   Attendant YES
Width
Maximum width of vehicle and lateral projections 4.3 metres
Width exceeds 2.55 metres
Police Notice - NO   Attendant NO   Max Speed 20MPH
Attendant   No
Width exceeds 3 metres
Police Notice - 24 hrs - required only where speed limit for the road is 40mph or less or where length of journey exceeds 5 miles. Attendant NO - Max Speed 20 MPH
Width 3.5m or more
Police Notice - 24 hrs - required only where speed limit for the road is 40mph or less or where length of journey exceeds 5 miles. Attendant - if over 3.5m. Max Speed 12 mph
Additional Requirements
Visibility and marking of projections requirements - *Schedule 8* - are the same as for Part 2 vehicles - *see earlier.*

Special Types movements
Part 4 Vehicles - Other Special Vehicles requiring Notifications or Attendants

Part 4 Articles 28 - 48 Road Vehicles (Authorisation of Special Types) (General) Order 2003

Part 4 details the requirements which apply to :-

- Articles 28 - 31 Vehicles carrying loads of exceptional width (exceeds 4.3 metres).
- Articles 32 - 35 Local excavation vehicles.
- Articles 36 - 40 Vehicles for tests, trials or non-UK use etc.
- Articles 41 - 44 Track-laying vehicles.
- Articles 45 - 48 Straddle carriers.

Part 5- Miscellaneous Vehicles

Part 5 Articles 50 - 63 Road Vehicles (Authorisation of Special Types) (General) Order 2003

Part 5 details the requirements which apply to :-

- Article 49 Vehicles with moveable platforms.
- Article 50 Pedestrian-controlled road maintenance vehicles.
- Article 51 Motor vehicles used for cutting grass or trimming hedges.
- Article 52 Trailers used for cutting grass or trimming hedges.
- Article 53 Operational military vehicles.
- Article 54 Track-laying vehicles belonging to Royal National Lifeboat Institution.
- Article 55 Highway testing vehicles.
- Article 56 Vehicles propelled by natural gas.
- Article 57 to 62 Longer semi-trailers.

Height Restrictions
Height Notifications

There are no height restrictions stipulated in the construction regulations (apart from a bus) or the STGO however if the load exceeds :-

- 15' - 4.57m (16' - 4.88m in some areas) - the abnormal loads officer in the police area may request notification,
- 16'6" - 10 days notice to national grid area office and regional electricity companies - Electricity Supply Regulations 1988,
- 17'6" - notice to BT.

Bridges below 16'6" (5.03 metres) normally display a bridge height sign but this is not always the case.

Chapter 15 Drivers Hours

Drivers Hours Rules

EU rules retained as UK legislation (UKRet) apply, irrespective of the country of registration of the vehicle, to carriage by road undertaken in the United Kingdom where that carriage is undertaken exclusively within the United Kingdom or the area consisting of the United Kingdom, the European Union and Switzerland[1].

AETR rules - apply, irrespective of the country of registration of the vehicle, to carriage by road undertaken in the United Kingdom where that carriage is part of international road transport operations undertaken in part outside the area consisting of the United Kingdom, the European Union or Switzerland[1]. This includes journeys to, from or which pass through any EEA country which is not also an EU member state - such countries include Iceland, Liechtenstein and Norway.

GB domestic rules - apply to any person who drives vehicles in Great Britain (England, Wales and Scotland) in the course of their employment, or for the purpose of a trade or business carried on by that person (unless EU or *AETR* rules apply to that vehicle or journey within Great Britain - *different rules apply in Northern Ireland*).

*A tachograph is required to be fitted and used in vehicles operating under EU*UKRet *Rules or AETR Rules.*

Temporary Relaxation of EU Drivers Hours

Article 14 EU Regulation 561/2006 UKRet

In urgent cases Member States may grant a temporary exception for a period not exceeding 30 days.

Emergency and Rescue operations

Article 3(d) EU Regulation 561/2006 UKRet

Vehicles used in connection with emergency or rescue operations would be exempt from the EU rules for the duration of the emergency.

This exception may be used by those undertaking retained fire and rescue work, volunteer police work or voluntary emergency or rescue services (e.g. RNLI, mountain rescue) where the situation is deemed to be an emergency.

Drivers who have interrupted a rest period to attend an emergency would be required to commence or complete a qualifying rest period before recommencing work.

 # EU Rules
Scope

Article 2 EU Regulation 561/2006 UKRet

This regulation applies to the carriage by road :-

- of goods where the maximum permissible mass[1] of the vehicle, including any trailer, or semi-trailer, exceeds 3.5 tonnes, or
- from 01/07/2026, of goods in international transport operations or in cabotage operations[2], where the maximum permissible mass of the vehicle, including any trailer, or semi-trailer, exceeds 2.5 tonnes, or
- of passengers by vehicles constructed or permanently adapted for carrying more than nine persons including the driver, and are intended for that purpose.

[1] *Maximum permissible mass means the maximum authorised operating mass of a vehicle when fully laden. It is not necessary for a vehicle or its trailer to be laden.*

[2] *Cabotage is the loading and unloading of goods, for hire or reward, between 2 points in a country by a vehicle that is not registered in that country.*
Cross-trade is the haulage of goods, for hire or reward, between 2 countries by a vehicle registered in a different country.

Transport Undertakings

Article 10 EU Regulation 561/2006 UKRet
Article 11(5) AETR

A transport undertaking shall not give drivers it employs or who are put at its disposal any payment, even in the form of a bonus or wage supplement, related to distances travelled, the speed of delivery and/or the amount of goods carried if that payment is of such a kind as to endanger road safety and/or encourages infringement of this Regulation.

A transport undertaking shall organise the work of drivers referred to in paragraph 1 in such a way that the drivers are able to comply with *Regulation (EU) No 165/2014 and Chapter II of this Regulation*. The transport undertaking shall properly instruct the driver and shall make regular checks to ensure that *Regulation (EU) No 165/2014* and *Chapter II of this Regulation* are complied with.

Undertakings, consignors, freight forwarders, tour operators, principal contractors, subcontractors and driver employment agencies shall ensure that contractually agreed transport time schedules respect this Regulation.

EU Rules
EU Exemptions - National and International Journeys

Article 3 EU Regulation 561/2006 UKRet

This Regulation shall not apply to carriage by road by :-

(a) vehicles used for the carriage of passengers on regular services where the route covered by the service in question does not exceed 50 kilometres,

(aa) vehicles or combinations of vehicles with a maximum permissible mass not exceeding 7.5 tonnes, only within a 100 km radius from the base of the undertaking and on the condition that driving the vehicle does not constitute the driver's main activity and transport is not carried out for hire or reward, used for :-

- ○ carrying materials, equipment or machinery for the driver's use in the course of the driver's work, or

- ○ delivering goods which are produced on a craft basis, (not *AETR*),

(b) vehicles with a maximum authorised speed not exceeding 40 km/h,

(c) vehicles owned or hired without a driver by the armed services, civil defence services, fire services, and forces responsible for maintaining public order when the carriage is undertaken as a consequence of the tasks assigned to these services and is under their control, (n*ot commercial operations contracted by these bodies),*

(d) vehicles used in the non-commercial transport of humanitarian aid or used in emergencies or rescue operations,

(e) specialised vehicles used for medical purposes,

(f) specialised breakdown vehicles operating within 100 km of base,

(g) vehicles undergoing road tests for technical development, repair or maintenance purposes, and new or rebuilt vehicles which have not yet been put into service,

(h) vehicles or combinations of vehicles with a maximum permissible mass not exceeding 7,5 tonnes used for the non-commercial carriage of goods,

(ha) vehicles with a maximum permissible mass, including any trailer, or semi-trailer exceeding 2,5 tonnes but not exceeding 3,5 tonnes that are used for the transport of goods, where the transport is not effected for hire or reward, and where driving does not constitute the main activity of the person driving the vehicle,

(i) commercial vehicles which are used for the non-commercial carriage of passengers or goods and which have a historic status.

Vehicles exempt from the EU legislation may still be subject to British Domestic regulations.

EU Rules
EU Exemptions National journeys only

Community Drivers' Hours and Recording Equipment Regs 2007

- Royal Mail delivery vehicles not exceeding 7.5 tonnes m.a.m, within 100km of base, driving does not constitute the driver's main activity.
- Any vehicle owned or hired without a driver by a public authority to undertake carriage by road otherwise than in competition with private transport undertakings. (eg NHS,Coastguard, Network Rail).
- England and Wales - any vehicle used or hired without a driver by an agricultural, horticultural, forestry, farming or fishery undertaking for carrying goods within 100km of base.
- Any tractor used for agricultural or forestry work within 100km of base.
- Any vehicle which operates exclusively on an island not exceeding 2300km² not linked to mainland GB.
- Any vehicle which is used by an undertaking for the carriage of goods within a 100km of base, propelled by gas or electricity, m.a.m, including any trailer or semi-trailer drawn by it, not exceeding 7500kg.
- Any vehicle being used for driving instruction and examination.
- Any vehicle which is being used in connection with :-
  - sewerage, flood protection, water, gas or electricity maintenance,
  - road maintenance or control,
  - door-to-door household refuse collection or disposal,
  - telegraph or telephone services,
  - radio or television broadcasting, or
  - the detection of radio or television transmitters or receivers.
- Any vehicle with not more than 17 seats, including the driver's seat, used exclusively for the non-commercial carriage of passengers.
- Any specialised vehicle used for circus or funfair equipment.
- Any specially fitted mobile project vehicle the primary purpose of which is use as an educational facility when stationary.
- Any vehicle which used for the collection of milk from farms or for the return to farms of milk containers or animal feed.
- Any vehicle which used to carry animal waste or carcasses which are not intended for human consumption.
- Any vehicle used exclusively on roads inside hub facilities.
- Any vehicle used to carry live animals between farm or slaughterhouse and market, within 100 km.
- Any vehicle which is being used by the Royal National Lifeboat Institution for the purpose of hauling lifeboats.
- Any vehicle which was manufactured before 01/01/1947.
- Any vehicle which is propelled by steam.

Exempted vehicles may still be subject to British Domestic Rules.

EU Rules
Daily and Weekly Driving Time

Article 4 EU Regulation 561/2006 UKRef

'**Driving time**' means the duration of driving activity recorded automatically or semi-automatically by recording equipment or manually.

'**Daily driving time**' means the total accumulated driving time between the end of one daily rest period and the beginning of the following daily rest period or between a daily rest period and a weekly rest period.

'**Weekly driving time**' means the total accumulated driving time during a week.

A '**week**' means the period of time between 00.00 on Monday and 24.00 on Sunday.

'**Other work**' means all activities which are defined as working time *regulation 2 of the Road Transport (Working Time) Regulations 2005* in England and Wales and Scotland, except 'driving', including any work for the same or another employer, within or outside of the transport sector.

Article 6 EU Regulation 561/2006

The **daily driving time** shall not exceed nine hours.

However, the daily driving time may be extended to at most 10 hours not more than twice during the week.

The **weekly driving time** shall not exceed 56 hours and shall not in relation to England and Wales and Scotland, result in the maximum weekly working time laid down in the Road Transport (Working Time) Regulations 2005 being exceeded.

The **total accumulated driving time** during any two consecutive weeks shall not exceed 90 hours.

Daily and weekly driving times shall include all driving time, whether within or outside the United Kingdom.

A driver shall record as other work any time spent doing activities which are defined as working time as well as any time spent driving a vehicle used for commercial operations that do not fall within the scope of this Regulation, and shall record any periods of availability since his last daily or weekly rest period. This record shall be entered either manually on a record sheet or printout or by use of manual input facilities on recording equipment.

Driving off the public road does not normally count as driving time merely other work.

EU Rules
Continuous Driving - Breaks during or after 4 1/2 hours driving

Article 4 EU Regulation 561/2006 UKRet

'**Driving period**' means the accumulated driving time from when a driver commences driving following a rest period or a break until he takes a rest period or a break. The driving period may be continuous or broken.

'**Multi-manning**' means the situation where, during each period of driving between any two consecutive daily rest periods, or between a daily rest period and a weekly rest period, there are at least two drivers in the vehicle to do the driving. For the first hour of multi-manning the presence of another driver or drivers is optional but for the remainder of the period it is compulsory.

Article 7 EU Regulation 561/2006 UKRet

After a driving period of four and a half hours a driver shall take an uninterrupted break of not less than 45 minutes, unless he takes a rest period.

This break may be replaced by a break of at least 15 minutes followed by a break of at least 30 minutes each distributed over the period in such a way as to comply with the provisions of the first paragraph.

A driver engaged in multi-manning may take a break of 45 minutes in a vehicle driven by another driver provided that the driver taking the break is not involved in assisting the driver driving the vehicle.

Extensions

Article 12 EU Regulation 561/2006 UKRet
To enable a vehicle to reach a suitable stopping place

Provided that road safety is not thereby jeopardised and to enable the vehicle to reach a suitable stopping place, the driver may depart from *Articles 6 to 9* to the extent necessary to ensure the safety of persons, of the vehicle or its load.

To reach the operating centre or driver's residence (Not *AETR*)

Provided that road safety is not thereby jeopardised, in exceptional circumstances, the driver may also depart from *Article 6(1) and (2)* and *Article 8(2)* by exceeding the daily and weekly driving time by up to one hour in order to reach the employer's operational centre or the driver's place of residence to take a weekly rest period.

A driver may exceed the daily and weekly driving time by up to two hours, provided that an uninterrupted break of 30 minutes was taken immediately prior to the additional driving.

It is not permitted to interrupt the additional driving with other work unless it is necessary to ensure the safety of persons, the vehicle or its load.

The driver shall indicate the reason for such departures manually on the record sheet of the recording equipment or on a printout from the recording equipment or in the duty roster, at the latest on arrival at the destination or suitable stopping place.

EU Rules
Daily Rest

Article 4 EU Regulation 561/2006 ^{UKRet}

'**Daily rest period**' means the daily period during which a driver may freely dispose of his time and covers a 'regular daily rest period' and a 'reduced daily rest period'.

'**Regular daily rest period**' means any period of rest of at least 11 hours. Alternatively, this regular daily rest period may be taken in two periods, the first of which must be an uninterrupted period of at least 3 hours and the second an uninterrupted period of at least nine hours,

'**Reduced daily rest period**' means any period of rest of at least nine hours but less than 11 hours.

'**Multi-manning**' means the situation where, during each period of driving between any two consecutive daily rest periods, or between a daily rest period and a weekly rest period, there are at least two drivers in the vehicle to do the driving. For the first hour of multi-manning the presence of another driver or drivers is optional but for the remainder of the period it is compulsory.

Article 8 EU Regulation 561/2006 ^{UKRet}

1. A driver shall take daily and weekly rest periods.
2. Within each period of 24 hours after the end of the previous daily rest period or weekly rest period a driver shall have taken a new daily rest period.
   If the portion of the daily rest period which falls within that 24 hour period is at least nine hours but less than 11 hours, then the daily rest period in question shall be regarded as a reduced daily rest period.
3. A daily rest period may be extended to make a regular weekly rest period or a reduced weekly rest period.
4. A driver may have at most three reduced daily rest periods between any two weekly rest periods.
5. By way of derogation from paragraph 2, within 30 hours of the end of a daily or weekly rest period, a driver engaged in multi-manning must have taken a new daily rest period of at least nine hours.

Daily rest periods away from base may be taken in a vehicle, as long as it has suitable sleeping facilities for each driver and the vehicle is stationary.

 # EU Rules
Weekly Rest

Article 4 EU Regulation 561/2006 UKRet

'**Weekly rest period**' means the weekly period during which a driver may freely dispose of his time and covers a 'regular weekly rest period' and a 'reduced weekly rest period'.

'**Regular weekly rest period**' means any period of rest of at least 45 hours,

'**Reduced weekly rest period**' means any period of rest of less than 45 hours, which may, subject to the conditions laid down in Article 8(6), be shortened to a minimum of 24 consecutive hours.

A '**week**' means the period of time between 00.00 on Monday and 24.00 on Sunday.

'**Multi-manning**' means the situation where, during each period of driving between any two consecutive daily rest periods, or between a daily rest period and a weekly rest period, there are at least two drivers in the vehicle to do the driving. For the first hour of multi-manning the presence of another driver or drivers is optional but for the remainder of the period it is compulsory.

Article 8 EU Regulation 561/2006
Amended by The Drivers' Hours and Tachographs (Amendment)
Regulations 2021 (03/03/2021)

1. A driver shall take daily and weekly rest periods.

2. Within each period of 24 hours after the end of the previous daily rest period or weekly rest period a driver shall have taken a new daily rest period.
   If the portion of the daily rest period which falls within that 24 hour period is at least nine hours but less than 11 hours, then the daily rest period in question shall be regarded as a reduced daily rest period.

3. A daily rest period may be extended to make a regular weekly rest period or a reduced weekly rest period.

4. A driver may have at most three reduced daily rest periods between any two weekly rest periods.

5. By way of derogation from paragraph 2, within 30 hours of the end of a daily or weekly rest period, a driver engaged in multi-manning must have taken a new daily rest period of at least nine hours.

6. In any two consecutive weeks a driver shall take at least :-
   (a) two regular weekly rest periods, or
   (b) one regular weekly rest period and one reduced weekly rest period of at least 24 hours.

A weekly rest period shall start no later than at the end of six 24-hour periods from the end of the previous weekly rest period.

EU Rules
Weekly Rest - *continued*

6b. Any reduction in weekly rest period shall be compensated by an equivalent period of rest taken en bloc before the end of the third week following the week in question.

7. Any rest taken as compensation for a reduced weekly rest period shall be attached to another rest period of at least nine hours.

8. The regular weekly rest periods and any weekly rest period of more than 45 hours taken in compensation for previous reduced weekly rest periods shall not be taken in a vehicle. They shall be taken in suitable gender-friendly accommodation with adequate sleeping and sanitary facilities.

Any costs for accommodation outside the vehicle shall be covered by the employer.

8a. Transport undertakings shall organise the work of drivers in such a way that the drivers are able to return to the employer's operational centre where the driver is normally based and where the driver's weekly rest period begins, or to return to the drivers' place of residence, within each period of four consecutive weeks, in order to spend at least one regular weekly rest period or a weekly rest period of more than 45 hours taken in compensation for reduced weekly rest period.

9. A weekly rest period that falls in two weeks may be counted in either week, but not in both.

Any period of extension of driving in order to reach the employer's operational centre or the driver's place of residence to take a weekly rest period shall be compensated by an equivalent period of rest taken en bloc with any rest period, by the end of the third week following the week in question.

Ferries and Trains
Article 9 EU Regulation 561/2006 UKRet

1. By way of derogation from Article 8, where a driver accompanies a vehicle which is transported by ferry or train and takes a regular daily rest period or a reduced weekly rest period, that period may be interrupted not more than twice by other activities not exceeding one hour in total. During that regular daily rest or reduced weekly rest period the driver shall have access to a sleeper cabin, bunk or couchette at their disposal.

With regard to regular weekly rest periods, that derogation shall only apply to ferry or train journeys where :-

    (a) the journey is scheduled for 8 hours or more, and

    (b) the driver has access to a sleeper cabin in the ferry or on the train.

continued over

EU Rules
Weekly Rest - *continued*

2. Any time spent travelling to a location to take charge of a vehicle falling within the scope of this Regulation, or to return from that location, when the vehicle is neither at the driver's home nor at the employer's operational centre where the driver is normally based, shall not be counted as a rest or break unless the driver is on a ferry or train and has access to a sleeper cabin, bunk or couchette.

3. Any time spent by a driver driving a vehicle which falls outside the scope of this Regulation to or from a vehicle which falls within the scope of this Regulation, which is not at the driver's home or at the employer's operational centre where the driver is normally based, shall count as other work.

Under AETR rules it is currently only permitted to interrupt regular daily rest periods not weekly rest periods.

Any time spent travelling to a location to take charge of a vehicle falling within the scope of this Regulation, or to return from that location, when the vehicle is neither at the driver's home nor at the employer's operational centre where the driver is normally based, shall not be counted as a rest or break unless the driver is on a ferry or train and has access to a sleeper cabin, bunk or couchette.

Any time spent by a driver driving a vehicle which falls outside the scope of this Regulation to or from a vehicle which falls within the scope of this Regulation, which is not at the driver's home or at the employer's operational centre where the driver is normally based, shall count as other work.

Concession for members of a volunteer force and instructors in the Cadet Corps (Not *AETR*)
Concessions from the daily and weekly rest requirements apply to professional drivers who are also members of a volunteer reserve force (e.g. the Army Reserve) or are an instructor in the Cadet Corps subject to conditions.

There are no such concessions for those undertaking retained fire and rescue work, volunteer police work or voluntary emergency or rescue services (e.g. RNLI, mountain rescue) unless the situation is deemed to be an emergency.

AETR Rules

Accord Européen relatif au Travail des équipages des véhicules effectuant des transports internationaux par Route

AETR rules apply to the whole journey, (including the UK, EU member states and Switzerland which are transited as part of the journey to or from any other country) to drivers of in scope vehicles on international journeys between the UK and countries outside the EU or Switzerland. This includes journeys to, from or which pass through any EEA country which is not also an EU member state - such countries include Iceland, Liechtenstein and Norway.

The provisions of the *AETR* are now, for the most part, the same as the EU rules on drivers' hours with some exceptions. These differences include :-

- extensions in driving time to reach the operating centre or the driver's place of residence only under EC rules,
- allowances to take two consecutive reduced weekly rest periods only under EC rules,
- interruption of weekly rest period to board or disembark a ferry or train (under *AETR* rules it is currently only permitted to interrupt regular daily rest periods),

Tachographs must be used in all vehicles operating under the AETR except those from non-AETR countries.

AETR signatory countries		
Albania	Kazakstan	Russia
Andorra	Liechtenstein	San Marino
Armenia	Monaco	Serbia
Azerbaijan	Montenegro	Turkey
Belarus	Moldova	Turkmenistan
Bosnia-Herzegovina	North Macedonia	Ukraine
Georgia	Norway	Uzbekistan

GB Domestic Drivers Hours Rules
Application

Part VI Transport Act 1968

British Domestic Rules rules apply to any person who drives a vehicle on public roads in Great Britain in the course of their employment, or for the purpose of a trade or business carried on by that person.

The rules apply to goods vehicles, public service vehicles and other passenger carrying vehicles constructed or adapted to carry more than 12 passengers, unless the EU or AETR Rules apply.

The requirements differ between goods vehicles and passenger vehicles.

Exemptions

- Driving under EU or *AETR* rules.
- All driving is off the public roads.
- Private driving.
- Vehicles used by Armed Forces, Police, Fire Brigade.
- Drivers who do not drive for more than 4 hours a day in any week. (Drivers may drive more than 4 hours for up to 2 days in any week providing all working duties start and finish within a 24 hour period, they have 10 consecutive hours of rest immediately before the first duty and immediately after the last duty, and they must obey the rules on driving times and length of working day.)
- Drivers of goods vehicles not exceeding a maximum permitted gross weight of 3.5 tonnes and dual purpose vehicles (Landrovers etc.) - Light goods vehicles - are exempt from the duty but not the driving limit requirements when used :-
  - by doctors, dentists, nurses, midwives or vets,
  - for any service of inspection, cleaning, maintenance, repair, installation or fitting,
  - by commercial travellers when carrying goods (other than personal effects) only for the purpose of soliciting orders,
  - by the AA, RAC or RSAC,
  - for cinematography or radio and television broadcasting.
- Whilst dealing with emergencies.

The Domestic rules which should be followed will depend on the type of vehicle (Goods or Passenger vehicle) driven most on that day or in that week.

Combined Domestic and EU Rules

- When working under EU Rules the driver must also record driving under Domestic Rules as periods of other work.
- When working under Domestic Rules the driver must count driving under EU Rules as periods of driving.
- The driver and operator can choose to undertake all of the work under the EU Drivers' Hours Regulations.

GB Domestic Drivers Hours
Passenger Vehicles

Section 96 Transport Act 1968

Type	Requirement	Exceptions
Continuous Or Accumulated Duty	5h 30m - driver must take a 30 minute break unless it is the end of the working day. Or, 8h 30m - driver must have accumulated 45 mins rest during the day and then take a 30 minute break (unless it's the end of the working day).	
Daily Driving	10 hours	Except whilst dealing with emergencies

Daily Duty	16 hours	There is no daily duty limit :-
		• if a driver drives for less than 4 hours each day for the whole week, or
		• drivers of dual purpose vehicles which are used solely in connection with the following jobs :-
		  ◦ a doctor, nurse, midwife, dentist or vet,
		  ◦ a maintenance, repair, cleaning, fitting or inspection service,
		  ◦ a commercial traveller,
		  ◦ the AA, RAC, or RSAC,
		  ◦ film, radio, or television broadcasting.

Daily Rest	10hrs To be taken between periods of work (not necessarily within a 24 hour period). Allowance - May be reduced to 8.5 hrs up to three times per week.	
Weekly Rest	24hrs in a 2 week period	Unless a driver only drives for less than 4 hours each day or is otherwise exempt as above.
Driver Records	Record book or tachograph	Exempt whilst exclusively or mainly driving passenger vehicles

GB Domestic Drivers Hours
Goods Hauling and Goods Carrying Vehicles
Section 96 Transport Act 1968
Drivers' Hours (Goods Vehicles) Modification Order 1986 SI 1459/86

Type	Requirement	Exceptions
Daily Driving	10 hours	Except whilst dealing with emergencies
Daily Duty	11 hours	There is no daily duty limit :- • if a driver drives for less than 4 hours each day for the whole week, or • drivers of goods vehicles not exceeding 3.5 tonnes, and dual purpose vehicles either of which are used solely in connection with the following jobs :- - a doctor, nurse, midwife, dentist or vet, - a maintenance, repair, cleaning, fitting or inspection service, - a commercial traveller, - the AA, RAC, or RSAC, - film, radio, or television broadcasting. • on any non-driving working day.
Driver Records	Record book or tachograph	Except whilst driving Goods vehicles :- ○ which are exempt from Operator Licensing (not Crown vehicles over 3500kg), or ○ within 50km of base on a day when the driver drives not more than 4hrs on road

Driver's Hours - Enforcement
Powers to stop
Stopping Officers (DVSA)
Section 99ZG Part VI Transport Act 1968

If a vehicle appears to a stopping officer to be one to which this Part could apply the officer may direct the driver to stop the vehicle for the purpose of enabling an authorised examiner to exercise their powers.

Stopping officers - offences
Section 66C(1) Road Traffic Act 1988 - level 5 fine

A person commits an offence if the person, with intent to deceive, impersonates a stopping officer or makes any statement or does any act calculated falsely to suggest that the person is a stopping officer.

Section 66C(2) Road Traffic Act 1988 - 1 month and/or level 3 fine

A person commits an offence if the person resists or wilfully obstructs a stopping officer who is exercising the powers of a stopping officer.

Driver's Hours - Enforcement - *continued*
Police and Traffic Officers

Section 163 Road Traffic Act 1988 - fixed penalty offence - level 5 fine

A person driving a mechanically propelled vehicle on a road must stop on being required to do so by a constable in uniform or a traffic officer.

In addition to prosecution in the courts a report can be sent to the traffic commissioners, who have the power to take action against the driver.

Powers to Direct

There are no powers to direct a vehicle to another place for the purpose of inspecting or downloading driver records however a vehicle may be directed to another place for other reasons whereupon these powers may be exercised such as for :-

* inspection of the vehicle[1] under *Section 68 Road Traffic Act 1988,*
* where it is believed the recording equipment has been interfered with[1] under *Section 99ZB Transport Act 1968,*

[1]The distance directed cannot exceed 5 miles.

* weighing a vehicle[2] under *Section 78 Road Traffic Act 1988.*

[2] If no offences are subsequently found compensation may be claimed by the operator where the distance directed exceeded 5 miles.

Inspection of Records

Part VI Transport Act 1968

Powers under the *Transport Act 1968* allow an officer to inspect recording equipment and records and download data from a digital tachograph and a driver card.

Prohibition

Where it appears there has been a contravention of *Sections 96 to 98 Transport Act 1968* (EU, *AETR* and Domestic drivers hours rules, tachographs and records) or where there will be a contravention if the vehicle is driven on a road, an authorised person may prohibit the driving on a road of :-

Section 99A Transport Act 1968

* a UK registered vehicle (not MoD or vehicles used for police or fire brigade purposes),

Section 1(2) Road Traffic (Foreign Vehicles) Act 1972

* a foreign goods vehicle or foreign public service vehicle.

Section 90D Road Traffic Offenders Act 1988
A constable or vehicle examiner may prohibit the driving of any vehicle of which a person was in charge at the time of an offence on whom a financial penalty deposit requirement is imposed who does not make an immediate payment of the appropriate amount.

Driver's Hours - Enforcement - *continued*
Immobilisation, Removal and Disposal of Prohibited Vehicles

Schedule 4 Road Safety Act 2006
Road Safety (Immobilisation, Removal and Disposal of Vehicles)
  Regulations 2009

Where the driving of a vehicle has been prohibited under :-

• *section 99A(1) of the Transport Act 1968* (drivers' hours),

• *section 1 of the Road Traffic (Foreign Vehicles) Act 1972* (foreign goods and public service vehicles),

• *section 69 or 70 of the Road Traffic Act 1988* (unfit or overloaded vehicles), or

• *section 90D of the Road Traffic Offenders Act 1988* (failure to make financial penalty deposit payment),

an authorised person, or a person acting under the direction of an authorised person may immobilise, remove and subsequently dispose of the vehicle in accordance with the regulations.

These Regulations do not apply in relation to a vehicle if a current disabled person's badge or current recognised badge is displayed on that vehicle.

Authorised person

Where the driving of the vehicle has been prohibited under :-

• *section 99A(1) Transport Act 1968, section 1(2) of the Road Traffic (Foreign Vehicles) Act 1972 or section 69 Road Traffic Act 1988* :-

  ◦ an examiner appointed by the Secretary of State under *section 66A of the Road Traffic Act 1988*, or

  ◦ a constable authorised by or on behalf of a chief officer of police to act for the purposes of the provision under which the driving of the vehicle has been prohibited.

• *section 1(3) of the Road Traffic (Foreign Vehicles) Act 1972* :-

  ◦ A person authorised to exercise the powers of *section 78 of the Road Traffic Act 1988* with respect to the weighing of motor vehicles and trailers.

• *section 70 of the Road Traffic Act 1988* :-

  ◦ an examiner appointed by the Secretary of State under *section 66A of the Road Traffic Act 1988*,

  ◦ a constable authorised by or on behalf of a chief officer of police to act for the purposes of the provision under which the driving of the vehicle has been prohibited,

  ◦ a person authorised with the consent of the Secretary of State to act by a highway authority other than the Secretary of State, or a local roads authority in Scotland.

• *section 90D of the Road Traffic Offenders Act 1988* :-

  ◦ an examiner appointed by the Secretary of State under *section 66A of the Road Traffic Act 1988*, or a constable.

Offences and Penalties
Failure to comply with EU or AETR Rules

Under EU or AETR rules enforcement action can be taken against operators and drivers for offences detected in Great Britain but committed in another country, provided that the offender has not already been penalised.

Section 96(11A) Transport Act 1968 - level 4 fine - fixed penalty offence

It is an offence for a driver of a motor vehicle, the driver's employer, and any other person to whose orders the driver was subject, to contravene, in the United Kingdom or another contracting country, any requirement of the applicable Community rules (EU or *AETR*) as to periods of driving, duty or distance driven.

Defences
Section 96(11B) Transport Act 1968

A person shall not be liable to be convicted under (11A) above if :-

(a) he proves that the contravention was due to unavoidable delay in the completion of a journey arising out of circumstances which he could not reasonably have foreseen), or

(b) being charged as the offender's employer or a person to whose orders the offender was subject he proves :-

- ○ that the contravention was due to the fact that the driver had for any particular period or periods driven or been on duty otherwise than in the employment of that person, or
- ○ as the case may be, otherwise than in the employment in which he is subject to the orders of that person,

and that the person charged was not, and could not reasonably have become, aware of that fact, or

(c) being charged as the offender's employer or a person to whose orders the offender was subject in respect of a contravention of a provision of EU rules, the person proves :-

- ○ (i) that at the time of the contravention he was complying with requirements of distance-related payments etc and organisation of drivers' work etc, and
- ○ (ii) that he took all reasonable steps to avoid the contravention, or

(d) being charged as the offender's employer or a person to whose orders the offender was subject in respect of a contravention of a provision of the *AETR*, the person proves :-

- ○ (i) that at the time of the contravention the person was complying with the requirements of organisation of drivers' work, distance-related payments etc, and
- ○ (ii) that the person took all reasonable precautions to avoid the contravention.

Driver's Hours - Offences and Penalties - *continued*
Failure to comply with GB Domestic Rules

Section 96(11) Transport Act 1968 - level 4 fine - fixed penalty offence

If any of the requirements of the domestic drivers' hours code, is contravened in the case of any driver :-

(a) that driver, and

(b) any other person (being that driver's employer or a person to whose orders that driver was subject) who caused or permitted the contravention,

shall be liable on summary conviction to a fine not exceeding level 4 on the standard scale.

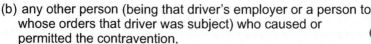
Cause and Permit are not fixed penalty offences.

Defences

A person shall not be liable to be convicted under this subsection if he proved to the court :-

(i) that the contravention was due to unavoidable delay in the completion of a journey arising out of circumstances which he could not reasonably have foreseen, or

(ii) in the case of a person charged under paragraph (b) of this subsection, that the contravention was due to the fact that the driver had for any particular period or periods driven or been on duty otherwise than in the employment of that person or, as the case may be, otherwise than in the employment in which he is subject to the orders of that person, and that the person charged was not, and could not reasonably have become, aware of that fact.

Fixed Penalties

Schedule 3 Road Traffic Offenders Act 1988
Fixed Penalty Order 2000

The scope of the fixed penalty scheme includes most drivers hours offences - EU, *AETR* and Domestic.

Section 54 Road Traffic Offenders Act 1988

Fixed penalties may be issued :-

• where a person is committing or has on that occasion committed a fixed penalty offence, or

• where a person has, within the period of 28 days before the day of that occasion, committed a Community drivers' hours offence except where the constable or vehicle examiner has reason to believe that :-

  ○ a fixed penalty notice has already been given under this section to the person in relation to the offence,

  ○ a conditional offer has already been issued to the person under *section 75 of this Act* in relation to the offence,

  ○ proceedings have already been initiated against the person for the offence, or

Driver's Hours - Offences and Penalties - *continued*

○ any other penalty has already been imposed on, or other proceedings have already been initiated against, the person in respect of the relevant breach (of the applicable Community rules which constitutes the Community drivers' hours offence concerned) in Northern Ireland, an EU member State or a contracting third country.

Community drivers hours offence

A person commits a 'Community drivers hours offence' if the person commits a fixed penalty offence (whether occurring in the United Kingdom, an EU member State, or a contracting third country) under :-

- *section 96(11A) Transport Act 1968* (permitted driving time and periods of duty),
- *section 98(4)(b)Transport Act 1968* (written records - except where recording equipment which has been repaired otherwise than in accordance with the Community Recording Equipment Regulation),
- *section 99C(1) Transport Act 1968* (failure to comply with prohibition), where the prohibition is imposed under *section 99A(1)(b)(ii)*, or
- *section 3(1) Road Traffic (Foreign Vehicles) Act 1972* (enforcement provisions) where the offence arises as a result of a contravention of the applicable Community rules.

Some of these penalties are graduated according to severity of the offence. Penalties relating to commercial vehicles can now also be imposed by vehicle examiners.

Financial Penalty Deposit Scheme

Section 90A Road Traffic Offenders Act 1988
Road Safety (Financial Penalty Deposit) Order 2009
Road Safety (Financial Penalty Deposit) (Appropriate Amount) Order 2009

This scheme allows enforcement officers (police and vehicle examiners) to require an immediate financial deposit from driver who he believes has committed an offence in relation to a motor vehicle on a road or public place and who is unable to provide a satisfactory address in the UK.

The amount of the deposit is listed in the above order and may be graduated according to severity. Failure to pay renders the vehicle liable to immediate prohibition and further powers permit immobilisation, removal and disposal of such vehicles.

Driver's Hours - Working Time Directives
Horizontal Amending Directive (HAD)

Working Time Regulations 1998,
Working Time (Amendment) Regulations 2003,
EC Directive 34/2000

This directive applies to employers of drivers and crew of goods and passenger vehicles which are not subject to EU drivers hours and tachograph regulations - generally drivers of smaller vehicles and other vehicles that are exempt from the EU requirements.
Provisions include :-

• 48 hour average working week (workers may opt-out of this provision),

• four weeks paid annual leave,

• regular health checks for night workers, and

• the need for adequate rest.

Road Transport Directive (RTD)

Road Transport (Working Time) Regulations 2005,
EC Directive 15/2002

This directive applies to employers of drivers and crew of goods and passenger vehicles which are subject to EU drivers hours and tachograph regulations. The requirements of the directive include :-

• 48 hour average working week subject to a 60 hour maximum in a single week,

• maximum 10 hours night work in a 24 hour period - night work includes any work undertaken between 0000 and 0400 for goods vehicles or 0100 and 0500 for passenger vehicles - (this limit can be removed by agreement with the work force),

• breaks - conformity for drivers with EU drivers hours requirements, and for other workers a break after 6 hours of working time of 30 minutes for 6-9 hours work and 45 minutes for over 9 hours. Breaks can be divided into 15 minute slots,

• rest - as EU drivers hours requirements or the *AETR* Agreement - also applies to trainees.

Powers

Schedule 3 Working Time Regulations 1998
Schedule 2 Road Transport (Working Time) Regulations 2005

Inspectors have powers of entry at any reasonable time (or at any time if he considers the situation to be dangerous) to any premises in order to enforce the regulations together with powers of seizure of documents and the issue of improvement and prohibition notices.

Enforcement of the directives will be undertaken by DVSA - penalties range from a fine up to 2 years imprisonment.

Chapter 16 Drivers Records

The Tachograph

Tachographs may be Analogue (pre 01/05/2006 vehicles) or Digital.

The latest units are Smart Digital Tachographs fitted in all EU in scope vehicles since 15/06/2019.

EU requirements

Article 3 EU Regulation 165/2014 UKRet

Tachographs shall be installed and used in vehicles which are used for the carriage of passengers or goods by road and to which Regulation (EU) No 561/2006 UKRet applies - (in scope vehicles)

The exception to this requirement is driving a vehicle collecting sea coal (the driver must still comply with the drivers hours rules).

AETR requirements

Article 10 AETR

A control device conforming to *Council Regulation (EEC) No.3821/85* as regards construction, installation, use and testing shall be considered as conforming to the requirements of this Agreement and the Annex and Appendices thereto.

GB Domestic requirements

Regulation 4 The Drivers' Hours (Goods Vehicles) (Keeping of Records) Regulations 1987

Vehicles operating under GB Domestic Rules are not required to be fitted with tachographs.

The only exception applies to Royal Mail vehicles :-

- which have a maximum permissible mass exceeding 3.5 tonnes but not exceeding 7.5 tonnes,
- which are being used to deliver items as part of a universal (postal) service,
- which are being used within a 100 kilometre radius from the base of the operator, and
- the driving of which does not constitute the driver's main activity.

The driver must use a tachograph but comply with GB Domestic rules on driving, duty and rest periods.

A tachograph may be used in place of manual records.

- If a tachograph is used in circumstances where a record is required to be kept, all rules on the fitment and use of the tachograph must be complied with.
- If a tachograph is fitted to a vehicle subject to the domestic rules but is not used to produce a legally required record, the tachograph should be properly calibrated and sealed but does not have to be recalibrated provided the seals remain intact and the vehicle remains out of scope of the EU rules.

Digital Records

Digital Tachographs retain a full record of activity for at least 12 months within the tachograph unit and will also record details of any faults, interference, errors and over speeding that occur.

Driver cards

Article 27-34 EU Regulation 165/2014[UKRet]
Annex Chapter 3 Article 11,12 AETR

Issued by DVLA to drivers, these cards are valid for 5 years and allow the recording of driving time and rest periods both on the tachograph unit and the card. Up to 28 days data will be recorded on the card.

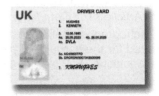

A driver card (or cards if multi-manned), similar in size to a photocard driving licence, inserted into the front of the unit also records data from the tachograph unit.

- Drivers shall use driver cards every day on which they drive, starting from the moment they take over the vehicle. The driver card shall not be withdrawn before the end of the daily working period unless its withdrawal is otherwise authorised or is necessary in order to enter the symbol of the country after having crossed a border. No driver card may be used to cover a period longer than that for which it is intended.
- Drivers shall adequately protect the driver cards, and shall not use damaged driver cards.
- When, as a result of being away from the vehicle, a driver is unable to use the tachograph fitted to the vehicle, the periods of 'other work', 'availability' and breaks, rest, annual leave or sick leave, shall if the vehicle is fitted with a digital tachograph, be entered onto the driver card using the manual entry facility provided for in the tachograph.
- Where there is more than one driver on board a vehicle fitted with a digital tachograph, each driver shall ensure that his driver card is inserted into the correct slot in the tachograph.
- Except where a smart tachograph is installed the driver shall enter in the digital tachograph the symbols of the countries in which the daily working period started and finished.

The driver shall also enter the symbol of the country that the driver enters after crossing a border of a Member State at the beginning of the driver's first stop in that Member State. That first stop shall be made at the nearest possible stopping place at or after the border.

Where the crossing of the border of a Member State takes place on a ferry or train, the driver shall enter the symbol of the country at the port or station of arrival.

Analogue Records

Analogue units produce recordings on a waxed chart placed within the unit by the driver. Three recordings are produced simultaneously by styli within the tachograph head :-

- speed,
- time spent driving, resting or doing other work (Mode),
- distance covered.

Record Sheets

*Article 34 EU Regulation 165/2014*UKRet
Annex Chapter 3 Article 12 AETR

- Drivers shall use record sheets every day on which they drive, starting from the moment they take over the vehicle. The record sheet shall not be withdrawn before the end of the daily working period unless its withdrawal is otherwise authorised.No record sheet may be used to cover a period longer than that for which it is intended.
- Drivers shall adequately protect the record sheets and shall not use dirty or damaged record sheets.
- When, as a result of being away from the vehicle, a driver is unable to use the tachograph fitted to the vehicle, the periods of 'other work', 'availability' and breaks, rest, annual leave or sick leave, shall, if the vehicle is fitted with an analogue tachograph, be entered on the record sheet, either manually, by automatic recording or other means, legibly and without dirtying the record sheet.
- Where there is more than one driver on board the drivers shall amend the record sheets as necessary, so that the relevant information is recorded on the record sheet of the driver who is actually driving.
- Drivers shall ensure that the time recorded on the record sheet corresponds to the official time in the country of registration of the vehicle, and operate the switch mechanisms to record separately and distinctly the different modes of use.
- Each driver shall enter the following information on his record sheet :-
  - on beginning to use the record sheet - his surname and first name,
  - the date and place where use of the record sheet begins and the date and place where such use ends,
  - the registration number of each vehicle used,
  - the start/end odometer readings,
  - the time of any change of vehicle,
  - the symbols of the countries in which the daily working period started and finished (as per digital record requirements).

Manual Records

Drivers of in scope goods vehicles are required to keep records under the GB domestic rules, there is no requirement for drivers of passenger vehicles to keep records. A person driving both passenger and goods vehicles should keep records of hours of duty and driving of goods vehicles.
Records may be kept manually or using a tachograph.

Exemptions
Regulations 12 and 13 The Drivers' Hours (Goods Vehicles) (Keeping of Records) Regulations 1987

- Where a driver during any working day only drives goods vehicles which are exempted from the requirement to have an operator's licence (or in the case of a vehicle in the public service of the Crown, would still be exempt if were it not a Crown vehicle).
- In any working day a driver does not drive a goods vehicle for more than four hours[1] and does not drive any such vehicle outside a radius of 50 kilometres from the operating centre of the vehicle.
- During any working day a driver does not spend all or the greater part of the time when he is driving vehicles to which Part VI of the Act applies in driving goods vehicles, then he and, if he is an employee-driver, his employer shall be exempted for that working day from the specified requirements, however a person who in any working week drives both passenger and goods vehicles should keep records of hours of duty and of driving of goods vehicles.
- Certain Royal Mail vehicles which are fitted with a tachograph and operating within 100km of base.

[1] For the purposes of computing the period of four hours mentioned above no account shall be taken of any time spent :-

- in driving a vehicle elsewhere than on a road if the vehicle is being so driven in the course of operations of agriculture, forestry or quarrying, or
- in the course of carrying out work in the construction, reconstruction, alteration or extension or maintenance of, or of a part of, a building, or of any other fixed works of construction of civil engineering (including works for the construction, improvement or maintenance of a road).

Where the vehicle is being driven on, or on a part of, a road in the course of carrying out of any work for the improvement or maintenance of, or of that part of, that road, it shall be treated as being driven elsewhere than on a road.

Records to be carried and produced by the driver

EU and AETR records

Article 36 EU Regulation 165/2014UKRet
Annex Chapter 3 Article 12(7)(b) AETR

Analogue Tachograph

Where a driver drives a vehicle fitted with an analogue tachograph, he shall be able to produce, whenever a control officer so requests :-

- the record sheets for the current day and those used by the driver in the previous 28 days,
- the driver card, if one is held, and
- any manual records and printouts made during the current day and the previous 28 days as required under this Regulation and Regulation (EC) No 561/2006.

Digital Tachograph

Where the driver drives a vehicle fitted with a digital tachograph, he shall be able to produce, whenever a control officer so requests :-

- his driver card,
- any manual records and printouts made during the current day and the previous 28 days as required under this Regulation and Regulation (EC) No 561/2006,
- the record sheets corresponding to the same period during which he drove a vehicle fitted with an analogue tachograph.

GB Domestic records

Regulation 10 The Drivers' Hours (Goods Vehicles)
(Keeping of Records) Regulations 1987

A driver shall have his current driver's record book (including all unused record sheets) in his possession at all times when he is on duty.

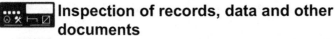 Inspection of records, data and other documents

Officer

Sections 99(8) and 103 Transport Act 1968

An officer means :-

- an examiner appointed under *section 66A of the Road Traffic Act 1988* and any person authorised for the purposes of this Part by a traffic commissioner,
- a police constable, who shall not, if wearing uniform, be required to produce any authority.

GB Domestic Rules

Section 99 Transport Act 1968

An officer may, on production if so required of his authority, require any person to produce, and permit him to inspect and copy :-

- any book or register which that person is required to carry or to be carried on any vehicle of which that person is the driver,
- any book or register which that person is required to preserve,
- if that person is the owner, any other document of that person which the officer may reasonably acquire to inspect,

and that book, register or document shall, if the officer so requires by notice in writing served on that person, be produced at the office of the traffic commissioner specified in the notice within such time (not being less than ten days) from the service of the notice as may be so specified.

Power of Entry

An officer may, on production if so required of his authority :-

- at any time, enter any vehicle to which this Part of this Act applies and inspect that vehicle and any recording equipment installed in it and inspect and copy any record sheet,
- at any time which is reasonable having regard to the circumstances of the case, enter any premises on which he has reason to believe that such a vehicle is kept or that any such record sheets, books, etc, and inspect any such vehicle, and inspect and copy any such record sheet, book, register or document, which he finds there.

Detention of Vehicles

For the purpose of exercising his powers above an officer may detain the vehicle in question during such time as is required for the exercise of that power.

Seizure of Documents

If an officer has reason to believe that an offence has been committed in respect of any record or document inspected by him under this section, he may seize that record or document.

Inspection of records, data and documents

EU or AETR Rules

Section 99ZA Transport Act 1968

An officer may, on production if so required of his authority, require any person to produce, and permit him to inspect, remove, retain and copy :-

- if that person is the owner of a vehicle, any document which the officer may reasonably require to inspect for the purpose of ascertaining whether the provisions of this Part of this Act have been complied with,
- any record sheet or hard copy of electronically stored data which that person is required to retain or to be able to produce,
- any book, register or other document required or which the officer may reasonably require to inspect for the purpose of ascertaining whether the requirements have been complied with,
- to produce and permit him to inspect any driver card which that person is required to be able to produce, and
- to permit the officer to copy the data stored on the driver card (and to remove temporarily the driver card for the purpose of doing so).

Power of entry and Inspection - vehicles

Section 99ZB Transport Act 1968

An officer may, on production if so required of his authority, at any time enter any vehicle to which the EU or *AETR* Rules apply in order to inspect that vehicle and any recording equipment in or on it and may :-

- inspect, remove, retain and copy any record sheet or hard copy of data that he finds there,
- inspect, remove, retain and copy any other document that he finds there for the purpose of ascertaining whether the requirements have been complied with,
- inspect and copy the data on any driver card or digital recording equipment that he finds there and remove and retain the copy,
- inspect any recording equipment that is in or on the vehicle and, if necessary remove it from the vehicle and retain it as evidence if he finds that it has been interfered with,
- inspect the vehicle for the purpose of ascertaining whether there is in or on the vehicle any device which is capable of interfering with the proper operation of any recording equipment in or on the vehicle,
- inspect anything in or on the vehicle which he believes is such a device and remove it from the vehicle and retain it as evidence.

For the purposes of :-

- exercising any of his powers under this section in relation to a vehicle or anything found in or on a vehicle, or
- exercising any of his powers in respect of a document or driver card carried by the driver of a vehicle,

an officer may detain the vehicle during such time as is required for the exercise of that power.

Inspection of records, data and documents
EU or AETR Rules
Direction of Vehicle to another place
Section 99ZB(3) Transport Act 1968

Where any examiner appointed under section 66A of the Road Traffic Act 1988, or any constable enters any vehicle under this section, he may, if he has reason to believe that :-

- any recording equipment in or on the vehicle has been interfered with so as to affect its proper operation, or
- there is in or on the vehicle any device which is capable of interfering with the proper operation of any recording equipment in or on the vehicle,

require the driver or operator of the vehicle to take it to an address specified by the officer or constable for the purposes of enabling an inspection of the recording equipment, the vehicle or any device in or on it to be carried out. *(If more than 5 miles and no evidence of offences under the tachograph regulations found the operator may claim compensation.)*

Power to seize documents
Section 99ZF Transport Act 1968

(1) If an officer has reason to believe an offence under *section 99ZE of this Act* (false records) has been committed in respect of any document inspected by him under *section 99ZA or 99ZB of this Act*, he may seize that document.

Prohibition of Vehicles
Section 99A Transport Act 1968 (UK Registered Vehicles)
Section 1 Road Traffic (Foreign Vehicles) Act 1972 (Foreign Vehicles)

If :-

- the driver of vehicle obstructs an authorised person in the exercise of his powers under the *Transport Act 1968* or the *Road Traffic (Foreign Vehicles) Act 1972* or fails to comply with any requirement made by an authorised person under those Acts in relation to the inspection of records etc. as above, or
- it appears to an authorised person that there has been a contravention of any of the provisions of :-
  - *sections 96 to 98 of this Act* and any orders or regulations under those sections, or
  - the applicable Community rules,

    or that there will be such a contravention if the vehicle is driven on a road, or
- it appears to an authorised person that an offence under *section 99(5), or section 99ZE (false records) of this Act* has been committed in respect of a UK vehicle or its driver,

the authorised person may prohibit the driving of the vehicle on a road either for a specified period or without limitation of time.

Offences

Using vehicle in contravention of requirements relating to installation, use or repair of recording equipment

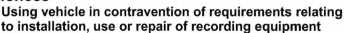

See Act for defences

EU Rules

Section 97(1)Transport Act 1968 - fixed penalty offences - level 5 fine

No person shall use, or cause or permit[1] to be used, a vehicle to which this section applies (in scope vehicles) :-

- unless there is in the vehicle recording equipment which :-
  - ○ has been installed in accordance with the *EU Tachographs Regulation* or the equivalent EU Regulation,
  - ○ complies with the EU Tachographs Regulation (including the relevant technical specifications),
  - ○ is being used as provided by *Articles 27 to 29 and 32 to 37 of that Regulation*, or
- in which there is recording equipment which has been repaired (whether before or after installation) otherwise than in accordance with the *EU Tachographs Regulation* or the equivalent EU Regulation.

[1] *Cause and Permit offences are not fixed penalty offences.*

Employer Offence

Section 97(4C) Transport Act 1968 - fine

Where a person (the driver) in the course of the driver's employment :-

- uses a vehicle in contravention of subsection (1) above, and
- is liable to be convicted under that subsection in respect of that use,

the employer also commits an offence and shall be liable on summary conviction to a fine.

AETR Rules

Section 97ZA(1) Transport Act 1968 - fixed penalty offences - level 5 fine

No person shall use, or cause or permit to be used, a vehicle to which this section applies :-

- unless there is in the vehicle recording equipment which :-
  - ○ has been installed in accordance with the *AETR*,
  - ○ complies with the *AETR* (including the relevant Appendices to the Annex to the *AETR*),
- in which there is recording equipment which has been repaired (whether before or after installation) otherwise than in accordance with the *AETR*.

Offences

 Inspection of records and other documents or obstructing an officer

GB Domestic Rules

Section 99(4) Transport Act 1968 - level 3 fine

It is an offence for any person who :-

- fails to comply with any requirement under *Section 99(1) Transport Act 1968* (requirement to produce, inspect and copy books or registers) of this section, or

- obstructs an officer in the exercise of his powers under *Section 99(2) (Power of Entry) or 99(3) (Detention of vehicle) of this section,*

EU or AETR Rules

Section 99ZD Transport Act 1968 - level 5 fine

A person commits an offence if he :-

- fails without reasonable excuse to comply with any requirement imposed on him by an officer under any of *sections 99ZA to 99ZC of this Act,* (inspection of documents, powers of entry), or

- obstructs an officer in the exercise of his powers under *section 99ZB or 99ZF (powers of entry and seizure) of this Act.*

False Records

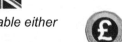

GB Domestic Rules

Section 99(5) Transport Act 1968 - indictable (triable either way) offence - 2 years/ £200 fine

It is an offence for any person who makes, or causes to be made, any entry in a book, register or document kept or carried for the purposes of regulations under *section 98* thereof which he knows to be false or, with intent to deceive, alters or causes to be altered any such record or entry.

EU or AETR Rules

Section 99ZE Transport Act 1968 - maximum fine / 2 years - indictable (triable either way) offence (level 5 fine for permitting)

It is an offence for any person :-

- if he makes, or causes or permits to be made, a relevant record or entry which he knows to be false,

- if, with intent to deceive, he alters, or causes or permits to be altered, a relevant record or entry,

- if he destroys or suppresses, or causes or permits to be destroyed or suppressed, a relevant record or entry, or

- if he fails without reasonable excuse to make a relevant record or entry, or causes or permits such a failure.

Offences

False Records - *continued*

A 'relevant record or entry' is :-

* any record or entry required to be made by or for the purposes of the *EU Tachographs Regulation* or the *AETR* or *section 97 or 97ZA of this Act*, or
* any entry in a book, register or document kept or carried for the purposes of the applicable Community rules.

Forgery, etc of seals on recording equipment

Section 97AA Transport Act 1968 - maximum fine / 2 years - indictable (triable either way) offence

It is an offence for a person who, with intent to deceive, forges, alters or uses any seal on recording equipment installed in, or designed for installation in, a vehicle to which *section 97 or 97ZA (EU or AETR Rules) of this Act applies.*

Recording or causing or permitting to be recorded false data on recording equipment or driver card, etc.

Section 99ZE Transport Act 1968 - maximum fine / 2 years - indictable (triable either way) offence (level 5 fine for permitting)

A person commits an offence :-

* if he records or causes or permits to be recorded any data which he knows to be false on recording equipment or on a driver card,
* if he records or causes or permits to be recorded any data which he knows to be false on any hard copy of data previously stored on recording equipment or on a driver card,
* if, with intent to deceive, he alters, or causes or permits to be altered, any data stored on recording equipment or on a driver card or appearing on any copy of data previously so stored,
* if, with intent to deceive, he produces anything falsely purporting to be a hard copy of data stored on recording equipment or on a driver card,
* if he destroys or suppresses, or causes or permits to be destroyed or suppressed, any data stored in compliance with the requirements of the applicable Community rules on recording equipment or on a driver card, or
* if he fails without reasonable excuse to record any data on recording equipment or on a driver card, or causes or permits such a failure.

Offences
Failure to comply with prohibition - UK vehicles

Section 99C Transport Act 1968 - level 5 fine - fixed penalty offence

It is an offence for any person who :-

- drives a vehicle on a road in contravention of a prohibition imposed under *section 99A(1) of this Act,*
- causes or permits[1] a vehicle to be driven on a road in contravention of such a prohibition, or
- refuses or fails to comply within a reasonable time with a direction given under *section 99A(2) of this Act.*

[1] Cause and Permit offences are not fixed penalty offences.

Exemptions

- Motor vehicles owned by the Secretary of State for Defence and used for naval, military or air force purposes.
- Motor vehicles used for naval, military or air force purposes while being driven by persons for the time being subject to the orders of a member of the armed forces of the Crown.
- Motor vehicles while being used for police or fire brigade purposes.
- Tramcars or trolley vehicles operated under statutory powers.

Failure to comply with prohibition - Foreign Vehicles

Section 3 Road Traffic (Foreign Vehicles) Act 1972 - level 5 fine - fixed penalty offence

It is an offence for any person who :-

- drives a vehicle on a road in contravention of a prohibition imposed under *section 1 of this Act,* or
- causes or permits[1] a vehicle to be driven on a road in contravention of such a prohibition, or
- refuses, neglects or otherwise fails to comply within a reasonable time with a direction given under *subsection (4) of that section.*

[1] Cause and Permit offences are not fixed penalty offences.

Where a constable in uniform has reasonable cause to suspect the driver of a vehicle of having committed an offence above, the constable may detain the vehicle, and for that purpose may give a direction, specifying an appropriate person and directing the vehicle to be removed by that person to such place and subject to such conditions as are specified in the direction, and the prohibition shall not apply to the removal of the vehicle in accordance with that direction.

Chapter 17 Goods Vehicle Operators Licences

Requirement for an Operator's Licence

Section 2 Goods Vehicles (Licensing of Operators) Act 1995

A Goods Vehicle Operator's Licence is required to use a goods vehicle on a road for the carriage or haulage of goods :-

- for hire or reward, or
- for or in connection with any trade or business carried on the operator.

Exceptions

Vehicles used for hire or reward

A goods vehicle or vehicle combination used for hire or reward :-

- with a maximum laden weight (*see over*) not exceeding 2.5 tonnes, or
- with a maximum laden weight (*see over*) not exceeding 3.5 tonnes if it is used only for national transport operations.

Vehicles used in connection with any trade or business carried on by the operator

A goods vehicle or a vehicle combination :-

- if it does not form part of a vehicle combination and :-
  - has a relevant plated weight not exceeding 3.5 tonnes, or
  - if it does not have a relevant plated weight, has an unladen weight not exceeding 1525 kilograms,
- if it forms part of a vehicle combination, other than an articulated combination, and the combination is such that :-
  - in a case where all the vehicles comprised in it have relevant plated weights, the aggregate of the relevant plated weights of those vehicles does not exceed 3.5 tonnes (ignore any trailer having an unladen weight not exceeding 1020 kilograms),or
  - in any other case, the aggregate of the unladen weights of the vehicles comprised in the combination does not exceed 1525 kilograms (ignore any trailer having an unladen weight not exceeding 1020 kilograms),
- if it forms part of an articulated combination which is such that :-
  - in a case where the trailer comprised in the combination has a relevant plated weight, the aggregate of :-
    - the unladen weight of the motor vehicle comprised in the combination, and
    - the relevant plated weight of that trailer,
    does not exceed 3.5 tonnes, or
  - in any other case, the aggregate of the unladen weights of the motor vehicle and the trailer comprised in the combination does not exceed 1525 kilograms.

Local or public authorities functions constitute the carrying on of a business.

Maximum laden weight

Section 58 Goods Vehicles (Licensing of Operators) Act 1995
Schedule 6 Part IV Road Traffic Regulation Act 1984

Maximum laden weight in relation to a vehicle or a combination of vehicles means :-

- in the case of a vehicle, or combination of vehicles, in respect of which a gross weight not to be exceeded in Great Britain is specified in construction and use requirements, that weight,
- in the case of any vehicle, or combination of vehicles, in respect of which no such weight is specified in construction and use requirements, the weight which the vehicle, or combination of vehicles, is designed or adapted not to exceed when in normal use and travelling on a road laden.

A vehicle will not come in scope of the requirement for Operator Licensing if the only reason it does so is because it exceeds the legal requirements relating to its weight.

Transport goods in and out of the UK using vans or car and trailers

A standard international goods vehicle operator licence to transport goods for hire or reward in the EU, Iceland, Liechtenstein, Norway and Switzerland is required when using :-

- vans with a maximum authorised mass (m.a.m.) over 2,500kg (2.5 tonnes) and up to and including 3,500kg (3.5 tonnes),
- vans towing a trailer with a gross train weight (GTW) over 2.5 tonnes and up to and including 3.5 tonnes,
- cars towing a trailer with a GTW over 2.5 tonnes and up to and including 3.5 tonnes,

except :-

- for use only in the UK, or
- transporting goods on a non-commercial basis (not for 'hire or reward').

These vehicles will also have to be fitted with tachographs from 01/7/2026. Operators of such vehicles working wholly within the UK are not affected.

Types of licences

Licences issued by the Traffic Commissioner for the area in which the operating centre is located are :-

- **Restricted** (orange identity disc) - own goods nationally and internationally.
- **Standard National** (blue identity disc) - hire and reward transportation nationally only.
- **Standard International** (green identity disc) - hire and reward transportation nationally and internationally.
- **Interim** or **Temporary** (yellow identity disc).

Categories of Licence

Each Operator's Licence above will be issued in one of two categories :-

- heavy goods vehicle licence[1] that authorises the use of one or more heavy goods vehicles (whether or not it also authorises the use of one or more light goods vehicles, or
- light goods vehicle licence[2] that authorises the use of only one or more light goods vehicles.

[1] 'Heavy goods vehicle' means a goods vehicle, or a vehicle combination including a goods vehicle, that has a maximum laden weight exceeding 3.5 tonnes.

[2] 'Light goods vehicle' means a goods vehicle, or a vehicle combination including a goods vehicle, that has a maximum laden weight not exceeding 3.5 tonnes.

Standard-national and Restricted Licences for Light Goods Vehicles are not required but may be issued.

Restricted licence

Allows operators to carry their own goods on their own account within Great Britain and the EU.

Standard National licence

Allows operators to carry their own goods on their own account, or other people's goods for hire or reward, in Great Britain and to carry their own goods on their own account abroad. This allows an operator to haul loaded trailers to or from ports within Great Britain as long as the towing or hauling vehicle does not actually leave Great Britain.

Standard International licence

Allows operators to carry their own goods and goods for other people for hire or reward, both in Great Britain and on international journeys.

Production of Licence

Regulation 26 Goods Vehicles (Licensing of Operators) Regulations 1995

An examiner, authorised person or a constable may require the licence holder to produce the licence for inspection.

The licence holder may produce the licence at any operating centre covered by the licence or at his head or principal place of business within that traffic area or if the request is from a police constable, at a police station chosen by the licence holder, in any event within 14 days of day of the requirement.

Enforcement Powers

Section 40, 41 Goods Vehicles (Licensing of Operators) Act 1995

An examiner, authorised person or a constable may :-

• at any reasonable time, enter any premises of the holder of or an applicant for a licence and inspect any facilities for maintaining the vehicles,

• seize any operators licence, document, plate or mark used to show authorisation to be used under such a licence which is carried on or by the driver of a vehicle which he has reason to believe has been forged altered or used with intent to deceive.

Examiner - Appointed under Sec 66A RTA 1988.
Authorised person - Authorised by the traffic commissioner for any area.

No Operators Licence

Section 2(5) Goods Vehicles (Licensing of Operators) Act 1995 - level 5 fine - fixed penalty

It is an offence for a person to use a goods vehicle on a road for the carriage of goods :-

• for hire or reward, or

• for or in connection with any trade or business carried on by him,

except under an operator's licence granted under this Act.

Fail to Display Disc

Section 57(9) Goods Vehicles (Licensing of Operators) Act 1995 - level 1 fine

It is an offence for a licence holder to fail to display an operators licence identity disc in a waterproof container in the front nearside of the windscreen, or on a vehicle without a windscreen, front nearside in a conspicuous position.

Fail to Produce Licence

Section 57(9) Goods Vehicles (Licensing of Operators) Act 1995 - level 1 fine

It is an offence for a licence holder to fail to produce an operators licence.

Carrying goods for hire or reward with a Restricted Licence

Section 3(6) Goods Vehicles (Licensing of Operators) Act 1995 - fine £500

It is an offence for a person to use a goods vehicle under a restricted licence for carrying goods for hire or reward.

International Operations with a National Licence

Section 3(7) Goods Vehicles (Licensing of Operators) Act 1995 - fine £500

It is an offence for a person to use a goods vehicle for carrying goods for hire or reward on international transport operations under a standard national licence.

Forgery

Section 38 Goods Vehicles (Licensing of Operators) Act 1995 - maximum fine / 2 years - indictable (triable either way) offence

It is an offence for a person, with intent to deceive, to forge, alter, use, lend, make or possess any operators licence, document, plate, mark identifying a vehicle as being authorised or anything closely resembling such a document.

UK Licence for the Community

Operators who are issued with standard international licences will also receive a UK Licence for the Community. These are required for all hire or reward operations in, or through EU countries and are documents required to be carried on the vehicle at such times.

Registration of road haulage journeys within Europe

Operators of vans or other light goods vehicles, cars towing trailers, and HGVs which transport goods between 2 points in the EU, Iceland, Liechtenstein and Norway for commercial purposes must register the journey via an online EU portal before the journey starts.

This is not an Operator Licence Condition it is an EU requirement and applies to commercial journeys including those where the operator and vehicle is exempt from Operator Licencing.

Detention of Vehicles and Goods

Schedule 1A Goods Vehicles (Licensing of Operators) Act 1995
Goods Vehicles (Enforcement Powers) Regulations 2001

Where an authorised person[1] has reason to believe that a goods vehicle is being, or has been, used on a road in contravention of *section 2* (no operators licence), he may :-

• detain the vehicle and its contents (*Regulation 3*),
• fix an immobilisation device to the vehicle in the place where the vehicle has been detained, an Immobilisation Notice should be fixed to the vehicle (*Regulation 5*), or
• move the vehicle, or require it to be moved, to a more convenient place and fix an immobilisation device (*Regulation 5*),
• remove the vehicle and goods into the custody of a specified person (*Regulation 8*).

Obstruction

Regulation 20 Goods Vehicles (Enforcement Powers) Regulations 2001 - level 3 fine

It is an offence for a person to intentionally obstruct an authorised person[1] in the exercise of his powers under *regulation 3 or 8 above.*

[1]Authorised person - an examiner appointed by the Secretary of State under section 66A of the Road Traffic Act 1988, or a person acting under the direction of such an examiner.

Release of detained vehicles

Regulation 4 Goods Vehicles (Enforcement Powers) Regulations 2001

An authorised person[1] shall release a detained vehicle, or shall direct that a detained vehicle be released if :-

• the operator holds an operators licence (even if the vehicle itself is not authorised, or specified), or
• the vehicle is exempt from operator licence requirements.

Removal of Immobilisation Notice or Device

Regulation 6 Goods Vehicles (Enforcement Powers) Regulations 2001

It is an offence for a person to :-

• remove or interfere with an immobilisation notice, *level 2 fine*, or
• remove or attempt to remove an immobilisation device fixed to a vehicle, *level 3 fine*,

except by or under the direction or authority of an authorised person[1].

False declaration to secure return of vehicle

Regulation 21 Goods Vehicles (Enforcement Powers) Regulations 2001 - level 5 fine / 2 years - indictable (triable either way) offence

It is an offence for a person to make a declaration which he knows to be false, or is in any material respect misleading with a view to securing the return of a vehicle.

Chapter 18 Driving Licences

Photocard Driving Licence
Section 99 Road Traffic Act 1988

- Full driving licences are pink.
- Provisional driving licences are green.
- A counterpart is no longer issued or required.
- The licence requires renewal at the end of the administrative validity period (AVP) for an updated photograph to be entered if required and/ or a renewed medical declaration to be made or medical certificate to be provided.

The **administrative validity period** (AVP) is valid :-

- in the case of group 1 licences (vehicles other than prescribed classes of goods or passenger-carrying vehicles), up to 10 years (3 years for drivers over the age of 70),
- in the case of group 2 (vocational) licences (Categories C, CE, C1, C1E, D, DE, D1 or D1E), up to 5 years (1 year for drivers over the age of 65).

Shorter AVPs may apply on grounds of disability.

The expiry date of the licence (AVP) is shown on the front of the licence in section 4b. An expired AVP does not invalidate the entitlement to drive, there is a separate offence for driving with an expired AVP.

The expiry date of the entitlement to drive each category of vehicle is shown on the back of the licence.

The front of the licence details surname, first names, date and place of birth, driver licence and issue number, administrative validity period (AVP) of the licence and an electronic copy of the holder's photograph and signature as well as the vehicles the holder is entitled to drive.

The back of the licence shows the vehicle categories the holder can drive together with the associated entitlement period (valid from and valid to dates).

Driver entitlements and endorsements are held by DVLA on the Driver Record. Individuals can access their own record on-line using their driving licence number, National Insurance number and the postcode on the driving licence.

Paper Driving Licence

'Old Style' green Paper licences have not been issued since 1998 having been replaced by the photocard licence although they remain valid and generally don't expire until the holders 70th birthday.

Driver Number

The driver number consists of 16 characters plus an issue number and is unique to the holder.

Example

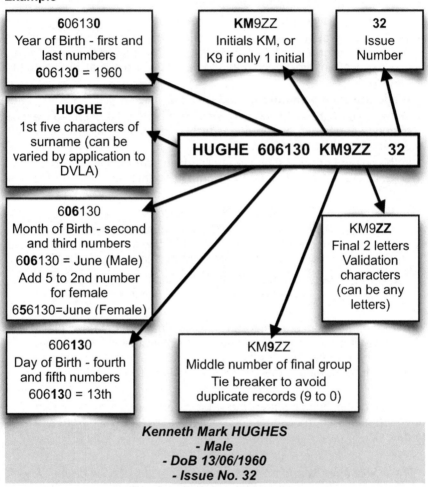

606130	KM9ZZ	32
Year of Birth - first and last numbers	Initials KM, or K9 if only 1 initial	Issue Number
606130 = 1960		

HUGHE
1st five characters of surname (can be varied by application to DVLA)

HUGHE 606130 KM9ZZ   32

606130
Month of Birth - second and third numbers
606130 = June (Male)
Add 5 to 2nd number for female
656130=June (Female)

KM9**ZZ**
Final 2 letters
Validation characters
(can be any letters)

606**13**0
Day of Birth - fourth and fifth numbers
606**13**0 = 13th

KM**9**ZZ
Middle number of final group
Tie breaker to avoid duplicate records (9 to 0)

Kenneth Mark HUGHES
- Male
- DoB 13/06/1960
- Issue No. 32

Medical Requirements

Licences are separated into 2 groups :-

- Group 1 licences - For categories A, B, BE, F, G, H, K, L, and AM
- Group 2 licences - For any other category - C1, C1E, C, CE, D1, D1E, D, DE

A health declaration is required by all applicants for a new licence or renewal of an existing driving licence.

Additionally a medical examination is required for applicants for Group 2 Licences.

All existing licence holders must notify DVLA where they become aware of a new or worsening disability (health condition).

'Disability' includes disease and the persistent misuse of drugs or alcohol, whether or not such misuse amounts to dependency.

Check the DVLA website to see a list of health conditions (disabilities) which need to be declared or notified.

Driving following failure to declare health information when applying for a licence
Section 92(10) Road Traffic Act 1988 - level 4 fine - 3 to 6 points

It is an offence for a person who has been granted a licence based on an application which he knew to be false, to drive a motor vehicle on a road.

Notification of a new or worsening health condition
Section 94(3) Road Traffic Act 1988 - level 3 fine

It is an offence for a person who holds a valid driving licence to fail, without reasonable excuse, to notify the Secretary of State (DVLA) in writing forthwith if he becomes aware :-

- that he is suffering from a previously undisclosed relevant or prospective disability, or
- that a previously disclosed disability has become more acute.

The requirement to notify does not apply if the disability is one from which he has not previously suffered, and he has reasonable grounds for believing that the duration of the disability will not exceed three months.

Driving after failure to notify a health condition
Section 94(3A) Road Traffic Act 1988 - level 3 fine - 3 to 6 points

It is an offence for a person who was required to notify the Secretary of State of a health condition but has failed without reasonable excuse to do so, to drive a motor vehicle on a road.

Medical Requirements *continued*
Disability Assessment Licence
Regulation 3,16(11A) Motor Vehicles (Driving Licences)
Regulations 1999

A driver whose full licence has been revoked on medical grounds may have on-road retraining and an assessment of medical fitness to drive.

A 'disability assessment licence' will be issued which is a provisional licence granted to enable him to drive a motor vehicle for the purposes of preparing for, and taking, a disability assessment test. The licence expires on completion of the test.

Eyesight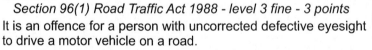
Requirements
Regulation 72 Motor Vehicles (Driving Licences) Regulations 1999 as amended by *Regulation 3 Motor Vehicles (Driving Licences) (Amendment) Regulations 2013*

In good daylight to read, with the aid of corrective lenses if worn, a motor vehicle number plate of the prescribed size[1] at a distance of :-

- 20.0 metres, or
- 12.0 metres - Category K only

[1] Prescribed size - Character height 79 mm, Character width 50 mm (this size is standard on new style plates issued post Sep 2001 fitted on cars and larger vehicles).

DVLA can be notified of failures electronically Monday - Friday 0800-2100 for immediate licence revocation action to be taken.

There are further visual acuity requirements for drivers of Group 2 (vocational) licences. These cannot be assessed roadside.

Offences
Section 96(1) Road Traffic Act 1988 - level 3 fine - 3 points
It is an offence for a person with uncorrected defective eyesight to drive a motor vehicle on a road.

Police Power
A constable having reason to suspect that a person driving a motor vehicle may be guilty of an offence of driving with uncorrected defective eyesight may require him to submit to a test.
Section 96(3) Road Traffic Act 1988 - level 3 fine - 3 points
It is an offence for a person to refuse to submit to such a test.

The test must be carried out in good daylight.

Information / Restriction Codes

Code	Description
01	Eyesight correction
02	Hearing or communication aid
10	Modified transmission
15	Modified clutch
20	Modified braking systems
25	Modified accelerator systems
30	Combined braking and accelerator systems (for licences issued before 28/11/2016)
31	Pedal adaptations and pedal safeguards
32	Combined service brake and accelerator systems
33	Combined service brake, accelerator and steering systems
35	Modified control layouts
40	Modified steering
42	Modified rear-view mirrors
43	Modified driving seats
44	Motorcycle modification (1 to 12)
45	Motorcycle combinations only
46	Tricycles only (licences issued before 29/06/2014)
70	Exchange licence
71	Duplicate licence
78	Automatic Transmission
79 (...)	Misc restriction shown in brackets
96	Allowed to drive a vehicle and trailer where the trailer weighs at least 750kg, and combined weight of the vehicle + trailer is between 3,500kg and 4,250kg
97	Not allowed to drive category C1 vehicles which are required to have a tachograph fitted
101	Not for hire or reward (that is, not to make a profit)
102	Drawbar trailers only
103	Subject to certificate of competence
105	Vehicle not more than 5.5 metres long
106	Restricted to vehicles with automatic transmissions
107	Not more than 8,250 kilograms
108	Subject to minimum age requirements
110	Limited to transporting persons with restricted mobility
111	Limited to 16 passenger seats
113	Limited to 16 passenger seats except for automatics
114	With any special controls required for safe driving
115	Organ donor
118	Start date is for earliest entitlement
119	Weight limit for vehicle does not apply
121	Restricted to conditions specified in the Secretary of State's notice
122	Valid on successful completion: Basic Moped Training Course
125	Tricycles only (for licences issued before 29/06/2014)

Driving Licence Categories
Motorcycles and Mopeds

Schedule 2 Motor Vehicles (Driving Licences) Regulations 1999

Category		Class of Vehicle
AM		**Moped** • Two or three-wheel vehicles with a maximum design speed exceeding 25km/h and not exceeding 45km/h, or **Light Quadricycle*** • Unladen mass not exceeding 350kg* (not including batteries in case of electric vehicles), • maximum design speed exceeding 25km/h (15.5 mph) and not exceeding 45 km/h (28 mph).
q		**Moped** A motor vehicle with fewer than four wheels which, if propelled by an internal combustion engine, has a cylinder capacity not exceeding 50cc and, if not equipped with pedals by means of which the vehicle is capable of being propelled, has a maximum design speed not exceeding 25km/h (15.5mph). Includes e-scooters on trial.
p		**Moped** A motor vehicle with fewer than four wheels with a maximum design speed exceeding 45km/h (28mph) but not exceeding 50km/h (31mph) and which, if propelled by an internal combustion engine, has a cylinder capacity not exceeding 50cc.
A1		**Motorcycles** • A motorcycle with a cylinder capacity not exceeding 125cc, of a power not exceeding 11kW and with a power to weight ratio not exceeding 0.1kW per kg. • A motor tricycle with a power not exceeding 15kW.
A2		A motorcycle of a power not exceeding 35kW, with a power to weight ratio not exceeding 0.2kW per kg and not derived from a vehicle of more than double its power.
A		• A motorcycle of a power exceeding 35kW or with a power to weight ratio exceeding 0.2kW per kg. • A motorcycle of a power not exceeding 35kW with a power to weight ratio not exceeding 0.2kW per kg and derived from a vehicle of more than double its power. • A motor tricycle with a power exceeding 15kW.

*Light Quadricycle L6e unladen mass 425kg differs from above.

See Chapter 2 Page 4.

Driving Licence Categories
Cars and Light Vans

Schedule 2 Motor Vehicles (Driving Licences) Regulations 1999

Category	Class of Vehicle
B	**Cars and Light Vans** • Motor vehicles not exceeding 3,500kg m.a.m., designed and constructed for the carriage of no more than eight passengers in addition to the driver. • As above with a trailer not exceeding 750kg m.a.m. • As above with a trailer exceeding 750kg m.a.m. where the total permissible weight of the combination does not exceed 3,500kg m.a.m.
BE[1]	Combinations of vehicles consisting of a vehicle in category B and a trailer, where the combination does not come within category B, and the m.a.m. of the trailer or semi-trailer does not exceed 3,500kg m.a.m.
BE[2]	Combinations of a motor vehicle and trailer where the tractor vehicle is in category B but the combination does not fall within that category.
B96 (Not issued in UK)	Combinations of a motor vehicle and trailer where :- • the tractor vehicle is in category B, • the maximum authorised mass of the trailer exceeds 750 kilograms, and • the maximum authorised mass of the combination exceeds 3.5 tonnes but does not exceed 4.25 tonnes.
B1	**Four wheeled light vehicles** Motor vehicles with four wheels not exceeding 400kg unladen weight (550kg for vehicles intended for carrying goods).
B1[2]	Motor vehicles having three or four wheels, and an unladen weight not exceeding 550 kilograms (old category).

[1] Category B holders are now automatically entitled to category BE (even if not endorsed on the licence).

[2] Where entitlement existed before (Grandfather rights).

m.a.m. = Maximum authorised mass = g.v.w gross vehicle weight.

Note - notwithstanding the entitlement to drive a motor vehicle and trailer in categories B and BE above other requirements may apply under the Construction regulations (*see Chapter 4*) :-

• In respect of trailers not exceeding 750kg total design axle weight - if the weight of the trailer + load exceeds half the kerbside weight of the drawing vehicle, brakes are required on the trailer.

• If the trailer weighs more than 750kg brakes are required (subject to exceptions).

Driving Licence Categories
Goods Vehicles, Tractors, Rollers and Mowing Machines

Schedule 2 Motor Vehicles (Driving Licences) Regulations 1999

Category	Class of Vehicle
C1	**Medium sized vehicles** • Vehicles exceeding 3,500kg not exceeding 7,500kg m.a.m., designed and constructed for the carriage of no more than eight passengers in addition to the driver. • As above with a trailer not exceeding 750kg m.a.m.
C1E	**Medium sized vehicles and trailers** • As Category C1 above with a trailer exceeding 750kg m.a.m., or • As Category B with a trailer exceeding 3500kg m.a.m. In either case provided that the maximum authorised mass of the combination does not exceed 12,000kg.
C1E (8.25 tonnes)[1]	As Category C1 above but with a Trailer exceeding 750 kg m.a.m. providing the total maximum authorised weight of the combination does not exceed 8250kg. The m.a.m. of the trailer may exceed unladen weight of motor vehicle.
C	**Large goods vehicles** • Vehicles exceeding 3,500kg m.a.m. designed and constructed for the carriage of no more than eight passengers in addition to the driver. • As above with a trailer not exceeding 750kg m.a.m.
CE	**Large goods vehicles with trailers** As Category C above but with a trailer exceeding 750kg m.a.m.
f	**Agricultural Tractors** Agricultural or forestry tractors, including any such vehicle drawing a trailer but excluding any motor vehicle included in category h.
g	**Road Rollers**
h	**Tracked Vehicles**
k	**Ride on mowers and pedestrian controlled vehicles** excluding pedestrian controlled mowers.

Driving Licence Categories
Passenger Vehicles

Schedule 2 Motor Vehicles (Driving Licences) Regulations 1999

Category	Class of Vehicle
D1	**Minibuses** • Motor vehicles designed and constructed for the carriage of not more than 16 passengers not including the driver and with a maximum length not exceeding 8 metres. • As above with a trailer not exceeding 750kg m.a.m.
D1E	**Minibuses with trailers** As Category D1 above but with a trailer exceeding 750kg m.a.m. but not the unladen weight of the tractor vehicle.
D1(not for hire or reward)[1]	• Passenger vehicles with 9 - 16 seats (not including the driver) driven otherwise than for Hire or Reward. • As above with a trailer not exceeding 750kg m.a.m.
D1E (not for hire or reward)[1]	As Category D1 (not for hire or reward) above but with a trailer exceeding 750 kg m.a.m. The maximum authorised mass of the trailer may exceed unladen weight of motor vehicle.
D	**Buses** • Motor vehicles designed and constructed for the carriage of more than eight passengers in addition to the driver. • As above with a trailer not exceeding 750kg m.a.m.
DE	**Buses with trailers** As Category D above but with a trailer exceeding 750kg m.a.m.

[1] Where entitlement existed before 01/01/1997 (grandfather rights).

m.a.m. = Maximum authorised
mass = g.v.w gross vehicle weight.

Minimum Age Requirements
Section 101 Road Traffic Act 1988
Regulation 9 MV (Driving Licences) Regs 1999

Category	Minimum Age
Motorcycles and Mopeds	
AM, Q, P	16 years
A1	17 years (16 years if already holds a full A1 licence - eg visitors)
A2	19 years or 2 years after passing Cat A (not A1) test which was taken before 19/01/2013 or 18 years if already holds a full A2 licence, or17years if **MoD**[1].
A Motorcycle	24 years or 2 years after passing Cat A (not A1) test taken before 19/01/2013, or 21 years in a case where has held a full A2 licence for at least 2 years, 20 years if already holds a full A or A3 licence, 17 years if **MoD**[1], 17 years if passes B or A2 or A3 driving test after 18/01/2013 and was previously entitled to a licence to drive a motor bicycle with an engine having a maximum net power output exceeding 25 kilowatts or a power to weight ratio exceeding 9.16 kilowatts per kilogram.
A Tricycle	24 years, or 21 years if has held a full A2 licence for at least 2 years, 20 years in the case of a person holding an A or A3 licence, 17 years if **MoD**[1], 17 years if the person was, before 19/01/2013, entitled to drive vehicles having 3 or 4 wheels and unladen weight not exceeding 550 kilograms.
Cars and Light Vans	
B, BE	17 years, or 16 yrs - where person in receipt of disability living allowance at the higher rate or personal independence payment which includes the mobility component at the enhanced rate, providing no trailer is drawn.
Invalid Carriages	
B1	16 years
Tractors, Rollers, Mowers etc	
F	17 years, (16 to/from test, or passed test providing wheeled, vehicle + trailer not ex 2.45m width, 2 wheeled or close coupled 4 wheel trailer.)
G	21 years 17 years if not steam, solid wheels, n/e 11.69 tonnes, not load carrying
H	17 years if the m.a.m. n/e 3,500kg or member of armed forces
K	16 years

> [1]**MoD** - Vehicle is being used for naval, military or air force purposes and is owned or operated by the Secretary of State for Defence, or is being driven by a person for the time being subject to the orders of a member of the armed forces of the Crown.

Minimum Age Requirements *continued*
Section 101 Road Traffic Act 1988
Regulation 9 MV (Driving Licences) Regs 1999

Category	Minimum Age
Goods Vehicles	
C1 C1E	21 years 18 years providing the maximum authorised mass of the combination does not exceed 7.5 tonnes, and 17/18 years as Cat C, CE below, 17 years if **MoD**[1].
C CE	21 years 18 yrs learners or full licence holders with driver CPC, NVT Training or acquired rights. 18 years where the vehicle is being used by the fire service or for maintaining public order or is undergoing road tests for repair or maintenance purposes. 18 years an incomplete large vehicle which has a working weight exceeding 3.5 tonnes but not exceeding 7.5 tonnes. 17 years - an incomplete large vehicle which has a working weight not exceeding 3.5 tonnes 17 years if **MoD**[1].
Passenger Vehicles	
D1 D1E	21 years 18 years provisional licence holder providing it is not engaged in the carrying of passengers (other than the supervisor and other trainees in the vehicle) whilst learning or undergoing driver CPC. 18 years full licence + CPC holder if the vehicle is a PSV using a PSV operators licence or a community bus permit. 17 years if **MoD**[1].
D DE	24 years 21 years where the vehicle is being used by the fire service or for maintaining public order or is undergoing road tests for repair or maintenance purposes. 21 years where a person under the age of 24 was entitled to a licence to drive a vehicle of that class before 19/01/2013. 20 years - full licence + CPC holder if the vehicle is a PSV using a PSV operators licence or a community bus permit and not on a regular service or route exceeds 50km. 18 years provisional licence holder providing it is not engaged in the carrying of passengers (other than the supervisor and other trainees in the vehicle) whilst learning or undergoing driver CPC. 18 years full licence + CPC holder if the vehicle is a PSV using a PSV operators licence or a community bus permit and the vehicle is engaged in the carriage of passengers on a regular service over a route not exceeding 50km. 18 years an incomplete large vehicle which has a working weight exceeding 3.5 tonnes but not exceeding 7.5 tonnes. 17 years an incomplete large vehicle which has a working weight not exceeding 3.5 tonnes. 17 years if **MoD**[1].

 **Grandfather Rights**

- Drivers who hold a car driving licence which was valid before 01/01/1997 retain rights to drive :-
  - ◦ small vehicles with large trailers BE,
  - ◦ motor vehicles 3500kg-7500kg m.a.m. with trailers up to a combined weight of 8250kg (7500kg if under 21yrs) C1 E, and
  - ◦ passenger vehicles with 9-16 passenger seats not used for hire or reward D1 and D1E,

  for the period of their licence.

Medical testing is not required. If their licence expires or becomes otherwise invalid they may lose these entitlements and will be required to pass a test to drive the larger vehicles together with a medical examination.

- Holders of a full motorcycle - Category A licence who passed their test before 19/01/2013 retain rights to drive Category B1 vehicles (3 or 4 wheel vehicles not exceeding 550kg unladen) as full licence holders.

- Holders of full car licences Category B who passed their test before 01/02/2001 retain rights to drive a moped in Category P as a full licence holder however since that date newly qualified drivers are required to undertake compulsory basic training before riding such a vehicle.

- Any person who held or was eligible to hold a Group M licence, authorising the driving of trolley vehicles used for the carriage of passengers with more than 16 passenger seats, under old regulations now revoked, may continue to drive vehicles of that class.

- Any person who held or was eligible to hold a Group N licence on 31/12/1996, authorising the driving of vehicles including those in group N - vehicles exempt from vehicle excise duty under old regulations now revoked, may continue to drive vehicles of that class.

- The test for a Category BE licence (car +trailer) was discontinued on 19/01/2023. All Category B licence holders are automatically entitled to drive BE vehicles (up to 3500kg m.a.m trailers subject to construction and use restrictions) from that date notwithstanding it does not appear on their licence. Category BE, will be added to photocard driving licences when they are renewed.

International Driving Permit

There are 3 types of International Driving Permit (IDP) :-

- The 1926 Paris Convention on Road Traffic IDP is recognised in Lichtenstein, Iraq, Somalia Mexico and Brazil.
- The 1949 Geneva Convention on Road Traffic IDP is valid for 12 months and is recognised in Ireland, Spain, Malta and Cyprus.
- The 1968 Vienna Convention on Road Traffic IDP is valid for 3 years, or the driving licence expiry date if earlier, and is recognised in all other EU countries, plus Norway and Switzerland.

An International Driving Permit (IDP) :-

- is a permit for use in conjunction a driving licence, not in place of it,
- makes it lawful for a person who is resident in a contracting country to drive in another contracting country,
- is not required by drivers from EU and EEA countries (although the reverse does not necessarily apply).

International Driving Permits (IDPs) issued in the UK :-

- are issued by the Post Office,
- may be issued to persons who hold a full UK licence who can present that licence at a Post Office. Provisional licences with test pass certificates are no longer accepted,
- are not valid for use in the UK,
- are not required by UK licence holders to drive when visiting the Republic of Ireland,
- may be required by UK licence holders travelling to other EU states as well as non-EU countries - *see UK GOV website*, (some EU countries will accept a full UK photocard licence alone). The correct type of International Driving Permit (IDP) must be obtained before departure and carried whilst driving for both commercial and private purposes.

An International Driving Permit (IDP) issued in the UK is not valid for use in the UK.

An International Driving Permit does not replace a driving licence or permit to drive - it is basically a standard form translation of the holders licence to enable the enforcement authorities to understand the entitlements it contains.

Drivers from abroad (including from EU and EEA countries) do not need an IDP when visiting the UK but one might come in useful for proving legitimacy if their driving licence is not an EU driving licence or otherwise not printed in English.

Provisional Licences
Breach of Provisional Licences Conditions

Section 87(1) Road Traffic Act 1988 - level 3 fine + 3 to 6 points - fixed penalty offence

Breach of the following conditions amounts to an offence of driving otherwise than in accordance with a licence.

Except where the holder has passed the appropriate test the holder of a provisional licence shall comply with the following conditions :-

Supervision
Regulation 16(2)(a) Motor Vehicles (Driving Licences) Regs 1999

• Shall be supervised by a qualified driver[1] (who is present with him in or on the vehicle) except when :-

- o driving a motor vehicle constructed to carry only one person which is not adapted to carry more than one person and is a vehicle in sub-category B1 (invalid carriages), a motor tricycle, a motor vehicle having four wheels and an unladen weight not exceeding 550 kilograms or a motor vehicle of a class included in category F, G, H or K, or

- o riding a moped or motor bicycle with or without a sidecar, a category P vehicle or a category Q vehicle, or

- o driving on an exempted island[3] (except categories C, CE, D, DE), or

- o undergoing a test.

[1] Qualified Driver
Regulation 17 Motor Vehicles (Driving Licences) Regulations 1999

A Qualified Driver means a full British (including Northern Ireland) or Community (EC) licence holder for the category of vehicle who is :-

• is at least 21 years of age (except in the case of the Armed Forces in the course of their duties), AND

• the holder of a full licence for that category of vehicle, AND

• has the relevant driving experience[2] (except in the case of the Armed Forces in the course of their duties).

A disabled supervisor must in addition be able to take control of the steering and braking functions in an emergency.

[2] Relevant driving experience means the qualified driver :-

• has held the relevant licence for a minimum period of 3 years, OR

• has held a full licence of the same category of vehicle being driven by the provisional licence holder for a minimum period of 1 year AND a full licence for a minimum period of 3 years for a corresponding category. Corresponding categories are C - D, C1 - D1, CE - DE, C1E - D1E and visa versa.

Provisional Licences

[1]**Exempted Island** means an island not connected to the mainland of Great Britain by bridge, tunnel, ford or other way suitable for the passage of motor vehicles but excluding Isle of Wight, St. Mary's (Isles of Scilly), Arran, Barra, Bute, Great Cumbrae, Islay, Lewis and Harris, Mainland Orkney, Mainland Shetland, Mull, North Uist, Benbecula and South Uist and Tiree.

Supervision - Motorbicycles exceeding 125cc 11kW
Regulation 16(7) Motor Vehicles (Driving Licences) Regulations 1999

A provisional licence holder shall not drive on the road except under the supervision of a certified direct access instructor on another machine.

Supervision - Mopeds and A1 Motorcycles
Regulation 16(7A) Motor Vehicles (Driving Licences) Regs 1999

A provisional licence holder shall not drive on a road when undergoing relevant training (CBT), unless the instructor is at all times present on another machine supervising only him or him and not more than 3 others.

'L' plates
Regulation 16(2)(b) Motor Vehicles (Driving Licences) Regs 1999

Display 'L' plates (or optionally 'D' plates in Wales) in such a manner as to be clearly visible to other persons using the road from a reasonable distance front and rear.

It is not an offence to display L or D plates when not required.

Trailers
Regulation 16(2)(c) Motor Vehicles (Driving Licences) Regs 1999

Shall not draw a trailer except when driving the following category of vehicle for which he holds a provisional licence :-

• BE, C1E, CE, D1E, DE,

• F - agricultural or forestry tractor. (A 16 yr old is limited to a two wheeled or close coupled (840mm) 4 wheel trailer, wheeled combination not exceeding 2.45m width and can drive on a road only to/from a test until test is passed - then is limited in size/width until 17th birthday).

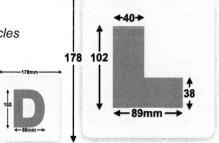

Provisional Licences

Passengers on Mopeds or Motorbicycles with or without sidecars

Regulation 16(6) Motor Vehicles (Driving Licences) Regulations 1999

A provisional licence holder on a moped or motorbicycle with or without a sidecar a category P vehicle, or a category Q vehicle shall not carry any other person on the vehicle (either as pillion or in a sidecar).

This condition does NOT apply to motor tricycles.

Passengers in Passenger-carrying Vehicles Cat D or D1

Regulation 16(8) Motor Vehicles (Driving Licences) Regulations 1999

No passengers may be carried except the qualified driver who is supervising, or any other PCV licence holders on the vehicle who are either instructors or trainees.

Use of a Motorway By Learner Drivers

Section 17(4) Road Traffic Regulation Act 1984 - level 4 fine - fixed penalty offence

Regulation 11 Motorways Traffic (England and Wales) Regulations 1982

The Motorways Traffic (England and Wales) (Amendment) Regulations 2018

No motor vehicle in Category A (motorcycles including A1) or B (cars including B1) is to be driven on a motorway by a provisional licence holder unless the holder has passed a driving test for the vehicle and is eligible to be granted a full licence except (from 04/06/2018) provisional licence holders may drive on a motorway when :-

- driving a category B vehicle the transmission of which may be disengaged, and the brakes operated, independently from the driver by a person sitting in the front passenger seat, and
- under the supervision of an approved driving instructor who is present with him in the vehicle and whose registration is not suspended.

Holders of a provisional licence which was in force before 01/01/1997 may not drive vehicles in Category B+E or C1 (since 01/01/1997 these categories no longer appear on a provisional licence).

Provisional licence holders (who have a full Cat B licence) may drive Cat C, C+E, C1, C1+E, D, D+E, D1, D1+E, B+E vehicles on the motorway - they must comply with provisional licence conditions, L-plates, supervision etc. (the Statutory Instrument introducing this is defective but the intention given is as above).

Vocational Licences

Additional licence entitlements are required to drive large vehicles :-

- Category C and C1 - Motor vehicles over 3500kg which do not fall into Categories D, F, G or H,
- Category D and D1 - Passenger vehicles with over 8 passenger seats,

subject to exemptions listed overleaf.

It is necessary to meet stringent medical requirements to obtain a category C, C1,D or D1 licence. A declaration of meeting the requirements may be made until the age of 45, thereafter a medical certificate must be provided.

Where the licence was issued before 19/01/2013 the licence entitlement lasts until the holders 45th birthday and subsequently every 5 years until the 65th birthday and then annually. If the AVP of the licence expires before the holders 45th birthday the licence must be renewed, a medical declaration of fitness made and the replacement licence will have an AVP of 5 years.

Where the licence was issued on or after 19/01/2013 the licence entitlement and AVP will last 5 years until the holder's 65th birthday and then annually. A declaration of meeting the medical standards must be made at each renewal until the age of 45 whereupon drivers are required to provide a medical examination report.

If a driver applies to DVLA to renew their photocard or their entitlement, they can continue to drive while DVLA is considering their application, providing they have not been told by their doctor or optician that they should not drive.
This temporary extension does not apply when driving abroad.

A driving test is required to obtain a full Cat C, C1, D or D1 licence (which includes entitlement to draw trailers not exceeding 750 kg m.a.m.) - further driving tests are required to draw larger trailers - Cat CE and Cat DE (or C1E and D1E).

Drivers who hold Cat C1, C1E or D1, D1E entitlements prior to 01/01/1997 can continue to drive such vehicles until their licence expires or is revoked without the need to take additional tests or medical examinations although the categories are now known as C1, C1E(8.25 tonnes), D1 (not for hire or reward) and D1E (not for hire or reward).

Professional bus, coach and lorry drivers are additionally required to hold a Driver Certificate of Professional Competence (Driver CPC).

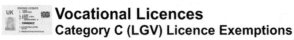 Vocational Licences
Category C (LGV) Licence Exemptions

Regs 7, 50, 51 Motor Vehicles (Driving Licences) Regulations 1999

The drivers of vehicles listed below are exempt from the requirement to hold a Large Vehicle licence but they must hold a **FULL** licence to drive vehicles in category B except as detailed.

- Vehicles in Category F, G, H or C1+E (8.25 tonnes) by holders of that category of licence.
- Vehicles manufactured before 01/01/1960 used unladen.
- Vehicles only used on Public Roads :-
  - in passing between land in the keepers occupation for aggregate distance not exceeding 9.7km/week, or
  - when used for agricultural, horticultural or forestry purposes whilst passing between land occupied by the same person when the journey does not exceed 1.5km on public roads.
- Mobile project vehicle - driver aged 21yrs or over and drive only on behalf of non-commercial body.
- Road Construction vehicle used or kept on road solely for conveyance of BUILT-IN road construction machinery with or without materials.
- Articulated goods vehicle not exceeding 3050 kg unladen.
- Visiting Forces vehicles.
- Engineering plant other than a mobile crane.
- Steam propelled vehicles.
- Works trucks and Industrial tractors.
- Agricultural motor vehicles not in Cat F (tractors).
- Digging machines.
- Haulage of lifeboats and equipment.
- PCV recovery vehicles by Cat D licence holder.
- Breakdown Vehicles - Specially fitted to raise and tow vehicles, used solely for disabled vehicles, unladen weight not exceeding 3050kg.
- Incomplete large vehicle - providing appropriate licence held.
- Exempted Military Vehicles.
- Any vehicle driven by a constable for the purpose of removing or avoiding obstruction to other road users or other members of the public, or for purpose of protecting life or property (including the vehicle and its load), or for other similar purposes.
- Alternatively fuelled vehicles 3,500kg - 4,250kg m.a.m. driven for the purpose of transporting goods, no trailer attached and providing the driver has undertaken a minimum of five hours training by a registered driving instructor on the driving of an alternatively fuelled vehicle with a m.a.m. exceeding 3,500kg.

Vocational Licences
Category D (PCV) Licence Exemptions

Regs 7, 8, 50 Motor Vehicles (Driving Licences) Regulations 1999

The drivers of vehicles listed below are exempt from the requirement to hold a Passenger Carrying Vehicle licence but they must hold a FULL Cat B except as detailed.

- Vehicles manufactured more than 30 years previously and not used for hire/reward or for the carriage of more than 8 passengers.
- Dual Purpose vehicles when used to carry passengers for naval, military or airforce purposes driven by members of armed forces providing licence held appropriate to m.a.m. of vehicle.
- A person who has held a full licence in category C for at least 2 years, may also drive vehicles included in category D which are :-
    - being driven to a place of repair of damage or defect or being road tested following repair,
    - not used for carriage of any person who is not connected with the repair or road testing.
- Any passenger carrying vehicle driven by a constable :-
    - for the purpose of removing or avoiding obstruction to other road users or other members of the public, or
    - for the purpose of protecting life or property (including the passenger carrying vehicle and its passengers), or
    - for other similar purposes.
- Tramcars (additionally if the driver was employed on duties which required the driving of tramcars on a road at any time during the one year period ending immediately before 01/07/1992 no licence at all is required) - *Regulation 8 Tramcars and Trolley Vehicles (Modification of Enactments) Regulations 1992.*
- Cat D1 Vehicles 9-16 seats (minibuses). Holders of a full Cat B (car) licence which was granted before 01/01/1997 will, subject to being at least 21 years old, continue to have entitlement to drive vehicles in Cat D1 and D1+E (not for hire or reward) during the validity of their licence. If the licence needs to be renewed at any time after 01/01/1998 the entitlement will be lost unless a medical examination is passed and application made, the licence will be re-issued for 3 years at a time.
- Permit Vehicles. A full Cat B licence holder over 21yrs who has held licence for at least 2 years and receives no payment other than expenses may drive Cat D1 vehicles on behalf of a non-commercial body for social purposes but not for hire or reward provided the vehicle does not exceed 3.5 tonnes M.a.m. (4.25 tonnes including specialist equipment for disabled) and no trailer is attached.If aged over 70 years then the driver must be able to comply with medical requirements for a D1 licence.

Certificates of Professional Competence (Driver CPC)

Vehicle Drivers (Certificates of Professional Competence) Regulations 2007

Professional bus, coach and lorry drivers are required to hold a Driver Certificate of Professional Competence in addition to their vocational driving licence. Drivers need to complete 35 hours of periodic training every five years to retain their Driver CPC. A driver qualification card (DQC) is issued to drivers who have completed the required training.

CPCs issued in EU countries and Switzerland are recognised in the UK.

Countries that use a Driver DQC card

Bulgaria, Cyprus, Czech Republic, Denmark, Estonia, Finland, France, Hungary, Ireland, Luxembourg (for non-resident drivers only), Norway, Portugal, Romania, Slovakia, Spain, Sweden and Switzerland.

Countries that use code 95 on the driving licence

Austria, Belgium, Finland, Germany, Greece, Iceland, Italy, Latvia, Lithuania, Luxembourg (for resident drivers only), Malta, Netherlands, Norway, Poland and Slovenia.

A new driver who has passed the theory and practical tests can enrol on an approved National Vocational Training (NVT) programme and defer taking the Driver Certificate of Professional Competence (Driver CPC) theory and practical tests for up to 12 months. An NVT concession card will be issued.

Production of Driver Qualification Card

Regulations 11(3) and 11(5) Vehicle Drivers (Certificates of Professional Competence) Regulations 2007 - level 3 fine

It is an offence for a driver to fail to carry their Driver Qualification Card (DQC) or equivalent document issued in an EC state, or driving licence if claiming acquired rights, or an NVT concession card (*Regulation 11(5)*), when driving a vehicle to which these regulations apply.

Regulation 11(7) Vehicle Drivers (Certificates of Professional Competence) Regulations 2007 - level 3 fine

It is an offence for a person to fail to produce that evidence or document when required to do so to a police constable or vehicle examiner.

Exemptions

- Non-EC nationals (unless they are employed or used by an undertaking established in a member State),
- Drivers of vehicles :-
  - limited by regulation to a maximum speed of 45km/h,
  - used by or under the control of the armed forces, a police force, the prison service, a fire and rescue authority, a local authority civil defence vehicle or an NHS ambulance service when the vehicle is being used as a consequence of a task assigned to the authority, force or service specified,
  - undergoing road tests for technical development, repair or maintenance purposes and whilst submitting it for such prearranged tests or when returning from such a test,
  - a new or rebuilt vehicle which has not yet been put into service,
  - being used in a state of emergency or is assigned to a rescue mission including non-commercial transport of humanitarian aid,
  - being used in the course of a driving lesson, a driving test, or additional driving training during work-based learning, for the purpose of enabling that person to obtain a driving licence or a CPC, provided :-

    - it is not also being used for the commercial carriage of goods or passengers, and

    - in the case of additional driving training during work-based learning, the driver is accompanied by a person who is a qualified driver of that vehicle,
  - being used for the non-commercial carriage of passengers or goods,
  - carrying material or equipment, including machinery, to be used by that person in the course of his work, provided that driving that vehicle is not his principal activity,
  - where the vehicle is being driven by a person whose principal work activity is not driving relevant vehicles and :-

    - the vehicle is being driven within a 100 kilometre radius of the driver's base and the driver is the only person being carried on the vehicle and no goods or burden are carried other than equipment, including machinery, that is permanently fixed to the vehicle, or

    - the vehicle is being used by an agricultural, horticultural, forestry, farming or fishery undertaking only for carrying goods in the course of that undertaking's business,
- Drivers undergoing an approved National Vocational Training programme in possession of an NVT concession card (valid for up to 12 months),
- Drivers of permit vehicles (*Sec 19 and 22*) and those driving under a Cat B licence.

Driving without a CPC

Regulation 10 Vehicle Drivers (Certificates of Professional Competence) Regulations 2007 - level 3 fine

It is an offence for a person to drive, or cause or permit another to drive, a vehicle in category C, CE, C1, C1E, D, DE, D1, D1E on a road without a current Driver CPC relating to that category of motor vehicle.

Forgery of Driver Qualification Card

Regulation 13 Vehicle Drivers (Certificates of Professional Competence) Regulations 2007 - 2 years and/or fine - indictable (triable either way) offence - Limitation of proceedings - within 6 month of evidence up to 3 years

It is an offence for a person, with intent to deceive, to :-

• forge, alter or use any driver qualification card or equivalent document,

• lend to, or allow to be used by, any other person such a document, or

• make or have in his possession any document so closely resembling such a document as to be calculated to deceive.

It is an offence for a person to knowingly make a false statement for the purpose of obtaining the issue of a driver qualification card.

Power to Seize

Regulation 14 Vehicle Drivers (Certificates of Professional Competence) Regulations 2007

If a constable or a vehicle examiner has reasonable cause to believe that a document carried in a motor vehicle, or by the driver of the vehicle, is a document in relation to which an offence has been committed under regulation 13, he may seize it.

Production of Driving Licence
Power to require production

Section 164(1) Road Traffic Act 1988

A **constable or a vehicle examiner**[1] may require production for examination the driving licence to drive a motor vehicle of :-

- a person driving a **motor vehicle** on a **road**, or
- a person whom a constable or vehicle examiner has reasonable cause to believe to have **been the driver** of a **motor vehicle** at a time when an **accident** occurred owing to its presence on a **road**, or
- a person whom a constable or vehicle examiner has reasonable cause to believe to **have committed** an **offence** in relation to the use of a **motor vehicle** on a **road**, or
- a person who **supervise**s the holder of a provisional licence granted under Part III of this Act while :-
    ◦ the holder is driving a **motor vehicle** on a **road**, or
    ◦ whom a constable or vehicle examiner has reasonable cause to believe was supervising the holder of such a licence while driving at a time when an **accident** occurred owing to the presence of the vehicle on a **road**, or
    ◦ whom a constable or vehicle examiner has reasonable cause to believe was supervising the holder of such a licence at a time when an **offence** is suspected of having been committed by the said holder in relation to the use of the vehicle on a **road**.

so as to enable the constable or vehicle examiner[1] to ascertain the name and address of the holder of the licence, the date of issue, and the authority by which it was issued, and he shall in prescribed circumstances (*see over*), on being so required by a constable, state his date of birth.

A person authorised by a traffic commissioner may, on production if so required of his authority, exercise in the case of goods vehicles or passenger-carrying vehicles of any prescribed class the above power as is exercisable by a constable. (Section 166 Road Traffic Act 1988)

[1] *Vehicle examiner means an examiner appointed under section 66A of the Road Traffic Act 1988.*

Fail to produce driving licence
Section 164(6) Road Traffic Act 1988 - level 3 fine

It is an offence for a person, when required to do so as above, to fail to produce his or her driving licence to a constable or vehicle examiner unless :-

- he produces a current receipt for the licence issued under *section 56 Road Traffic Offenders Act 1988* (fixed penalty receipt) and if required to do so produces the licence in person immediately on their return at a police station specified on that occasion, or

- within 7 days after that occasion produces such a receipt at the specified police station and then if required to do so produces the licence in person at that police station immediately on its return.

Defence
Section 164(8) Road Traffic Act 1988

In proceedings against any person for an offence of fail to produce a licence it shall be a defence for him to show that :-

- he produced it in person at the police station specified by him at the time they were required within 7 days, or

- he produced it in person there as soon as was reasonably practical, or

- it was not reasonably practical to produce it there before the day on which proceedings were commenced.

Date Of Birth

Section 164(2) Road Traffic Act 1988 Regulation 83(1)
Regulation 83(1) Motor Vehicles (Driving Licences) Regulations 1999

A police constable may require a person to state his date of birth :-

- where that person fails to produce forthwith for examination his licence on being required to do so by a constable under *section 164(1)*, or

- where, on being so required, that person produces a licence which the police constable in question has reason to suspect :-

  ○ was not granted to that person, or

  ○ was granted to that person in error, or

  ○ contains an alteration in the particulars entered on the licence made with intent to deceive, or where the driver number has been altered, removed or defaced, or

- where he suspects that the supervisor, at the time of driving, an accident or an offence relating to the use of the vehicle on a road, is under 21 years of age.

Fail To State Date Of Birth
Section 164(6) Road Traffic Act 1988 - level 3 fine

It is an offence for a person to fail to state his or her date of birth to a constable as required as above.

Proof of Date of Birth
Section 164(9) Road Traffic Act 1988 - level 3 fine

Where a person has stated his date of birth to a constable as required above, he may be served with a notice in writing requiring him to provide :-

- such evidence in that person's possession or obtainable by him as may be specified for the purpose of verifying that date, and
- if his name differs from his name at the time of his birth, with a statement in writing specifying his name at that time.

It is an offence for a person to knowingly fail to comply with such a notice.

Production of Motorcycle Training Certificate
Section 164(4A) Road Traffic Act 1988

Where a constable to whom a provisional licence has been produced by a person driving a **motor bicycle** has reasonable cause to believe that the holder was not driving it as part of the training being provided on a training course for motor cyclists, the constable may require him to produce the prescribed certificate of completion of a training course for motor cyclists.

Fail to produce certificate of completion of a training course
Section 164(6) Road Traffic Act 1988 - level 3 fine

It is an offence for a person, when required to do so as above, to fail to produce his or her certificate of completion of a training course to a constable unless he can show that :-

- he produced it in person at the police station specified by him at the time they were required within 7 days, or
- he produced it in person there as soon as was reasonably practical, or
- it was not reasonably practical to produce it there before the day on which proceedings were commenced.

A full Cat B (car) licence also conveys full Cat P (moped) entitlement however those who passed the Cat B test on or after 01/02/2001 must complete CBT before riding a moped on the road. The certificate does not have to be renewed.

There is no power to require production of CBT from a full licence holder.

There are no provisions for obtaining duplicate CBTs more than 2 years old nor is there a central register.
CBT undertaken in N Ireland is recognised in the rest of the UK.

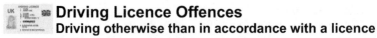 # Driving Licence Offences
Driving otherwise than in accordance with a licence

Includes no licence, breach of licence conditions, under age driving.

Endorsable Offence
Section 87(1) Road Traffic Act 1988 - level 3 fine - 3 to 6 points[1] - fixed penalty offence

It is an offence for a person to drive on a **road** a **motor vehicle** of any class otherwise than in accordance with a licence authorising him to drive a motor vehicle of that class.

[1] Obligatory endorsement in circumstances where the offender's driving would not have been in accordance with any licence that could have been granted to him.

Non-Endorsable Offence
Section 87(1) Road Traffic Act 1988 - level 3 fine - non endorsable[2] - fixed penalty offence

It is an offence for a person to drive on a **road** a **motor vehicle** of any class otherwise than in accordance with a licence authorising him to drive a motor vehicle of that class.

[2] Non-endorsable in circumstances where the offender's driving would have been in accordance with any licence that could have been granted to him (example - where the entitlement period to drive the category of vehicle had expired but where the driver would have been granted one had he applied).

Cause or Permit Offences
Section 87(2) Road Traffic Act 1988 - level 3 fine offence

It is an offence for a person to cause or permit another person to drive on a **road** a **motor vehicle** of any class, otherwise than in accordance with a licence authorising that other person to drive a motor vehicle of that class.

[1] Cause and Permit offences are not fixed penalty offences.

> *Where the administrative validity period (AVP) has expired (the photograph on the licence requires renewing every 10 years) but the entitlement period to drive the category of vehicle has not then use section 99(5) - next page - **NOT** Section 87 above.*

Power of Entry and Seizure
Section 165A Road Traffic Act 1988

See Page 2-19 for powers of entry and seizure where he has required a person under *section 164* to produce his driving licence for examination, the person fails to produce it, and he has reasonable grounds for believing that a **motor vehicle** is or was being driven by the person in contravention of *section 87*(1) (otherwise than in accordance with a licence.

Fail to Surrender Licence

Section 99(5) Road Traffic Act 1988 - level 3 fine

It is an offence for a person without reasonable excuse to fails to comply with a duty to surrender a licence in accordance with *Section 99* :-

- on or before the date of expiry of the administrative validity period (AVP), or
- having been served with a notice in writing revoking the licence and requiring its surrender because it was issued in error or with an error or omission or where the particulars no longer comply, or
- having been served with a notice in writing revoking the licence and requiring its surrender because it appears the licence holder is not lawfully resident in the UK, or
- where the name or address of the licence holder as specified on the licence ceases to be correct.

Driving Whilst Disqualified by a court

Section 103 Road Traffic Act 1988 - Extended Limitation of Proceedings

It is an offence for a person, whilst disqualified from holding or obtaining a licence, to :-

- *section 103(1)(a)* obtain a licence - *level 3 fine,*
- *section 103(1)(b)* - drive a motor vehicle on a road - *level 5 fine / 6 months / 6 points.*

A licence obtained by a person who is disqualified is of no effect or, where the disqualification relates only to vehicles of a particular class, is of no effect in relation to vehicles of that class.

There is no power of entry to arrest associated with this offence.

A driver of a motor vehicle may be disqualified by a court from holding or obtaining a licence for a given period of time, or from driving until the person passes a test for a particular category of vehicle (in which case any breach of provisional licence conditions amounts to a driving whilst disqualified offence *section 103* **NOT** *section 87*).

Drivers disqualified for less than 56 days will retain their licence and it will automatically become valid the day after expiry of the disqualification.

There is mutual recognition of driving disqualifications between Northern Ireland, Great Britain and the Isle of Man. Drivers normally resident in the UK but disqualified in the Republic of Ireland (Eire) may be served a notice and subsequently their disqualification will also apply within the UK.

Causing death - disqualified drivers

Section 3ZC Road Traffic Act 1988 - 10 years and or fine - 3 - 11 points - disqualification - indictable offence

It is an offence for a person to cause the death of another person by driving a **motor vehicle on a road** and, at that time is committing an offence under *section 103(1)(b) Road Traffic Act 1988* (driving while disqualified).

Causing death - unlicensed drivers

Section 3ZB Road Traffic Act 1988 - 2 years - 3 - 11 points - disqualification - indictable (triable either way)

It is an offence for a person to cause the death of another person by driving a **motor vehicle on a road** and, at the time when he is driving, the circumstances are such that he is committing an offence under *section 87(1) Road Traffic Act 1988* (driving otherwise than in accordance with a licence).

Causing serious injury - disqualified drivers

Section 3ZD Road Traffic Act 1988 - 4 years and or fine - 3 - 11 points - disqualification - indictable (triable either way)

It is an offence for a person to cause serious injury to another person by driving a **motor vehicle on a road** and, at that time is committing an offence under *section 103(1)(b) Road Traffic Act 1988* (driving while disqualified).

> Serious injury means, in England and Wales, physical harm which amounts *to* grievous bodily harm for the purposes of the Offences against the Person Act 1861 and
> in Scotland, severe physical injury.

Mobility Scooters and Electrically Propelled Cycles

The offences above do not apply to electrically propelled cycles or to mechanically propelled invalid carriages (mobility scooters) which comply with the prescribed requirements and are being used in accordance with the prescribed conditions as they are not classed as motor vehicles.

Change of Name or Address

Section 99(4) Road Traffic Act 1988

Where the name or address cease to be correct the holder of the licence must forthwith surrender the licence (to DVLA) and provide the correct details.

Section 99(5) Road Traffic Act 1988 - level 3 fine

It is an offence to fail without reasonable excuse to do so.

Duplicate Driving Licences

Section 102 Road Traffic Act 1988

A person is disqualified from obtaining a driving licence if he is already the holder of a licence for that category of vehicle whether it is suspended or not.

Section 103 Road Traffic Act 1988 - level 3 fine

It is an offence for a person, whilst disqualified from holding or obtaining a licence, to obtain a licence.

A replacement for a defaced or lost licence may be obtained however if the original is found it must be returned to DVLA as soon as possible.

Regulation 21B Motor Vehicles (Driving Licences) Regulations 1999

A person must not hold more than one Great Britain, Northern Ireland or EC driving licence.

Disqualification

Sections 34 and 35 Road Traffic Offenders Act 1988

- Obligatory - does not incur points nor count for 'totting-up'.
- Discretionary - can incur points and may count for 'totting-up'.
- Totting-up - for repeated offences - when a person accumulates 12 penalty points or more in any 3 year period. The period taken is from date of offence to date of offence.

Endorsement

Driving related drink/drive endorsements remain on licence for 11 years from date of conviction.

Dangerous driving, offences resulting in disqualification and disqualification until a test is passed, remain on licence for 4 years from date of conviction.

All other endorsements remain on the licence for 4 years from date of offence.

Probationary Periods

P

Road Traffic (New Drivers) Act 1995

If a driver first passes a driving test accumulates 6 or more penalty points on his driving licence within the first 2 years of passing a driving test as a result of offences committed before his test or within that 2 year period, his licence will be revoked by notice in writing and he must re-apply for a provisional licence and retake a driving test if a full licence is wanted.

Only penalty points gained from offences committed within the previous 3 years count. A green P plate is optional.

Drivers who hold a driving licence issued in Northern Ireland *must display 'restricted driver' orange 'R' Plates whilst driving in Northern Ireland for one year after passing their test and comply with certain restrictions during that period. This requirement does not apply elsewhere nor does it apply to drivers who hold licences issued outside Northern Ireland when driving within Northern Ireland.*

Driving Instruction

Regulation of motor car Driving Instructors is carried out by the Driver and Vehicle Standards Agency (DVSA).
Instructors must be registered or have a licence authorising them to give instruction.

Section 123(4) Road Traffic Act 1988 - level 4 fine

It is an offence for :-

- an unregistered or unlicensed person to give **paid instruction**[1] in the driving of a **motor car**[2],
- a person who employs such a person in that capacity.

[1] **Paid instruction** includes payment for money or moneys worth, or free instruction to a provisional licence holder by, or arranged by, a person whose business is the supply of motor cars and in connection with the supply of a motor car in the course of that business.

This requirement does not apply to the giving of instruction by a police instructor (police or civilian) in pursuance of arrangements made by or under the authority of a chief officer of police.

[2] **Motor car** means a motor vehicle, not an invalid carriage or motorcycle, which :-

- is not constructed or adapted to carry not more than 9 passengers including the driver, and
- has a maximum gross weight not exceeding 3.5 tonnes.

Exhibition of certificate of registration or licence

Section 123(6) Road Traffic Act 1988 - level 3 fine

It is an offence to give paid driving instruction in a motor car unless a certificate of registration or a current licence is exhibited on the motor car in the required manner.

Regulation 16 Motor Cars (Driving Instruction) Regulations 1989

The certificate or licence shall be fixed to the front nearside windscreen, and exhibited so that the particulars on the back of the certificate are clearly visible in daylight from outside the motor car and the particulars on the front of the certificate or licence are visible from the front nearside seat of the vehicle.

Chapter 19 Foreign Driving Licences

EU Licences (Community or EEA Licence)

Full EU (or EEA) licence holders can continue to use their licence after becoming resident and can supervise others to drive as for a UK licence holder. An EU licence holder can also apply to be an ADI (approved driving instructor).

Provisional licences issued outside the UK are not valid in the UK.

Non-Residents

Section 99A(1) Road Traffic Act 1988

An EU or EEA licence valid in the member state of issue is valid in this country for a motor vehicle of any class (UK or Foreign registered) including a medium or large goods vehicle or passenger carrying vehicle which his permit or licence authorises him to drive without time limitation UNLESS the licence was issued in an EU or EEA country in exchange for a non-EEA licence in which case it is valid for driving in Great Britain for 12 months only.

GB Residents

Those who take up residence in Great Britain may continue to use their ordinary EU or EEA licence (except vocational entitlements) until expiry at 70 years of age. (If a person is 67 or over when they become resident they can drive for 3 years from that time). This now includes returning drivers who are holders of EEA licences obtained by exchanging a UK licence which was issued on or after 01/01/2021 for such a licence.

An EU licence issued in an EU or EEA country in exchange for a non-EEA licence is valid for driving in GB for 12 months only unless it was exchanged for a UK licence post brexit (returning drivers).

If a holder wants to drive other classes of vehicle as a provisional licence holder they can apply to DVLA for the same provisional entitlements as a UK licence holder.

Those who take up residence in Great Britain may continue to use their vocational EU licence until :-

- if they are younger than 45, until their 45th birthday or until they have lived in Great Britain for five years, whichever is longer.
- if they are over 45 years but under 65 years, until they are 66 or have lived in Great Britain for five years, whichever is sooner,
- if they are aged 65 or over, until they have lived in Great Britain for 12 months.

A UK driving licence must be obtained to continue driving vehicles with a vocational licence in Great Britain after these periods.

The holder of an EU/EEA vocational licence **MUST** register their details with the DVLA within 12 months of coming to live in Great Britain.

Holders of EU/EEA ordinary licences do not have to register, but can do so if they wish.

EU Countries

Austria	France	Malta
Belgium	Germany	Netherlands
Bulgaria	Greece	Poland
Croatia	Hungary	Portugal
Cyprus	Ireland	Romania
Czech Republic	Italy	Slovakia
Denmark	Latvia	Slovenia
Estonia	Lithuania	Spain
Finland	Luxembourg	Sweden

EEA Countries

Iceland, Liechtenstein, Norway

If an EU or EAA licence is held by a UK resident their driver records can be endorsed by British courts. Holders are subject to the same medical and, for vocational licences, conduct requirements, as a UK licence holder.

Other (Non-EU or Non-EEA) Licences

Article 2 Motor Vehicles (International Circulation) Order 1975
Regulation 80 Motor Vehicles (Driving Licences) Regulations 1999

A **full** and valid permit or licence of a non-EC or non-EEA foreign country is valid for :-

- Residents of The Isle of Man, Jersey and Guernsey to drive any class of vehicle including UK registered goods or passenger vehicles which their licence permits.
- Other Visitors - for 12 months from last entry to this country as a visitor to drive :-
    - any vehicle **brought temporarily into Great Britain** which the permit or licence authorises him to drive., or
    - any UK registered vehicle which his permit or licence authorises him to drive **except** UK registered goods vehicles which exceed 3.5 tonnes or passenger vehicles which exceed 9 passenger seats.
- GB Residents - for 12 months* from becoming resident to drive any UK registered vehicle which the permit or licence authorises him to drive **except** goods vehicles which exceed 3.5 tonnes or passenger vehicles which exceed 9 passenger seats.

*The 12 month period starts from the time a person first takes up residence. Just because a person may return to their home country on occasions does not reset the clock.

Other (Non-EU or Non-EEA) Licences - *Continued*

> *Visiting forces personnel may use expired licences and may use their permit without limit of time.*

A person who becomes resident may, after 6 months residence, :-
- apply for a British provisional licence, or
- if eligible (*see later*) - apply for an exchange licence,

but may continue to use his **full** foreign licence for the first 12 months.

Ukrainian Licences

Regulation 80A Motor Vehicles (Driving Licences) Regulations 1999

Holders of a valid Ukraine driving licence may continue to drive in Great Britain for 3 years after becoming resident if they :-
- have a Ukraine Family Scheme visa, Ukraine Sponsorship Scheme visa or Ukraine Extension Scheme visa,
- came to the UK on a Ukraine visa scheme and then switched to a different type of visa.

Minimum Age Requirements

Article 2(4) Motor Vehicles (International Circulation) Order 1975

The minimum age requirements in the UK apply to drivers of all vehicles except drivers of :-
- large goods vehicles operating under EU or *AETR* regulations, (if driven by a person not resident in an EU or EEA State, the Isle of Man, Jersey or Guernsey, the vehicle must be brought temporarily into Great Britain),
- all other classes of vehicle with a minimum 21 year age requirement registered in a foreign Convention (non-EU or *AETR*) country,

when the minimum age requirement of 21 may be reduced to 18 years providing the holder is a non-resident and holds a suitable certificate of competence.

UK residents driving foreign registered vehicles

> *UK residents of any nationality are not entitled to drive foreign registered vehicles in the UK with some exceptions.*
> *See Chapter 11 Page 1.*

Exchange Licences
Isle of Man, Jersey and Guernsey

Holders of licences issued on or after 01/04/1991 from The Isle of Man, Jersey and Guernsey may exchange their ordinary and vocational licence within 12 months of becoming resident in the UK.

Designated Countries

Section 108(2)(b) Road Traffic Act 1988
Driving Licences (Exchangeable Licences) Orders 1984 to 2021

If a full valid licence or permit from a designated country is held, it may be exchanged for an equivalent Full British licence in Categories A, AM, A1, A2, A3, B, BE, F, K, P or Q within 5 years of becoming resident (the original licence or permit is still only valid to drive within the first year).

Vocational licences are not exchangeable except where indicated.

Andorra	Gibraltar G	South Africa
Australia	Hong Kong	Switzerland S
Barbados	Japan	Taiwan T
British Virgin Islands	Korea K	Ukraine U
Canada	Monaco	United Arab Emirates UAE
Cayman Islands C	New Zealand	Zimbabwe
Falkland Islands F	North Macedonia M	
Faroe Islands	Singapore	

C Cayman Islands - A1, AM, B, BE, B1, F, K and P,
F Faroe Islands (not motorcycles),
G Gibraltar - Vocational licences,
K Republic of Korea (not motorcycles),
M Republic of North Macedonia - B, B1, BE, F, K and P,
S Switzerland - Vocational licences,
T Taiwan - B, B1, BE, F, K and P,
U Ukraine - B, B1, BE, F, K and P,
UAE United Arab Emirates - A1, AM, B, B1, BE, F, K and P.

EU and EAA Licences

EU and EAA Licence holders who take up residence in Great Britain may continue to use their licence during its period of validity in Great Britain after which time it MUST be exchanged for a GB licence in order to keep driving. An EU licence issued in another EU or EEA country in exchange for a non-EEA licence from :-

• a designated country is valid for driving in GB for 12 months only and is acceptable for exchange purposes,
• a non-designated country is valid for driving in GB for 12 months only and is not valid for exchange purposes.

International Driving Permits are not exchangeable.

Chapter 20 Vehicle Registration and Licensing

Registration of Mechanically Propelled Vehicles

Section 21 Vehicle Excise and Registration Act 1994

Mechanically propelled vehicles used on a public road within the UK must be registered, subject to certain exceptions which include military vehicles, visiting forces vehicles, temporary imported vehicles used by non-residents, electrically assisted pedal cycles, pedestrian controlled vehicles and class 2 invalid carriages.

A vehicle will be registered and allocated a vehicle registration number at the same time as the first vehicle licence is issued.

Vehicles used exclusively off-road may be registered voluntarily to aid recovery in case of theft - such vehicles registered for off road use will be allocated a Q or QNI prefix registration number.

Unregistered or Incorrectly Registered Vehicles

Section 43C Vehicle Excise and Registration Act 1994 - level 3 fine - fixed penalty offence

It is an offence for a person to use a vehicle on which vehicle excise duty is chargeable (or which is exempt but requires a nil licence) on a public road or in a public place if the name and address of the keeper are not recorded in the register, or any of the particulars recorded in the register are incorrect.

It is a defence for a person to show :-

- that there was no reasonable opportunity to furnish the name and address of the keeper of the vehicle, or
- that there was no reasonable opportunity to correct the particulars, or
- that he had reasonable grounds for believing, or it was reasonable to expect, that the details were correctly recorded in the register, or that any exception prescribed in regulations is met.

Public Road

Section 62(1) Vehicle Excise and Registration Act 1994

A Public Road means :-

- in England and Wales and Northern Ireland, means a road which is repairable at the public expense, and
- in Scotland, has the same meaning as in the *Roads (Scotland) Act 1984*, (a road which a roads authority have a duty to maintain).

Keeper Obligations

Regulations 12 - 23 Road Vehicles (Registration and Licensing) Regulations 2002

The keeper of a vehicle must :-

- produce the registration document for inspection if he is at any reasonable time required to do so by a police officer or a person acting on behalf of the Secretary of State, *Regulation 12 - level 2 fine*
- where he believes that the particulars in the registration document are, or have become, inaccurate, he shall forthwith notify DVLA of the inaccuracy. *Regulation 14 - level 2 fine*

Keeper in relation to a vehicle means the person by whom that vehicle is kept.

The registered keeper of a vehicle must :-

- where a registration document has been, or may have been, lost, stolen, destroyed or damaged, or it contains any particulars that have become illegible, he shall apply to DVLA for the issue of a replacement document, *Regulation 13 - level 2 fine*
- where any alteration is made to a vehicle so as to make any of the particulars set out in the registration document incorrect, he shall notify the alteration to DVLA, *Regulation 16 - level 3 fine*
- when the vehicle is destroyed or sent permanently out of Great Britain he shall immediately notify DVLA of that fact and shall at the same time surrender the registration document, *Regulation 17- level 3 fine*
- if he changes address he shall forthwith notify DVLA and return the registration document, *Regulation 18 - level 3 fine*
- where there is a change of keeper, give the new keeper part 10 of the V5C (the V5C/2), complete and return the rest to DVLA, or where the new keeper is a motor trader, complete part 9 and send to DVLA, give the trader the remainder of the V5C - the motor trader does not have to register the vehicle in his name for 3 months providing it is not used on a road other than under a trade licence or kept on the road at any time. *Regulations 22 and 23 - level 3 fine*

Registered keeper in relation to a vehicle means the person for the time being shown in the register as the keeper of that vehicle.

Offence

Section 59(1) Vehicle Excise and Registration Act 1994 - level 2 or 3 fine

It is an offence for a person to contravene or fail to comply with a requirement of the *Road Vehicles (Registration And Licensing) Regulations 2002.*

Production of Registration Document by User

Section 28A Vehicle Excise and Registration Act 1994 - level 2 fine

It is an offence for a person using a vehicle in respect of which a registration document has been issued to fail to produce the document for inspection on being so required by a constable, or an authorised person, unless :-

- the person produces it, in person, at a police station specified by him at the time of the request, within 7 days after the date of the request or as soon as is reasonably practicable, or
- where the vehicle is subject to a lease or hire agreement and the vehicle is not registered or required to be registered in the name of the lessee or hirer providing the person produces appropriate evidence of the agreement to the constable or authorised person at the time of the request or, in person, at a police station specified by him at the time within 7 days after the date of the request, or as soon as is reasonably practicable, and the person has reasonable grounds for believing, or it is reasonable for him to expect, that the person from whom the vehicle has been leased or hired is able to produce the registration document, or
- where any exception prescribed in regulations is met.

An authorised person must, if so requested, produce evidence of his authority to exercise the power - when required to produce to an authorised person, a vehicle testing station may be specified instead of a police station.

Forgery / Fraudulent Use or Alteration of a Registration Document

Section 44(1) Vehicle Excise and Registration Act 1994 - maximum fine / 2 years - indictable (triable either way)

It is an offence for a person to :-

- forge, or
- fraudulently alter, or
- fraudulently use, or
- fraudulently lend, or
- fraudulently allow to be used by any person,

a registration document.

Trailer Registration Document or Certificate (VTRC)
Haulage Permits and Trailer Registration Act 2018
Trailer Registration Regulations 2018

This Act makes provision to support UK hauliers to continue to operate internationally post Brexit. *The Vienna Convention on Road Traffic 1968* has been ratified by the UK Government and came into force in March 2019

Registration is required for :-

- Commercial trailers weighing over 750kg, and
- Non-commercial trailers weighing over 3,500kg,

travelling to or through countries which have ratified the 1968 Convention which are :-

> **UK trailer registration certificate**

Albania	France	Netherlands
Andorra	Georgia	Norway
Armenia	Germany	Poland
Austria	Greece	Portugal
Azerbaijan	Hungary	Romania
Belarus	Italy	Russia
Belgium	Kazakhstan	San Marino
Bosnia and Herzegovina	Latvia	Serbia
Bulgaria	Lithuania	Slovakia
Croatia	Luxembourg	Slovenia
Czech Republic	Macedonia	Sweden
Denmark	Moldova	Switzerland
Estonia	Monaco	Ukraine
Finland	Montenegro	

Additionally abnormal load trailers used abroad are required to have a keeper's certificate.

Smaller, common non-commercial trailers, such as caravans and horse trailers, may be registered by their keepers if they wish.

Trailers that are only used in the UK or for journeys between the UK and Ireland do not need to be registered.

Regulation 19(f) Trailer Registration Regulations 2018 - level 3 fine

It is an offence for a person to fail to produce the registration document for a trailer for inspection if required to do so by :-

- an examiner appointed under *section 66A of the Road Traffic Act 1988*, or an examiner appointed under *Article 74 of the Road Traffic (Northern Ireland) Order 1995*, or
- an officer appointed under *section 66B of the Road Traffic Act 1988*,

carrying out any function under any enactment in relation to the same trailer or the motor vehicle that is drawing it.

See also Chapter 21 Page 9.

Requirement to be licensed

Section 1 Vehicle Excise and Registration Act 1994

A Vehicle Licence is required on every mechanically propelled vehicle[1] :-

- which is registered under the Act, or
- which is not registered but is used, or kept, on a public road (a road repairable at public expense).

[1] ***Mechanically propelled vehicle*** *includes any thing (whether or not it is a vehicle) that once was a mechanically propelled vehicle.*

Licences are not transferable, the keeper of a vehicle is required to purchase a new licence for a vehicle when it is acquired and then renew every 6 months or annually.

A refund on the existing period of validity of a licence may be claimed by a person who disposes of a vehicle.

Using or Keeping an Unlicensed Vehicle

Section 29 Vehicle Excise and Registration Act 1994 - level 3 fine or 5 x the vehicle excise duty (VED)

It is an offence for a person to use or keep a mechanically propelled vehicle[1] :-

- which is registered but unlicensed (where no vehicle licence or trade licence is in force for or in respect of the vehicle), or
- which is not registered but is used, or kept, on a public road in the United Kingdom.

except :-

- an exempt vehicle :-
  - ○ which has a nil licence in force in respect of the vehicle, or
  - ○ that does not require require a nil licence to be in force.
- a vehicle which is being neither used nor kept on a public road, and a SORN declaration has been made and the terms of the declaration have at no time been breached, or
- a vehicle kept by a motor trader or vehicle tester at business premises.

Vehicles becoming chargeable to duty at higher rate

Section 15 Vehicle Excise and Registration Act 1994
Section 37 Vehicle Excise and Registration Act 1994 - level 3 fine or 5 x VED

It is an offence for a person to use or keep a mechanically propelled vehicle which is used, or altered, that a higher rate of duty is due than has been paid.

Exempt Vehicles

Section 5, Schedule 2 Vehicle Excise and Registration Act 1994

- Historic vehicles - not goods or passenger vehicles in commercial use.
- Trams - vehicles used on tram lines.
- Electrically assisted pedal cycles which comply with the regulations,.
- Vehicles not for carriage.
- Police,Fire, Ambulances and health service vehicles.
- Mine rescue vehicles.
- Lifeboat haulage vehicles.
- Road rollers.
- Invalid carriages not exceeding 508kg unladen.
- Vehicles for disabled people - vehicles used by or for disabled persons.
- Vehicles used only for agricultural, horticultural or forestry purposes and only used on public roads when passing between land occupied by the same person on journeys not exceeding 1.5km on public roads.
- Agricultural and Off-road tractors, Light agricultural vehicles.
- Agricultural engines.
- Mowing machines.
- Steam powered vehicles.
- Electrically propelled vehicles - except light passenger vehicles registered on or after 01/04/2017 whose price exceeds £40,000.
- Snow ploughs and Gritters.
- Vehicles used in relation to an MoT, Goods Vehicle Test, vehicle identity check, or a vehicle weight test :-
  - when submitting the vehicle for a test by previous arrangement for a specified time on a specified date, or
  - bringing it away from any such test or check, or
  - when it is being used by an authorised person in the course of such a test (including warming the engine up), or
  - following failure of a test, delivering it (by previous arrangement for a specified time on a specified date) at a place where relevant work is to be done on it, or
  - bringing it away from a place where relevant work has been done.
- Vehicles for export.
- Vehicles imported and used by members of visiting forces and their dependants.
- Light passenger vehicles with low CO2 emissions- conditions apply.
- Foreign registered vehicles temporarily imported by a person who is not a UK resident.
- Crown Vehicles and Diplomatic or Consular vehicles - D or X plates.

A Nil licence may be issued in some cases.

Statutory Off-Road Notification - SORN

Section 22(1D) Vehicle Excise and Registration Act 1994
Road Vehicles (Statutory Off-Road Notification) Regulations
1997

A system of continuous licencing is now in effect regardless of use or periods off the roads unless a SORN declaration has been made (form V11 or V85/1).

Section 59(1) Vehicle Excise and Registration Act 1994 - level 2 fine

A person who :-

- surrenders a vehicle licence, or a nil licence for a vehicle registered and kept in Great Britain, or
- does not renew a vehicle licence, or a nil licence for such a vehicle kept by him, or
- keeps such a vehicle while unlicensed,

must make a declaration in writing that the vehicle will not be used or kept on a public road.

> *Once a statutory off-road notification is made it will have effect indefinitely or until such time as a vehicle licence or nil licence is taken out for that vehicle or the vehicle keeper is changed. If the new vehicle keeper wishes to keep the vehicle unlicensed, the new vehicle keeper will have to make a new statutory off-road notification.*

Failing to Renew Licence

Section 31A Vehicle Excise and Registration Act 1994 - level 3 fine or 5 x VED if still unlicensed at start of proceedings

The registered keeper of a vehicle is guilty of an offence if the vehicle is unlicensed unless :-

- he is no longer the keeper and has notified change of ownership as required, or
- he is the keeper but the vehicle is neither kept nor used on a public road, and he has made a SORN declaration to that effect, or
- the vehicle has been stolen and not recovered, and it was reported stolen as required by regulations, or
- he renews the licence within one month.

This section does not apply to :-

- exempt vehicles which require a NIL Licence where a NIL licence is in force, and
- exempt vehicles which do not require a NIL licence, and
- vehicles used under a Trade Licence.

A charge or supplement may also be made for late renewal of licence.

Failure to have nil licence for exempt vehicle.

Section 43A Vehicle Excise and Registration Act 1994 - level 2 fine or compounded if still unlicensed at start of proceedings

It is an offence for a person to use, or keep, on a public road :-

- an exempt vehicle which is one in respect of which regulations under this Act require a nil licence to be in force, and
- a nil licence is not for the time being in force in respect of the vehicle.

Using an incorrectly registered vehicle

Section 43C Vehicle Excise and Registration Act 1994 - level 3 fine

It is an offence for a person to use, on a public road or in a public place :-

- a vehicle on which vehicle excise duty is chargeable, or
- which is an exempt vehicle in respect of which regulations under this Act require a nil licence to be in force,

in respect of which :-

- the name and address of the keeper are not recorded in the register, or
- any of the particulars recorded in the register are incorrect.

Duty To Give Information

Section 46(4) Vehicle Excise and Registration Act 1994 - level 3 fine

It is an offence for :-

- the person keeping the vehicle to fail to give information as to the identity of the driver or person who used the vehicle or kept the vehicle on the road unless he shows that he did not know and could not with reasonable diligence ascertain it,
- any another person to fail to give information as it is in his power to give and which may lead to the identification of the driver of the vehicle or any person who used the vehicle or kept the vehicle on a road,
- any person alleged to have used an unlicensed vehicle on a road to fail to give information as it is in his power to give as to the identity of the person by whom was is kept,

which is required by or on behalf of a Chief of Police or the Secretary of State where an offence under Section 29 (no licence) has been alleged.

False Information

Section 45 Vehicle Excise and Registration Act 1994 - maximum fine / 2 years - indictable (triable either way)

It is an offence for a person who :-

- in connection with an application for a licence makes a declaration, or
- being required to furnish particulars relating a vehicle or the keeper of a vehicle to furnish any particulars,

which to his knowledge is false or in any material respect misleading.

Clamping and Removal of Untaxed Vehicles

Regulation 5 Vehicle Excise Duty (Immobilisation, Removal and Disposal of Vehicles) Regulations 1997
Regulation 9 Vehicle Excise Duty (Immobilisation, Removal and Disposal of Vehicles) Regulations 1997

If a vehicle is stationary in any place except :-

- within the curtilage of, or in the vicinity of, a dwelling-house, mobile home or houseboat and which is normally enjoyed with it, or
- within the curtilage of, or in the vicinity of, a building consisting of two or more dwellings and which is normally enjoyed only by the occupiers of one or more of those dwellings,

an authorised person[1], if he has reason to believe a *section 29* offence (unlicensed vehicle) is being committed as regards the vehicle, may :-

- fix an immobilisation device to the vehicle either in situ or in the same road or another public road, (a notice must be fixed to the vehicle), then remove such an immobilised vehicle after 24 hours if it has not been released, or
- remove such a vehicle immediately.

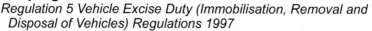

[1] An authorised person is one authorised by the Secretary of State for the purposes of these Regulations. They may be a local authority, an employee of a local authority, a member of a police force or any other person.

Exemptions

- A current disabled persons badge is displayed.
- Exempt vehicles.
- British Medical Association car badge is displayed.
- PSV being used for the carriage of passengers.
- Abandoned vehicles.
- Post Office or Royal Mail liveried vehicles used for postal delivery or collection.
- Vehicles being used for removal of obstruction to traffic, maintenance of public roads, repair or cleaning of sewers, traffic signs, gas, water, electricity and telephone infrastructure.
- a stationary vehicle which has already been immobilised or removed under these Regulations and less than 24 hours have elapsed since it was released or removed.

Interference with clamp or notice

Regulation 7(2), (3) Vehicle Excise Duty (Immobilisation, Removal and Disposal of Vehicles) Regulations 1997 - level 2/3 fine

It is an offence for a person, without authority, to :-

- remove or interfere with an immobilisation notice, or
- remove or attempt to remove an immobilisation device fixed to a vehicle in accordance with these Regulations.

HGV Road User Levy

HGV Road User Levy Act 2013

The HGV road user levy applies time based charges for using or keeping a heavy goods vehicle weighing 12 tonnes or more on a public road in the UK and applies to heavy goods vehicles (HGV) of 12 tonnes or more. The levy aims to make sure these vehicles contribute to reducing the wear and tear of the road network. The levy amount varies according to the vehicles :-

• weight,

• axle configuration,

• levy duration.

The charge is levied at the same time as vehicle excise duty for UK registered vehicles. Vehicles registered abroad must make levy payments before entering the UK.

Section 11 HGV Road User Levy Act 2013 - level 5 fine - fixed penalty offence

It is an offence for a person to use or keep a heavy goods vehicle on a public road on a day in respect of which the HGV road user levy charged in respect of the vehicle has not been paid.

Exemptions

Exemptions include :-

• use in England on the M6 Toll road and in Northern Ireland the A37 and the two sections of A3 to the west of Clones,

• vehicles used on trade plates,

• rigid vehicles and articulated tractive units charged vehicle excise duty at the basic goods vehicle rate (showman's vehicles, vehicles used on islands and learner training vehicles).

Chapter 21 Registration Marks

ZD73 ZLK

Requirements

Section 23 Vehicle Excise and Registration Act 1994
Regulation 3, 4, 29 Road Vehicles (Display of Registration Marks) Regulations 2001

ZD73 ZLK

All **mechanically propelled vehicles used on public roads** require a registration mark except :-

- electrically assisted pedal cycles,
- vehicles kept by the Crown used or appropriated for use for naval, military or air force purposes,
- invalid vehicles, unladen weight not exceeding 254 kilograms and which are specially designed and constructed, and not merely adapted, for the use of a disabled person and solely used by that person,
- pedestrian-controlled vehicles, unladen weight not exceeding 450 kilograms neither constructed nor adapted for the carriage of a driver or passenger.

Regulations

The Road Vehicles (Display of Registration Marks) Regulations 2001

These regulations detail the requirements for the format, fixing and display of registration marks on vehicles.

Offences

Contravene a requirement of the regulations

Section 59(1) Vehicle Excise and Registration Act 1994 - level 3 fine - fixed penalty

It is an offence for :-

- the person driving the vehicle, or,
- where it is not being driven, the person keeping it,

to contravene or fail to comply with a requirement of The Road Vehicles (Display of Registration Marks) Regulations 2001.

See page 8 for offences of :-

- *No registration plate.*
- *Obscured registration plate.*
- *Forgery etc. of plates.*

ZD73 ZLK **Offences**
Number and Position
Regulations 5 to 8 Road Vehicles (Display of Registration Marks) Regulations 2001
Position

Plates must be fixed :-

• on the front and rear of the vehicle (rear only on motorcycles),
• vertically or as close to vertical as is reasonably practicable,

and in such a position that in normal daylight the characters of the registration mark are easily distinguishable from every part of the relevant area (see *Visibility of Registration Plates - Page 4).*

Front Plates - must be fixed on the front of the vehicle.

Rear Plates - must be fixed on the rear of the vehicle but may be fixed in the space provided on vehicles constructed in accordance with relevant type-approval directives and lit in a manner provided for in those directives.

Number

Motorcycles and motor tricycles (unless they have a car type body) :-

• 1 rear plate,
   ○ optional front plate if first registered before 01/09/2001,
   ○ no front plate permitted if first registered on or after 01/09/2001.

Works truck, road roller or an agricultural machine :-

• 1 rear plate or 1 plate on each side.

Trailers :-

• Where a vehicle is towing a trailer(s), a plate on is required the rear of the rearmost trailer (a plate is not required on rear of towing vehicle).
• Where the towing vehicle is an agricultural machine the plate on the trailer may relate to any other agricultural machine kept by the keeper of the towing vehicle.
• The plate fixed to a trailer must conform to the same requirements as those which apply to the towing vehicle Regulation 2(2).

Additional requirements apply to some trailers used on international operations.

Other vehicles :-

• 1 front plate and 1 rear plate.

Style of characters

Regulation 15 and Schedule 4 Road Vehicles (Display of Registration Marks) Regulations 2001

A prescribed character font (based on Charles Wright font) is required on new and replacement plates issued on or after 01/09/2001 (except where the vehicle was first registered before 01/01/1973).

All older plates must either be in the prescribed font or in a style which is substantially similar. The characters must be easily distinguishable, with or without serifs but not :-

- italic, or non vertical,
- where the curvature or alignment of the lines of the stroke is substantially different from the prescribed font,
- multiple or broken strokes,
- formed in such a way as to make a character or characters appear like a different character or characters.

Lighting of rear registration plates

Regulation 9 Road Vehicles (Display of Registration Marks) Regulations 2001

Where a vehicle is being used on a road between sunset and sunrise the registration plate fixed on the rear of :-

- a vehicle, or
- where the vehicle is towing a trailer, the trailer or,
- where the vehicle is towing more than one trailer, the rearmost trailer,

must be lit so that it is easily distinguishable from every part of a relevant area having a diagonal length :-

- in the case of a plate displaying a mark having characters with a width of 44 millimetres, of 15 metres, and
- in any other case, of 18 metres,

except :-

- works trucks,
- road rollers,
- agricultural machines, and
- vehicles first registered before 01/10/1938 in Great Britain or 01/01/1948 in Northern Ireland.

Where a vehicle or, trailer has been constructed so as to satisfy the requirements of a relevant type-approval directive that plate may be lit by a lamp which complies with those requirements but if it is not so lit it must be lit in the manner required above.

Note - having a defective rear registration plate light does not constitute a 'moving traffic offence' for the purposes of Section 6 Road Traffic Act - preliminary tests.

ZD73 ZLK Visibility of Registration Plates

Regulations 5 to 9 Road Vehicles (Display of Registration Marks) Regulations 2001

Vehicle	Daylight / Sunset to Sunrise
Works Trucks, road rollers, agricultural machines and vehicles 1st registered before 01/01/1933	Easily distinguishable / No requirement
Other vehicles	
Size of Characters	**Diagonal length of the Relevant Area (x)**
Character width 57mm (pre 01/09/2001)	22 metres / 18 metres
Character width 50mm-standard on new car plates	21.5 metres / 18 metres
Character width 44mm	18 metres / 15 metres
The plate(s) must be fixed on the front and rear of the vehicle (rear only on motorcycles) vertically or, where that is not reasonably practicable, in a position as close to the vertical as is reasonably practicable, and in such a position that in normal daylight the characters of the registration mark are easily distinguishable from every part of the relevant area.	

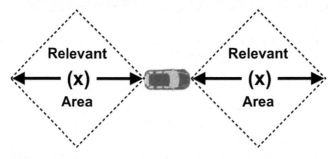

Zero-tailpipe emissions vehicles

Regulation 16(4A) Road Vehicles (Display of Registration Marks) Regulations 2001

An eligible vehicle[1] may display a plate or device which is green in colour :-

- made from retro-reflective material,
- colour Pantone 7481c (green) or a colour match that is as close as possible to this colour,
- no less than forty millimetres and no more than fifty millimetres in width.

[1] **Eligible Vehicle**

A vehicle to which these regulations apply and which cannot produce any tailpipe emissions including the plate or other device fixed to a trailer drawn by that vehicle.

No other vehicle may display a plate or other device which is green in colour.

Specification of Registration Plates
Requirements for Registration Plates

Regulation 10 Road Vehicles (Display of Registration Marks) Regulations 2001

Schedule 2

- **Part A1** Vehicles registered and new replacement registration plates fitted (except to historic vehicles) **on or after 21/09/2021** (mandatory specification) (BS AU 145e).
- **Part 1** Vehicles registered **on or after 01/09/2001 and before 01/09/2021** (mandatory specification) (BS AU 145d).
- **Part 2** Vehicles registered **on or after 01/01/1973 and before 01/09/2001** (optional specification) or comply with any of the above parts.
- **Part 3** Vehicles registered **before 01/01/1973** (optional specification) or comply with any of the above parts.

Layout of Registration Marks

Regulations 12, 13 and 14 Road Vehicles (Display of Registration Marks) Regulations 2001

Schedule 3

- **Part 1** Table A Permitted layouts for registration marks.
- **Part 2** Diagrams showing permitted layouts.
- **Part 3** Table B Stroke and character width, spacing and margins.

Vehicles registered and plate replacements issued on or after 01/09/2001		
ZD73 ZLK	Any vehicle	Optional for Motorcycles, tricycles, quadricycles, agricultural machines, works trucks road rollers.
Height (+/- 1mm)	79mm	64mm
Width (+/- 0.5mm)	50mm	44mm
Stroke	14mm	10mm
Margins Upper/lower (minimum)	11mm	11mm
Margins Side (minimum)	11mm	11mm
Space between characters	11mm	10mm
Space between No.1's or I's	11 - 54mm	10 - 40mm
Space between 1 or I and another character	11 - 33mm	10 - 25mm
Space between groups	33mm	30mm
Space between rows	19mm	13mm

Dimensions must be within :-

- 1mm for height, and
- 0.5mm in any other case.

ZD73 ZLK International distinguishing sign (Dual Purpose Plate)

Regulation 16 Road Vehicles (Display of Registration Marks)
Regulations 2001
The Road Vehicles (Display of Registration Marks) (Amendment)
Regulations 2009

An approved international distinguishing sign or Country Identifier (UK) may be applied to the extreme left hand edge of a plate.

If a plate does not have the UK sign incorporated, a separate UK sticker should be displayed on the rear of the vehicle when used outside the UK or Ireland (and it is advised to cover the GB or other identifier).

England, ENG, Eng, SCOTLAND, Scotland, SCO, Sco, CYMRU, Cymru, CYM, Cym, WALES or Wales are permitted together with the national flags of the Great Britain, England, Scotland or Wales.
Northern Ireland or NI is not permitted.

Height minimum 98 mm, width 40 - 50 mm or proportionately smaller for plates with 2 rows of characters.

Unless it forms part of a dual purpose plate, a registration plate may not be combined with a plate or device of any kind containing material which would not be permitted to be displayed on a dual purpose plate provided the plate or other device was originally fixed to the vehicle and complied with the requirements before 2300 hrs 31/12/2020.

Personalised Registrations

Personalised Plates may be displayed on vehicles providing they do not show that the vehicle is newer than it actually is.

Applications and authorisations for transfer are made via DVLA.

A number plate can be withdrawn by DVLA when they have been informed of a plate not conforming with the regulations being used on the road. Usually a warning letter will be sent to the registered keeper before doing so.

Further requirements

Regulation 11 and 16 Road Vehicles (Display of Registration Marks) Regulations 2001

- No bolt, screw or other fixing or treatment to a plate shall make the characters less easily distinguishable or prevent or impair the making of a photograph - *Regulation 11.*
- No reflex-reflecting material may be applied to a plate other than an international sign - *Regulation 11.*
- The surface must not comprise or incorporate any design, pattern or texture, or be treated in any way which gives to any part of the plate the appearance of a design, pattern or texture - *Regulation 11.*
- Two-tone/3D fonts of any kind are not permitted on new plates conforming to BS AU 145e.
- No material other than a registration mark may be displayed on a registration plate except material which complies with the BS or EEA equivalent standards (eg: an approved dual purpose plate, a Zero-tailpipe emissions vehicle plate, the BS standard and the maker/supplier name and postcode or identifying mark are the only other items permitted on the plate - car logos, graphics, other wording etc are not permitted) - *Regulation 16.*

Sale and Supply of Registration Plates

The sale and supply of Registration Plates is regulated by the Vehicles (Crime) Act 2001. Suppliers must be registered with DVLA.

Offences include supply of plates that do not comply with the Regulations as well as selling and supplying.counterfeit plates.

Entry and Inspection

Section 26 Vehicles (Crime) Act 2001

A constable or an authorised person may at any reasonable time enter and inspect premises for the time being entered in the register as premises which are occupied by a person carrying on business as a registration plate supplier and :-

- require production of, and inspect, any registration plates kept at the registered premises, and
- require production of, inspect and take copies of or extracts from any records which the person is required to keep.

No force may be used to enter premises unless a warrant to enter under section 26(4) Vehicles (Crime) Act 2001 is obtained when, if necessary, reasonable force may be used.

ZD73 ZLK ## Offences

No registration plate

Section 42(1) Vehicle Excise and Registration Act 1994 - level 3 fine - fixed penalty offence

If a registration mark is not fixed on a vehicle which is required to be fitted with one the person driving the vehicle, or where the vehicle is not being driven, the keeper, shall be guilty of an offence except where the vehicle is unregistered and was, at the first reasonable opportunity :-

- being driven on a road for the purpose of being registered, or
- being driven in connection with an M.O.T. test prior to registration (e.g. import or ex M.o.D. vehicle).

Obscured registration plate

Section 43(1) Vehicle Excise and Registration Act 1994 - level 3 fine - fixed penalty offence

If a registration mark fixed on a vehicle is in any way obscured or rendered or allowed to become not easily distinguishable :-

- the person driving, or
- where the vehicle is not being driven, the keeper,

shall be guilty of an offence.

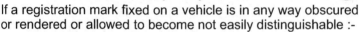

It is a defence to prove that all steps reasonably practicable to prevent the mark being obscured or rendered not easily distinguishable were taken.

Contravene a requirement of the regulations

Section 59(1) Vehicle Excise and Registration Act 1994 - level 3 fine - fixed penalty offence

It is an offence for :-

- the person driving the vehicle or,
- where it is not being driven, the person keeping it,

to contravene or fail to comply with a requirement of *The Road Vehicles (Display of Registration Marks) Regulations 2001.*

Forgery etc. of plates

Section 44(1) Vehicle Excise and Registration Act 1994 - maximum fine / 2 years - indictable (triable either way) offence

It is an offence for a person to :-

- forge, or
- fraudulently alter, or use, or allow to be used by any person, or lend, any registration mark.

International Trailer Registration Marks

Requirement

Registration and display of a registration plate in the UK is required for :-

- Commercial trailers weighing over 750kg, and
- Non-commercial trailers weighing over 3,500kg,

which are on international journeys.

Trailers that are only used in the UK or for journeys between the UK and Ireland do not need to be registered.

These registration plates are required in addition to the requirement to display the towing vehicle registration plate on UK registered vehicles.

Specification

Reg 16, Schedule 2 Trailer Registration Regs 2018

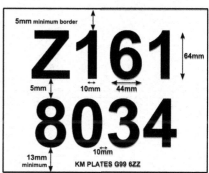

The registered keeper or the user of a registered trailer must not use it on a road, or cause or permit it to be so used, unless a registration plate (displaying its assigned registration mark) is fixed on the trailer in compliance with this regulation.

Fitting of registration marks

Regulation 17 Trailer Registration Regulations 2018

The registration plate must be fixed :-

- on the rear of the trailer,
- vertically or, where that is not reasonably practicable, in a position as close to the vertical as is reasonably practicable,
- in a position that is as far as reasonably practicable from the position of any plate that is required to be fixed to the trailer by the *Road Vehicles (Display of Registration Marks) Regulations 2001*, and
- in such a position that in normal daylight the characters of the registration mark are easily distinguishable from behind the trailer.

If it is not possible to fix a registration plate on the rear of the trailer, a registration plate must be fixed to both sides of the trailer and in such positions that in normal daylight the characters of the registration mark are easily distinguishable from either side of the trailer.

Illumination of the trailer registration plate/mark is not required.

Reg 19(g) and (h) Trailer Registration Regulations 2018 - level 3 fine

It is an offence for a person to contravene or fail to comply with :-

- *reg 16(1)* (duty to fix a registration plate on a registered trailer), or
- *reg 16(3)* (prohibition on displaying an unassigned registration mark on a trailer).

ZD73 ZLK Registration Marks - system

SUFFIX	ZLK 732V						
A	Feb 63	H	Aug 69	R	Aug 76
B	Jan 64	J	Aug 70	S	Aug 77
C	Jan 65	K	Aug 71	T	Aug 78
D	Jan 66	L	Aug 72	V	Aug 79
E	Jan 67	M	Aug 73	W	Aug 80
F	Aug 67	N	Aug 74	X	Aug 81
G	Aug 68	P	Aug 75	Y	Aug 82

PREFIX	V732 ZLK						
A	Aug 83	H	Aug 90	R	Aug 97
B	Aug 84	J	Aug 91	S	Aug 98
C	Jan 85	K	Aug 92	T	Mar 99
D	Jan 86	L	Aug 93	V	Sep 99
E	Jan 87	M	Aug 94	W	Mar 00
F	Aug 88	N	Aug 95	X	Sep 00
G	Aug 89	P	Aug 96	Y	Mar 01

AGE IDENTIFIERS			TAG	DVLA Office	ID
Year	Mar- Aug	Sep- Feb			
2001/02	-	51	A	Peterborough / Norwich Ipswich	A - N / O - U V - Y
2002/03	2	52	B	Birmingham	A-Y
2003/04	3	53	C	Cardiff / Swansea / Bangor	A - O / P - V / W - Y
2004/05	4	54	D	Chester / Shrewsbury	A-K / L-Y
2005/06	5	55	E	Chelmsford	A-Y
2006/07	6	56	F	Nottingham / Lincoln	A-P / R-Y
2007/08	7	57	G	Maidstone / Brighton	A-O / P-Y
2008/09	8	58	H	Bournemouth / Portsmouth	A-J / K-Y
2009/10	9	59	K	Luton / Northampton	A-L / M-Y
2010/11	10	60	L	Wimbledon / Stanmore Sidcup	A - J / K - T U - Y
2011/12	11	61	M	Manchester	A-Y
2012/13	12	62	N	Newcastle / Stockton	A-O / P-Y
2013/14	13	63	O	Oxford	A-Y
2014/15	14	64	P	Preston / Carlisle	A-T / U-Y
2015/16	15	65	R	Reading	A-Y
2016/17	16	66	S	Glasgow / Edinburgh Dundee / Aberdeen Inverness	A - J / K - O P - T / U - W X, Y
2017/18	17	67			
2018/19	18	68			
2019/20	19	69	V	Worcester	A-Y
2020/21	20	70	W	Exeter / Truro / Bristol	A-J / K, L / M-Y
2021/22	21	71	Y	Leeds Sheffield Beverley	A - K / L - U / V - Y
2022/23	22	72	Z	Not Allocated.	D
2023/24	23	73	TAG = Z	ZD73 ZLK	
2024/25	24	74	ID = D		

Chapter 22 Trade Licences

161
80

Trade Licences allow businesses who generally have mechanically propelled vehicles in their possession for short periods of time, to use them on public roads without the need to register (in the case of a new vehicle) or tax them provided they adhere to certain conditions and restrictions of use.

More than one licence may be held at any one time.

Public Road means a road which is repairable at the public expense.

Issue of licences

16180

Section 11 Vehicle Excise and Registration Act 1994

Regulation 39 Road Vehicles (Registration and Licensing) Regulations 2002

Trade Licences are issued to :-

- Vehicle Testers - a person, other than a motor trader, who regularly in the course of his business engages in the testing on roads of vehicles belonging to other persons,
- Motor Traders - a manufacturer or repairer of, or dealer in, vehicles including the business of modifying vehicles, whether by the fitting of accessories or otherwise and the business of valeting vehicles and a dealer includes a business consisting wholly or mainly of collecting and delivering vehicles (including hire, leasing, finance and hire purchase companies), and not including any other activities except activities as a manufacturer or repairer of, or dealer in, vehicles,

who use the licence for vehicles temporarily in their possession in the course of their business as a motor trader or in the case of a motor manufacturer who may also use vehicles for research and development.

- A paper licence is no longer issued.
- A 'general registration mark' is assigned to the licence holder which is displayed on the Trade Plates.
- A set of Trade Plates are issued for each licence held.
- All Trade licences require renewal at the end of June or December each year.

161° Trade Licence Conditions
80
Schedule 6 Part I Road Vehicles (Registration and Licensing) Regulations 2002

The holder of a trade licence :-

- shall notify any change of name or address to the Secretary of State forthwith,
- shall not, and shall not permit any person to, alter, deface, mutilate or add anything to a trade plate,
- shall not, and shall not permit any person to, exhibit on any vehicle any trade plate :-
  ○ which has been altered, defaced mutilated or added to,
  ○ upon which the figures or particulars have become illegible, or
  ○ the colour of which has altered whether by fading or otherwise,
- shall not, and shall not permit any person to, exhibit on any vehicle anything which could be mistaken for a trade plate,
- shall not permit any person to display any trade plates on a vehicle except a vehicle which that person is using for the purposes of the holder under the licence,
- shall not, and shall not permit any person, to display any trade plates on any vehicle unless :-
  ○ that vehicle is of a specified class (*section 11 VERA 1994*) ie: a manufacturer (vehicles in his temporary possession and for research and development and testing), a vehicle tester (for testing purposes) and a motor trader (vehicles in his temporary possession), and
  ○ the vehicle is being used for one or more of the prescribed purposes,
- shall not display any trade plate on a vehicle used under the licence unless that trade plate shows the general registration mark assigned to the holder in respect of that licence.

Trade Licence Prescribed Purposes
Schedule 6 Part II Road Vehicles (Registration and Licensing) Regulations 2002

A Motor Trader shall NOT use any vehicle on a public road by virtue of a trade licence UNLESS :-

- it is a business purpose,
- no goods or burden of any description are carried except **specified loads[1]**,
- no person is carried on the vehicle or any trailer drawn by it except in connection with such purposes listed above and below, and
- it is a purpose listed below :-
  ○ for test or trial of vehicle or accessories or equipment during or after construction, modification or repair,

Prescribed Purposes - *continued*

- o return journeys to public weighbridge to ascertain its weight or for registration or inspection by Secretary of State,
- o test or trial by prospective purchaser or proceeding to or returning from a place for trial by prospective purchaser,
- o for test or trial for benefit of person interested in promoting publicity, or proceeding to or returning from such a place at the instance of such interested person,
- o delivery to place where purchaser intends to keep it,
- o for demonstrating its operation or the operation of its accessories or equipment when being handed over to the purchaser,
- o delivering it from one part of his premises to another part of his premises or to premises of or part of premises of another manufacturer or repairer or dealer, or removing the said vehicle to his own premises from such a manufacturer etc.,
- o proceeding to or returning from a workshop in which a body or a special type of equipment or accessory is to be or has been fitted to it or in which it is to be or has been painted, valeted or repaired,
- o proceeding from manufacturers to dealers or repairers premises to a place from which it is to be transported by train, ship or aircraft to or proceeding to that persons premises having been transported,
- o proceeding to or returning from any garage, auction room or other place to which vehicles are usually stored or usually or periodically offered for sale and where the vehicle is to be stored or offered for sale or has been so stored or offered,
- o going to or returning from a place where it is to be or has been tested or likewise to be broken up or otherwise disposed of.

[1]Specified Loads

A specified load is one of the following kinds of load :-

- load carried to test or demonstrate the vehicle or accessories or equipment where the load is to be returned to place of loading except for unloading when demonstrating equipment or in the case of an accident, or where the load consists of water, fertiliser or refuse,
- in the case of a vehicle which is being delivered or collected and is being used for a relevant (prescribed) purpose, a load consisting of another vehicle used or to be used for travel from or to the place of delivery or collection, or
- a load built into or permanently attached to a vehicle,
- a load consisting of a trailer or of parts, accessories or equipment designed to be fitted to the vehicle and tools for fitting them to the vehicle.

Manufacturers and Vehicle Testers may use a load for testing providing it is returned to point of loading.

Offences
Display Of Trade Plates

Section 59(1) Vehicle Excise and Registration Act 1994 - level 3 fine

Reg 42 Road Vehicles (Registration and Licensing) Regulations 2002

Trade plates shall be fixed to and displayed on a vehicle such that, if it were a registration mark assigned to the vehicle, the provisions of the *Road Vehicles (Display of Registration Marks) Regulations 2001* would be complied with.

Misuse Of A Trade Licence

Section 34(1) Vehicle Excise and Registration Act 1994 - level 3 fine or 5 x VED - fixed penalty offence

The holder of a trade licence is guilty of an offence if he :-

• uses more vehicles on a public road at any one time than he is authorised to use by virtue of the trade licences he holds (unless the vehicles have a current vehicle licence in force),

• uses a vehicle (under a trade licence) on a public road for a purpose other than a prescribed purpose, or,

• keeps any vehicle (under a trade licence) on a public road unless authorised, if it is not being used thereon, (A vehicle must not be parked on a public road except for emergencies)[1].

• *[1] This offence attracts the same level of penalty as a section 29 unlicensed vehicle offence but unlike the section 29 offence there is no power of removal.*

Forgery / Alteration of Trade Plate

Section 44(1) Vehicle Excise and Registration Act 1994 - maximum fine / 2 years - indictable (triable either way) offence

It is an offence for a person to :-

• forge, or fraudulently alter, use or lend, or

• fraudulently allow to be used by another person,

any trade plate (including a replacement trade plate).

False Declaration / Details

Section 45 Vehicle Excise and Registration Act 1994 - maximum fine / 2 years - indictable (triable either way) offence

It is an offence to :-

• make any declaration which he knows to be false or in any material respect misleading, or

• furnish any false or misleading particulars when required by the act to furnish details of or relating to the keeper.

Chapter 23 Insurance

Requirement for Insurance

Section 143(2) Road Traffic Act 1988 - level 5 fine / 6 to 8 points - Extended Limitation of Proceedings to 3 years - £300 fixed penalty offence

It is an offence for any person to :-

• use, cause, or permit any other person to use, or

• aid and abet the use of (*section 44 Magistrates' Courts Act 1980*),

a **motor vehicle** on a **road** or **other public place** unless there is in force in relation to the use of the vehicle by that person, or that other person, a policy of insurance in respect of third party risks.

Cause,Permit and Aid and Abet offences are not fixed penalty offences.

Defence

To prove to a court that :-

• the vehicle did not belong to him nor was hired by him under a contract of hiring or loan, and

• the vehicle was being used in the course of his employment, and

• he neither knew nor had reason to believe that the vehicle was not insured.

Exceptions

• Invalid Carriages (not exceeding 254 kg unladen).

• Vehicles owned by local authorities and driven under their control.

• Vehicles owned by police authorities and driven under their control.

• Any vehicle used for police purposes driven by or under the direction of a constable.

• Salvage vehicles under *Merchant Shipping Act 1894*.

• Vehicles requisitioned by the armed forces.

• Vehicles owned by a health service body and driven under their control.

• An ambulance owned by a National Health Service trust and driven under their control.

• Vehicles made available to persons or groups by the Secretary of State for Health.

• Vehicles and persons in the public service of the Crown.

• Vehicles of visiting Armed Forces and driven under their control.

• Vehicles owned by the Care Quality Commission and driven under their control.

A policy of insurance must be issued by an authorised insurer (member of Motor Insurers Bureau).

Automated Vehicles
Automated and Electric Vehicles Act 2018

This Act makes provision for the creation of a new liability scheme for insurers in relation to automated vehicles.

Green Card

A green card is an international certificate of insurance proving visiting motorists have the minimum compulsory insurance cover required.

Where a motor vehicle remains in the United Kingdom after the expiry of the period of validity specified in the card the green card shall not be regarded as having ceased to be in force.

A green card issued in the UK is only valid for use outside the UK.

Motor Insurers Bureau

The MIB (Motor Insurers' Bureau) assists victims of uninsured or untraced drivers and UK residents involved in accidents with foreign-registered vehicles, either in the UK or elsewhere in Europe.

A Motor Insurance Database (MID) is maintained by the MIB and is updated by UK insurers. It can be accessed by the public to check that their own vehicle is registered on the database - free of charge or, in the event of an accident, to check the insurance details of another vehicle which is involved - a small charge is made. *http://www.askmid.com/*.

Validity of Insurance

Section 148 Road Traffic Act 1988

Failure to comply with a condition of an insurance policy shall not invalidate the policy if it relates to :-

- the age or physical or mental condition of persons driving the vehicle,
- the condition of the vehicle,
- the number of persons that the vehicle carries,
- the weight or physical characteristics of the goods that the vehicle carries,
- the time at which or the areas within which the vehicle is used,
- the horsepower or cylinder capacity or value of the vehicle,
- the carrying on the vehicle of any particular apparatus, or
- the carrying on the vehicle of any particular means of identification other than any means of identification required to be carried by or under the *Vehicle Excise and Registration Act 1994*.

An Insurer may terminate a policy if it is made aware of a breach of a policy condition including one of the above but the policy may remain valid until the insurers have taken steps to 'avoid it' (voidable policy). Even where a driver has obtained a policy of insurance by misrepresentation or non-disclosure, the policy may remain valid so far as liability under *section 143 of the Road Traffic Act 1988* is concerned (Adams v Dunn [1978] CLR 365). In other cases the insurance contract may be declared vitiated ab initio (void from the beginning).

Production of Insurance
Power to require production of Insurance
Section 165 Road Traffic Act 1988

A constable or a vehicle examiner[1] may require :-

- a person driving on a **road** a **motor vehicle** (other than an invalid carriage),
- a person whom he has reasonable cause to believe to have been the driver of a motor vehicle (other than an invalid carriage) at a time when an accident occurred owing to its presence on a road or other public place[2],
- a person whom he has reasonable cause to believe to have committed an offence in relation to the use on a road of a motor vehicle (other than an invalid carriage),

to produce for examination[3] the relevant certificate of insurance.

A person authorised for the purpose by a traffic commissioner appointed under the *Public Passenger Vehicles Act 1981*, may, on production if so required of his authority, exercise in the case of goods vehicles or passenger-carrying vehicles of any prescribed class all such powers as are, under *section 165 of this Act*, exercisable by a constable. (*Section 166 RTA 1988*)

[1] *Vehicle examiner means an examiner appointed under section 66A of the Road Traffic Act 1988.*

[2] *Although insurance is required for motor vehicles in public places there is no power to stop them other than on a road and the only power to require production of insurance in a public place is following an accident.*

[3] *This now includes providing electronic access to a copy of the certificate or a legible printed copy of the certificate. Nothing requires a constable or examiner to provide the equipment needed to access the certificate.*

Offence
Section 165(3) Road Traffic Act 1988 - level 3 fine

It is an offence for a person to fail to produce insurance as required.

Defence
- To produce insurance in person at the police station (specified by him at the time it was required) within 7 days.
- To produce insurance in person at the police station (specified by him at the time it was required) as soon as was reasonably practical.
- To prove it was not reasonably practical to produce insurance there before the day on which proceedings were commenced.

Uninsured Vehicles
Continuous Insurance Enforcement

Section 144A Road Traffic Act 1988 - level 3 fine - fixed penalty offence

It is an offence for the registered keeper of a motor vehicle registered under the *Vehicle Excise and Registration Act 1994* to keep a vehicle which is not covered by a current policy of insurance in respect of third party risks as complies with the requirements of this Act.

The vehicle may be in any place - public or private.

Exceptions
Section 144B Road Traffic Act 1988

- The vehicle is exempt from the requirement to be insured.
- The registered keeper is not at the relevant time the person keeping the vehicle, and if previously he was the person keeping the vehicle, he has complied with any requirements relating to furnishing of particulars or the making of declarations.
- The registered keeper is at the relevant time the person keeping the vehicle, but the vehicle is not used on a road or other public place, and he has complied with any requirements relating to furnishing of particulars or the making of declarations. (SORN)
- The vehicle has been stolen and not been recovered and the registered keeper has complied with any requirements relating to furnishing of particulars or the making of declarations.
- The registered keeper is at the relevant time the person keeping the vehicle, and neither a licence nor a nil licence under the *Vehicle Excise and Registration Act 1994* was in force for the vehicle on 31/01/1998 nor has one been taken out for the vehicle since that date and the vehicle has not been used or kept on a public road since that date.

The Motor Vehicles (Insurance Requirements) Regulations 2011 stipulate the nature and timing of the furnishing of particulars and declarations to be made.

False Statements
Section 174(5) Road Traffic Act 1988 - level 5 fine / 2 years - indictable (triable either way) offence

It is an offence for a person to :-
- make a false statement, or
- withhold any material information,

for the purpose of obtaining a certificate of insurance.

Power to Immobilise Uninsured Vehicles

Regulation 5 Motor Vehicles (Insurance Requirements)
(Immobilisation, Removal and Disposal) Regulations 2011

Where an authorised person[1] has reason to believe that an offence under *section 144A* (keeping an uninsured vehicle) is being committed as regards a vehicle which is **stationary on a road or other public place**, the authorised person or a person acting under the direction of the authorised person may :-

- fix an immobilisation device to the vehicle while it remains in the place where it is stationary, or
- move it from that place to another place on the same or another road or public place and fix an immobilisation device to it in that other place.

Where an immobilisation device is fixed to a vehicle in accordance with this regulation, the person fixing the device must also fix to the vehicle an immobilisation notice.

[1]Authorised person - a person authorised by the Secretary of State for the purposes of these Regulations (may include a local authority, an employee of a local authority, a member of a police force or any other person).

Exemptions

These Regulations do not apply where :-

- a current disabled person's badge is displayed on the vehicle[2],
- the vehicle appears to have been abandoned,
- the vehicle is a public service vehicle being used for the carriage of passengers,
- the vehicle is being used for the purpose of the removal of any obstruction to traffic, the maintenance, improvement or reconstruction of a public road, or the laying, erection, alteration, repair or cleaning in or near a road of any traffic sign or sewer or of any main, pipe or apparatus for the supply of gas, water or electricity, or of any telegraph or telephone wires, cables, posts or supports, or
- the vehicle is being used by a universal service provider in relation to the provision of a universal postal service and each side of the vehicle is clearly marked with the name of the universal service provider concerned.

[2] If however the vehicle is not being used in accordance with regulations under section 21 of the Chronically Sick and Disabled Persons Act 1970 in circumstances where a disabled person's concession would be available, the person in charge of the vehicle is guilty of an offence under regulation 8 - level 3 fine.

continued over

Power to Immobilise Uninsured Vehicles *continued*
Release

The immobilisation device may only be released by, or under the direction of, an authorised person where :-

- the release charge has been paid, and
- evidence of insurance for the person who is driving the vehicle away is produced, and
- the registered keeper is not, at the point of release, guilty of an offence of keeping an uninsured vehicle as regards the vehicle.

Removal of or interference with an immobilisation notice or device

Motor Vehicles (Insurance Requirements) (Immobilisation, Removal and Disposal) Regulations 2011 - level 2/3 fine

It is an offence for a person, except by or under the authority or direction of an authorised person,

- to remove or interfere with an **immobilisation notice,** *Regulation 7(2)*
- to remove or attempt to remove an **immobilisation device** fixed to a vehicle in accordance with these Regulations. *Regulation 7(3)*

Power to Remove Vehicles

Regulation 9 Motor Vehicles (Insurance Requirements) (Immobilisation, Removal and Disposal) Regulations 2011

Where an authorised person has reason to believe that an offence under *section 144A* (keeping an uninsured vehicle) :-

- is being committed as regards a vehicle which is stationary on a road or other public place, or
- was being committed as regards a vehicle at the time when an immobilisation device which is fixed to the vehicle was fixed to it in accordance with these Regulations, and :-
  - 24 hours have elapsed since the device was fixed to the vehicle, and
  - the vehicle has not been released in accordance with these Regulations,

the authorised person or a person acting under the authorised person's direction, may remove the vehicle.

The owner will be notified and may reclaim the vehicle upon payment of removal and storage charges and/or fines. In some circumstances the vehicle may be scrapped.

Seizure of vehicles driven without insurance
Section 165A Road Traffic Act 1988

A constable in uniform may seize a motor vehicle (not an invalid carriage) where :-

- he has required a person under *section 165 Road Traffic Act 1988*, to produce evidence that a **motor vehicle** is not or was not being driven in contravention of *section 143* (no insurance), the person fails to produce such evidence and the constable has reasonable grounds for believing that the vehicle is or was being so driven, or
- the person fails to stop the vehicle when required to do so by a constable in uniform under *section 163 Road Traffic Act 1988*, or to stop the vehicle long enough for the constable to make such lawful enquiries as he considers appropriate, and the constable has reasonable grounds for believing that the vehicle is or was being driven in contravention of *section 143* (no insurance).

Before seizing a motor vehicle, the constable must warn the driver that he will seize it if the person does not produce his licence immediately, or as the case may be, with evidence that the vehicle is insured or exempt from insurance unless the circumstances make it impracticable for him to do so.

If the vehicle has failed to stop as requested or has driven off, he may seize it at any time within the period of 24 hours beginning with the time at which the condition in question is first satisfied.

The constable may enter any premises (other than a private dwelling house) on which he has reasonable grounds for believing the vehicle to be and may use reasonable force, if necessary, to seize the vehicle or enter the premises.

Private dwelling house does not include any garage or other structure occupied with the dwelling house, or any land appurtenant (related) to the dwelling house.

Seizure Notice
Regulation 4 Road Traffic Act 1988 (Retention and Disposal of Seized Motor Vehicles) Regulations 2005

A constable, on seizing a vehicle shall give a seizure notice to the driver of the vehicle being seized unless the circumstances make it impracticable for him to do so.

Causing death by driving: uninsured drivers
Section 3ZB Road Traffic Act 1988 - 2 years - 3 - 11 points - disqualification - indictable offence

It is an offence for a person to **cause** the **death** of another person by **driving** a **motor vehicle** on a **road** and, at the time when he is driving, the circumstances are such that he is committing an offence under *section 143 Road Traffic Act 1988* (no insurance).

Obligations relating to insurance following an accident

Duty of a driver to produce insurance and report to the police following an injury accident.

Section 170 Road Traffic Act 1988

Where an accident occurs due to the presence of a **mechanically propelled vehicle** on a **road** or other **public place** whereby personal injury is caused to a person other than the driver of that vehicle - the **driver** of a **motor vehicle** must produce a certificate of insurance to a constable or to some other person having reasonable grounds for requiring him to produce it, or if he does not he must :-

- **report** the accident to a police station or a police constable **as soon as reasonably practicable** (in any case within 24 hours), and
- **produce** that certificate there or within 7 days at a police station specified by him when the accident was reported.

Offence

Section 170(7) Road Traffic Act 1988 - level 3 fine

It is an offence for a person to fail to produce insurance or report an accident as required.

Duty of an owner to prove insurance cover

Where a driver of a **motor vehicle** was required to produce insurance under *section 165* (by a police officer, vehicle examiner or other authorised person) or *section 170* (following an injury accident) the owner of a vehicle must give such information in order to prove insurance cover of that vehicle on that occasion as he may be required to give by or on behalf of a chief officer of police.

Offence

Section 171(2) Road Traffic Act 1988 - level 4 fine

It is an offence for a person to fail to give such information as is required.

Duty to provide insurance information

Section 154(2) Road Traffic Act 1988 - level 4 fine

It is an offence for a person against whom a claim is made in respect of any liability required to be covered by an insurance policy **(injury** to a person **or damage** to property) without reasonable excuse to fail to :-

- state whether or not, in respect of that liability, he was insured, or he would have been insured if the insurer had not cancelled his policy,
- give the particulars on the insurance certificate, or where no certificate was delivered, to give the registration mark of the vehicle, the number or identifying particulars of the policy, the name of the insurer, the period of insurance cover,

on demand by or on behalf of the person making the claim, or wilfully make a false statement in reply to any such demand.

This requirement is over and above any accident obligations a driver may have and can take place some time after an accident.

Chapter 24 Testing Vehicles

MOT testing

The MOT test is a regular inspection to ensure that vehicles meet roadworthiness and environmental standards.

Requirement for a test certificate

Section 47(1) Road Traffic Act 1988 - level 3 fine (level 4 passenger vehicle with more than 8 passenger seats) - fixed penalty offence

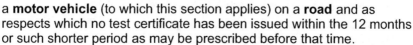

It is an offence for a person to :-

* use, cause[1], or permit[1] to be used, or
* aid and abet, counsel or procure the commission by another person, the use of, *section 44 Magistrates' Courts Act 1980*

a **motor vehicle** (to which this section applies) on a **road** and as respects which no test certificate has been issued within the 12 months or such shorter period as may be prescribed before that time.

[1] Cause and Permit offences are not fixed penalty offences.

Test certificates are required and must be renewed annually after :-

* 3 years, or
* 1 year in the case of motor vehicles used for the carriage of passengers with more than 8 passenger seats, taxis used to ply for hire (hackney cabs) and ambulances,

after date of 1st registration, or date of manufacture if used otherwise.

Public Service Vehicles must be approved prior to entering service. They will have type approval, a certificate of conformity or a Certificate of Initial Fitness (COIF).

Exemptions

Regulation 6(2) Motor Vehicles (Tests) Regulations 1981

* Vehicles travelling to a pre-arranged test.
* During a test itself by the examiner or an authorised person.
* Where a test has been failed :-
  * whilst being driven from the test, or
  * driving to by previous arrangement or from a place where work is to be done or has been done on it to remedy defects discovered on a previous test which led to a failure, or
  * towing it to a place where the vehicle is to be broken up for scrap.
* Vehicles being removed under a statutory power of removal.
* Vehicles being tested under a Trade licence.
* Vehicles subject to goods vehicle testing.
* An imported vehicle whilst it is being driven from the port of entry to the residence of the owner.
* Vehicles which have been detained or seized by a Police Constable or Customs and Excise.

Vehicles exempt from MOT testing

Regulation 6(1), (1A) Motor Vehicles (Tests) Regulations 1981
•Vehicles subject to goods vehicle testing *(Reg 6(2)) see over,*

- Heavy locomotive, Light locomotive, Motor tractor, Tracked vehicle.
- An articulated vehicle not being an articulated bus.
- Vehicle used only to travel between land in a persons occupation, used not exceeding 6 miles /week aggregate on public roads.
- Works truck.
- Pedestrian controlled vehicle.
- Invalid carriage not exceeding 306 kgs u/w (510 kgs if NHS supplied).
- A foreign vehicle temporarily in Great Britain within 12 months of entry.
- Vehicle proceeding to a port for export.
- Visiting forces vehicle or imported Armed forces vehicles.
- A vehicle provided for police purposes by the police authority and maintained in approved workshops.
- A vehicle with a current Northern Ireland Test Certificate.
- An electrically propelled goods vehicle, the design gross weight of which does not exceed 3500 kgs 1st registered before 01/03/2015.
- Licensed hackney carriages and private hire cars which are required to undergo testing conducted by the local authority.
- Agricultural motor vehicle.
- Street cleansing, refuse and gully cleaning vehicles which are specially constructed, not adapted and :-
  - 3 wheeled, or
  - maximum design speed not exceeding 20 m.p.h., or
  - with an inside track width less than 810mm.
- Tramcar and trolley vehicles.
- A public service vehicle having a date of manufacture before 01/01/1960 and which has not undergone substantial changes in the technical characteristics of its main components.
- Certain classes of vehicle when used on isolated islands.
- Military and Crown vehicles (as they are unregistered).
- A vehicle max speed 15.5 miles per hour on level.
- A vehicle of historical interest* other than a public service vehicle.

* A vehicle of historical interest means a vehicle which is considered to be of historical interest to Great Britain and which :-

- *was manufactured or registered for the first time at least 40 years previously, and is of a type no longer in production, and*
- *has been historically preserved or maintained in its original state and has not undergone substantial changes in the technical characteristics of its main components.*

Goods vehicle plating and testing

Section 53 Road Traffic Act 1988 - level 4 fine

It is an offence for a person to use, cause, or permit to be used, on a road a vehicle to which this section applies without a plating certificate in force or a valid goods vehicle test certificate.

Red paper Plating Certificates (aka Ministry Plates)are issued within 14 days of registration to standard construction vehicles.

Blue paper Plating Certificates are issued to Non standard vehicles following a test to determine permissible weights or to any vehicles at annual inspection where the permissible weights are altered.

Weights detailed on the Plating Certificate supersede any weights displayed on a manufacturers plate (normally a metal plate).

Test certificates must be renewed annually after the end of the month following the first anniversary of first registration for a motor vehicle, or of its sale by retail in the case of a trailer.

Vehicles Which Require Annual Testing

Goods Vehicles (Plating and Testing) Regulations 1988

Goods vehicles being :-

• goods vehicles with a gross weight of more than 3,500 kg,
• vehicles that are built or have been adapted to form part of an articulated vehicle,
• semi-trailers,
• horseboxes with a gross weight of more than 3,500kg,
• 'A' frame trailers and converter dollies manufactured on or after 01/01/1979,
• trailers with an unladen weight of more than 1,020kg with powered braking systems (instead of standard overrun brakes and as well as the required parking brake).

Vehicles exempt from goods vehicle testing

Schedule 2 Goods Vehicle (Plating and Testing) Regulations 1988

Some vehicles don't have to take an HGV annual test including tractors and vehicles less than 1 year old.

A full list of exempt vehicles are listed in the schedule or https://www.gov.uk/government/publications/exemption-from-heavy-goods-vehicle-hgv-annual-testing-v112g.

Trailer Test Date Discs

Reg 73 Road Vehicles (Construction and Use) Regulations 1986

In addition to a Goods Vehicle Test Certificate trailers are issued with a Test Date Disc with the expiry date of the test certificate marked thereon which must be displayed in a legible condition in a conspicuous and readily accessible position clearly visible from the nearside of the road in daylight.

Production of Test Certificate, Plating certificate and Goods Vehicle Test certificate
Section 165(1) Road Traffic Act 1988

A constable or a vehicle examiner[1] may require :-

- a person driving on a **road** a **motor vehicle** (other than an invalid carriage),
- a person whom he has reasonable cause to believe to have been the driver of a motor vehicle (other than an invalid carriage) at a time when an accident occurred owing to its presence on a road or other public place,
- a person whom he has reasonable cause to believe to have committed an offence in relation to the use on a road of a motor vehicle (other than an invalid carriage),

to produce for examination[2] :-

- a test certificate if it is required,
- in relation to a goods vehicle which requires a plating certificate or goods vehicle test certificate, any such certificate issued in respect of that vehicle or any trailer drawn by it.

A person authorised by a traffic commissioner may, on production if so required of his authority, exercise the above power in the case of goods vehicles or passenger-carrying vehicles -section 166 RTA 1988.

[1] Vehicle examiner means an examiner appointed under *section 66A of the Road Traffic Act 1988.*

[2] This now includes providing electronic access to a copy of the certificate or a legible printed copy of the certificate. Nothing requires a constable or examiner to provide the equipment needed to access the certificate.

Offence
Section 165(3) Road Traffic Act 1988 - level 3 fine
It is an offence to fail to produce a test certificate, plating certificate or goods vehicle test certificate(s) as required above.

Defence

- to produce them in person at the police station specified by him at the time they were required, within 7 days,
- to produce them in person there as soon as was reasonably practical,
- it was not reasonably practical to produce them there before the day on which proceedings were commenced.

Chapter 25 Documents

Identity of Driver or Rider
Section 172 Road Traffic Act 1988

Where a driver of a **vehicle** or rider of a **cycle** is alleged to be guilty of an offence to which this section applies a person on behalf of the Chief Officer of Police may require :-

- the person keeping the vehicle to give such information as to the identity of the driver as may be required,
- any other person to give any information which is in his power to give and may lead to the identification of the driver.

This section applies to :-

- any offence under the *Road Traffic Act 1988* except offences concerned with Driving Instruction, Regulation of motoring events, Wearing of protective headgear (motorcyclists), Obstructing authorised examiners, Driving with uncorrected defective eyesight, L.G.V. and P.C.V. trainee driver schemes,
- *sections 25,26 and 27 Road Traffic Offenders Act 1988* (information and production of licence to a court),
- offences against any other enactment relating to the use of vehicles on roads,
- manslaughter by the driver of a motor vehicle.

Section 172(3) Road Traffic Act 1988 - level 3 fine / 6 points - fixed penalty offence - £200

It is an offence for a person to fail to comply with a requirement to give information.

It is a defence to shows he did not know and could not with reasonable diligence have ascertained who the driver of the vehicle was.

Written notice

The requirement to supply information may be made by written notice served by post.and require information to be supplied within 28 days from the day on which the notice is served.

If the person on whom the notice is served can show that it was not reasonably practicable to give it or he gave it as soon as reasonably practicable after the 28 days, he shall not be guilty of an offence.

Liability of Company Directors etc.

Where a body corporate is guilty of an offence under this section and the offence is proved to have been committed with the consent or connivance of, or to be attributable to neglect on the part of, a director, manager, secretary or other similar officer of the body corporate, or a person who was purporting to act in any such capacity, he, as well as the body corporate, is guilty of that offence. No defence will be available unless it is shown that no record was kept of the persons who drove the vehicle and that the failure to keep a record was reasonable.

Forgery And Use Of Documents
Section 173 (1) Road Traffic Act 1988 - maximum fine / 2 years - indictable (triable either way) offence

It is an offence for a person with intent to deceive to :-
- forge, alter or use, a document or other thing,
- lend to another or allow another to use, a document or other thing,
- make or have in possession any document or other thing so closely resembling a document or other thing as to be calculated to deceive.

A Document Or Other Thing for this section is :-
- Licence issued under *Road Traffic Act 1988*, or, in the case of a licence to drive, any counterpart of such a licence.
- Counterpart of a Community licence.
- Test certificate, goods vehicle test certificate, plating certificate, certificate of conformity or Minister's approval certificate.
- Seatbelt exemption certificate.
- Speed limiter seal.
- VIN plate, type approval plate, other plate required to be marked on a vehicle by regulations under *section 41 Road Traffic Act 1988.*
- Document evidencing the appointment of an examiner under *section 66A Road Traffic Act 1988.*
- Operators records of inspection of a goods vehicle.
- Driving test pass certificate.
- Document evidencing the successful completion of a compulsory driver training course.
- Driving instructor certificate or badge.
- Certificate of insurance or other document produced in lieu.
- International road haulage permit.
- Certificate of completion of course for drink drive offenders.

Issue Of False Documents
Section 175 Road Traffic Act 1988 - level 4 fine

It is an offence for a person to issue a :-
- certificate of insurance,
- test certificate,
- goods vehicle test certificate,
- goods vehicle plating certificate,

when the document or certificate so issued is to his knowledge false in a material particular.

False Statements

Section 174 Road Traffic Act 1988 - level 5 fine / 2 years -
indictable (triable either way) offence

It is an offence for a person to make a false statement :-

- to obtain, prevent the grant of or impose conditions on, a driving licence,
- to secure entry or retention on a register of approved driving instructors,
- when supplying information for type approval, alteration of plated weights, testing of goods vehicles, application for vehicle excise licences,
- to obtain the grant of an international road haulage permit,
- to obtain a document evidencing successful completion of a compulsory driver training course,

or withhold any material information for the purpose of obtaining a certificate of insurance.

Julian Calendar

Document dating system based on day of year			
January	001 - 031	July	182 - 212
February *	032 - 059	August	213 - 243
March	060 - 090	September	244 - 273
April	091 - 120	October	274 - 304
May	121 - 151	November	305 - 334
June	152 - 181	December	335 - 365

* In leap years add 1 to all days after February 28th.

Example

- Driving Licence Document Number (found in bottom right hand corner of licence)
- Issue No. 08 3741H017 **96218**1420638
- Year of Issue = 96
- 218 = Day of Issue
- So Date of Issue = 5th August 1996

Seizure of Documents and Plates
Section 176(1) and (1A) Road Traffic Act 1988

If a constable has reasonable cause to believe that a document produced to him is a document in relation to which an offence has been committed under *section 173, 174 or 175 of this Act* or under *section 115 of the Road Traffic Regulation Act 1984* (parking meter tickets etc.), he may seize the document.

Section 176(4) Road Traffic Act 1988

A constable or an examiner appointed under *section 66A of the Road Traffic Act 1988* may seize a document or plate carried on a motor vehicle or by the driver of the vehicle if he has reasonable cause to believe it is a document or plate in relation to which an offence has been committed under *sections 173, 174 or 175 of the Road Traffic Act 1988* in so far as they apply :-

- to documents evidencing the appointment of examiners under *section 66A of this Act*, or
- to goods vehicle test certificates, plating certificates, certificates of conformity or Minister's approval certificates, or
- to plates containing plated particulars or containing other particulars required to be marked on goods vehicles by sections *54 to 58 Road Traffic Act 1988* or regulations made under them (type approval), or
- to records required to be kept by virtue of *section 74 of this Act* (records of Inspection of goods vehicles by operator), or
- to international road haulage permits.

When a document or plate is seized under *subsection 176(4)* above, either the driver or owner of the vehicle shall if the document or plate is still detained and neither of them has previously been charged with an offence in relation to the document or plate under *section 173, 174 or 175 of this Act,* be summoned before a magistrates' court or, in Scotland, the sheriff to account for his possession of, or the presence on the vehicle of, the document or plate.

Seize includes a power to detach from a vehicle.

Chapter 26 Penalties

Prosecution and Punishment of Offences

Schedule 2 Road Traffic Offenders Act 1988

The mode of prosecution and punishment for offences under the Road Traffic Acts are detailed in *Schedule 2 to Road Traffic Offenders Act 1988*. The measures include imprisonment, fines, disqualification from driving and the award of penalty points on the driving licence.

Prosecution authorities can also issue fixed penalty tickets, offer attendance on suitable courses or impose vehicle defect rectification requirements as alternatives to prosecution. The courts may stipulate mandatory attendance on courses, mandatory testing in the case of drink or drug offenders and impose the requirement to re-take a driving test. 'endorse' driving record penalty points if convicted of a motoring and some other offences.

Offences in this guide are summary offences except where specified.

Endorsements stay on the driving record for 4 or 11 years.

A driver who accumulates 12 or more penalty points within a period of 3 years can be disqualified.

Disqualification

Section 34 Road Traffic Offenders Act 1988

A person can be disqualified from driving by a court if :-

• they are convicted of certain driving offences, or
• they get 12 or more penalty points on their driving licence within 3 years.

Disqualification for less than 56 days

A person does not need to apply for a new licence before they can drive again.

Disqualification for 56 days or more

A person who has been disqualified for 56 days or more must apply for a new licence before driving again.

National Driver Offender Retraining Scheme (NDORS)

This scheme provides an alternative to prosecution for minor moving road traffic offences (usually those for which a fixed penalty may be issued) whereby the driver/rider pays for the cost of the course in lieu of the penalty for the offence and upon successful completion of the course no conviction is recorded against them.

A driver can only access a course once in 3 years.

Offer of a course as an alternative to a fixed penalty or court proceedings is at the discretion of the police force.

Fixed Penalty Offences

Section 51, Schedule 3 Road Traffic Offenders Act 1988

Fixed penalty offences are specified in Schedule 3 (Schedule 5 in Scotland) to this Act.

An offence is not a fixed penalty offence if it is committed by causing or permitting a vehicle to be used by another person in contravention of any provision made or restriction or prohibition imposed by or under any enactment.

Fixed Penalty Notices

Fixed penalty offences, may be dealt with by way of the issue of a fixed penalty notice which provides the opportunity to pay a fixed fine instead of going to court. If the fine is not paid within 28 days it will be increased by 50% and recovered by the courts. A person may request a court appearance if the reason for issue of the notice is disputed.

Non-Endorsable Notices

May be issued to persons who commit fixed penalty offences which do not attract endorsement on a driving licence.

- A notice of intended prosecution is not required if a notice is issued to a person.
- They can be issued to a person or left on a vehicle.

Endorsable Notices

These are issued to persons who commit fixed penalty offences which attract endorsement on a driving licence.

- A notice of intended prosecution is not required if a notice is issued.
- They cannot be left on a vehicle.
- They attract a higher penalty.

The constable or vehicle examiner may only give a fixed penalty notice in respect of the offence if satisfied, on accessing information held on the person's driving record, that the person would not be liable to be disqualified under *section 35 of this Act* (totting up) if convicted of that offence.

A period of disqualification due to totting up wipes the slate clean, in other cases the penalty points remain valid for 3 years.

Conditional Offer of a Fixed Penalty (COFP)

Section 75 Road Traffic Offenders Act 1988

A constable or a vehicle examiner who has reason to believe that a fixed penalty offence has been committed, and no fixed penalty notice in respect of the offence has been given under *section 54 of this Act* or fixed to a vehicle under *section 62 of this Act*, may send a notice (a conditional offer of a fixed penalty) to the alleged offender.

Additional Offences Open to Conditional Offer in Scotland are listed at *Schedule 5 Road Traffic Offenders Act 1988.*

Issue of Fixed Penalty Notices
Non-Endorsable Notices on Stationary Vehicles
Section 62(1) Road Traffic Offenders Act 1988

A constable (in uniform or otherwise) or a vehicle examiner may attach such a notice to a stationary vehicle if he has reason to believe a non endorsable fixed penalty offence is or has on that occasion been committed in respect of that vehicle.

Section 62(2) Road Traffic Offenders Act 1988 - level 2 fine

It is an offence for a person, without the authority of the driver or person in charge of the vehicle, to remove or interfere with a fixed penalty notice fixed to that vehicle.

Issue of Fixed Penalty Notice to a person
Section 54 Road Traffic Offenders Act 1988

A constable in uniform (or a vehicle examiner who produces his authority) may give a fixed penalty notice (non-endorsable or endorsable as applicable) to a person who he has reason to believe :-

- is committing or has on that occasion committed a fixed penalty offence[1], or
- has, in the previous 28 days, committed a Community drivers' hours offence[1] unless he has reason to believe a penalty notice or other penalty has already been issued, a conditional offer made or proceedings initiated against the person for the offence.

[1] A person commits a **'Community drivers' hours offence'** if the person commits a fixed penalty offence in the United Kingdom, an EU member State, or a contracting third country under :-

- *section 96(11A) Transport Act 1968* (permitted driving time and periods of duty),
- *section 98(4)(b) Transport Act 1968* (written records - except where recording equipment which has been repaired otherwise than in accordance with the Community Recording Equipment Regulation),
- *section 99C(1) Transport Act 1968* (failure to comply with prohibition), where the prohibition is imposed under *section 99A(1)(b)(ii)*, or
- *section 3(1) Road Traffic (Foreign Vehicles) Act 1972* (enforcement provisions) where the offence arises as a result of a contravention of the applicable Community rules.

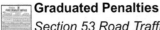 **Graduated Penalties**

Section 53 Road Traffic Offenders Act 1988
Road Safety (Financial Penalty Deposit) (Appropriate
Amount) Order 2009

Certain penalties may be graduated to reflect the nature and severity of offence as well as the time or location of the contravention. The level of fine as well as the number of penalty points may vary.

Graduated Fixed Penalty Offences listed in the Order include :-

• *Transport Act 1968* - Domestic and EC drivers' hours and recording equipment offences.

• *Road Traffic Act 1988* - Construction and Use offences :-

  ◦ Tyres - less than 1mm tread - *regulation 27(1)(g)*,

  ◦ Excess weight: goods and passenger vehicles,

  ◦ Speed limiter offences,

  ◦ Danger or nuisance offences involving maintenance, security of load etc. - *regulation 100*.

Further measures scheduled for introduction include graduated penalties with a range of penalty points according to given criteria in respect of excess speed and motorway offences.

An offence committed by causing or permitting a vehicle to be used by another person in contravention of any provision made or restriction or prohibition imposed by or under any enactment is not a fixed penalty offence.

Financial penalty deposit

Sections 90A - C Road Traffic Offenders Act 1988
Road Safety (Financial Penalty Deposit) Order 2009
Road Safety (Financial Penalty Deposit) (Appropriate Amount) Order 2009

A constable in uniform or vehicle examiner (on production of his authority) may impose a financial penalty deposit requirement on a person on any occasion if he has reason to believe that the person :-

• is committing or has on that occasion committed a specified Financial Penalty offence relating to **a motor vehicle or trailer**, or

• has, within the period of 28 days before the day of that occasion, committed an offence relating to **a motor vehicle** which is a Community drivers' hours offence (*see previous page*) unless he has reason to believe a financial penalty deposit requirement or other penalty has already been imposed or proceedings initiated against the person for the offence,

and the person fails to provide a satisfactory address (an address in the United Kingdom at which the constable or vehicle examiner considers it likely that it would be possible to find the person whenever necessary to do so in connection with the proceedings, fixed penalty notice or conditional offer).

Financial penalty deposit *continued*

The person must be :-

- given written notification that it appears likely that proceedings will be brought against him in respect of the offence, or
- (if the offence is a fixed penalty offence) either given such notification or given a fixed penalty notice (or, in Scotland, handed a conditional offer) in respect of the offence.

Payments may be made by cash, debit or credit card. The 'appropriate amount' is equal to the sum payable of the fixed penalty notice or the minimum fine normally imposed by the Courts for other offences.

The amounts may be fixed or graduated according to the number or severity of the offence(s) and mirror the penalties contained in the Fixed Penalty Order 2000.

Prohibition
Section 90D Road Traffic Offenders Act 1988

Where a person on whom a financial penalty deposit requirement is imposed does not make an immediate payment of the appropriate amount the constable or vehicle examiner may prohibit the driving on a road of any vehicle of which the person was in charge at the time of the offence by giving to the person notice in writing of the prohibition - a direction may be given to move the vehicle to a specified place and subject to conditions.

Offence
Section 90D(6) Road Traffic Offenders Act 1988 - fixed penalty offence

It is an offence for a person to :-

- drive or cause or permit a vehicle to be driven in contravention of a prohibition under this section, or
- fail to comply within a reasonable time with any direction given.

1 Cause and Permit offences are not fixed penalty offences.

The prohibition shall come into force as soon as the notice is given, and continue in force until :-

- payment of the appropriate amount or where a fixed penalty notice was given, or a conditional offer handed, payment of the fixed penalty,
- the person is convicted or acquitted of the offence or informed that he is not to be prosecuted, or
- the coming to an end of the prosecution period.

Other Fixed Penalties

Fixed Penalty Notices issued by or on behalf of the police should not be confused with :-

- Penalty Charge Notices issued by a council usually for parking offences, bus lane infringements etc.
- Parking Charge Notices issued by a private parking company in private car parks.

Local Authority Penalty Charge Notices

Local Authorities may use civil parking enforcement (CPE) powers in their area and Civilian Enforcement Officers may issue penalty charge notices on behalf of the authority for a wide range of non-endorsable offences relating to parking, bus lane infringements etc.

Additionally, under various Acts, they may have powers to issue notices within their area for :-

Section 3 Clean Neighbourhoods and Environment Act 2005

- Exposing vehicles for sale on a road.

Section 4 Clean Neighbourhoods and Environment Act 2005

- Repairing vehicles on a road.

Section 2A Refuse Disposal (Amenity) Act 1978 (c. 3)

- Abandoned vehicles.

Road Traffic (Vehicle Emissions) (Fixed Penalty) (England) Regulations 2002

- Vehicle Emissions.

A power to require the name and address of the person to whom the notice is to be issued is usually granted together with an offence of failing to provide it or for giving false details.

Parking Charge Notices

Parking Charge Notices may be issued by private parking companies on private land. These are generally civil matters of trespass or breach of contract.

Powers of removal or clamping may exist where there are Acts of Parliament or bye-laws in effect such as car parks owned by local authorities, at railway stations and major airports.

Chapter 27 Proceedings

Notice Of Intended Prosecution
Bar to proceedings
Section 1 Road Traffic Offenders Act 1988

A person shall not be convicted of an offence to which this section applies (*see below*) unless :-

- he was warned (verbally or in writing) at the time of the offence that the question of prosecuting him would be taken into consideration, or
- within 14 days of the offence a summons was served, or
- within 14 days of the offence a notice of intended prosecution (N.O.I.P.) which specifies the nature of the alleged offence and the time and place, was served on him or the registered keeper.

A notice will be deemed to have been served if it was sent by registered post or recorded delivery addressed to him at his last known address, notwithstanding that the notice was returned as undelivered or otherwise not received by him.

Exceptions
Service of a notice will not be required in relation to an offence if :-

- at the time of an offence or immediately after an accident occurs owing to the presence on a road of a vehicle in respect of which the offence was committed, (except where the defendant was unaware that there had been an accident Bentley v Dickinson [1983] RTR 356),
- a fixed penalty notice has been issued for the offence,
- neither the name and address of the accused nor the name and address of the registered keeper could, with reasonable diligence, be ascertained in time for a summons or notice to be served or sent,
- the accused by his own conduct contributed to the failure,
- the offence was reduced to a lesser charge after a not guilty finding on the more serious allegation (i.e. dangerous to careless driving) (providing a N.O.I.P was served for the original allegation).

Application
Section 1 and Schedule Road Traffic Offenders Act 1988

A Notice of Intended Prosecution is required for breach of the following offences except where an accident[1] has occurred or a fixed penalty notice issued :-

- Dangerous Careless and Inconsiderate Driving and Cycling. *Sections 1,3, 28, 29 Road Traffic Act 1988.*
- Leaving a Vehicle in a Dangerous Position. *Section 22 RTA 1988.*
- Failing to Comply with Traffic Directions of a police officer engaged in the regulation of traffic or at a traffic survey. *Section 35 RTA 1988.*
- Failing to Comply with a Traffic Sign. *Section 36 RTA 1988.*
- Speed offences. *Sections 16,17(4), 88(7) or 89(1) RTRA 1984.*
- Aid and Abet the above offences.

Limitation of proceedings for Summary Offences
Section 127 Magistrates' Court Act 1980
Section 136 Criminal Procedure (Scotland) Act 1995

An information must be laid within 6 calendar months of the commission of a summary offence, except where any other Act expressly provides otherwise.

The court must be informed of the complaint within the 6 month period, the issue and service of a summons and the subsequent trial may all occur outside that period.

In computing the limitation period the day on which the offence was committed is not included.

The requirement does not apply to either-way offences or indictable only offences.

Many road traffic offences are purely summary and in most cases proceedings are taken by laying an information and the issue of a summons.

Proceedings must be brought within six months from the date on which sufficient evidence came to the knowledge of the prosecutor (usually the investigating police officer) to warrant proceedings but, in any event, they must not be brought more than three years after the commission of the offence.

Any such prosecution must not be brought more than three years after the commission of the offence.

Exceptions to the Six Month Time Limit

The six months' time limit applies to most summary road traffic offences, but statutory exceptions include :-

Section 6 and Schedule 1 Road Traffic Offenders Act 1988

- driving after making a false declaration as to physical fitness,
- failing to notify Secretary of State of onset or deterioration of disability,
- driving after such a failure,
- driving after refusal of licence under *section 92 or 93*,
- failure to surrender licence following revocation,
- obtaining driving licence, or driving, whilst disqualified,
- using an uninsured motor vehicle,
- making a false statement to obtain a driving licence or certificate of insurance,
- issuing false documents,
- aiding and abetting the above offences,

Section 37 Vehicles (Crime) Act 2001

- unauthorised taking of a mechanically propelled vehicle.

Chapter 28 Parking

Wilful Obstruction of the Highway

Section 137(1) Highways Act 1980 - 6 months[1] and/or level 3 fine - fixed penalty offence if vehicle

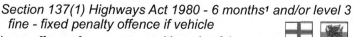

It is an offence for a person, without lawful authority or excuse, if they in any way wilfully obstruct the free passage along a highway.

See Chapter 1 Page 9 for further details.

Unnecessary Obstruction

Section 42 Road Traffic Act 1988 - level 3 fine (level 4 fine goods vehicles and passenger vehicles with more than 8 passenger seats) - fixed penalty offence Regulation 103 Road Vehicles (Construction and Use) Regulations 1986

It is an offence for a person in charge of a **motor vehicle or trailer** to cause or permit the vehicle to stand on a **road** so as to cause any unnecessary obstruction.

Leaving vehicles in a Dangerous Position

Motor Vehicles

Section 22 Road Traffic Act 1988 - level 3 fine - 3 points - Notice of Intended Prosecution - fixed penalty offence

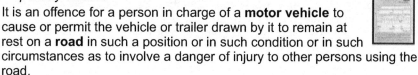

It is an offence for a person in charge of a **motor vehicle** to cause or permit the vehicle or trailer drawn by it to remain at rest on a **road** in such a position or in such condition or in such circumstances as to involve a danger of injury to other persons using the road.

Other Vehicles

Section 22 Road Traffic Act 1988 - level 3 fine - Notice of Intended Prosecution - fixed penalty offence

It is an offence for a person in charge of any other **vehicle** to cause or permit the vehicle or trailer drawn by it to remain at rest on a **road** in such a position or in such condition or in such circumstances as to involve a danger of injury to other persons using the road.

Failing to switch off engine and set parking brake (Quitting)
Section 42 Road Traffic Act 1988 - level 3/4 fine - fixed penalty
Reg 107 Road Vehicles (C&U) Regs 1986

It is an offence for a person to leave or cause or permit to be left, on a **road** a **motor vehicle** which is not attended by a person licensed to drive it unless :-

• the engine is stopped, and

• any parking brake which is required to be fitted is effectively set.

Exemptions to stopping engine
• A vehicle being used for ambulance, fire or police purposes, or

• a vehicle in such a position and condition as not to be likely to endanger any person or property and engaged in an operation which requires its engine to be used to :-

   ○ drive machinery forming part of, or mounted on the vehicle and used for purposes other than driving the vehicle, or

   ○ maintain the electrical power of the batteries at a level required for driving that machinery or apparatus.

See also Chapter 4 Page 37 - Stopping Engine when stationary.

Leaving Trailers at Rest
Section 42 Road Traffic Act 1988 - level 3/4 fine - fixed penalty
Reg 89 Road Vehicles (Construction and Use) Regs 1986

It is an offence for a person in charge of a **motor vehicle, or trailer** drawn thereby, to cause or permit such trailer to stand on a **road** when detached from the drawing vehicle unless at least one of it's wheels are prevented from revolving by the setting of a brake or use of a chain, chock or other efficient device.

See also Chapter 3 Lights.

Parking Restrictions
Civil Enforcement Powers or Road Traffic Regulation Act 1984

Waiting Restrictions
Single Yellow lines - No waiting at certain times - see upright sign.

Double Yellow lines - No waiting at any time - No sign required.

Loading Restrictions
Single kerb marking - No loading or unloading at certain times - see upright sign.

Double kerb marking - No loading or unloading at any time[1].

Yellow carriageway and kerb markings are not required in a Controlled Parking Zone CPZ (an area where on-street parking is restricted during specified times).

Parking On The Footway

Section 19A Road Traffic Act 1988 - NOT IN FORCE

There is no national prohibition on footway (pavement adjacent to carriageway) parking except in relation to heavy commercial vehicles - see below. If the parking amounts to an obstruction action may be taken by the police or local council.

Local authorities may implement a Traffic Regulation Order to restrict or prohibit parking on the footway or designate a locality a 'Special Parking Area' in order to take enforcement measures.

See also Driving or riding on footways at the side of the carriageway, Chapter 30 Page 9.

No parking
on footway
except where
signed

Parking Heavy Commercial Vehicles On The Footway

Section 19(1) Road Traffic Act 1988 - level 3 fine - fixed penalty offence

It is an offence for a person to park a heavy commercial vehicle wholly or partly :-

- on the verge of a road, or
- on any land situated between two carriageways and which is not a footway, or
- on a footway.

It is a defence prove to the satisfaction of the court :-

- that it was parked with the permission of a constable in uniform, or
- that it was parked for the purpose of saving life or extinguishing fire or meeting any other like emergency, or
- that it was parked on the verge or footway for the purpose of loading and unloading, and :-
  - such loading or unloading could not have been carried out satisfactorily if not so parked, and
  - that the vehicle was not left unattended at any time whilst so parked.

Heavy commercial vehicle means a goods vehicles which has a max laden weight (or train weight if towing a trailer) exceeding 7.5 tonnes.

Parking Restrictions relating to lights

Road Vehicles Lighting Regulations 1989

- Restrictions on the Use of Headlights when parked.
- Parking without lights between sunset and sunrise.
- Parking on the nearside between sunset and sunrise.

See Chapter 3 Pages 23, 24.

Parking on cycle tracks

Section 21(1) Road Traffic Act 1988 - level 3 fine

It is an offence for a person, without lawful authority, to park a **mechanically propelled vehicle** wholly or partly on a **cycle track**.

Section 129(6) Roads (Scotland) Act 1984 - level 2 fine

It is an offence for a person to park a **motor vehicle** wholly or partly on a cycle track.

Exceptions include maintenance vehicles.see Chapter 30 Page9.

Parking in Bus and Cycle Lanes

Traffic Regulation Orders - see Chapter 33 Page 16, or Section 36(1) Road Traffic Act 1988 see Chapter 33 Pages 3 and 9.

Builders Skips

Section 139 Highways Act 1980 - level 3 fine

Section 85 Roads (Scotland) Act 1984 - fixed penalty

It is an offence for a person to :-

• deposit a skip on a highway without the permission of the highway authority for the area,

• fail to properly light the skip during the hours of darkness, remove it as soon as practicable after it has been filled or to fail to comply with the conditions of the permission.

It is a defence to show that the offence was due to an act or default of another person and that he took all reasonable precautions and exercised all due diligence to avoid the commission of the offence by himself or any other person under his control.

Where an offence is due to the act or default of some other person, that other person is guilty of the offence.

Temporary Signs placed by the police

Section 67 Road Traffic Regulation Act 1984

A constable or person acting under the instructions of a chief officer of police may place signs indicating prohibitions, restrictions or requirements relating to vehicular traffic to prevent or mitigate congestion or danger to or from traffic in consequence of extraordinary circumstances.

Such signs may only be maintained up to 7 days (28 days if placed in connection with terrorism or the prospect of terrorism).

Section 36 Road Traffic Act 1988 - level 3 fine - NOIP - fixed penalty offence

It is an offence for a person to fail to comply with a traffic sign placed in circumstances above.

Clearways
Stopping on Clearways

Clearways, where no stopping is allowed, are established using Traffic Regulation Orders which detail the extent of the prohibition or restriction, the period of operation and the exemptions which apply.

Such orders can be extended to prohibit waiting on the adjacent verges and footways.

Contravention of the order are offences in various sections of the Road Traffic Regulation Act 1984 - most commonly section 5(1) below.

See also Chapter 33.

Section 5(1) Road Traffic Regulation Act 1984 - level 3 fine - fixed penalty offence

Common Exemptions
- Building operations or demolition.
- Removal of obstruction or potential obstruction to traffic.
- Maintenance and improvement work to the carriageway.
- Erection, maintenance, removal testing etc. of apparatus in, on, under or over the carriageway.
- Fire, police, coastguard or ambulance purposes.
- Postal collections or deliveries.
- Dustbin collections, refuse and cesspool clearance.
- Public Service Vehicles providing a local service stopping at authorised stopping places.
- Waiting to gain access to premises with the vehicle.
- Required by law to stop.
- Upon the direction or with the permission of a constable in uniform.
- To avoid accident.
- Prevented from proceeding by circumstances outside his control.

Trading on Trunk and Principal roads
Article 6 The Various Trunk Roads (Prohibition of Waiting) (Clearways) Order 1963

Section 147A Highways Act 1980 - level 3 fine

Section 97 Roads (Scotland) Act 1984 - level 3 fine

This legislation prohibits selling from a vehicle or stall on verges, lay-bys or unenclosed land within 15 metres of any part of a trunk road where it is likely to cause danger or interrupt any user of the road except with the consent in writing of the roads/highway authority and in accordance with such reasonable conditions as the authority think fit.

Removal and Disposal of Vehicles
Regulation 3(2) Removal and Disposal of Vehicles Regulations 1986

A constable may require the owner, driver or other person in control or charge of a **vehicle** :-

- which has broken down, or been permitted to remain at rest, on a **road or other land** in such a position, condition or circumstances as to cause an obstruction or as to be likely to cause danger of injury to any person,
- which has been permitted to remain at rest or has broken down on a **road or other land** in contravention of a prohibition or restriction,

to move the vehicle or to cause it to be moved.

Regulation 4 Removal and Disposal of Vehicles Regulations 1986

A constable may remove or arrange for the removal of such broken down or stationary vehicle as above or which is on a road or other land, and appears to a constable to have been abandoned without lawful authority.

Abandoned vehicles etc.
Section 2 Refuse Disposal (Amenity) Act 1978 - fine and/or 3 months - local authority fixed penalty notice

It is an offence for a person to abandon on **any land in the open air**, or on **any other land forming part of a highway** (or road in Scotland) :-

- a **motor vehicle or anything which formed part of a motor vehicle** and was removed from it in the course of dismantling the vehicle on the land, or
- **any thing other than a motor vehicle**, being a thing which he has brought to the land for the purpose of abandoning it there.

Vehicle clamping
Police Power
Section 104(1) Road Traffic Regulation Act 1984

Where a constable finds a **vehicle on a road** which has been permitted to remain at rest there in contravention of any prohibition or restriction he or any person under his direction may :-

- fix an immobilisation device in situ,
- move the vehicle to another place and fix an immobilisation device.

A notice must be affixed to the vehicle once immobilised.

Exemptions from immobilisation

- a current disabled persons badge is displayed,
- the vehicle is within a meter bay unless :-
  - the meter bay was not authorised for use when the vehicle was parked, or
  - the initial charge was not made, or
  - there is an overstay of more than 2 hours.

Removal of Notice or Clamp

Section 104(5), (6) Road Traffic Regulation Act 1984 - level 2/3 fine

It is an offence for a person,

- without the authority of the person in charge of the vehicle or the person who placed it there, to remove or interfere with a notice affixed in accordance with this section,
- without being authorised to do so, to remove or attempt to remove an immobilisation device fixed in accordance with this section.

Powers of other bodies

Where Local Authorities operate DPE (deCriminalised parking enforcement) schemes, powers to clamp derive from *section 79 Traffic Management Act 1984.*

Clamping powers are also exercisable by the local authorities, DVSA and DVLA for enforcement of a range of measures including illegal parking, obstruction, abandoned vehicles, unroadworthy vehicles, no vehicle excise licence, traveller encampments, local authority car parks, car parks at airports and railway stations.

Enforcement Agents (Bailiffs) have a mix of statutory and common law powers to immobilise and tow away vehicles for the purposes of enforcing debts.

Illegal Clamping

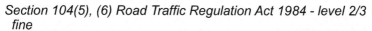
Private contractors can no longer clamp vehicles parked on private land.

Mishandling of parking documents

Section 115 Road Traffic Regulation Act 1985 - indictable (triable either way offence), level 5 fine/ 2 years

This section provides an offence for a person, with intent to deceive, to use, or lend to, or allow to be used by, any other person any local authority parking ticket, permit, token or similar authorisation.

This includes :-

- blue badges issued to disabled persons, and
- residents, visitor and business parking permits.

P Parking Concessions For Disabled And Blind People

Blue Badge Scheme

The Blue Badge is a Central Government Scheme administered by Local Authorities. The disabled persons badge provides exemption from waiting restrictions on yellow lines up to 3 hours (no limit in Scotland) but parking is prohibited in areas where there is a loading or unloading prohibition or in bus lanes, clearways and cycle lanes during their hours of operation.

The badge should be exhibited on the dashboard of the vehicle so that the so that the front of the badge is clearly legible from the outside of the vehicle. A badge issued to an individual may be displayed on a vehicle while it is parked if it has been driven by the holder, or has been used to carry the holder, to the place where it is parked or is to be driven by the holder, or is to be used to carry the holder, from that place.

Production of badge

A constable, or an enforcement officer (a civil enforcement officer, a parking attendant or an authorised enforcement officer on production of his authority) may require any person who is in the vehicle, or appears to have been in, or to be about to get into, the vehicle, to produce the badge for inspection.

Section 21(4BD) Chronically Sick and Disabled Persons Act 1970 - level 3 fine

It is an offence for a person who without reasonable excuse fails to produce a badge when required to do so.

Misuse of badge

Section 21(4B) and (4BZA) Chronically Sick and Disabled Persons Act 1970 - level 3 fine

It is an offence for a person to drive a motor vehicle on a road at a time when a badge is displayed on the vehicle unless the badge is issued under this section and displayed in accordance with regulations made under it and has not been cancelled or has not been returned as required.

Section 117(1) Road Traffic Regulation Act 1984 - level 3 fine

A person who at any time acts in contravention of, or fails to comply with, any provision relating to the parking of motor vehicles is guilty of an offence if at that time :-

• there is displayed a badge, and
• he was using the vehicle in circumstances where a disabled person's concession would be available to a disabled person's vehicle,

unless the badge was issued and displayed in accordance with regulations.

Chapter 29 Speed Limits

Generally speed limits apply only to drivers of **motor vehicles** however some temporary limits and limits at special events imposed by orders **may** apply to drivers or riders of all vehicles including cycles. Some local by-laws, particularly in public parks, may also apply to cyclists.

	Offence	Driving Licence Code
1	**Restricted Roads - 30mph (20mph Wales)**	
	Section 89(1) Road Traffic Regulation Act 1984 - level 3 fine / 3 to 6 points - fixed penalty offence	SP30
2	**Speed Limits on other roads (not motorways) - 20/30/40/50/60mph**	
	Section 89(1) Road Traffic Regulation Act 1984 - level 3 fine / 3 to 6 points - fixed penalty offence	SP30
3	**Motorway Speed Limits - Fixed and Variable**	
	Section 17(4) Road Traffic Regulation Act 1984 - level 4 fine / 3 to 6 points - fixed penalty offence	SP50
4	**Vehicle Class Speed Limits - Various**	
	Section 89(1) Road Traffic Regulation Act 1984 - level 3 fine / 3 to 6 points - fixed penalty offence	SP10/20 /40
5	**Speed Limits at Roadworks etc. - Various**	
	Section 16(1) Road Traffic Regulation Act 1984 - level 3 fine / 3 to 6 points - fixed penalty offence	SP30
6	**National Speed Limits - 50/60/70mph**	
	Section 89(1) Road Traffic Regulation Act 1984 - level 3 fine / 3 to 6 points - fixed penalty offence	SP30
7	**Minimum Speed Limits - Various**	
	Section 88(7) Road Traffic Regulation Act 1984 - level 3 fine - fixed penalty offence	Not endorsable
8	**Exceeding C and U Plated Speed Restrictions 40/50mph**	
	Section 42(b) Road Traffic Act 1988 - level 4 fine for goods vehicles - fixed penalty offence	Not endorsable
9	**Speed Limits at Events - Various**	
	Section 16C(1) Road Traffic Regulation Act 1984 - level 3 fine	Not endorsable

A Notice of Intended Prosecution (N.O.I.P.) is required for offences 1 to 7 above unless a Fixed Penalty Notice is issued at the time.

1 Restricted Roads - 20/30mph

Sections 81 - 83 Road Traffic Regulation Act 1984
A restricted road is a road (not being a motorway) :-

- in England and Wales, with a system of street lighting furnished by lamps placed not more than 200 yards (183 metres) apart, or
- in Scotland, with a system of carriageway lighting furnished by means of lamps placed not more than 185 metres apart and the road is a Class C or unclassified road, or
- where a traffic authority for a road has directed that the road which is not a restricted road (by virtue of a system of street lighting as above) shall become a restricted road (speed restriction signs are required).

A traffic authority may de-restrict a road - signs required.

Drivers are expected to know that a system of street lighting means that a road carries a 30 m.p.h. speed limit in England and Scotland or 20 m.p.h. in Wales unless signs show otherwise.

2 Speed limits on other roads (not motorways) - 20/30/40/50/60mph

Section 84 Road Traffic Regulation Act 1984

Traffic Regulation Orders (TROs) made under *section 84(1)* by a Traffic Authority are of a permanent nature. Most permanent speed limits (except on motorways or restricted roads) of 20, 30, 40, 50mph and, on dual carriageways, 60mph are authorised under this section.

Section 88(1)(a) Road Traffic Regulation Act 1984

Orders made under *section 88(1)(a)* by the Secretary Of State in England or a Minister in Wales or Scotland can impose speed limits on all roads, or on all roads in a specified area or on all roads of a specified class, or on all roads other than roads of a specified class or on any specified road. Orders made under *section 88* are temporary in nature and require renewal after 18 months.

3 Motorway Speed limits - Fixed and Variable

The Motorways Traffic (Speed Limit) Regulations 1974

These Regulations impose a maximum speed limit of 70 miles per hour on the driving of motor vehicles on motorways, except on specified lengths of motorway which are for the time being subject to speed limits lower than 70 m.p.h.

Various (Variable Speed Limits) Regulations

Modifications to these regulations are made to allow the use of variable speed limits on smart motorways.

Speed restrictions at roadworks on motorways are authorised under section 14 (see item 5 - next page) not this section.

4 Vehicle Classes Speed Limits - Various

Section 86 Road Road Traffic Regulation Act 1984
Schedule 6 Traffic Regulation Act 1984

Schedule 6 prescribes the maximum speeds permissible in relation to each class of vehicle, *see page 7.* The Secretary Of State in England or a Minister in Wales or Scotland has the power to vary the limit except for vehicles which are :-

- constructed solely for the carriage of passengers and their effects, and
- not adapted to carry more than 8 passengers exclusive of driver, and
- neither a heavy motor car nor an invalid carriage, and
- not drawing a trailer, and
- fitted with pneumatic tyres on all its wheels.

5 Speed Limits at Roadworks etc. - Various

Section 14 Road Traffic Regulation Act 1984

The traffic authority for a road may **by order** under *section 14* restrict or prohibit temporarily the use of that road, or of any part of it, by vehicles, or vehicles of any class, or by pedestrians, to such extent and subject to such conditions or exceptions as they may consider necessary :-

- because works are being or are proposed to be executed on or near the road, or
- because of the likelihood of danger to the public, or of serious damage to the road, which is not attributable to such works, or
- for the purpose of litter clearing and cleaning to be discharged.

The traffic authority for a road may at any time **by notice** restrict or prohibit temporarily the use of the road, or of any part of it, by vehicles, or vehicles of any class, or by pedestrians, where it appears to them that it is :-

- necessary or expedient because works are being or are proposed to be executed on or near the road or for the purpose of litter clearing and cleaning to be discharged, or
- necessary because of the likelihood of danger to the public, or of serious damage to the road, which is not attributable to such works,

that the restriction or prohibition should come into force without delay.

This includes imposing speed restrictions on all types of roads including motorways.

A Notice of Intended Prosecution (N.O.I.P.) is required for offences 1 to 5 above unless a Fixed Penalty Notice is issued at the time.

6 National Speed Limits[1] - 50/60/70mph

Section 88(1)(a) Road Traffic Regulation Act 1984
The 70 mph, 60 mph and 50 mph (Temporary Speed Limit) Order 1977

The maximum speed limits on single and dual carriageway roads(except restricted roads and motorways) are set by the Secretary of State in England or a Minister in Wales or Scotland. These limits are currently the same across Great Britain.

- Dual Carriageway roads 70mph.
- Single carriageway roads 60 mph.

Named roads specified as having lower limits are also listed in the Order.

The order specifying these limits is temporary in nature and must be renewed every 18 months, this is achieved automatically by *The 70 miles per hour, 60 miles per hour and 50 miles per hour (Temporary Speed Limit) (Continuation) Order 1978*.

7 Minimum Speed Limits[1] - Various

Section 88(1)(b) Road Traffic Regulation Act 1984

The relevant authority in the interests of safety or for the purpose of facilitating the movement of traffic, may, by order prohibit, for a period not exceeding 18 months, the driving of motor vehicles on any road (except a motorway) specified in the order, at a speed less than the speed specified in the order, subject to such exceptions as may be so specified.

8 Exceeding Plated Speed Restrictions - 40/50mph

Regulation 100A Road Vehicles (Construction and Use) Regulations 1986

These regulations impose speed restrictions of 40mph on vehicles displaying a low platform trailer **LL plate** and 50 mph on a restricted speed vehicle displaying **50 plate**.

9 Speed Limits at Events - Various

Section 16A Road Traffic Regulation Act 1984

A *section 16A* Order may be made by a Traffic Authority for facilitating the holding of a sporting event, social event or entertainment which is held on a road. Usually limited to 3 day duration.

[1]A Notice of Intended Prosecution (N.O.I.P.) is required for offences 6 and 7 above unless a Fixed Penalty Notice is issued at the time.

Requirement for signs

Section 85 Road Traffic Regulation Act 1984
Schedule 10 Traffic Signs Regulations and General Directions 2016

A person shall not be convicted of driving a motor vehicle on a road in excess of the speed limit unless the limit is indicated by traffic signs which are erected and maintained as required, except on :-

- restricted roads with a system of street lighting which are subject to a speed limit of 30 m.p.h, (20 m.p.h in Wales), or
- roads subject to the national speed limit of 60 m.p.h. on single carriageways or 70 m.p.h. on dual carriageways.

A minimum of one terminal sign must still be placed as close as practicable to the point where a limit begins and ends.
There is no requirement to place repeater signs along a speed limit at all. The onus is on traffic authorities to determine the appropriate level of signing provision on a case by case basis having regard to existing guidance.
A lack of signage or unclear/obscured signage could form the basis for a defence.

Evidence

A person shall not be liable to be convicted solely on the evidence of one witness to the effect that, in the opinion of the witness, the person prosecuted was driving the vehicle at a speed exceeding a specified limit. Corroboration is required which can include :-

- The independent opinion of a second police officer.
- A calibrated speed detection instrument, such as a radar gun or a vehicle speedometer.

Evidence of fact does not require corroboration (such as speed from tyre marks or from a tachograph chart given by expert witnesses or from an approved calibrated camera).

Employers encouraging speed offences

Section 89(4) Road Traffic Regulation Act 1984

If a person who employs other persons to drive motor vehicles on roads publishes or issues any time-table or schedule, or gives any directions, under which any journey, or any stage or part of any journey, is to be completed within some specified time, and it is not practicable in the circumstances of the case for that journey (or that stage or part of it) to be completed in the specified time without the commission of an offence of exceeding a speed limit, the publication or issue of the time-table or schedule, or the giving of the directions, may be produced as prima facie evidence that the employer procured or (as the case may be) incited the persons employed by him to drive the vehicles to commit such an offence.

Exemptions From Speed Limits
(70) Emergency Vehicles

Section 87 Road Traffic Regulation Act 1984

No statutory provision imposing a speed limit on motor vehicles shall apply to any vehicle on an occasion when it is being used for :-

- fire and rescue authority purposes,
- ambulance[1] purposes, including vehicles that, although not being used for ambulance purposes, are being used for the purpose of providing a response to an emergency at the request of an NHS ambulance service[2], or
- National Crime Agency purposes by a person who has been trained in driving vehicles at high speeds, or for training persons to drive vehicles for use for National Crime Agency purposes, or
- police purposes,

if the observance of that provision would be likely to hinder the use of the vehicle for the purpose for which it is being used on that occasion.

[1] An ambulance is a vehicle which is constructed or adapted and used for the purposes of conveying sick, injured or disabled persons.
[2]An NHS ambulance service means an NHS trust or NHS foundation trust which has a function of providing ambulance services or the Scottish Ambulance Service Board.

Special Forces

Regulation 2 Road Traffic Exemptions (Special Forces) (Variation and Amendment) Regulations 2011

Vehicles used by Special Forces for training and national security emergencies are exempt from speed limits.

Class Speed Limit exemptions

The Motor Vehicle (Variation of Speed Limit) Regulations 1947

- Motor vehicles owned by the Secretary of State for Defence and used for naval, military or air force purpose or which are so used while being driven by persons for the time being subject to the orders of any member of the armed forces of the Crown or which are vehicles in the service of visiting force and are constructed or adapted :-
  - for actual combative purposes, or training in connection therewith,
  - for the conveyance of personnel, or
  - for use with, or for the carriage or drawing of guns or machine guns, ammunition, equipment or stores,
  - as Mobile cranes constructed or adapted for the raising of aircraft,
  - as Fire tenders,
  - as Ambulances.
- Motor vehicles used for salvage - *Merchant Shipping Act 1894.*

Vehicle Class Speeds

Vehicle	Carriageway Type
	Single/Dual/M-way
Motorcycle	60/70/70
Motorcycle + Trailer	50/60/60
Invalid Carriage (not exceeding 254kg)	20/20/-
Passenger vehicle, Motor caravan, Dual purpose vehicle :- *none of which exceed 3050 kg unladen or 8 passenger seats, or* A car derived van	60/70/70
As above + Trailer	50/60/60
Passenger vehicle, Dual purpose vehicle, Motor caravan :- *which exceeds 3050 kg unladen or 8 passenger seats but does not exceed 12 metres length*	50/60/70
As above + Trailer	50/60/60
Passenger vehicle, Dual purpose vehicle Motor caravan *which exceeds 3050 kg unladen or 8 passenger seats and exceeds 12 metres length*	50/60/60
As above + Trailer	50/60/60

Dual purpose vehicle - A vehicle constructed or adapted for the carriage both of passengers and of goods, maximum unladen weight not exceeding 2040kg, and is either :-

- constructed or adapted so that the driving power of the engine is, or can be selected to be, transmitted to all wheels of the vehicle (eg: Land Rovers etc.), or
- permanently fitted with a rigid roof, at least one row of transverse passenger seats to the rear of the driver's seat and fitted with both side and rear windows - there must also be a minimum ratio between the size of passenger and stowage areas (eg: some estate cars).

Unladen weight - the weight of a vehicle or trailer inclusive of the body and all parts (the heavier being taken where alternative bodies or parts are used) which are necessary to or ordinarily used with the vehicle or trailer when working on a road, but exclusive of the weight of water, fuel or accumulators used for the purpose of the supply of power for the propulsion of the vehicle or, as the case may be, of any vehicle by which the trailer is drawn, and of loose tools and loose equipment.

Car derived van - A goods vehicle which is constructed or adapted as a derivative of a passenger vehicle which has a maximum laden weight not exceeding 2000kg.

Vehicle Class Speeds *continued*

Vehicle	Carriageway Type Single/Dual/M-way
	🏴󠁧󠁢󠁥󠁮󠁧󠁿 🏴󠁧󠁢󠁷󠁬󠁳󠁿 🏴󠁧󠁢󠁳󠁣󠁴󠁿
Goods vehicle not exceeding 7.5 tonnes maximum laden weight, not articulated vehicle or car derived van.	50/60/70
As above + Trailer.	50/60/60
Articulated goods vehicle not exceeding 7.5 tonnes maximum laden weight.	50/60/60
Rigid Goods vehicle exceeding 7.5 tonnes maximum laden weight in England and Wales.	50/60/60 🏴󠁧󠁢󠁥󠁮󠁧󠁿
As above + Trailer in England and Wales.	🏴󠁧󠁢󠁷󠁬󠁳󠁿
Articulated goods vehicle exceeding 7.5 tonnes maximum laden weight in England and Wales.	
Rigid Goods vehicle exceeding 7.5 tonnes maximum laden weight in Scotland.	40¹/50/60 🏴󠁧󠁢󠁳󠁣󠁴󠁿
As above + Trailer in Scotland.	
Articulated goods vehicle exceeding 7.5 tonnes maximum laden weight in Scotland.	
¹ All Goods vehicles exceeding 7.5 tonnes maximum laden weight - on specified stretches of the A9 single carriageway road in Scotland.	50/50/60 🏴󠁧󠁢󠁳󠁣󠁴󠁿
	🏴󠁧󠁢󠁥󠁮󠁧󠁿 🏴󠁧󠁢󠁷󠁬󠁳󠁿 🏴󠁧󠁢󠁳󠁣󠁴󠁿
Motor tractor or locomotive without trailer or with not more than 1 trailer.	30/30/30
Motor tractor or locomotive with more than 1 trailer.	20/20/20
Agricultural motor vehicle (with or without trailer).	40/40/40
Works trucks (with or without trailer).	18/18/18
Tracked vehicles fitted with springs and resilient material between the rollers of the track or vehicles towing such vehicles.	20 (40 mph for military vehicles)
Tracked vehicles not fitted with springs and resilient material between the rollers of the track or vehicles towing such vehicles.	5

Chapter 30 Manner of Driving

Dangerous Driving

Manner of driving

Section 2A(1) Road Traffic Act 1988

A person is to be regarded as driving dangerously if :-

- the way he drives falls far below what would be expected of a competent and careful driver, and
- it would be obvious to a competent and careful driver that driving in that way would be dangerous.

But this subsection does not apply where a designated person who has undertaken prescribed training is driving for police purposes.

Manner of driving: constables etc

Section 2A(1B) Road Traffic Act 1988

A designated person is to be regarded as driving dangerously if :-

- the way the person drives falls far below what would be expected of a competent and careful constable who has undertaken the same prescribed training, and
- it would be obvious to such a competent and careful constable that driving in that way would be dangerous.

__Designated Person__ includes constables (but not Port constables) and members of police staff and, subject to conditions, National Crime Agency officers.

__Prescribed Training__ - see Road Traffic Act 1988 (Police Driving: Prescribed Training) Regulations 2023.

Condition of Vehicle

Section 2A(2) Road Traffic Act 1988

A person is also to be regarded as driving dangerously if it would be obvious to a competent and careful driver that driving the vehicle in its current state would be dangerous.

In determining the state of a vehicle, regard may be had to anything attached to or carried on or in it and to the manner in which it is attached or carried.

Dangerous

Section 2A (3)Road Traffic Act 1988

'Dangerous' refers to danger either of injury to any person or of serious damage to property, and in determining what would be expected of, or obvious to, a competent and careful driver or constable (as the case may be) in a particular case, regard shall be had not only to the circumstances of which he could be expected to be aware but also to any circumstances shown to have been within the knowledge of the accused.

Dangerous Driving *continued*
Dangerous Driving - offence

Section 2 Road Traffic Act 1988 - 2 years/fine - 3 - 11 points - disqualification period and disqualified until test passed - (NOIP) - indictable (triable either way) offence

It is an offence for a person to drive a **mechanically propelled vehicle** dangerously on a **road** or other **public place**.

Causing Serious Injury by Dangerous Driving

Section 1A Road Traffic Act 1988 - 5 years - 3 - 11 points - disqualification period and disqualified until test passed - indictable (triable either way) offence

It is an offence for a person to cause **serious injury** to another person by driving a **mechanically propelled vehicle** dangerously on a **road** or other **public place**.

Serious Injury means physical harm which amounts to grievous bodily harm for the purposes of the Offences against the Person Act 1861 or in Scotland, severe physical injury.

Causing Death by Dangerous Driving

Section 1 Road Traffic Act 1988 - Imprisonment for life - 3 - 11 points - disqualification and disqualified until test passed - indictable

It is an offence for a person to cause the **death** of another person by driving a **mechanically propelled vehicle** dangerously on a **road** or other **public place**.

Manslaughter

Common Law - Life - indictable offence

An unlawful homicide without malice aforethought.

If the standard of driving has been grossly negligent on the part of the driver, a charge of gross negligence manslaughter may be considered.

Corporate Manslaughter

Section 1 Corporate Manslaughter and Corporate Homicide Act 2007 - unlimited fine

It is an offence for any corporation, department or listed government body, police force or a partnership, trade union or employers' association that is an employer, where the way in which its activities are managed or organised causes the death of a person, and

- it amounts to a gross breach of a relevant duty of care owed to the deceased, and
- the management or organisation is a substantial element in the breach.

Careless, or Inconsiderate, driving
Meaning of careless, or inconsiderate, driving

Section 3ZA(2) Road Traffic Act 1988

A person is to be regarded as driving without due care and attention if (and only if) the way he drives falls below what would be expected of a competent and careful driver.

But this subsection does not apply where a designated person who has undertaken prescribed training is driving for police purposes.

Manner of driving: constables etc
Section 3ZA(2B) Road Traffic Act 1988

A designated person is to be regarded as driving without due care and attention if (and only if) the way the person drives falls below what would be expected of a competent and careful constable who has undertaken the same prescribed training.

Designated Person includes constables (but not Port constables) and members of police staff and, subject to conditions, National Crime Agency officers.

Prescribed Training
The Road Traffic Act 1988 (Police Driving: Prescribed Training) Regulations 2023

Careful and competent driver or constable
Section 3ZA(3) Road Traffic Act 1988

In determining what would be expected of a careful and competent driver or constable (as the case may be) in a particular case, regard shall be had not only to the circumstances of which he could be expected to be aware but also to any circumstances shown to have been within the knowledge of the accused.

Reasonable Consideration
Section 3ZA(4) Road Traffic Act 1988

A person is to be regarded as driving without reasonable consideration for other persons only if those persons are inconvenienced by his driving.

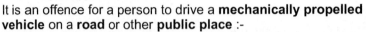

Careless, or Inconsiderate, driving *continued*
Careless Driving - offence

Section 3 Road Traffic Act 1988 - level 5 fine - 3 to 9 points - discretionary disqualification - (NOIP) - fixed penalty offence

It is an offence for a person to drive a **mechanically propelled vehicle** on a **road** or other **public place** :-

- without due care and attention, or
- without reasonable consideration for other persons using the road or place.

Causing serious injury by careless, or inconsiderate, driving

Section 2C(1) Road Traffic Act 1988 - 2 years and or fine, 3 - 11 points - disqualification period - indictable (triable either way) offence

A person who causes serious injury to another person by driving a **mechanically propelled vehicle** on a **road** or other **public place** without due care and attention, or without reasonable consideration for other persons using the road or place, is guilty of an offence.

Serious injury means :-

- in England and Wales, physical harm which amounts to grievous bodily harm for the purposes of the *Offences against the Person Act 1861*, and
- in Scotland, severe physical injury.

Power to Seize vehicles used to cause alarm, distress or annoyance

Section 59 Police Reform Act 2002
Section 126 Antisocial Behaviour etc. (Scotland) Act 2004

A constable in uniform may seize a **motor vehicle** where he has reasonable grounds for believing that it is being used or has been used :-

- in contravention of *section 3 Road Traffic Act 1988* (careless and inconsiderate driving), or *section 34 Road Traffic Act 1988* (prohibition of off-road driving), and
- is causing, or is likely to cause, alarm, distress or annoyance to members of the public.

He may, if the **motor vehicle** is moving, order the person driving it to stop the vehicle.

See Chapter 2 page 18 for full details.

Careless, or Inconsiderate, driving *continued*
Causing Death by Careless Driving

Section 2B Road Traffic Act 1988 - 5 years - 3 - 11 points - disqualification - indictable (triable either way)

It is an offence for a person to cause the death of another person by driving a **mechanically propelled vehicle** on a **road** or other **public place** :-

• without due care and attention, or
• without reasonable consideration for other persons using the road or place.

Causing Death by Careless Driving when under influence of Drink or Drugs

Section 3A Road Traffic Act 1988 - Imprisonment for life - 3 - 11 points - disqualification - indictable offence

It is an offence for a person to cause the **death** of another person by **driving** on a **road** or other **public place** :-

• without due care and attention, or
• without reasonable consideration for other persons using the road or place,

a vehicle which is :-

• a **mechanically propelled vehicle** and he is, at time when he is driving, unfit to drive through drink or drugs, or
• a **motor vehicle** and :-
  ○ he has consumed so much alcohol that the proportion of it in his breath, blood or urine at that time exceeds the prescribed limit, or
  ○ he has in his body a specified controlled drug and the proportion of it in his blood or urine at that time exceeds the specified limit for that drug, or
  ○ he is, within 18 hours after that time, required to provide a specimen (breath - at a police station, blood or urine - at a police station or hospital) in pursuance of *section 7 Road Traffic Act 1988,* or
  ○ he is required by a constable to give his permission for a laboratory test of a specimen of blood taken from him under *section 7A Road Traffic Act 1988*, but in either case, without reasonable excuse, fails to provide it.

Dangerous and Careless Driving - Application

Dangerous Driving and Careless or Inconsiderate Driving offences apply to a person who **drives a mechanically propelled vehicle on a road or other public place** in a particular manner or condition.

Electrically assisted pedal cycles

Electrically assisted pedal cycles are classed as **mechanically propelled vehicles** so both dangerous and careless driving offences apply where they take place on a road or other public place.

e-Scooters

e-Scooters are classed as **mechanically propelled vehicles** (and possibly **motor vehicles**) so both dangerous and careless driving offences apply where they take place on a road or other public place.

Mobility Scooters

Sections 1 to 4 Road Traffic Act 1988 **do not apply** to Class II and III mechanically propelled invalid carriages which comply with the prescribed requirements and are being used in accordance with the prescribed conditions.

Where injury is involved consider 'Wanton or furious driving'.

Vehicles participating in Authorised (Off Road) Motoring Events

Section 13A Road Traffic Act 1988

A person shall not be guilty of an offence under *sections 1,1A, 2, 2B, 2C or 3 Road Traffic Act 1988* by **driving a vehicle** in a **public place other than a road** if he shows that he was driving in accordance with an authorisation for a motoring event given under regulations made by the Secretary of State.

See The Motor Vehicles (Off Road Events) Regulations 1995.

Other Offences
Causing death - unlicensed or uninsured drivers

Section 3ZB Road Traffic Act 1988 - 2 years - 3 - 11 points - disqualification - indictable (triable either way)

It is an offence for a person to **cause the death** of another person by **driving** a **motor vehicle** on a **road** and, at the time when he is driving, the circumstances are such that he is committing an offence under :-

- *section 87(1) Road Traffic Act 1988* (driving otherwise than in accordance with a licence), or
- *section 143 Road Traffic Act 1988* (using a motor vehicle without insurance).

Causing death - disqualified drivers

Section 3ZC Road Traffic Act 1988 - 10 years and or fine - 3 - 11 points - disqualification - indictable offence

It is an offence for a person to **cause the death** of another person by driving a **motor vehicle** on a **road** and, at that time is committing an offence under *section 103(1)(b) Road Traffic Act 1988* (driving while disqualified).

Causing serious injury - disqualified drivers

Section 3ZD Road Traffic Act 1988 - 4 years and or fine - 3 - 11 points - disqualification - indictable (triable either way)

It is an offence for a person to **cause serious injury** to another person by driving a **motor vehicle** on a **road** and, at that time is committing an offence under *section 103(1)(b) Road Traffic Act 1988* (driving while disqualified).

Serious injury means in England and Wales, physical harm which amounts to grievous bodily harm for the purposes of the Offences against the Person Act 1861, and in Scotland, severe physical injury.

Application
Electrically Assisted Pedal Cycles and Mobility Scooters
Sections 3ZB, 3ZC and 3ZD above **do not apply to** :-

- electrically assisted cycles prescribed by regulations, and
- Class II and III Invalid carriages which comply with the prescribed requirements and used in accordance with the prescribed conditions,

as they are not classed as motor vehicles.

Where injury is involved consider 'Wanton or furious driving'.
Where drink is involved consider 'Drunk in charge of a carriage'.

Other Offences *continued*
Motor Racing on a Public Way

Section 12, 12A-I Road Traffic Act 1988 - level 4 fine, 3 - 11 points

It is an offence to promote or take part in a race or trial of speed between **motor vehicles** on a **public way** except where :-

- a permit has been issued to the promoter of the event by an authorised motor sport governing body, and
- an order has been granted by the highway authority for the area (or areas) in which the event is to take place.

> **Public Way**
> In England and Wales, a Highway.
> In Scotland a Public Road.

Motoring Events on a Public Way

Motor Vehicles (Competitions and Trials) Regulations 1969
Section 13 Road Traffic Act 1988 - level 3 fine

It is an offence to promote or take part in a competition or trial involving the use of **motor vehicles** on a public way unless it is authorised, and conducted in accordance with any conditions imposed.

Unnecessary Reversing

Regulation 106 Road Vehicles (Construction and Use)
 Regulations 1986
Section 42 Road Traffic Act 1988 - level 3 fine

No person shall drive, or cause or permit to be driven, a motor vehicle backwards on a road further than may be requisite for the safety or reasonable convenience of the occupants of the vehicle or other traffic, unless it is a road roller or is engaged in the construction, maintenance or repair of the road.

Carriage of children in agricultural vehicles

Health and Safety at Work Act 1974
Prevention of Accidents to Children in Agriculture Regulations 1998

It is an offence for a person to cause or permit a child under 13 years of age to :-

- ride on a tractor, self-propelled agricultural machine, trailer, machine or agricultural implement mounted in whole or in part on, or towed or propelled by a tractor or other vehicle, or on a machine or agricultural implement drawn by an animal, (*Except a trailer where the child rides on its floor or on a load carried by it and where it has adequate means for preventing the child falling from it.*)
- drive a tractor, or self-propelled vehicle or machine,

while it is being used in the course of agricultural operations or is going to or from the site of such operations.

Defence for a person to prove that he used all due diligence to comply.

Other Offences *continued*
Driving on footpaths, bridlepaths and off the road

Section 34 Road Traffic Act 1988 - level 3 fine - fixed penalty

It is an offence for a person to drive a **mechanically propelled vehicle** :-

- on to or upon any **common land, moorland or other land** (of whatever description) not being land forming part of a road, or
- on any road being a **footpath, bridleway or restricted byway**.

except :-

- ○ for the purpose of parking on any land within 15 yards of a road, being a road on which a motor vehicle may be lawfully driven, or
- ○ for purpose of saving life, extinguishing fire or meeting any other like emergency.

This section does not apply to :-

- mechanically propelled grass cutters controlled by a pedestrian,
- other mechanically propelled vehicles controlled by a pedestrian which may be specified by regulations,
- electrically assisted pedal cycles prescribed by regulations, and

- Class II and III Invalid carriages which comply with the prescribed requirements and used in accordance with the prescribed conditions,

There may be other rights of access or easements in existence to allow access to land or for maintenance.

Driving or riding on footways at the side of the carriageway (pavements)

Section 72 Highways Act 1835 - level 2 fine - fixed penalty

It is an offence for a person to wilfully ride a **carriage** upon a **footway by the side of a road** made or set apart for the use or accommodation of foot passengers, except :-

- Local council vehicles used for maintenance, cleansing etc. of footpaths and verges.
- Class 1, 2 or 3 Invalid Carriages driven at a maximum of 4 m.p.h.

This offence relates to both cycles and motor vehicles and is complete even if committed for a few seconds. Force policies relating to children may vary and it would be wise to consult these before proceeding.

Driving in Bus Lanes and through Bus Gates

Various sections, Road Traffic Regulation Act 1984

It is an offence to contravene a Traffic Regulation Order

See Chapter 33 Pages 1, 3 and 16.

Other Offences *continued*
Driving or Parking on Cycle Tracks
Section 21(1) Road Traffic Act 1988 - level 3 fine

It is an offence for a person, without lawful authority, to drive, or park a **mechanically propelled vehicle** wholly or partly on a cycle track.

It is a **defence** to prove to a court that :-

• the vehicle was driven or parked for the purpose of saving life, extinguishing fire or meeting any other like emergency,

• the vehicle was owned or operated by or on behalf of the highway authority and was driven or parked in connection with cleansing, maintenance, improvement, removal of obstructions, preventing nuisances etc. or other work on the track or it's verges,

• the vehicle was owned or operated by or on behalf statutory undertakers and was driven or parked in connection with works.

Cycle track
Section 329(1) Highways Act 1980

A highway or part of a highway with a public right of way on pedal cycles and electrically assisted pedal cycles. Pedestrians may have a right of way (examine the definitive map).

Parking on a cycle track may be dealt with under Civil Enforcement.

Driving in Cycle Lanes

Section 36 Road Traffic Act 1988 (mandatory with flow cycle lanes) OR Various sections Road Traffic Regulation Act 1984

It is an offence to fail to comply with a *section 36* Sign or contravene a Traffic Regulation Order.

See Chapter 33 Pages 9 and 16.

Sites of Special Scientific Interest (SSSI's)

It is an offence for a person (other than the responsible authority acting in the exercise of its functions) to, without reasonable excuse :-

Sections 28P(6) Wildlife and Countryside Act 1981 - indictable (triable either way offence) - fine

• knowing that he is within a site of special scientific interest to intentionally or recklessly destroy or damage any of the flora, fauna, or geological or physiographical features by reason of which land is of special interest, or intentionally or recklessly disturbs any fauna, or

Sections 28P(6A) Wildlife and Countryside Act 1981 - level 4 fine

• intentionally or recklessly destroy or damage any of the flora, fauna, or geological or physiographical features by reason of which a site of special scientific interest is of special interest, or

• intentionally or recklessly disturbs any of those fauna.

Prosecution by Natural England or with permission of DPP.

Other Offences *continued*
Wanton or furious driving or racing

Section 35 Offences Against the Person Act 1861 - 2 years - indictable offence - 3 to 9 points if mechanically propelled vehicle

It is an offence for any person having charge of **any carriage or vehicle**, by wanton or furious driving, or racing, or other wilful misconduct, or by wilful neglect, doing, or causing to be done any bodily harm to any person.

Danger of Injury

Section 40A Road Traffic Act 1988 - level 5 fine for goods vehicles or vehicles adapted to carry more than 8 passengers - level 4 fine in any other case - 3 points, - fixed penalty offence

A person is guilty of an offence if he uses, causes or permits another to use a **motor vehicle or trailer** on a road when :-

- *section 40A(a)* the condition of the motor vehicle or trailer, or of its accessories or equipment, or
- *section 40A(b)* the purpose for which it is used, or
- *section 40A(c)* the number of passengers carried by it, or the manner in which they are carried, or
- *section 40A(d)* the weight, position or distribution of its load, or the manner in which it is secured,

is such that the use of the **motor vehicle or trailer** involves a danger of injury to any person.

Cause and permit offences are not fixed penalty offences.

Proper Control

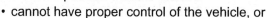

Regulation 104 Road Vehicles (Construction and Use) Regulations 1986
Section 41D(a) Road Traffic Act 1988 - level 3/4 fine

No person shall drive or cause or permit any other person to drive, a motor vehicle on a road if the driver is in a such a position that the driver :-

- cannot have proper control of the vehicle, or
- cannot have a full view of the road and traffic ahead.

[1] Cause and Permit offences are not fixed penalty offences.
See Chapter 4 Page 2.

Use of Mobile Phones

Regulation 110 Road Vehicles (Construction and Use)
Regulations 1986
Section 41D(b) Road Traffic Act 1988 - level 3/4 fine

(1) No person shall drive a motor vehicle on a road if he is using :-

(a) a hand-held mobile telephone, or

(b) a hand-held device of a kind specified in paragraph (4).

(2) No person shall cause or permit any other person to drive a motor vehicle on a road while that other person is using :

(a) a hand-held mobile telephone, or

(b) a hand-held device of a kind specified in paragraph (4).

(3) No person shall supervise a holder of a provisional licence if the person supervising is using :-

(a) a hand-held mobile telephone, or

(b) a hand-held device of a kind specified in paragraph (4),

at a time when the provisional licence holder is driving a motor vehicle on a road.

(4) A device referred to in paragraphs (1)(b), (2)(b) and (3)(b) is a device, other than a two-way radio, which is capable of transmitting and receiving data, whether or not those capabilities are enabled.

Two way radios which can also operate on mobile telephone frequencies are not exempt even when being used as a two way radio.

Exceptions

Regulation 110(5, 5A, 5B) Road Vehicles (Construction and Use)
Regulations 1986

A person does not contravene a provision of this regulation if, at the time of the alleged contravention :-

• the person is using the telephone or other device to call the police, fire, ambulance or other emergency services in response to a genuine emergency, and it is unsafe or impracticable to cease driving in order to make the call,

• that person is using the mobile telephone or other device only to perform a remote controlled parking function within 6 metres of the motor vehicle, or

• that person is using the mobile telephone or other device to make a contactless payment for goods or service which is received at the same time as, or after, the contactless payment is made and the motor vehicle is stationary, (ie: paying at a toll booth).

Definitions
Regulation 110(6) Road Vehicles (Construction and Use) Regulations 1986

Hand-Held
A mobile telephone or other device is to be treated as hand-held if it is, or must be, held at some point while being used.

Using
Using includes :-
- illuminating the screen, or unlocking the device,
- checking the time,
- checking notifications,
- making, receiving, or rejecting a telephone or internet based call,
- sending, receiving or uploading oral or written content,
- sending, receiving or uploading a photo or video,
- utilising camera, video, or sound recording functionality,
- drafting any text,
- accessing any stored data such as documents, books, audio files, photos, videos, films, playlists, notes or messages,
- accessing an application, or the internet.

A phone or other applicable device mounted in a cradle is permitted providing it can be operated without holding it (the driver can still operate the buttons without holding the device), however if the driver is distracted when operating the device consider other offences such as proper control, careless, or dangerous driving.

Road can include verges and lay-bys.
Driving can include when the vehicle is stationary.

See Chapter 4 Page 2

The Highway Code

The latest version of the Highway Code can be found on-line at :-

https://www.gov.uk/guidance/the-highway-code

Liability
Section 38(7) Road Traffic Act 1988

A failure on the part of a person to observe a provision of the Highway Code shall not of itself render that person liable to Criminal proceedings of any kind but any such failure may in any proceedings (whether civil or Criminal) be relied upon by any party to the proceedings as tending to establish or to negate any liability which is in question in those proceedings.

Maintenance and use of vehicles so as not to be a danger

Regulation 100 Road Vehicles (Construction and Use) Regulations 1986
Section 42 Road Traffic Act 1988 - level 3 fine

Condition, Passengers and Loading - *R100(1)*

Every **motor vehicle and any trailer drawn by it** shall at all times be in such condition that no danger is caused or is likely to be caused to any person in or on the vehicle or trailer or on a road, and

• the number of passengers carried* by such a vehicle or trailer, or
• the manner in which any passengers are carried in or on such vehicle or trailer, and
• the weight, distribution, packing and adjustment of the load of such vehicle or trailer,

shall at all times be such, that no danger is caused or is likely to be caused to any person in or on the vehicle or trailer or on a road.

The number of passengers carried shall not apply to a vehicle to which the Public Service Vehicles (Carrying Capacity) Regulations 1984 apply.

Security of Loads - *R100(2)*

The load carried by a **motor vehicle or trailer** shall at all times :-

• be so secured, if necessary by physical restraint other than its own weight, and
• be in such a position,

that neither danger nor nuisance is likely to be caused to any person or property by reason of the load or any part thereof falling or being blown from the vehicle or by reason or any other movement of the load or any part thereof in relation to the vehicle.

Unsuitable Use - *R100(3)*

No **motor vehicle or trailer** shall be used for any purposes for which it is so unsuitable as to cause or be likely to cause danger or nuisance to any person in or in the vehicle or trailer or on a road.

The nature of the route used may be considered.

Securing of suspended implements

Regulation 108 Road Vehicles (Construction and Use) Regulations 1986
Section 42 Road Traffic Act 1988 - level 3 fine

Where a vehicle is fitted with any apparatus or appliance designed for lifting and part of the apparatus or appliance consists of a suspended implement, the implement shall at all times while the vehicle is in motion on a road and when the implement is not attached to any load supported by the appliance or apparatus be so secured either to the appliance or apparatus or to some part of the vehicle that no danger is caused or is likely to be caused to any person on the vehicle or on the road.

Chapter 31 Impairment

Unfit Through Drink Or Drugs
Mechanically Propelled Vehicles

Section 4(1) and (2) Road Traffic Act 1988 - level 4 to 5 fine, 3 to 6 months, 3 - 11 points, disqualification

It is an offence for a person when :-

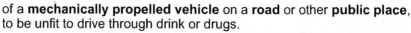

- driving, or
- attempting to drive, or
- in charge,

of a **mechanically propelled vehicle** on a **road** or other **public place**, to be unfit to drive through drink or drugs.

Unfit means a person's ability to drive properly is for the time being impaired (no prescribed or specified limit).
Drug includes any intoxicant other than alcohol.

Defence to being unfit when in charge

A person shall be deemed not to have been in charge of a mechanically propelled vehicle if he proves that at the material time the circumstances were such that there was no likelihood of his driving it so long as he remained unfit to drive through drink or drugs. The Court may disregard any injury to him and any damage to the vehicle.

See Page 8 for Preliminary Tests.

Power of Entry and Arrest

Powers of arrest exist under :-

- *Section 6D Road Traffic Act 1988* following a positive preliminary test,
- *Section 1 Criminal Justice (Scotland) Act 2016,*
- *Section 24 Police and Criminal Evidence Act 1984,*

and a power of entry to arrest can be found at :-

- *Section 17(1)(c)(iiia) Police and Criminal Evidence Act 1984.*

Mobility Scooters

Sec20(1)(b) Chronically Sick and Disabled Persons Act 1970

In the case of a vehicle which is a Class 2 or 3 invalid carriage complying with the prescribed requirements and which is being used in accordance with the prescribed conditions *section 4 of the Road Traffic Act 1988* **shall not apply** to it.

Electrically Assisted Pedal Cycles

Section 4 **does apply** to riders of electrically assisted pedal cycles as although not classed as motor vehicles they still fall within the definition of mechanically propelled vehicle.

e-Scooters

Section 4 **does apply** to riders of e-scooters as they fall within the definition of mechanically propelled vehicle.

Unfit Through Drink Or Drugs *continued*
Cycles

Section 30 Road Traffic Act 1988 - level 3 fine

It is an offence for a person, when riding a **cycle** on a **road** or other **public place** to be unfit to ride through drink or drugs (that is to say under the influence of drink or a drugs to such an extent as to be incapable of having proper control of the cycle).

Power of arrest under Section 24 Police and Criminal Evidence Act 1984, or in Scotland, Section 30(2) Road Traffic Act 1988.

Carriages

Section 12 Licensing Act 1872 - level 1 fine /1 month

It is an offence for a person to be drunk on a **highway** or other **public place** while in charge of a carriage (*see Chapter 2 Page 3*).

A person liable to be charged with an offence under section 4, 5, 7 or 30 of the Road Traffic Act 1988 is not liable to be charged with this offence.

Shipping

Sections 78(2) Railways and Transport Safety Act 2003

It is an offence for a :-

- professional master of a ship, or
- a professional pilot of a ship, or
- a professional seaman in a ship while on duty,

if his ability to carry out his duties is impaired because of drink or drugs.

Rail and Tramways

Section 27(1) Transport and Works Act 1992

It is an offence for a person to work on a transport system used for the carriage of members of the public :-

- as a driver, guard, conductor or signalman or any other capacity in which he can control or affect the movement of a vehicle,
- or in a maintenance capacity or as a supervisor of, or look-out for, persons working in a maintenance capacity,

when he is unfit to carry out that work through drink or drugs.

A person shall be taken to be unfit to carry out any work if his ability to carry out that work properly is for the time being impaired.

Aircraft

Section 92(1) Railways and Transport Safety Act 2003

It is an offence for a person to perform an aviation function, or an ancillary function when his ability to perform the function is impaired because of drink or drugs.

Excess Alcohol
Motor Vehicles

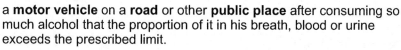

Section 5 Road Traffic Act 1988 - level 4/5 fine, 3/6 months, disqualification, 3 - 11 points

It is an offence for a person to :-

• drive,

• attempt to drive, or

• be in charge of,

a **motor vehicle** on a **road** or other **public place** after consuming so much alcohol that the proportion of it in his breath, blood or urine exceeds the prescribed limit.

Defence to exceeding the limit when in charge

A person prosecuted for having been in charge of a motor vehicle with excess alcohol can claim a defence if he proves that at the material time the circumstances were such that there was no likelihood of his driving the vehicle whilst the proportion of alcohol in his breath, blood or urine remained likely to exceed the prescribed limit.

See Page 8 for Preliminary Tests.

Mobility Scooters

Section 5 **does not apply** to drivers or riders of Class 2 or 3 invalid carriages which comply with the prescribed requirements and which are being used in accordance with the prescribed conditions as they are not classed as motor vehicles.

Electrically Assisted Pedal Cycles

Section 5 **does not apply** to riders of electrically assisted pedal cycles which comply with the prescribed requirements as they are not classed as motor vehicles.Consider instead unfit to drive through drink or drugs.

e-Scooters

Section 5 **does apply** to the rider of an e-scooter classed as a motor vehicle.

Where there is some doubt as to classification as a motor vehicle - for example a privately owned scooter not in a trial which is found in a public place which is not a road and where there is no evidence of road use, consider 'Unfit to drive through drugs' - *Section 4* as they are still classed as mechanically propelled vehicles.

Excess Alcohol *continued*
Shipping

Sections 78(3) Railways and Transport Safety Act 2003

It is an offence for a :-

• professional master of a ship, or
• a professional pilot of a ship, or
• a professional seaman in a ship while on duty,

if the proportion of alcohol in his breath, blood or urine exceeds the prescribed limit.

Rail and Tramways

Section 27 Transport and Works Act 1992

It is an offence for a person to work on a transport system used for the carriage of members of the public :-

• as a driver, guard, conductor or signalman or in any other capacity in which he can control or affect the movement of a vehicle, or
• in a maintenance capacity or as a supervisor of, or look-out for, persons working in a maintenance capacity,

after consuming so much alcohol that the proportion of it in his breath, blood or urine exceeds the prescribed limit.

Aircraft

Section 93(1) Railways and Transport Safety Act 2003

It is an offence for a person to perform :-

• an aviation function[1], or
• an activity which is ancillary to an aviation function,

at a time when the proportion of alcohol in his breath, blood or urine exceeds the prescribed limit.

Aviation Function includes pilot, flight navigator, flight engineer, flight radio-telephony operator and member of the cabin crew of an aircraft during flight, attending the flight deck of an aircraft during flight to give or supervise training, to administer a test, to observe a period of practice or to monitor or record the gaining of experience, licensed air traffic controller and licensed aircraft maintenance engineer.

Excess Alcohol *continued*
Prescribed Limits

Motor Vehicles	Breath	Blood	Urine
Motor Vehicles (England & Wales) *Section 11 Road Traffic Act 1988*	35	80	107
Motor Vehicles (Scotland) *Section 11 Road Traffic Act 1988*	22	50	67
Shipping	**Breath**	**Blood**	**Urine**
Shipping (Professional seamen only) *Section 81 Railways and Transport Safety Act 2003*	25	50	67
Rail	**Breath**	**Blood**	**Urine**
Rail (Applies to drivers, guards, conductors, signalmen and rail or vehicle maintenance workers) *Sec 38 Transport and Works Act 1992*	35	80	107
Aircraft	**Breath**	**Blood**	**Urine**
Aircraft (Applies to air crew and air traffic controllers) *Section 93(2) Railways and Transport Safety Act 2003*	9	20	27
Aircraft (Applies to licensed aircraft maintenance engineers) *Section 93(3) Railways and Transport Safety Act 2003*	35	80	107

Units
- Breath - micrograms of alcohol in 100 millilitres.
- Blood or Urine milligrams of alcohol in 100 millilitres.

Hip Flask Defence

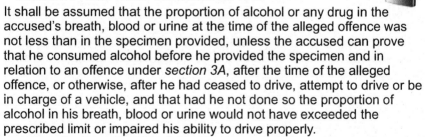

Section 15 Road Traffic Offenders Act 1988

It shall be assumed that the proportion of alcohol or any drug in the accused's breath, blood or urine at the time of the alleged offence was not less than in the specimen provided, unless the accused can prove that he consumed alcohol before he provided the specimen and in relation to an offence under *section 3A*, after the time of the alleged offence, or otherwise, after he had ceased to drive, attempt to drive or be in charge of a vehicle, and that had he not done so the proportion of alcohol in his breath, blood or urine would not have exceeded the prescribed limit or impaired his ability to drive properly.

To substantiate or disprove any such claim the following evidence should be gathered including relevant times, type and amount of alcohol, glasses, bottles used, the accused's sex, age, height, weight, build, food consumed, quantity and time, witness corroboration.

Excess Drugs
Offence

Section 5A Road Traffic Act 1988 - level 4/5 fine, 3/6 months, disqualification, 3 - 11 point

It is an offence for a person to :-

- drive, or
- attempt to drive, or
- be in charge of,

a **motor vehicle** on a **road** or other **public place** if the proportion of a specified controlled drug in his blood or urine exceeds the specified limit for that drug.

See Page 8 for Preliminary Tests.

Specified Controlled Drugs

Drug Driving (Specified Limits) (England and Wales) Regulations 2014
The Drug Driving (Specified Limits) (Scotland) Regulations 2019

Limit (micrograms per litre of blood)

[1]Amphetamine	**250**	[1]Lysergic Acid Diethylamide	**1**
[1]Benzoylecgonine	50	Methadone	500
Clonazepam	50	[1]Methylamphetamine	10
[1]Cocaine	**10**	[1]Methylenedioxymethamphetamine	10
[1]Delta-9-Tetrahydrocannabinol	2	[1]6-Monoacetylmorphine	**5**
Diazepam	**550**	Morphine 80	80
Flunitrazepam	300	Oxazepam	**300**
[1]Ketamine	**20**	Temazepam	1000
Lorazepam	100		

[1] The threshold values for these drugs are set just above the 'lowest accidental exposure limit' and reflect the government policy of zero tolerance to these 'illegal' drugs and consequently the limits are below the level at which an increased risk to road safety is expected to exist.

Medical Defence

To show that he was in lawful possession of the drug which had been prescribed or supplied to him for medical or dental purposes and was taken as prescribed or supplied or in accordance with any manufacturers instructions and in accordance with advice or instructions concerning the time elapsed between taking the drug and driving.

Excess Drugs *continued*
Defence to exceeding the limit when in charge

A person shall be deemed not to have been in charge of a mechanically propelled vehicle if he proves that at the material time the circumstances were such that there was no likelihood of his driving it whilst the proportion of specified controlled drug in his blood or urine remained likely to exceed the specified limit for that drug.

> *The Court may disregard any injury to him and any damage to the vehicle.*

Mobility Scooters

Section 5A **does not apply** to Class 2 or 3 invalid carriages (mobility scooters) complying with the prescribed requirements as they are not classed as motor vehicles.

Electrically assisted pedal cycles

Section 5A **does not apply** to electrically assisted pedal cycles which comply with the prescribed requirements as they are not classed as motor vehicles. Consider 'Unfit to drive through drugs'

e-scooters

Section 5A **does apply** to e-scooters classed as motor vehicles.

Where there is some doubt as to classification as a motor vehicle - for example a privately owned scooter not in a trial which is found in a public place which is not a road and where there is no evidence of road use, consider 'Unfit to drive through drugs' -as they are still classed as mechanically propelled vehicles.

Preliminary Tests
Motor Vehicles

Section 6(1-5) Road Traffic Act 1988

Where a constable (in uniform or not) reasonably suspects that a person :-

- who is driving, attempting to drive or is in charge of a **motor vehicle** on a **road** or other **public place**, has alcohol or a drug in his body or is under the influence of a drug - *section 6(2)*, or

- has been driving or attempting to drive or been in charge of a **motor vehicle** on a **road** or other **public place** with alcohol or a drug in his body or while unfit to drive because of a drug, and still has alcohol or a drug in his body or is still under the influence of a drug - *section 6(3)*, or

- who is or has been driving or attempting to drive or in charge of a **motor vehicle** on a **road** or other **public place** and has committed a traffic offence[1] whilst the vehicle was in motion - *section 6(4), or*

- was driving, attempting to drive or in charge of a **motor vehicle** at the time an accident occurs owing to the presence of the motor vehicle on a **road** or other **public place** - *section 6(5),*

he may require that person to co-operate with any one or more preliminary tests administered to the person by that constable or another constable.

*A constable may **administer** a preliminary test only if he is in uniform unless the test follows a requirement made pursuant to an accident owing to the presence of a motor vehicle on a road or other public place.*

[1] **Traffic Offence** means an offence under :-

- any provisions of *Part II of the Public Passenger Vehicles Act 1981,*
- any provision of the *Road Traffic Regulation Act 1984,*
- any provision of the *Road Traffic Offenders Act 1988 except Part III,*
- any provision of the *Road Traffic Act 1988 except Part V* (Approved Driving Instructors).

It does not include vehicle registration offences, no number plate etc.

A person does not co-operate with a preliminary test or provide a specimen of breath for analysis unless his co-operation or the specimen is sufficient to enable the test or the analysis to be carried out, and is provided in such a way as to enable the objective of the test or analysis to be satisfactorily achieved.

Section 6A(2) Road Traffic Act 1988

A preliminary breath test administered in reliance on section 6(2) to (4) may be administered only at or near the place where the requirement to co-operate with the test is imposed.

Preliminary Tests *continued*
Offence
Section 6(6) Road Traffic Act 1988 - level 3 fine, 4 points, discretionary disqualification

It is an offence for a person, without reasonable excuse, to fail to co-operate with a preliminary test.

Mobility Scooters

Section 6 **does not apply** to riders of Class 2 or 3 invalid carriages (mobility scooters) which comply with the prescribed requirements and are being used in accordance with the prescribed conditions as they are not classed as motor vehicles.

Electrically assisted pedal cycles

Section 6 **does not apply** to electrically assisted pedal cycles which comply with the prescribed requirements as they are not classed as motor vehicles.

e-scooters

Section 6 **does apply** to e-scooters which are classed as motor vehicles.

Shipping
Section 83 Railways and Transport Safety Act 2003

This section replicates certain provisions of the *Road Traffic Act 1988*, amended where appropriate to apply to shipping, adopting in relation to mariners the same procedures for taking specimens as are applicable to motorists. The section also replicates, similarly amended, the provisions in relation to preliminary impairment tests and preliminary drug tests.

Rail and Trams
Sections 29 to 33 Transport and Works Act 1992

Similar powers to those provided under the *Road Traffic Act 1988* for the taking of breath tests and samples for analysis are provided in the *Transport and Works Act 1992*.

Aviation
Section 96 Railways and Transport Safety Act 2003

This section replicates certain provisions of the *Road Traffic Act 1988* and the *Road Traffic Offenders Act 1988*, amended where appropriate to apply to aviation. It also replicates provisions in relation to preliminary impairment tests and preliminary drug tests, amended where appropriate to apply to aviation.

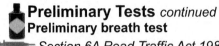

Preliminary Tests *continued*
Preliminary breath test

Section 6A Road Traffic Act 1988

A preliminary breath test is a procedure whereby the person to whom the test is administered provides a specimen of breath to be used for the purpose of obtaining, by means of an approved device, an indication whether the proportion of alcohol in the person's breath or blood is likely to exceed the prescribed limit.

A preliminary breath test may be only be administered at or near the place where the requirement to co-operate with the test is imposed except following an accident owing to the presence of a motor vehicle on a road or other public place, where, if the constable who imposes the requirement thinks it expedient, it may be administered at a police station specified by him.

Preliminary impairment test

Section 6B Road Traffic Act 1988

A preliminary impairment test (known as a FIT Test) is a procedure whereby the constable administering the test observes the person to whom the test is administered in his performance of tasks specified by the constable, and makes such other observations of the person's physical state as the constable thinks expedient.

A preliminary impairment test may be administered at or near the place where the requirement to co-operate with the test is imposed, or if the constable who imposes the requirement thinks it expedient, at a police station specified by him. A constable must be approved by the Chief Constable and must have regard for the Code of Practice.

Preliminary drug test

Section 6C Road Traffic Act 1988

A preliminary drug test is a procedure by which a specimen of sweat or saliva is obtained, and used for the purpose of obtaining, by means of an approved device, an indication whether the person to whom the test is administered has a drug in his body and if so whether it is a specified controlled drug and if it is, whether the proportion of it in the person's blood or urine is likely to exceed the specified limit for that drug. Up to three preliminary drug tests may be administered.

A preliminary drug test may be administered at or near the place where the requirement to co-operate with the test is imposed, or if the constable who imposes the requirement thinks it expedient, at a police station specified by him.

Preliminary Tests *continued*
Power of arrest

Section 6D Road Traffic Act 1988

A constable may arrest a person without warrant (unless he is a hospital patient) if :-

- as a result of a preliminary breath test the constable reasonably suspects that the proportion of alcohol in the person's breath or blood exceeds the prescribed limit, or
- as a result of a preliminary drug test the constable reasonably suspects that the person has a specified controlled drug in his body and the proportion of it in the person's blood or urine exceeds the specified limit for that drug, or
- the person fails to co-operate with a preliminary test (of any kind) and the constable reasonably suspects that the person has alcohol or a drug in his body or is under the influence of a drug.

A person arrested under this section may, instead of being taken to a police station, be detained at or near the place where the preliminary test was, or would have been, administered, with a view to imposing on him there a requirement under *section 7 of this Act* (breath tests for analysis or blood or urine sample for laboratory test).

The fact that specimens of breath for analysis may have been provided under *section 7 of this Act* by the person concerned does not prevent the power of arrest above having effect if the constable who imposed on him the requirement to provide the specimens has reasonable cause to believe that the device used to analyse the specimens has not produced a reliable indication of the proportion of alcohol in the breath of the person.

Power of Entry - injury accident

Section 6E Road Traffic Act 1988

Following an accident in a case where a constable reasonably suspects that the accident involved injury of any person he may enter any place (using reasonable force if necessary) for the purpose of :-

- requiring a person to provide a preliminary test, or
- arresting a person under *section 6D* above (following a positive preliminary breath test or drug test or failure to co-operate with any preliminary test if reasonably suspect that the person has alcohol or a drug in his body or is under the influence of a drug).

This section does not extend to Scotland.

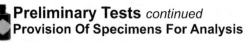

Preliminary Tests *continued*
Provision Of Specimens For Analysis
Power to require specimens
Section 7 Road Traffic Act 1988

In the course of an investigation into whether a person has committed an offence under s*ections 3A, 4, 5 or 5A* a constable may require him to :-

- (**alcohol**) provide two specimens of breath for analysis by an approved device, or
- (**alcohol or drugs**) to provide a specimen of blood or urine for a laboratory test.

A requirement to provide specimens of breath for analysis can only be made :-

- at a police station,
- at a hospital, or
- at or near a place where a preliminary breath test has been administered to the person concerned or would have been so administered but for his failure to co-operate with it (in these circumstances the constable must be in uniform unless the requirement is in accordance with *section 6(5)* - following a road traffic accident).

There is no need for preliminary breath test before evidential breath test under this section.

A requirement to provide a specimen of blood or urine can only be made at a police station or at a hospital, and cannot be made at a police station unless :-

- the constable has reasonable cause to believe that for medical reasons a specimen of breath cannot be provided or should not be required, or
- specimens of breath for analysis have not been provided elsewhere and at the time of the requirement a device or a reliable device is not available at the police station or it is then for any other reason not practicable to use such a device there, or
- as a result of the administration of a preliminary drug test, the constable making the requirement has reasonable cause to believe that the person required to provide a specimen of blood or urine has a drug in his body, or
- in the case of *section 3A, 4 or 5A* offences a medical practitioner has advised that the condition of the person might be due to some drug.

This request may be made notwithstanding that the person has already provided or been required to provide two samples of breath. The choice of blood or urine is made by the constable unless the medical practitioner or registered health care professional is of the opinion, for medical reasons, that blood should not be taken. The medical practitioner may override the decision of the health care professional.

Preliminary Tests *continued*
Provision Of Specimens For Analysis *continued*

Breath

The lower of any two breath analysis readings is used and the higher disregarded. If the reading does not exceed 39 micrograms of alcohol in 100 ml of breath, current policy is not to prosecute however a person may still be detained under *section 10* below.

Blood

A specimen of blood may only be taken by a medical practitioner or by a registered health care professional.

Urine

A specimen of urine shall be provided within one hour of the requirement for its provision being made and after the provision of a previous specimen of urine.

Warnings

A constable must, on requiring any person to provide a specimen, warn him that a failure to provide the specimen may render him liable to prosecution.

Failure to provide specimen of breath, blood or urine

Section 7(6) Road Traffic Act 1988 - 3 to 6 months, level 4 or 5 fine, disqualification, 3-11 points

It is an offence for a person, without reasonable excuse, to fail or refuse to provide a specimen for analysis in pursuance of *section 7*.

Detention Of Persons

Section 10 Road Traffic Act 1988

A person required to provide a specimen of breath, blood or urine for analysis may afterwards be detained at a police station, or if not already at the police station, arrested and taken there and detained[1], until it appears to a constable that, were that person then driving or attempting to drive a mechanically propelled vehicle on a road, he would not be committing an offence under *sections 4, 5 or 5A* unless it appears to a constable that there is no likelihood of his driving or attempting to drive a mechanically propelled vehicle whilst :-

- his ability to drive properly is impaired,
- the proportion of alcohol in his breath, blood or urine exceeds the prescribed limit, or
- the proportion of a specified controlled drug in the person's blood or urine exceeds the specified limit for that drug.

If a person's ability to drive properly is or might be impaired through drugs a medical practitioner must be consulted and his advice must be acted upon.

[1] A person who is at a hospital as a patient shall not be arrested and taken to a police station if it would be prejudicial to his proper care and treatment as a patient.

Preliminary Tests *continued*
Provision Of Specimens For Analysis *continued*
Hospital patients

Section 9 Road Traffic Act 1988

A constable may request a preliminary test under *section 6* and/or a specimen of breath, blood or urine for analysis under *section 7* or a specimen of blood under *section 7A*.

A person at a hospital as a patient shall not be required to co-operate with a preliminary test or to provide a specimen for analysis (or the specimen shall not be taken without his consent) unless the medical practitioner in immediate charge of the case has been notified and does not object on the grounds that the requirements for, co-operation with, provision of, or warnings given relating to the test would be prejudicial to the proper care and treatment of the patient.

Persons incapable of consenting

Section 7A Road Traffic Act 1988

A constable may make a request to a medical or health care practitioner for him to take a specimen of blood from a person without that persons consent if :-

- the constable would otherwise be entitled under section 7 to require the specimen, and
- it appears to that constable the person has been involved in an accident subject of his investigation, and
- it appears to that constable that the person is or may be incapable of giving a valid consent due to medical reasons.

The request shall be made to a police medical or health care practitioner or if not reasonably practicable another a practitioner other than a police medical or health care practitioner neither of whom are responsible for the clinical care of the person concerned.

The specimen shall not be analysed unless the person from whom it was taken has been informed that it was taken, has been required by a constable to give his permission for a laboratory test of the specimen and has given his permission.

A constable must, on requiring any person to give his permission for a laboratory test of a specimen already taken, warn him that a failure to give the permission may render him liable to prosecution.

Failure to give permission for sample to be analysed

Section 7A(6) Road Traffic Act 1988 - 3 to 6 months, level 4 /5 fine, disqualification, 3-11 points

It is an offence for a person, without reasonable excuse, to fail to give his permission for a laboratory test of a specimen of blood taken from him under *section 7A*.

Chapter 32 Accident Obligations

All Accidents

Section 170 Road Traffic Act 1988

Where, owing to the presence of a **mechanically propelled vehicle**[1] on a **road or other public place**, an accident occurs by which :-

- **personal injury** is caused to a person other than the driver of that vehicle (*Section 170(1)(a)*), or
- **damage** is caused :-
  - to another vehicle other than that vehicle or its trailer (*Section 170(1)(b)(i)*), or
  - to an animal[2] other than one being carried in that vehicle or its trailer (*Section 170(1)(b)(ii)*), or
  - to any property constructed on, fixed to, growing in or otherwise forming part of the land on which the road or place is situated or adjacent land (*Section 170(1)(b)(iii)*),

the driver must :-

- **STOP** and
- if required to do so by any person having reasonable grounds for requiring it give :-
  - his/her name and address and the vehicle owner's name and address, and
  - the identification marks of the vehicle.

The duty to stop means to stop sufficiently long enough to exchange the particulars above (Lee v Knapp [1966] 3 All ER 961).

If for any reason the driver does not give his name and address he must report the accident at a police station or to a constable **as soon as reasonably practicable** and in any case within 24 hours.

This does not mean the driver can delay reporting without good reason (Bulman v Bennett [1974] RTR 1).

Section 170 does not apply to Class 2 and 3 Invalid Carriages which comply with the prescribed requirements and are being used in accordance with the prescribed conditions.

See Chapter 2 Page 2.

[1] *Mechanically propelled vehicle includes electrically assisted pedal cycles, e-scooters and invalid carriages*

other than Class 2 and 3 Invalid Carriages above.

[2] *Animal means horse, cattle, ass, mule, sheep, pig, goat, dog.*

Injury accidents

Section 170 Road Traffic Act 1988

Where, owing to the presence of a **mechanically propelled vehicle** on a **road** or other **public place**, an accident occurs by which **injury is caused to a person other than the driver of that vehicle** the driver of a **motor vehicle**[3], in addition to the obligations on the previous page, **MUST** produce a certificate of insurance[4] (*Sec 170(5)*) to :-

• a constable, or

• any person having reasonable grounds for requiring it.

If, at the time of the accident, the driver does not produce proof of insurance he **must** report the accident and produce a certificate of insurance or other evidence of insurance [4/5] (*Sec 170(6)*) :-

• at a police station, or

• to a constable,

as soon as reasonably practicable and in any case within 24 hours.

This does not mean the driver can delay reporting without good reason (Bulman v Bennett [1974] RTR 1).

Section 170 does not apply to Class 2 and 3 Invalid Carriages which comply with the prescribed requirements and are being used in accordance with the prescribed conditions (see Chapter 2 Page 2).

Section 170(5) above does not apply to other invalid carriages.

[3] *Motor Vehicle does not include electrically assisted pedal cycles prescribed by regulations but may include e-scooters.*

[4] *An electronic or clearly printed copy of a certificate is acceptable.*

[5] *A further 7 days to produce insurance is allowed providing the accident has been reported to police.*

Duty to give insurance details where a claim is made
Section 154(1) Road Traffic Act 1988

A person making a claim in respect of compulsory insurance liability arising from the use of a **motor vehicle** on a **road** or other **public place** may require particulars specified on a certificate of insurance or where no certificate was delivered, identifying particulars of the vehicle and policy.

This requirement is independent of the accident obligation offences listed above and relates to both injury and damage only accidents.

Accident Obligation Offences

Fail to stop and give details and report if required - all accidents

Section 170(4) Road Traffic Act 1988 - level 5 fine / 6 months / 5-10 points

It is an offence for the driver of a **mechanically propelled vehicle**, involved in an accident on a **road or other public place** whereby damage or injury is caused (to a 3rd party) :-

- to fail to stop, and
- if required to do so by any person having reasonable grounds for so requiring :-
    - to fail to give his name and address, and
    - to fail to give the name and address of the owner of the vehicle, and
    - to fail to give the identifying marks of the vehicle, and
- if the driver does not give his name and address, to fail to report the accident at a police station or to a constable **as soon as reasonably practicable** and in any case within 24 hours.

Fail to report - insurance not produced - injury accident

Section 170(7) Road Traffic Act 1988 - level 3 fine

It is an offence for the driver of a **motor vehicle** involved in an accident involving injury to another on a **road or other public place** who has not produced proof of insurance to a constable or any person having reasonable grounds for requiring it. (*section 170(5)*) to then fail to report the accident at a police station or to a constable **as soon as reasonably practicable** and in any case within 24 hours and produce the insurance certificate or other evidence of cover.

A further 7 days from the time of the accident to produce insurance is allowed providing the accident has been reported to the police.

Duty to give insurance details where a claim is made

Offence

Section 154(2) Road Traffic Act 1988 - level 4 fine

It is an offence for a person, without reasonable excuse, to fail to supply details required or to wilfully make a false statement in reply to such a demand.

POLICE ACCIDENT Accident Obligation Examples

	Scenario	Offence
1	Motor car on a road strikes wild deer - deer killed, occupants not injured, car damaged - no other damage. Car fails to stop.	No obligations, no offences.
2	Motor car on a road strikes sheep - sheep killed, occupants not injured, car damaged - no other damage. Car fails to stop and driver does not report accident.	Offence - Fail to stop and give name and address.*S170(4)*. Offence - Fail to report accident as soon as is reasonably practicable - *S170(4)*.
3	Motor car on a road strikes pedestrian causing minor injury, car not damaged. Car stops. Driver gives his name and address, that of the owner and the registration number of the car but does not have any insurance details on him. Driver does not report accident to police.	Offence - fail to report accident as soon as is reasonably practicable and give insurance details - *S170(7)*.
4	Pedal Cycle on a pavement (footway) strikes pedestrian causing injury to pedestrian. Cyclist fails to stop and does not report the accident.	No Accident Obligation Offence Consider Cycling on the footway, Dangerous or careless cycling.
5	Electrically Assisted Pedal Cycle Pedal Cycle complying with regulations on a pavement (footway) strikes pedestrian causing injury to pedestrian. Cyclist fails to stop and does not report the accident.	Offence - Fail to stop and give name and address etc. *S170(4)* Offence - Fail to report accident as soon as is reasonably practicable. *S170(4)* Consider Cycling on the footway, Wanton or furious riding, dangerous or careless driving or cycling.
6	e-scooter privately owned and not forming part of a trial (and any other unregistered powered transporter) on a pavement (footway) strikes pedestrian causing injury to pedestrian. Rider fails to stop and does not report the accident.	Offence - Fail to stop and give name and address etc. *S170(4)* Offence - Fail to report accident as soon as is reasonably practicable. *S170(4)* Offence -Fail to report accident and give insurance details - *S170(7)* if motor vehicle. Consider Wanton or furious riding, dangerous or careless driving. Additional offences may be committed - fail to register, no insurance, driving licence offence, if motor vehicle.

Chapter 33 Traffic Signs

Failure to comply with a sign

There are basically 2 types of offences relating to signs :-

1. Failure to comply with a sign where an Act, Regulation, Order, Bylaw, Resolution or Notice or other condition gives legal effect to the sign (*section 36 signs*), and

2. Contravention of an Act, Regulation, Order, Bylaw, Resolution or Notice where a sign gives legal effect to the Act, Regulation, Order, Notice etc.

Fail to Comply with Section 36 Signs (NOIP)

Section 36(1) Road Traffic Act 1988 - level 3 fine - 3 points where specified[1] - fixed penalty offence

Where a traffic sign of the prescribed size, colour and type, or authorised character, has been **lawfully placed** on or near a **road**, a person driving or propelling a **vehicle** who fails to comply with the indication given by the sign is guilty of an offence.

Lawfully placed means :-

- the indication given by the sign is an indication of a statutory prohibition, restriction or requirement, or

- it is **expressly provided** by or under any provision of the Traffic Acts that this section shall apply to the sign or to signs of a type of which the sign is one.

[1] Specified Signs

*Where a provision in an Act, Regulation, Authorisation or Order stipulates that contravention of a sign by the driver of a **motor vehicle** attracts an endorsement on a driving licence.*

Contravening Acts, Regulations, Orders etc.

Various - Road Traffic Regulation Act 1984 - level2/3 fine - endorsable or non-endorsable mainly fixed penalty offences

It is an offence for a person to contravene, or use a **vehicle**, or cause or permit a **vehicle** to be used in contravention of an Order made under the Road Traffic Regulation Act 1984.

Cause or permit offence are not fixed penalty offences.

Signs subject to civil enforcement

Part 6 and Schedule 7 Traffic Management Act 2004 - non-endorsable - local authority Penalty Charge Notice

A civil charge may be imposed upon a person who fails to comply with the indication given by a traffic sign to which is subject to civil enforcement.

'Expressly provided' Section 36 Signs
Signs at traffic surveys

Where a traffic survey of any description is being carried out on or in the vicinity of a road, this section applies to a traffic sign by which a direction is given :-

- stop a vehicle,
- make it proceed in, or keep to, a particular line of traffic, or
- proceed to a particular point on or **near the road** on which the vehicle is being driven or propelled.

CENSUS STOP if directed

830.1

There is no requirement for a person to provide any information for the purposes of the survey.

Traffic signs for bridges and other structures

Vehicles exceeding height indicated in metric and imperial units prohibited from passing under, into or through a bridge, tunnel or other structure.

3.2 m
10'6"

629.2A Specified Sign

A Traffic Order is not required for this sign.

Signs that indicate regulatory requirements for moving traffic

Vehicular traffic must proceed in the direction indicated by the arrow.

606

The sign must only be placed to indicate the effect of an Act, order, regulation, bylaw, resolution or notice except when placed on the central island of a roundabout or in combination with a plate displaying the legend 'Dual carriageway'.

Vehicular traffic must **turn ahead** in the direction indicated by the arrow.

609

The sign must only be placed to indicate the effect of an Act, order, regulation, bylaw, resolution or notice except when placed on a road approaching its junction with a dual carriageway road.

'Expressly provided' Section 36 Signs *continued*
Signs that indicate regulatory requirements for moving traffic *continued*

Keep Left/Right - Vehicular traffic (except tramcars or trolley vehicles) passing the sign must keep to the side of the sign indicated by the downward pointing arrow (includes temporary keep right signs on emergency or breakdown vehicles).

610

Exemptions for emergency vehicles used for the purposes of :-

• fire and rescue, ambulance, blood service,

• bomb disposal, special forces,

• police, National Crime Agency.

Priority must be given to vehicles from the opposite direction.

The sign must not be placed unless accompanied by its associated plate.

Give way to oncoming vehicles

615

A Traffic Order is not required for this sign.

No entry for vehicular traffic.

The sign must only be placed to indicate the effect of an Act, order, regulation, bylaw, resolution or notice which prohibits or restricts the use of the road by traffic.

616
Specified
Sign

Bus and Tram Routes and Bus Gates

Route for use only by traffic indicated.

953 - 953.1

The sign must only be placed to indicate the effect of an Act, order, regulation, bylaw, resolution or notice which prohibits or restricts the use of the road by traffic.

The symbols for Motorcycles, Cycles or Taxis may be omitted.

'Expressly provided' Section 36 Signs *continued*
**Regulatory signs at junctions and
miscellaneous regulatory signs**

Stop

Every vehicle must stop before crossing the
transverse line, or if that line is not clearly visible,
before entering the major road (or level crossing) in
respect of which the stop sign has been provided, and

601.1
Specified Sign

* no vehicle must cross the transverse line, or if that line is not
  clearly visible, enter the major road (or level crossing) in respect of
  which the stop sign has been provided :-

    o in respect of a road - so as to be likely to endanger any person, or
      to cause the driver of another vehicle to change its speed or
      course in order to avoid an accident, or to cause the driver to
      change speed in order to avoid an accident, or

    o in respect of a level crossing - so as to be likely to endanger the
      driver of, or any passenger in, any railway vehicle or tramcar or to
      cause that driver to change speed in order to avoid an accident.

*A Traffic Regulation Order is not required for this sign.
NB: There are no exemptions for emergency vehicles.*

Give-Way - Major Road - No vehicle shall cross the
give-way line, or if that is not clearly visible, enter the
major road so as to be likely to endanger any person,
or to cause the driver of another vehicle to change its
speed or course in order to avoid an accident.

602

Give-Way - Level Crossing - No vehicle must cross the give-way line,
or if that line is not clearly visible, enter the level crossing, so as to be
likely to endanger the driver of, or any passenger in, any railway vehicle
or tramcar or to cause that driver to change the speed of his or her
vehicle in order to avoid an accident.

Road markings may be used with or without sign.

A Traffic Regulation Order is not required for this sign.

'Expressly provided' Section 36 Signs *continued*
Regulatory signs at junctions and miscellaneous regulatory signs - *continued*

Priority to right sign (Mini-Roundabout) -
Vehicles entering the junction must give priority to vehicles from the right at the give-way line, or, if that is not clearly visible, at the road junction **AND** proceed past the centre marking on the left unless the size of the vehicle or the layout of the junction makes it impracticable to do so.

611.1 1003.4

No vehicle shall pass the give way line in a manner or at a time likely to endanger any person, or to cause the driver of another vehicle to change its speed or course in order to avoid an accident.

A Traffic Regulation Order is not required for this sign.

Vehicles exceeding the maximum gross weight indicated prohibited from crossing the bridge or other structure.

WEAK BRIDGE

7.5 t m g w

In the case of vehicles not required to be marked with their maximum gross weight but required to be marked with their unladen weight, the unladen weight must not exceed the gross weight indicated on the sign.

626.2A

The sign must only be placed to indicate the effect of a statutory provision which restricts the use of the road carried by a bridge or other structure.

Permission to cross sign - No abnormal transport unit shall proceed across onto or over a level crossing unless the driver has telephoned and received permission to cross and proceeds as instructed UNLESS the phone appears to be working but is not answered within 2 minutes or it appears to be broken and he then drives over with reasonable expedition when no scheduled services are due.

784.1
Specified
Sign

Abnormal transport unit - (dimensions, inclusive of the load)
- length exceeds 61 feet 6 inches (18.75 m), or
- width, exceeds 9 feet 6 inches (2.9 m), or
- maximum gross weight exceeds 44 tonnes, or
- any vehicle incapable or unlikely to proceed, at a speed exceeding 5 m.p.h.

A Traffic Regulation Order is not required for this sign.

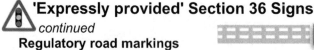

'Expressly provided' Section 36 Signs

continued

Regulatory road markings

1003A/B

Give Way marking

- No vehicle may proceed past the transverse line which is the nearer to the major road (or level crossing) into that road in a manner or at a time likely to endanger the driver of, or any passenger in, a vehicle on the major road (or railway vehicle or tramcar)or to cause the driver of such a vehicle to change its speed or course in order to avoid an accident,
- where the transverse lines are placed in advance of a point in the road where the width of the carriageway narrows significantly, that no vehicle may proceed past such one of those lines as is nearer to the point of narrowing in a manner or at a time likely to endanger the driver of, or any passenger in, a vehicle that is proceeding in the opposite direction to the first-mentioned vehicle, or cause the driver of such a vehicle to change its speed or course in order to avoid an accident,
- where the transverse lines are placed in advance of a length of the carriageway of the road where a cycle track crosses the road along a route parallel to the transverse lines, that no vehicle may proceed past such one of those lines as is the nearer the cycle track, in a manner or at a time likely to endanger any cyclist proceeding along the cycle track or to cause such a cyclist to change speed or course in order to avoid an accident.

Cyclists give way

A cycle must not be ridden across the transverse line in a manner or at a time that is likely to endanger any person, or to cause the driver of another vehicle to change its speed or course in order to avoid an accident.

A Traffic Regulation Order is not required for these signs.

Traffic Segregation Markings

Division of traffic lanes on a length of carriageway, or between the main carriageway and slip road, of a motorway or all-purpose dual carriageway road, or part of the carriageway between two lanes at a roundabout which vehicular traffic must not enter except in emergency.

1042

A Traffic Regulation Order is not required for this sign.

'Expressly provided' Section 36 Signs *continued*
Regulatory road markings *continued*
Double White Line Systems

No stopping except :-
- to board/alight from vehicle,
- to load/unload goods,
- in connection with building/demolition or excavation or removal of obstruction to traffic, road maintenance or repair or works connected with the main utilities, or
- if required by law to stop, or
- to avoid an accident, or
- circumstances outside driver's control, or
- with permission of a police officer in uniform or traffic officer in uniform or on his directions or those of a traffic warden in uniform, or
- in a lay-by or on road with 2 or more lanes in each direction, or
- pedal cycles,

- vehicles used for the purposes of :-
  ◦ fire and rescue, ambulance, or ambulance response,
  ◦ bomb disposal, special forces,
  ◦ police, National Crime Agency, traffic officer.

> **1013.1-5**
> **Specified**
> **Signs**

No vehicle shall cross or straddle but shall keep to the left of a continuous white line nearest to the vehicle except where it is safe, and if necessary to do so :-
- to enter land or premises or a side road, or
- to pass a stationary vehicle, or
- owing to circumstances outside the control of the driver, or
- in order to avoid an accident, or
- to pass a road maintenance vehicle which is in use and moving at not more than 10 m.p.h. and displaying either of the keep rights shown here, or

- to pass a pedal cycle moving at not more than 10 m.p.h., or
- to pass a horse moving at not more than 10 m.p.h., or
- for the purpose of complying with any direction of a constable in uniform, a traffic officer in uniform or a traffic warden.

No vehicle should cross or straddle the broken line nearest to the vehicle unless it is seen by the driver of the vehicle to be safe to do so.

A Traffic Regulation Order is not required for this sign.

⚠️ 'Expressly provided' Section 36 Signs *continued*
Regulatory road markings *continued*

Box Junctions

No vehicle or part of a vehicle shall remain stationary within the box junction except :-

* to turn right (other than at a roundabout) whilst prevented from doing so by oncoming traffic or other vehicle which is stationary whilst waiting to complete a right turn,
* vehicles used for the purposes of :-
  ○ fire and rescue, ambulance, or ambulance response,
  ○ bomb disposal, special forces,
  ○ police and National Crime Agency.

  when the observance of the prohibition would be likely to hinder the use of that vehicle for that purpose.

| 1043 |

A Traffic Regulation Order is not required

Level Crossing Box Junctions

Area of carriageway at a level crossing which vehicles must not enter in a manner which then causes any part of the vehicle to remain at rest within the marked area due to the presence of stationary vehicles (on or beyond the crossing).

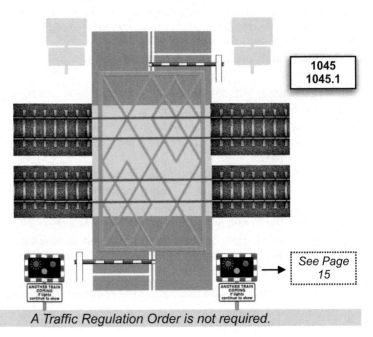

| 1045 |
| 1045.1 |

See Page 15

A Traffic Regulation Order is not required.

'Expressly provided' Section 36 Signs *continued*
Mandatory with-flow cycle lanes

Solid white line used to separate a cycle lane from another part of the carriageway where the direction of travel along the cycle lane and the part of the carriageway from which it is separated is the same. Cyclists do not have to use the lane.

| 1049B |

A Traffic Regulation Order is not required for this sign.

The marking conveys the requirement that a vehicle, other than a pedal cycle, must not be driven, or ridden, in the cycle lane during the cycle lane's hours of operation except a vehicle may cross into the part of the carriageway reserved for pedal cycles, or straddling the marking, if it is safe and necessary to do so :-

- in order to pass a stationary vehicle,
- to enable the vehicle to enter, from the side of the road on which it is proceeding, land or premises adjacent to the length of road on which the line is placed, or another road joining that road,
- due to circumstances outside the control of the driver,
- in order to avoid an accident, or
- for the purpose of complying with any direction of a constable in uniform or a traffic warden.

The prohibition does not apply to the driver of a vehicle being used for at least one of the purposes below and the observance of the prohibition would be likely to hinder the use of the vehicle for that purpose :-

- fire and rescue, ambulance, or ambulance response,
- bomb disposal, special forces,
- police and National Crime Agency.

Where a single solid white line is used as a boundary for a ***contra-flow cycle lane*** *it is not a marking to which section 36 applies nor is the sign to the right (a contraflow cycle lane in a two lane one-way street) and they must only be placed to indicate the effect of an Act, order, regulation, bylaw, resolution or notice which prohibits or restricts the use of the road by traffic.*
See Page 16.

'Expressly provided' Section 36 Signs *continued*
Temporary Signs

Keep Right/Left Sign

Traffic to keep to the Right/Left of vehicles carrying out mobile road works.

7403

The sign may only be placed in connection with the execution of works on or near a road, or a temporary obstruction.

Keep Right/Left Sign

Attached to the front or back of a road maintenance vehicle to indicate the side on which traffic should pass, or

610

Placed in relation to an emergency or breakdown vehicle which is temporarily obstructing the road to warn other traffic of the obstruction and to indicate the way past the vehicle.

A Traffic Regulation Order is not required for this sign.

Vehicular traffic must not proceed beyond the sign

The sign may only be placed :-

- in connection with a cycle race approved by or under regulations made under *section 31 of the 1988 Act* (regulation of cycle racing on public ways),

633.1

- by an accredited marshal acting under the instructions of the chief officer of police, and
- on a road which is subject to a speed limit of 60mph or less.

No Overtaking

Vehicular traffic must not overtake the vehicle used to escort other vehicles through road works if the sign shows 'No Overtaking

7029

Police No Waiting

Temporary prohibition of waiting except for loading and unloading

636

Such signs may only be maintained up to 7 days (28 days if placed in connection with terrorism or the prospect of terrorism).

See Chapter 28 Page 4.

'Expressly provided' Section 36 Signs *continued*
Manual Stop Signs

Manually operated Stop sign

Vehicular traffic must not proceed into a length of road where one-way working is temporarily necessary.

7023

 The sign comprises the STOP and GO symbols on opposite sides of the same sign.

The signs may only be placed :-

- where one-way working is necessary along a length of road because part of the width of the carriageway has been temporarily closed to traffic, and

- either there is no junction with another road along that length, or the traffic authority has given express written approval to the placing of the sign in relation to a length of road having a junction with another road.

Manually operated Stop sign

Vehicular traffic must not proceed beyond the sign when displayed for a short period during works on or near an all-purpose road (Double sided sign).

7031

The sign may only be placed in connection with the execution of works on or near a road, or a temporary obstruction.

School crossing patrol sign

A school crossing patrol wearing an approved uniform may require the person driving or propelling a vehicle which is approaching a place in a road where a person is crossing or seeking to cross the road, to stop by exhibiting the prescribed sign.

605.3
Specified
Sign

A Traffic Regulation Order is not required for this sign.

'Expressly provided' Section 36 Signs *continued*
Bus Stand and Bus Stop Clearways

A person driving a vehicle must not cause it to stop within the clearway.

Exceptions

• The driver of a bus to enable passengers to board or alight, to maintain a published timetable, or to enable a crew change.

• A vehicle that has stopped with the permission or at the direction of a constable in uniform, a traffic warden, or a traffic officer in uniform.

• A vehicle which is prevented from proceeding by circumstances beyond the driver's control or to avoid injury or damage to persons or property.

• A taxi for so long as may be reasonably necessary for a passenger to board or alight and to load or unload any luggage of the passenger (not on a red route).

• A marked royal mail vehicle for postal packets to be collected.

• A vehicle driven by a trainee bus driver.

• Any building, demolition or excavation operation.

• The removal of any obstruction to traffic.

• The maintenance, improvement or reconstruction of a road and street furniture including bus stop infrastructure.

1025.1

• Installation or repair or cleaning of sewers, gas, water or electricity, or communications apparatus.

• A vehicle being used for at least one of the following purposes :-

  ○ fire and rescue, ambulance, or ambulance response,

  ○ bomb disposal, special forces,

  ○ police and National Crime Agency.

A Traffic Regulation Order is not required for this sign/marking.

'Expressly provided' Section 36 Signs *continued*
School Entrances

When placed in conjunction with a 'No Stopping on entrance markings' sign it conveys the prohibition that a person driving a vehicle must not cause it to stop on that marking :-

- if the sign placed in conjunction with the marking does not show a time period, at any time, or
- if the sign shows a time period, during that period.

Exceptions

- Stopped with the permission or direction of a constable in uniform, a traffic warden, or, a traffic officer in uniform.
- A vehicle which is prevented from proceeding by circumstances beyond the driver's control or in order to avoid injury or damage to persons or property.
- A marked royal mail vehicle for postal packets to be collected.
- The removal of any obstruction to traffic.
- The maintenance, improvement or reconstruction of a road.
- Constructing, improving, maintaining or cleaning any street furniture.
- A vehicle being used for at least one of the following purposes :-
  - fire and rescue, ambulance, or ambulance response,
  - bomb disposal, special forces,
  - police, traffic officer and National Crime Agency.

A Traffic Regulation Order is not required for this sign/ marking.

If the marking is not accompanied by a sign it is advisory only and not enforceable under this section.

No stopping
Mon - Fri
8 am - 5 pm
on entrance
markings

SCHOOL — KEEP — CLEAR

1027.1

⚠ 'Expressly provided' Section 36 Signs *continued*
Traffic light signals for the control of vehicular traffic

A **green signal** indicates that vehicular traffic may proceed beyond the stop line and proceed straight on or to the left or to the right, except :-

- where the signal is an arrow, vehicles may only proceed in the direction indicated by the arrow, or
- where the signal is a pedal cycle symbol, only vehicles which are pedal cycles may proceed.

An **amber signal**, when shown alone, conveys the same prohibition as red, except that, as respects any vehicle which is so close to the stop line that it cannot safely be stopped without proceeding beyond the stop line, it conveys the same indication as the green signal which was shown immediately before it.

The **red signal** conveys the prohibition that vehicular traffic must not proceed beyond the stop line.

Red and amber signals illuminated together denote an impending change to green but conveys the same prohibition as the red signal.

3000 Specified Sign

Where a vehicle is being used for one of the following purposes and the observance of the prohibition would be likely to hinder the use of the vehicle for that purpose, the vehicle must not proceed beyond the stop line in such a manner or at such a time as to be likely to endanger any person or to cause the driver of another vehicle to change its speed or course in order to avoid an accident :-

- fire and rescue, ambulance, or ambulance response, blood service,
- bomb disposal, special forces, police and National Crime Agency.

Stop line at Traffic Lights - failure to stop at the Stop line is an offence of failing to comply with the light signal, not the line.

Vehicular traffic must not proceed beyond the line when required to stop by light signals or a constable in uniform.

Where there are 2 stop lines 'stop line' means :-

- the first stop line (the transverse white line below the pedal cycle symbol), or
- the second stop line (the transverse white line above the pedal cycle symbol) in the case of a pedal cycle, or a vehicle which has proceeded beyond the first stop line.

Drivers of motor vehicles must stop at the first white line reached if the lights are amber or red unless the vehicle has already proceeded over the first white line at the time that the signal goes red.

Where there is no stop line or it is not visible,:-

- stop before the 'WHEN RED LIGHT SHOWS WAIT HERE' sign, or,
- if no such sign, the post or other structure on which signal is mounted.

'Expressly provided' Section 36 Signs *continued*

Level crossings etc.

Level crossings, swing or lifting bridges, airfields or in the vicinity of premises used regularly by fire, police or ambulance vehicles.

**3014
Specified
Sign**

The **amber signal** conveys the prohibition that traffic must not proceed beyond the stop line or the road marking provided, except that a vehicle which is so close to the stop line that it cannot safely be stopped without proceeding beyond the stop line may proceed.

The **intermittent (flashing) red signals** convey the prohibition that traffic must not proceed beyond the stop line[1] or marking.

No entry for vehicular traffic

The sign may only be placed to indicate the effect of an Act, order, regulation, bylaw, resolution or notice which prohibits or restricts the use of the road by traffic.

**616
Specified
Sign**

Motorway and Dual Carriageway Gantry and Carriageway side mounted light signals

Vehicular traffic must not proceed in the lane or actively managed hard shoulder to which the sign relates and must not enter that lane or hard shoulder until one of the following signs is displayed on a matrix sign in relation to that lane or hard shoulder :-

**6031.1
Specified
Sign**

- a maximum speed limit sign,
- a national speed limit sign, or the legend 'END'.

5003.1

This is **NOT** a Specified Sign (*Regulation 36* does not apply to this sign)

Offence is driving on the hard shoulder contrary to the motorway regulations - used on Dynamic (hard shoulder running) motorways (*see Chapter 34*).

5003.1

Other signs to which Section 36 applies

But which are not 'expressly provided' by or under a provision of the Traffic Acts but **which indicate a statutory prohibition, restriction, or requirement** may be dealt with

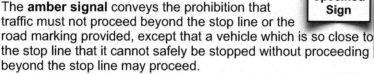

as an offence under *Section 36 Road Traffic Act 1988 or under the Road Traffic Regulation Act 1984* as a contravention of a Traffic Regulation Order or Notice (*see over*).

⚠ Traffic Regulation Orders and Notices

Traffic Regulation Orders or Designation Orders, Authorisations and Notices are required to give legal effect to many signs that impose restrictions on traffic such as :-

- Waiting and Loading, One-way streets,
- Weight and width restrictions,
- Access and turning restrictions, Road and Footway closures,
- Speed Limits, Bus lanes and contra-flow Cycle Lanes.

Types of Traffic Orders

Road Traffic Regulation Act 1984

- **Sections 1 and 6** - Traffic Regulation Orders - Permanent orders.
- **Section 9** - Experimental Traffic Orders (last up to 18 months).
- **Section 14** Orders - Temporary prohibitions or restrictions for roadworks, or likelihood of danger or damage and litter clearing.
- **Section 16A** Orders - Prohibition or restrictions in connection with certain events - usually limited to 3 day duration.
- **Section 18** Orders - One-way traffic on trunk roads.
- **Section 19** Orders - Regulation of use by public service vehicles.
- **Section 20** Orders - Prohibition or restriction of use of vehicles on roads of certain classes.
- **Section 22 and 22A** Orders - Traffic regulation for special areas in the countryside for conserving or enhancing the natural beauty of the area.
- **Section 22B** Orders - Traffic regulation on long distance routes.
- **Section 22BB** Orders - Traffic regulation on byways etc. in National Parks in England and Wales.
- **Section 22C** Orders - Prevention of Terrorism related.
- **Section 29** Orders - Prohibit traffic on roads used as playgrounds.
- **Sections 32 to 63A** Orders - Power of local authorities to provide parking places.
- **Part VI Speed Limit Orders**.

Each Order or Notice will detail the extent, restrictions, prohibitions and exemptions which apply as well as the offence and penalty for contravention of the requirements.

S29 and Part VI Order offences are endorsable fixed penalty offences.

S16A Order contraventions are not fixed penalty offences.

Other offences are non-endorsable fixed penalty offences.

Cause or permit offence are not fixed penalty offences.

Chapter 34 Motorways

Motorway Offences

Section 17(4) Road Traffic Regulation Act 1984 - level 4 fine - fixed penalty offences.

It is an offence for a person to use a special road (motorway) in contravention of this section or regulations made under this section :-

- Prohibited Traffic on Motorway - 3 points if motor vehicle.
- Stopping on hard shoulder - non endorsable.
- Other Motorway regulation offences - 3 points if motor vehicle.

Motorway Speed Offences - *see Chapter 29*
Section 17(4) Road Traffic Regulation Act 1984

- Fixed and Variable Speed offences (not roadworks) - 3 to 6 penalty points.

Section 16 Road Traffic Regulation Act 1984

- Speed offences at roadworks - 3 to 6 penalty points.

Carriageway means that part of a motorway which :-

- is provided for the regular passage of vehicular motor traffic along the motorway and includes the actively managed hard shoulder when it is treated as a lane of the carriageway, and
- where a hard shoulder is provided, has the approximate position of its left-hand or nearside edge marked with a continuous solid white line.

Central reservation means that part of a motorway which separates the carriageway to be used by vehicles travelling in one direction from the carriageway to be used by vehicles travelling in the opposite direction.

Emergency refuge area means a part of a motorway :-

- which is adjacent to and situated on the left-hand or near-side of the hard shoulder or carriageway, and
- whose boundary with the hard shoulder or carriageway is marked with a broken white line.

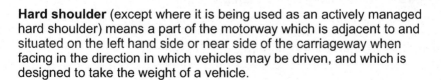

Hard shoulder (except where it is being used as an actively managed hard shoulder) means a part of the motorway which is adjacent to and situated on the left hand side or near side of the carriageway when facing in the direction in which vehicles may be driven, and which is designed to take the weight of a vehicle.

Motorway Traffic
Section 17(1) Road Traffic Regulation Act 1984
Schedule 4 Highways Act 1980 Schedule 3 Roads (Scotland) Act 1984

Authorised Traffic	
Class	**Type**
Class I	Heavy and light locomotives, motor tractors, heavy motor cars, motor cars and motor cycles which :- exceed 50cc, not controlled by a pedestrian, they and any trailers comply with general *Construction & Use regulations*, all the weight is transmitted to the road by wheels fitted with pneumatic tyres, and which are constructed as to be capable of attaining a speed of 25mph on the level under its own power, when unladen and not drawing a trailer.
Class II	Abnormal load and military vehicles authorised by Orders made under *s44 RTA 1988 and Article 16, 17 and 21 STGO* vehicles authorised under the STGO or any other Order under *s44 RTA 1988* which are capable of 25 mph as above
Excluded Traffic	
Class	**Type**
Class III	Motor vehicles controlled by pedestrians.
Class IV	All motor vehicles (other than invalid carriages and motorcycles less than 50cc) not in Class I, II or III.
Class V	Vehicles drawn by animals.
Class VI	Vehicles (other than pedal cycles, perambulators, pushchairs and other forms of baby carriage) drawn or propelled by pedestrians.
Class VII	Pedal cycles.
Class VIII	Animals ridden or led (other than dogs held on a lead).
Class IX	Pedestrians, Perambulators, pushchairs, and other forms of baby carriage, and Dogs held on a lead.
Class X	Motor cycles less than 50 c.c. (Class VII Scotland)
Class XI	Invalid carriages. (Class VII Scotland)

Use Of A Motorway By Excluded Traffic
Reg 15 Motorways Traffic (England and Wales) Regulations 1982
Regulation 13 Motorways Traffic (Scotland) Regulations 1995
Secretary of State Authorisation
The Secretary of State may authorise the use of a motorway by any excluded traffic on an occasion or in emergencies or for the purpose of enabling such traffic to cross a motorway or to secure access to premises abutting on or adjacent to a motorway.

Police Authorisation

The Chief Officer of Police of the Police area in which a motorway or any part of a motorway is situated, or any officer of or above the rank of Superintendent authorised in that behalf by the Chief Officer may, where by reason of any emergency the use of any road (not being a motorway) by any excluded traffic is rendered impossible or unsuitable :-

- authorise any excluded traffic to use that motorway or that part of motorway as an alternative road for the period which the use of the other road by that traffic is impossible or unsuitable, and
- relax any prohibition or restrictions imposed by these Regulations in so far as he considers it necessary to do so in connection with the use of that motorway or part of motorway by excluded traffic.

Maintenance vehicles

Class III or IV traffic may use a motorway for the maintenance, repair, cleansing or clearance of any part of a motorway.

Pedestrians

Pedestrians may use a motorway :-

- when it is necessary to do so as a result of an accident or emergency or as a result of a vehicle being at rest on a motorway in any of the following circumstances :-
  - by reason of a breakdown or mechanical defect or lack of fuel, oil or water, required for the vehicle, or
  - by reason of any accident, illness or other emergency, or
  - to permit any person carried in or on the vehicle to recover or move any object which has fallen on a motorway, or
  - to permit any person carried in or on the vehicle to give help which is required by any other person in any of the circumstances specified above, or
- where in accordance with any permission given by a constable, for the purpose of investigating any accident on or near a motorway,
- in the exercise of his duty as a constable or as a member of a fire brigade or an ambulance service,
- where it is necessary to do so to carry out in an efficient manner :-
  - the maintenance, repair, cleaning, clearance, alteration or improvement of any part of the motorway, or
  - the removal of any vehicle from any part of a motorway, or
  - the erection, laying, placing, maintenance, testing, alteration, repair or removal of any structure, works or apparatus in, on, under or over any part of a motorway,
- where it is necessary in connection with any inspection, survey, investigation or census which is carried out in accordance with any general or special authority granted by the Secretary of State,
- to place or recover a sign, cone, pyramid or triangle or warning lamp whilst acting in accordance with the *Traffic Signs (Temporary Obstructions) Regulations 1997.*

Motorway Regulations
Section 17(2) and (3) Road Traffic Regulation Act 1984

Regulations made under these sections with respect to the use of special roads may :-

- regulate the manner in which and the conditions subject to which special roads may be used by traffic authorised to do so,
- authorise, or enable the use of special roads on occasion or in an emergency or for the purpose as may be specified and by traffic other than that otherwise authorised,
- relax, or enable any authority so specified to relax, any prohibition or restriction imposed by the regulations,
- include provisions as may for the time being be indicated by traffic signs in accordance with the regulations,
- make provision with respect to special roads generally, or may make different provision with respect to special roads provided for the use of different classes of traffic, or may make provision with respect to any particular special road.

Exemptions from the Motorway Regulations

Reg 16 Motorways Traffic (England and Wales) Regulations 1982
Regulation 14 Motorways Traffic (Scotland) Regulations 1995

Nothing in these regulations shall preclude any person from using a motorway otherwise than in accordance with those provisions, in any of the following circumstances :-

- where he does so in accordance with any direction or permission given by a constable in uniform, [a traffic officer in uniform], or with the indication given by a traffic sign,
- where it is necessary for him to do so to avoid or prevent an accident or to obtain or give help required as the result of an accident or emergency and he does so in such manner as to cause as little danger or inconvenience as possible to other traffic on a motorway,
- where he does so in the exercise of his duty as [a traffic officer when in uniform], a constable or a member of an ambulance service or as an employee of a fire [and rescue authority or] brigade,
- where it is necessary to do so to carry out in an efficient manner :-
  - the maintenance, repair, cleaning, clearance, alteration or improvement of any part of a motorway,
  - the removal of any vehicle from any part of a motorway,
  - the erection, laying, placing, maintenance, testing, alteration repair, or removal of any structure, works or apparatus in, on under or over any part of a motorway,
- where it is necessary for him to do so in connection with any inspection, survey, investigation or census which relates to a motorway or any part thereof, and which is carried out in accordance with any general or special authority granted by the Secretary of State.

Items in [ ] in England and Wales only.

Motorway Regulations *continued*
Use of a Motorway By Learner Drivers

Reg 11 Motorways Traffic (England and Wales) Regulations 1982
Regulation 10 Motorways Traffic (Scotland) Regulations 1995

No motor vehicle in Category A (motorcycles including A1) or B (cars including B1) (or B+E or C1) is to be driven on a motorway by a provisional licence holder unless the holder has passed a driving test for the vehicle and is eligible to be granted a full licence except provisional licence holders may drive on a motorway when :-

- driving a category B vehicle the transmission of which may be disengaged, and the brakes operated, independently from the driver by a person sitting in the front passenger seat, and
- under the supervision of an approved driving instructor who is present with him in the vehicle and whose registration is not suspended.

Provisional licence holders (who have a full Cat B licence) may drive Cat C, C+E, C1, C1+E, D, D+E, D1, D1+E, B+E vehicles on the motorway - they must comply with provisional licence conditions, L-plates, supervision etc.

Driving elsewhere than on the carriageway

Regulation 5 Motorways Traffic (England and Wales) Regulations 1982
Regulation 4 Motorways Traffic (Scotland) Regulations 1995

Subject to the following provisions of these regulations, no vehicle shall be driven on any part of the motorway which is not a carriageway.

The relevant length of an actively managed hard shoulder shall be treated for the purposes of these Regulations as a lane of the carriageway. The start and end points of this section of hard shoulder is indicated by overhead gantry signs.

No Entry

Reg 6(1) (Motorways Traffic (England and Wales) Regulations 1982
Regulation 5(1) Motorways Traffic (Scotland) Regulations 1995

Where there is a traffic sign indicating that there is no entry to a carriageway at a particular place, no vehicle shall be driven or moved onto that carriageway at that place.

No left or right turn

Reg 6(2) Motorways Traffic (England and Wales) Regulations 1982
Regulation 5(2) Motorways Traffic (Scotland) Regulations 1995

Where there is a traffic sign indicating that there is no left or right turn into a carriageway at a particular place, no vehicle shall be so driven or moved as to cause it to turn left or right into the carriageway at that place.

Motorway Regulations *continued*
Driving in the wrong direction on main carriageway

Reg 6(3) Motorways Traffic (England and Wales) Regulations 1982
Regulation 5(3) Motorways Traffic (Scotland) Regulations 1995

Every vehicle on a length of carriageway which is contiguous to (alongside) a central reservation, shall be driven in such a direction that the central reservation is at all times on the right hand side of the vehicle.

Does not include the hard shoulder.

Driving in the wrong direction on slip road

Reg 6(4) Motorways Traffic (England and Wales) Regulations 1982
Regulation 5(4) Motorways Traffic (Scotland) Regulations 1995

Where traffic signs are so placed that there is a length of carriageway (being a length which is not contiguous to a central reservation) which can be entered at one end only, every vehicle shall be driven in such a direction only as to cause it to proceed away from that end of that length of carriageway.

U-turns

Reg 6(5) Motorways Traffic (England and Wales) Regulations 1982
Regulation 5(5) Motorways Traffic (Scotland) Regulations 1995

No vehicle which :-

• is on a length of carriageway on which vehicles are required by any of the foregoing provisions of this Regulation to be driven in one direction only and is proceeding in or facing that direction, or

• is on any other length of carriageway and is proceeding in or facing one direction,

shall be driven or moved so as to cause it to turn and proceed in or face the opposite direction.

Reversing

Regulation 8 Motorways Traffic (England and Wales) Regulations 1982
Regulation 7 Motorways Traffic (Scotland) Regulations 1995

No vehicle on a motorway shall be driven or moved backwards except in so far as it is necessary to back the vehicle to enable it to proceed forwards or to be connected to any other vehicle.

Includes the hard shoulder.

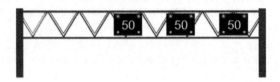

Motorway Regulations *continued*
Stopping on the carriageway

Reg 7(1) Motorways Traffic (England and Wales) Regulations 1982
Regulation 6 Motorways Traffic (Scotland) Regulations 1995

No vehicle shall stop or remain at rest on a carriageway except where it is necessary to stop :-

- by reason of any accident, illness or other emergency, or
- by reason of a breakdown or mechanical defect or lack of fuel, oil or water required for the vehicle, or
- to permit any person carried in or on the vehicle to recover or move any object which has fallen onto the motorway, or
- to permit any person carried in or on the vehicle to give help which is required by any other person in any of the above circumstances,

and the vehicle shall, as soon and in so far as is reasonably practicable, be driven or moved off the carriageway onto the hard shoulder or onto an emergency refuge area which is contiguous to that carriageway or hard shoulder.

Exception - because it is prevented from proceeding by the presence of any other vehicle, person or object.

Stopping or driving on the hard shoulder

Regulation 9 Motorways Traffic (England and Wales) Regulations 1982
Regulation 8 Motorways Traffic (Scotland) Regulations 1995

No vehicle shall be :-

- driven, or moved, or
- stop or remain at rest,

on any hard shoulder or emergency refuge area except :-

- by reason of any accident, illness or other emergency, or
- by reason of a breakdown or mechanical defect or lack of fuel, oil or water required for the vehicle, or
- to permit any person carried in or on the vehicle to recover or move any object which has fallen onto the motorway, or
- to permit any person carried in or on the vehicle to give help which is required by any other person in any of the above circumstances.

A vehicle which is at rest on a hard shoulder or emergency refuge area shall so far as is reasonably practicable be allowed to remain at rest in such position that no part of it or of its load shall obstruct or cause danger to vehicles using the carriageway.

A vehicle shall not remain at rest on a hard shoulder or emergency refuge area for longer than is necessary.
***Dynamic Hard Shoulder Running Smart Motorways** permit the use of the hard shoulder as a running lane in certain traffic conditions.*

Motorway Regulations *continued*
Use Of Central Reservation and Verges

Reg 10 Motorways Traffic (England and Wales) Regulations 1982
Regulation 9 Motorways Traffic (Scotland) Regulations 1995

No vehicle shall be driven, moved, stop or remain at rest on a central reservation or verge.

Restriction On Use Of Right Hand (Offside) Lane of a Motorway

Reg 12 Motorways Traffic (England and Wales) Regulations 1982
Regulation 11 Motorways Traffic (Scotland) Regulations 1995

The following vehicles shall not be driven, moved, stop or remain at rest on the right hand or offside lane of a length of carriageway which has 3 or more lanes open for use by traffic proceeding in the same direction (including, on Smart Motorways, an actively managed hard shoulder when it is in use as a lane of the carriageway) :-

- a goods vehicle with a maximum laden weight exceeding 7.5 tonnes,
- a goods vehicle with a maximum laden weight exceeding 3.5 tonnes but not exceeding 7.5 tonnes, required to be fitted with a speed limiter,
- a passenger vehicle with a maximum laden weight exceeding 7.5 tonnes constructed or adapted to carry more than 8 seated passengers in addition to the driver,
- a passenger vehicle with a maximum laden weight not exceeding 7.5 tonnes constructed or adapted to carry more than 8 seated passengers in addition to the driver, required to be fitted with a speed limiter,
- a motor vehicle drawing a trailer,
- a motor tractor, a light locomotive or a heavy locomotive,

except so far as is necessary :-

- ○ to enable the vehicle to pass another vehicle which is carrying or drawing a load of exceptional width, or
- ○ to enable a vehicle to change lane without involving danger of injury to any person or inconvenience to other traffic.

Animals Carried In Vehicles

Reg 14 Motorways Traffic (England and Wales) Regulations 1982
Regulation 12 Motorways Traffic (Scotland) Regulations 1995

A person in charge of any animal which is carried by a vehicle using a motorway shall, so far as is practicable secure that :-

- *Reg 14(a)* the animal shall not be removed from or permitted to leave the vehicle whilst on the motorway, and
- if it escapes from, or it is necessary for it to be removed from, or permitted to leave, the vehicle :-
  - ○ *Reg 14(b)(i)* it shall not go or remain on any part of the motorway other than a hard shoulder or emergency refuge area, and
  - ○ *Reg 14(b)(ii)* it shall, whilst it is not on or in the vehicle, be held on a lead or otherwise kept under proper control.

Smart Motorways

A smart motorway uses technology to actively monitor and manage the flow of traffic by use of variable mandatory speed limits and by either allowing use of the hard shoulder as an extra lane during busy times or by doing away with the hard shoulder entirely and using the extra width as a permanent lane for use by traffic.

There are three types of Smart Motorways in operation in England :-

- Controlled - *see below*.
- Dynamic Hard Shoulder Running.
- All Lane Running.

Controlled Motorways

These have 3 or more lanes with variable mandatory speed limits indicated by overhead gantry signs.

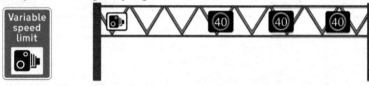

The hard shoulder is separated from live lanes by a solid white line and should only be used in a genuine emergency.

Dynamic Hard Shoulder Running

The hard shoulder is opened as a running lane to traffic at busy periods to ease congestion.

Motorways with dynamic hard shoulder running have a solid white line to differentiate the hard shoulder from the normal carriageway.

Hard Shoulder for Emergency Use Only

Offence - Contravening Motorway regulations - Driving on hard shoulder
S17(4) RTRA 1984
See Pages 1, 7 and Chapter 33 Page 15

Emergency refuge areas are spaced at 500m to 800m intervals.

Smart Motorways *continued*
All Lane Running

All Lane Running is a version of Smart Motorways where all lanes are used as permanent live running lanes for traffic.

There is no hard shoulder and all lanes are separated by broken white line markings.

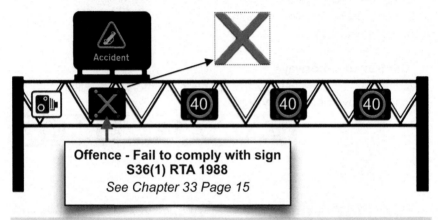

Offence - Fail to comply with sign S36(1) RTA 1988
See Chapter 33 Page 15

Lanes can be individually closed and variable speed limits set.
Any lane can be closed in an emergency.

Emergency refuges are provided which are spaced 2.5 km apart.

These types of motorway are commonly equipped with MIDAS (Motorway Incident Detection and Automatic Signalling) - Inductive loops detect the volume and speed of traffic and send data automatically to the local control centre and to overhead variable message gantries in the form of pre-set messages.

Chapter 35 Pedestrian Crossings

Types of Crossing

School crossings

Traffic is controlled by a School Crossing Patrol person wearing an approved uniform and displaying an approved, hand held, sign.

Zebra Crossings

This crossing has black and white stripes with orange flashing beacons.

- A zebra crossing gives the pedestrian right of way once their foot is on the crossing.
- A zebra crossing with a cycle crossing alongside is known as a Parallel pedestrian and cyclist crossing.

Pelican Crossings (Pedestrian Light Controlled Crossing)

- Pelican crossings are controlled by the pedestrian pressing the button on the WAIT box.
- Pedestrians should only cross when the green man lights up and all the traffic has stopped.
- Pelican crossings have a flashing green man for pedestrians and a flashing amber for drivers.

These crossings are being phased out.

Puffin Crossings (Pedestrian User Friendly Intelligent Crossing)

- A more modern type of Pelican Crossing with special sensors built in which can detect a pedestrian waiting and make sure that traffic remains stopped until all the pedestrians have crossed the road.
- One of the main differences is that the red and green man signals are just above the WAIT box and not on the other side of the road.
- Puffins do not have a flashing green man for pedestrians or a flashing amber for drivers.

Toucan Crossings (Two-Can Cross)

These crossings are provided for pedestrians and cyclists.

Equestrian (Pegasus) Crossings

These crossings are provided for mounted horse riders.

Puffin, Toucan and equestrian crossings do not have a flashing amber phase. The light sequence for traffic is the same as at traffic lights.

Crossings at Traffic light junctions

Crossings at a junction at which the priority between motor vehicles is regulated by traffic light signals and which allow pedestrians to cross during the red phase for vehicular traffic, found mainly in urban areas.

Light signals are mandatory for all vehicles (including cycles) travelling along the carriageway but advisory for pedestrians, cyclists and horse riders using the crossing.

School Crossings
Section 28(1) Road Traffic Regulation Act 1984

A school crossing patrol wearing an approved uniform may require the person driving or propelling a vehicle which is approaching a place in a road where a person is crossing or seeking to cross the road, to stop by exhibiting a prescribed sign.

Fail to stop at School Crossing Patrol Sign
Section 28(3) Road Traffic Regulation Act 1984
Section 36(1) Road Traffic Act 1988 - 3 points if motor vehicle
- fixed penalty offence

It is an offence for a person who has been required to stop to :-

- fail to cause the **vehicle** to stop before reaching the place where a person is crossing or seeking to cross and so as not to stop or impede that person crossing, or
- cause a **vehicle** to be put in motion whilst the sign is still exhibited.

Pelican Crossings
Offence
Section 25(5) Road Traffic Regulation Act 1984 - level 3 fine + 3 points if motor vehicle - fixed penalty offence

It is an offence for a **person** to contravene the *Zebra, Pelican and Puffin Pedestrian Crossings Regulations 1997* in respect of use of Pelican Crossings.

These crossings are being phased out.

The regulations remain in force in relation only to Pelican Crossings established prior to 22/10/2016.

Offences of stopping within the controlled area and within the limits of the crossing may be dealt with under Civil Enforcement Powers in certain areas.

Contraventions of the regulations include :-

- Pedestrians - Loitering on a crossing - *Regulation 19*.
- Stopping vehicles within the limits of a crossing - *Regulation 18*.
- Stopping vehicles in the controlled area - *Regulation 20*.
- Overtaking vehicles in the controlled area - *Regulation 24*.
- Contravening the Red Light - *Regulation 23*.
- Contravening the Amber flashing Light - *Regulation 26*.

Pelican crossings have a flashing green man for pedestrians and a flashing amber for drivers.

Zebra and Puffin Crossings
Offence

Section 25(5) Road Traffic Regulation Act 1984 - level 3 fine + 3 points if motor vehicle - fixed penalty offence

It is an offence for a **person** to contravene the requirements of the *Traffic Signs Regulations and General Directions 2016* in respect of use of a Zebra or Puffin Crossing (*Schedule 14 Part 5*).

Offences of stopping within the controlled area may be dealt with under Civil Enforcement Powers in certain areas.

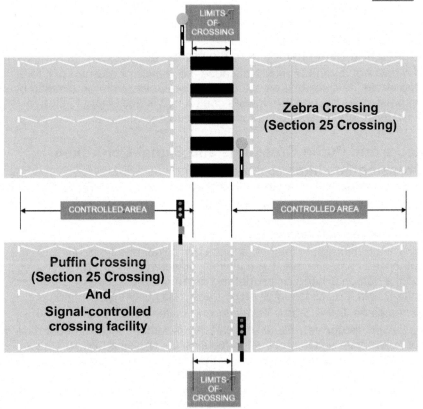

Zebra Crossing (Section 25 Crossing)

CONTROLLED AREA

CONTROLLED AREA

Puffin Crossing (Section 25 Crossing) And Signal-controlled crossing facility

LIMITS OF CROSSING

Puffin, Toucan and equestrian crossings do not have a flashing amber phase. The light sequence for traffic is the same as at traffic lights.

Zebra and Puffin Crossings *continued*
Sch 14 Pt 5 Traffic Signs Regulations and General Directions 2016

Pedestrian loitering on a crossing

A **pedestrian** must not remain on the carriageway within the limits of a crossing longer than is reasonably necessary for that pedestrian to pass over the crossing with reasonable despatch.

Precedence to Pedestrians (Zebra Crossings)

Every pedestrian who is on the carriageway within the limits of a Zebra crossing, which is not for the time being controlled by a constable in uniform, before any part of a **vehicle** has entered those limits has precedence within those limits over that vehicle and the driver must accord such precedence to any such pedestrian. (Where there is a refuge for pedestrians or central reservation on a Zebra crossing, the parts of the crossing situated on each side of the refuge or central reservation are to be treated as separate crossings.)

Stopping within the limits of the crossing

The driver of a **vehicle** must not cause the vehicle or any part of it to stop within the limits of a crossing unless prevented from proceeding by circumstances beyond the driver's control or it is necessary to stop to avoid injury or damage to persons or property.

Zebra and Puffin Crossings and Signal-Controlled Crossing Facilities *continued*

Overtaking within a controlled area

Fail to Comply with Section 36 Sign

Section 36(1) Road Traffic Act 1988 - level 3 fine - 3 points - fixed penalty offence

Where a traffic sign of the prescribed size, colour and type, or authorised character, has been lawfully placed on or near a road, a person d**riving or propelling a vehicle** who fails to comply with the indication given by the sign is guilty of an offence.

Schedule 14 Traffic Signs Regulations and General Directions 2016

Whilst any **motor vehicle** or any part of it is within the limits of a crossing controlled area and is proceeding towards the crossing to which the controlled area relates, the driver of the vehicle must not cause it or any part of it to pass ahead of the foremost part of :-

- **any other motor vehicle** proceeding in the same direction and nearest to the crossing to which the controlled area relates,
- **a vehicle** which is stationary and nearest to the crossing for the purpose of according precedence to a pedestrian on the crossing or for the purpose of complying with a traffic light signal for controlling vehicular traffic.

Zebra and Puffin Crossings and Signal-Controlled Crossing Facilities *continued*

Stopping in a controlled area

Fail to Comply with Section 36 Sign

Section 36(1) Road Traffic Act 1988 - level 3 fine - 3 points if motor vehicle - fixed penalty offence

Where a traffic sign of the prescribed size, colour and type, or authorised character, has been lawfully placed on or near a road, a **person driving or propelling** a **vehicle** who fails to comply with the indication given by the sign is guilty of an offence.

Offences of stopping within the limits of the crossing may be dealt with under Civil Enforcement Powers in certain areas.

Schedule 14 Traffic Signs Regulations and General Directions 2016

The driver of a **vehicle** must not cause it, or any part of it, to stop in a crossing controlled area except :-

• a pedal cycle, or

• a driver who stops a vehicle in a controlled area in any of the following circumstances :-

  ○ to accord precedence to a pedestrian on the crossing,

  ○ to comply with a light signal for the control of vehicular traffic or a direction of a constable in uniform, or a traffic officer in uniform,

  ○ the driver is prevented from proceeding by circumstances beyond driver's control or to avoid injury or damage to persons or property,

  ○ the vehicle is being used for purposes of :-

    ▪ fire and rescue authority or service,

    ▪ ambulance and ambulance response, blood service,

    ▪ bomb or explosive disposal, special forces,

    ▪ police, National Crime Agency.

  ○ the vehicle is stopped for no longer than is necessary for it to be used for the following purposes (but only if the vehicle cannot be used for those purposes without stopping in the controlled area) :-

    ▪ building, demolition or excavation,

    ▪ removal of any obstruction to traffic,

    ▪ the maintenance, improvement or reconstruction of a road, or

    ▪ the laying, erection, alteration, repair or cleaning of any sewer, or main, pipe or apparatus for the supply of gas, water or electricity, or electronic communications apparatus.

  ○ a public service vehicle local service waiting to take up or set down passengers having proceeded past the crossing,

  ○ the vehicle is stopped for the purpose of making a left or right turn.

Puffin Crossings and Signal-Controlled Crossing Facilities *continued*
Light Signals
Fail to Comply with Section 36 Sign
Section 36(1) Road Traffic Act 1988 - level 3 fine -
3 points if motor vehicle - fixed penalty offence

Where a traffic sign of the prescribed size, colour and type, or authorised character, has been lawfully placed on or near a road, a person **driving or propelling a vehicle** who fails to comply with the indication given by the sign is guilty of an offence.

> *When vehicular light signals at a Puffin crossing or Signal Controlled Crossing Facility are displaying a light signal which conveys a prohibition, the driver of a vehicle must not cause it to contravene that prohibition.*

Schedule 14 Traffic Signs Regulations and General Directions 2016

The light signals mean :-

- A **green signal** indicates that vehicular traffic may proceed beyond the stop line and proceed straight on or to the left or to the right, except :-
  - where the signal is an arrow, vehicles may only proceed in the direction indicated by the arrow,
  - where the signal is a pedal cycle symbol, only vehicles which are pedal cycles may proceed.
- An **amber signal, when shown alone**, conveys the same prohibition as red, except that, as respects any vehicle which is so close to the stop line that it cannot safely be stopped without proceeding beyond the stop line, it conveys the same indication as the green signal which was shown immediately before it.
- The **red signal** conveys the prohibition that vehicular traffic must not proceed beyond the stop line except where a vehicle is being used for at least one of the purposes below and the observance of the prohibition in would be likely to hinder the use of the vehicle for that purpose.
  Instead, the prohibition conveyed is that the vehicle must not proceed beyond the stop line in such a manner or at such a time as to be likely to endanger any person or to cause the driver of another vehicle to change its speed or course in order to avoid an accident.
  Those purposes are :-
    - fire and rescue authority or service,
    - ambulance, ambulance response service, blood service,
    - bomb or explosive disposal, special forces,
    - police, and National Crime Agency.
- **Red and amber signals** illuminated together denote an impending change to green but conveys the same prohibition as the red signal.

Chapter 36 Police Powers

Arrest without warrant : England and Wales
Section 24 Police and Criminal Evidence Act 1984

(1) A constable may arrest without a warrant anyone who is about to commit an offence, anyone who is in the act of committing an offence, anyone whom he has reasonable grounds for suspecting to be about to commit an offence or anyone whom he has reasonable grounds for suspecting to be committing an offence.

(2) If a constable has reasonable grounds for suspecting that an offence has been committed, he may arrest without a warrant anyone whom he has reasonable grounds to suspect of being guilty of it.

(3) If an offence has been committed, a constable may arrest without a warrant anyone who is guilty of the offence, anyone whom he has reasonable grounds for suspecting to be guilty of it.

(4) But the power of summary arrest conferred by *subsection (1), (2) or (3)* is exercisable only if the constable has reasonable grounds for believing that for any of the reasons mentioned in *subsection (5)* it is necessary to arrest the person in question.

(5) The reasons are :-

 (a) to enable the name of the person in question to be ascertained (in the case where the constable does not know, and cannot readily ascertain, the person's name, or has reasonable grounds for doubting whether a name given by the person as his name is his real name),

 (b) correspondingly as regards the person's address,

 (c) to prevent the person in question :-

   (i) causing physical injury to himself or any other person, or

   (ii) suffering physical injury, or

   (iii) causing loss of or damage to property, or

   (iv) committing an offence against public decency (subject to *subsection (6)*), or

   (v) causing an unlawful obstruction of the highway,

 (d) to protect a child or other vulnerable person from the person in question,

 (e) to allow the prompt and effective investigation of the offence or of the conduct of the person in question,

 (f) to prevent any prosecution for the offence from being hindered by the disappearance of the person in question.

(6) *Subsection (5)(c)(iv)* applies only where members of the public going about their normal business cannot reasonably be expected to avoid the person in question.

Arrest without warrant : Scotland
Section 1 Criminal Justice (Scotland) Act 2016

(1) A constable may arrest a person without a warrant if the constable has reasonable grounds for suspecting that the person has committed or is committing an offence.

(2) In relation to an offence not punishable by imprisonment, a constable may arrest a person under *subsection (1)* only if the constable is satisfied that it would not be in the interests of justice to delay the arrest in order to seek a warrant for the person's arrest.

(3) Without prejudice to the generality of *subsection (2)*, it would not be in the interests of justice to delay an arrest in order to seek a warrant if the constable reasonably believes that unless the person is arrested without delay the person will :-
 (a) continue committing the offence, or
 (b) obstruct the course of justice in any way, including by seeking to avoid arrest, or interfering with witnesses or evidence.

Index

0 - 9

DRIVING LICENCE OFFENCE CODES

Code	Offence	Penalty points
AC10	Failing to stop after an accident	5 to 10
AC20	Failing to give particulars or report an accident within 24 hours	5 to 10
AC30	Undefined accident offences	4 to 9
BA10	Driving while disqualified by order of court	6
BA30	Attempting to drive while disqualified by order of court	6
BA40	Causing death by driving while disqualified	3 to 11
BA60	Causing serious injury by driving while disqualified	3 to 11
CD10	Driving without due care and attention	3 to 9
CD20	Driving without reasonable consideration for other road users	3 to 9
CD30	Driving without due care and attention or without reasonable consideration for other road users	3 to 9
CD33	Causing serious injury by careless or inconsiderate driving	3 to 9
CD40	Causing death through careless driving when unfit through drink	3 to 11
CD50	Causing death by careless driving when unfit through drugs	3 to 11
CD60	Causing death by careless driving with alcohol level above the limit	3 to 11
CD70	Causing death by careless driving then failing to supply a specimen for alcohol analysis	3 to 11
CD80	Causing death by careless, or inconsiderate, driving	3 to 11
CD90	Causing death by driving: unlicensed, disqualified or uninsured drivers	3 to 11
CU10	Using a vehicle with defective brakes	3
CU20	Causing or likely to cause danger by reason of use of unsuitable vehicle or using a vehicle with parts or accessories (excluding brakes, steering or tyres) in a dangerous condition	3
CU30	Using a vehicle with defective tyre(s)	3
CU40	Using a vehicle with defective steering	3
CU50	Causing or likely to cause danger by reason of load or passengers	3
CU80	Breach of requirements as to control of the vehicle, such as using a mobile phone	3 to 6
DD10	Causing serious injury by dangerous driving	3 to 11
DD40	Dangerous driving	3 to 11
DD60	Manslaughter or culpable homicide while driving a vehicle	3 to 11
DD80	Causing death by dangerous driving	3 to 11
DD90	Furious driving	3 to 9
DR10	Driving or attempting to drive with alcohol level above limit	3 to 11
DR20	Driving or attempting to drive while unfit through drink	3 to 11
DR30	Driving or attempting to drive then failing to supply a specimen for analysis	3 to 11
DR31	Driving or attempting to drive then refusing to give permission for analysis of a blood sample that was taken without consent due to incapacity	3 to 11
DR61	Refusing to give permission for analysis of a blood sample that was taken without consent due to incapacity in circumstances other than driving or attempting to drive	10
DR40	In charge of a vehicle while alcohol level above limit	10
DR50	In charge of a vehicle while unfit through drink	10
DR60	Failure to provide a specimen for analysis in circumstances other than driving or attempting to drive	10
DR70	Failing to co-operate with a preliminary test	4

DRIVING LICENCE OFFENCE CODES

DG10	Driving or attempting to drive with drug level above the specified limit	3 to 11
DG60	Causing death by careless driving with drug level above the limit	3 to 11
DR80	Driving or attempting to drive when unfit through drugs	3 to 11
DG40	In charge of a vehicle while drug level above specified limit	10
DR70	Failing to co-operate with a preliminary test	4
DR90	In charge of a vehicle when unfit through drugs	10
IN10	Using a vehicle uninsured against third party risks	6 to 8
LC20	Driving otherwise than in accordance with a licence	3 to 6
LC30	Driving after making a false declaration about fitness when applying for a licence	3 to 6
LC40	Driving a vehicle having failed to notify a disability	3 to 6
LC50	Driving after a licence has been cancelled (revoked) or refused on medical grounds	3 to 6
MS10	Leaving a vehicle in a dangerous position	3
MS20	Unlawful pillion riding	3
MS30	Play street offences	2
MS50	Motor racing on the highway	3 to 11
MS70	Driving with uncorrected defective eyesight	3
MS80	Refusing to submit to an eyesight test	3
MS90	Failure to give information as to identity of driver etc	6
MW10	Contravention of special roads regulations (excluding speed limits)	3
PC10	Undefined contravention of pedestrian crossing regulations	3
PC20	Contravention of pedestrian crossing regulations with moving vehicle	3
PC30	Contravention of pedestrian crossing regulations with stationary vehicle	3
SP10	Exceeding goods vehicle speed limits	3 to 6
SP20	Exceeding speed limit for type of vehicle (excluding goods or passenger vehicles)	3 to 6
SP30	Exceeding statutory speed limit on a public road	3 to 6
SP40	Exceeding passenger vehicle speed limit	3 to 6
TS10	Failing to comply with traffic light signals	3
TS20	Failing to comply with double white lines	3
TS30	Failing to comply with 'stop' sign	3
TS40	Failing to comply with direction of a constable/warden	3
TS50	Failing to comply with traffic sign (excluding 'stop' signs, traffic lights or double white lines)	3
TS60	Failing to comply with a school crossing patrol sign	3
TS70	Undefined failure to comply with a traffic direction sign	3
UT50	Aggravated taking of a vehicle	3 to 11
MR09	Reckless or dangerous driving (whether or not resulting in death, injury or serious risk). *MR Codes - N Ireland or Isle of Man*	
MR19	Wilful failure to carry out the obligation placed on driver after being involved in a road accident (hit or run)	
MR29	Driving a vehicle while under the influence of alcohol or other substance affecting or diminishing the mental and physical abilities of a driver	
MR39	Driving a vehicle faster than the permitted speed	
MR49	Driving a vehicle whilst disqualified	
MR59	Other conduct constituting an offence for which a driving disqualification has been imposed by the State of Offence